ONE MORE DAY

EVERYWHERE

Crossing 50 Borders
on the Road to Global Understanding

GLEN HEGGSTAD

ECW Press

Published by ECW Press
2120 Queen Street East, Suite 200, Toronto, Ontario, Canada M4E 1E2
416.694.3348 / info@ecwpress.com

LIBRARY AND ARCHIVES CANADA CATALOGUING IN PUBLICATION

Heggstad, Glen
One more day everywhere : crossing fifty borders on the road to global understanding / Glen Heggstad.

ISBN 978-1-55022-882-3

1. Heggstad, Glen—Travel. 2. Cultural awareness. 3. Motorcycle touring. 4. Voyages around the world. I. Title.

G465.H44 2009   910.4'1092   C2009-902539-6

Cover design: Rachel Ironstone
Text design: Tania Craan
Typesetting: Mary Bowness
Photos: Glen Heggstad
Printing: Victor Graphics   2   3   4   5

This book has been printed on 30% PCW paper

PRINTED AND BOUND IN THE UNITED STATES

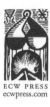

ECW PRESS
ecwpress.com

Table of Contents

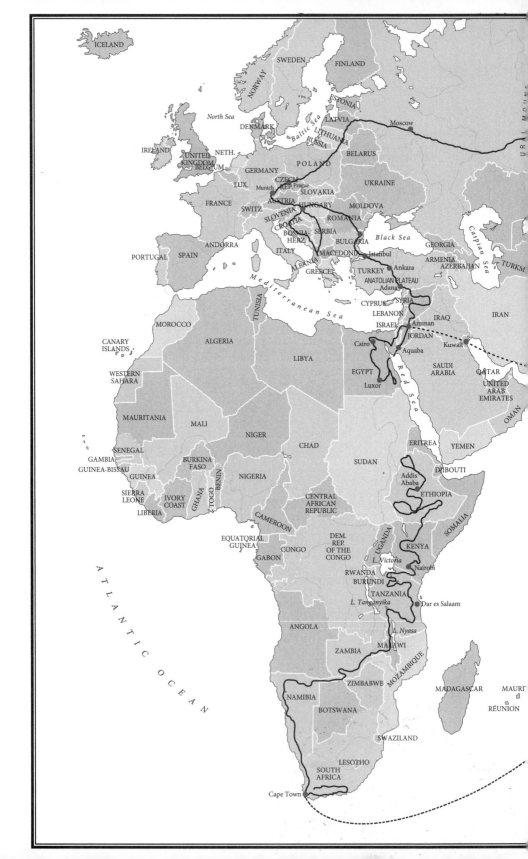

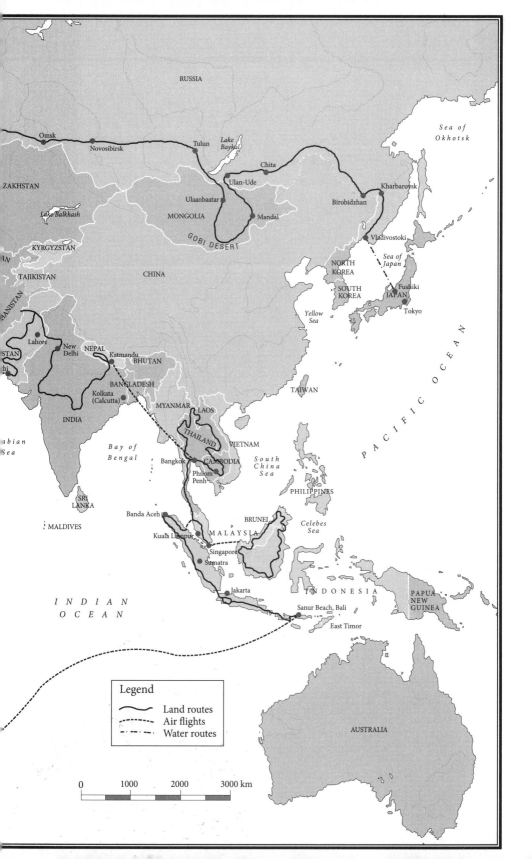

Dedicated to those who will change the world
Zoë and Scout

Introduction

In November 2001, while on a motorcycle ride from California to the tip of South America, capture by a Colombian terrorist army was not what I had in mind. Yet on one quiet, sunny afternoon, on a remote Andean highway, there wasn't a choice. Marched at gunpoint into the mountains outside of Medellín, after that moment I knew that life would never be the same. During five grueling weeks as an involuntary guest of the National Liberation Army, they eventually broke my spirit with head games and torture. When I was finally freed in a Christmas prisoner exchange with the Colombian government, as an ultimate act of defiance against my captors, I continued to pursue my original goal of riding to the tip of South America and back. But once returning to California, after one too many restless nights, I realized that recovery from that incident would be more difficult than anticipated, and although I was back in Palm Springs, it was still a long road home. After late evenings and early mornings of teeth-grinding turmoil, I eventually concluded the only way to restore my psychological health and dignity was to continue what I had been doing — riding motorcycles to exotic lands. My silent mantra illuminating the path to positive thought became "Living well is the best revenge." But since I had already tackled South America, the new goal would become traversing the entire globe, alone on a motorcycle. At first, friends and family still shaken by my Colombian ordeal couldn't accept what I needed to do, reminding me of the current headlines highlighting increasing international terrorism and an impatient world furious with American foreign policy.

But for me, still reeling from a firsthand experience of human madness, there was no other way to contend with such a festering wound of personal doubt and deepening emptiness. I needed to find out what was really out there and hopefully confirm a suspicion that humanity was not inherently evil.

Yet in a post-9/11 climate of fear, Western societies were growing increasingly alarmed with news of more terrorist plots. Jerked from a slumbering state of denial, on September 11, 2001, the United States of America had been savagely attacked with its own technology and more was promised. From bombings to kidnappings, evidence of constant threats in a volatile world was blasting across our TV screens. Terrorists wanted citizens to feel helpless and cringe in fear. When we hide at home, they win. In a frightening overreaction, would America ultimately strangle under its own self-imposed security? Unable to defeat the U.S. militarily, could Osama bin Laden and others like him win the most strategic battle, unwittingly aided by our own political masters?

As a nervous U.S. Congress inched toward smothering the Constitution, would an Orwellian prophecy become a reality? With a proliferation of street corner surveillance cameras and an abuse of wiretapping regulations, lawmakers, worried about appearing unpatriotic, were looking the other way. And Americans were beginning to accept the concept of Big Brother protecting us. After all, who would vote against bills cleverly labeled "The Patriot Act" and "Homeland Security"? Yet while struggling from paycheck to paycheck, Americans were either confronted with tales of terror or droned into complacency with celebrity gossip and reality TV. The lack of truthful, relevant information was numbing.

For me the decision was simple and final: I had to clear my head with a journey into the real world, the developing world, and examine that world through the eyes of those who lived there. For Westerners abroad during the most uncertain political climate in recent history, traveling the earth alone was more than an adventurous challenge; it was a direct message to terrorists wherever they lurked: We are not afraid. But more important, we refuse to hate.

On a 52,000-mile odyssey exclusively through developing nations across five continents, I stumbled upon a startling realization. We, the American people, have been deceived. Nearly every preconceived notion about the world fed to us by our national media was proved false. Meeting the people of planet earth face to face as a lone traveler becomes an opportunity to discover firsthand that we are all the same — and sometimes even related. Eventually, a truth surfaces: while governments may not get along, people do.

From lopsided Middle East horror stories to rumors of ruthless Russians, one by one, foolish myths were dispelled as poverty-stricken strangers invited this wandering motorcyclist into their wooden shacks, offering their last crumbs of bread. But riding the earth alone wasn't easy and plenty went wrong, contending with daily challenges of harsh weather, difficult terrain and explosive geopolitical events. Despite a year of planning, at times, given the steady changes in circumstance and necessity to take chances, I was nearly sucked over the edge. Enduring hypothermia while riding mud roads through Siberian tornadoes led to the blissful solitude of the Mongolian Plains, with an electrifying jolt into adventure and humanity. In a Munich hospital, my congested kidneys nearing failure, I wondered if there wasn't a safer way for a man to restore himself? Later, a reckless mid-winter crossing of eastern Turkey's frozen Anatolian Plateau nearly stalled the journey until spring.

Sitting cross-legged in a Syrian Bedouin's tent silently sipping tea while American fighter jets patrolled the skies over nearby Iraq, I pondered — *Who would have thought my odyssey would lead to this?* While traveling Egypt, eluding mandatory military escorts, my journey through the ancient Nile Valley was peaceful, with throngs of young Arabs gathering to shake my hand. A sunrise climb of Mount Sinai took my breath away, the same as it must have for Moses when he accepted the Ten Commandments. And later that night, with distant gazes into the dancing campfire, a nomadic Bedouin chieftain described life while previously under Israeli occupation as "Paradise."

After being granted a special-entry permit from the commander of Israeli Defense Forces, on election day in Gaza, I was cornered by Palestinian thugs from Hamas and the question arose — were my feet too close to the flames? Stranded in the Sadar District of Karachi while terrorists blew up mosques and hunted Westerners, fate was tempted once more when I flipped a coin to decide my next destination — India or Afghanistan?

On the Nepali border, coughing up black soot in a dollar-a-night flophouse, I was anxious to ride into the sporadic violence of civil disorder to escape the madness of Indian roadways. Brought to my knees while visiting the Killing Fields of Cambodia, it took the innocent smiles of bashful natives to eventually revive a wobbling faith in humanity. Weary from a year of tumultuous travel, the steamy massage parlors of Bangkok provided sensuous mid-journey relief before heading south to Indonesia, where the wilds of Borneo set my imagination ablaze while I established a world's record as the first person to circle the island on two wheels. But once in Sumatra I found that nothing could prepare me for the horrors of tsunami-ravaged Banda Aceh. Saving the best for last, it was the soft humility and alien ferocity of Africa that finally fulfilled a dream that began during my turbulent youth.

Prologue

Adventuring must be in my Norwegian blood. As a foolishly bold kid anxious to accept dares, life was always more interesting when challenging the norms. But eating worms, jumping off roofs or being the first to test out new rope swings was unsettling behavior for my hand-wringing parents. After spending more time in detention than studying and wearing down wood on the principal's bench, counselors were summoned. Standard warnings and punishments had no effect. To my mother's horror, at age 12, my father suggested constructing a homebuilt, mini-scooter using an old lawn mower engine. The freedom and power of a motorized bike was like a match to gasoline for a troubled young rebel growing up in the 60s. A lifetime lust for adventure had been ignited. Fiercely independent and anti-authority, I was constantly rejecting the status quo, and that made me feel more alive. In high school, while others were elected most likely to succeed, my teachers often remarked that I would surely spend life behind bars, and I did — handlebars.

Infected with motorcycle fever, sprawling California back roads merely made me crave more. After watching *Easy Rider* and reading Jack Kerouac's *On the Road*, barriers were shattered on a tumultuous highway that never ends. In that 1960s drug-crazed era, outlaw motorcyclists became unlikely counterculture heroes and represented the ultimate symbol of resisting authority. Huge and hairy, these modern barbarians on gleaming choppers turned obsession into reality with an insolent assault on societal norms. At the age of 20, my predicted destiny was fulfilled when I became the youngest member of the Hells Angels Motorcycle Club and later the sergeant-at-arms of the San Bernardino chapter.

During a short stint in jail, a long, painful view down the road convinced me the next time I arrived here it would be for an extended stay. A chance conversation with an unlikely source, a local kung fu master, made me believe that following specific, strict disciplines of the martial arts was the only way to disrupt my patterns of senseless aggression and harness my wild spirit. With goals of competing in the ring, I became a full-time student, training six hours a day, six days a week for six years. While I worried about surrendering my role as a sworn outlaw, in 1979 I cautiously retired from the club. Redirecting my scattered energies into karate, judo and Brazilian jujitsu became the pressure-relief valve for a life more conducive to freedom. In between winning national championships and backpacking through Asia, I squeezed in short motorcycle journeys. But they were never long enough, and, like most motorcyclists, I had tantalizing visions of some day canceling tomorrow to simply keep riding. But with life's complications, someday was in danger of becoming never. With a growing awareness that life does eventually end, I finally decided that as of October 1, 2001, my fate would be officially tossed to the wind. And those winds immediately turned into a hurricane.

A few weeks past the 9/11 attacks, my dream ride to the tip of South America was interrupted by capture in Colombia by violent rebels fighting the government. When I was finally freed, supporters from home sent new equipment, giving me a second chance to complete my ride to Argentina and back. Gringo-hating Marxist terrorists had used torture and starvation to break my spirit, but, in the end, setting a new goal was the only solution. Resisting all forms of negative emotion was my most potent weapon; publicly vowing to finish riding the world became a silent middle finger to former tormentors. It's true — what doesn't kill us only makes us stronger. Instead of collapsing under the weight of my Colombian ordeal, I used it as a springboard to the next level, with a journey into the evolving landscape of humanity. Yet even though I was now a more experienced rider, this was far easier said than done.

From California, there were no airfreight links into Siberia, so after flying to Tokyo, I crossed Japan to the western coast for a three-day sail to the once forbidden reaches of the former Soviet Union.

On July 16, 2004, the lifelong goal of riding the world quietly began near the North Korean border in Vladivostok, Russia.

The Russians, security minded as ever, made it complicated to enter the Motherland with a motorcycle and wander. Officials were concerned about spies, misfits or journalists who might report what the government preferred to keep secret. Organized tours are welcome, but overland travelers are forced to fill out lengthy visa applications supplemented by fictitious business proposals before being considered. The process was a hassle, expensive and risky because anyone in the chain of command could change their minds on a whim. My itinerary was purposely vague. Destinations were to be determined by weather or at fateful forks in the road. Let's call this a ride from California to Africa by way of Siberia, with photographs and stories of what happened in between.

It took a lifetime of hope and a solid year to plan for this adventure. Mr. Murphy constantly intervened with problems of logistics and legalities. Every issue required follow-up letters and phone calls just to be told no. A glowing laptop screen became the staging ground for research and preparation. Friends and relatives finally quit mumbling, "Gee Glen, are you sure of what you're doing?" They've resigned to the fact that they are now part of the lunacy and are warily watching the show. The plan was to have nothing to worry about or look back at, so to strengthen my resolve and properly cast my fate to the wind, I sold all of my earthly possessions, including a coveted mountain ranch. Whatever remained was given away. It was the ultimate state to be in — homeless on the road. What was important for survival, I crammed into a set of Jesse aluminum saddlebags bolted on the sides of a 650cc BMW motorcycle on loan from local dealers. Still, on the verge of plunging into the merry chaos of the developing world, I never felt more secure.

Although born in California, I grew up a traditional Norwegian — long lost relatives still live above the Arctic Circle, near Tromso in northern Norway. Viking blood pumping through my veins has constantly propelled me toward foreign lands and bizarre circumstances, but the physical conditioning and awareness honed from 25 years of martial arts often provides an edge. Still, the most effective weapon when traveling has been a big, stupid smile and an obvious gratitude merely to be there.

Sometimes serious problems arrive from nowhere, but we just have to roll with the punches, literally. There were U.S. State Department travel warnings about every country on my list, including some considered allies. Wandering strange lands alone is seldom comfortable but it's always rewarding, as every experience carries a lesson, even when it's a painful one. True adventurers admit we feel more alive when straddling the edge. But the measure of our passion is growth, and a motorcyclist's addiction intensifies while leaning through the next curve of a spiraling mountain road.

That's why it's called adventure travel — shit happens. Experiences on the road range from toe-curling ecstasy to sphincter-puckering fear while sampling the perils and pleasures on the two-wheeled path to nirvana. Yet that's the purpose of such journeys; if the challenge was easy, it wouldn't be worth the effort. In martial arts, we establish our goals and twist the perseverance dial according to what gets in the way, so I just applied the same principles to my beckoning odyssey. Adventuring is a great spiritual exercise. One thing for certain, you never give up.

At my going away party in a Palm Springs biker bar, an old friend, David Christian, handed me a three-by-three-inch, yellowed photograph of a smiling young child. He told me with misty eyes, "Here is my little brother and since he never got to go anywhere, please take him with you." This was confusing until David left and I read the writing on the back, "Phillip Dean Christian 1948–1951." With that thought in mind, my adventure was dedicated to Phillip, and his photo was tucked in my jacket, where he could be protected from the sandstorms of faraway deserts, the wilds of Siberia and the driving rains of the tropics but still enjoy the show.

THE ROUTE

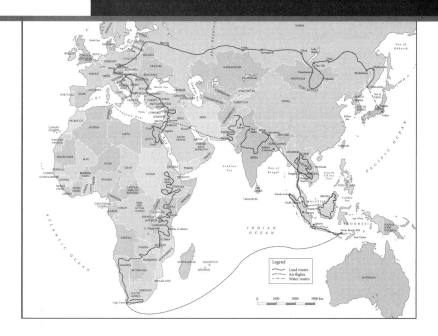

Leaving Home
July 4, 2004
Los Angeles, California
● ● ● ● ● ● ● ● ● ● ● ● ●

Up until now, it's been just planning and setbacks. But in 12 hours, the reality of roaming a planet full of dreams begins by disconnecting from the relative ease and familiarity of California and taking an anxious step into the unknown. To maximize the experience it's necessary to depart from the comfort zone for as long as tolerable, and who knows how long this experience will last or what will happen at home in my absence. But even if I wanted to, there's no turning back now.

There are so many questions and issues to ponder, both personal and global. Given the rate science advances, where will technology be when I return? In a multiyear absence from loved ones, interpersonal relationships are sure to change. Traveling alone on a motorcycle involves a certain vulnerability — from physical health to personal safety. In the event of a medical crisis, would I be subject to the developing world's blood supply? And what about the war on terror, or the one in Iraq? Will I encounter chanting mobs of churning masses angry with my government?

In this intensifying political climate, people constantly warn me that it's foolish to ride the earth alone, but passion conquers common sense — wanderers wander because they have to. Yet omens abound. There were many good excuses to postpone — the need to promote my new book with media interviews and book signings. The second of two surgical procedures had failed, leaving one last stone the diameter of a dime in my kidney and two thin plastic tubes shoved into my body to allow ailing organs to function until another procedure could be scheduled. At least my urologist, using ultrasonic waves, had pulverized the other four. But these foreign objects left in my bladder rubbed against urinary nerves, making it feel like I constantly had to pee.

I spent the final three weeks in California, visiting doctor's offices, hospital rooms and CAT-scan labs. Marching in smiling with chest out, I left with drooping shoulders. A line had to be drawn somewhere — no more needles, pills or tests.

Hardest of all: parting kisses with Jodie. With her seductive balance of beauty and brilliance, she was the woman of my dreams. But because of my self-centered determination, her contagious happiness and delicate laughter have turned to mangled sorrow. For the last year, in the throes of committed love, we both buried the inevitable parting as something too far away to imagine. Just halfway through her medical degree and restricted by an overprotective, conservative and religious family, Jodie was torn between her loyalty for me and inescapable cultural constraints. Realizing this could be the last time we'd ever be together was a thought we tried to deny with unrealistic pledges to meet next year in India. Her last words socked me into twisted guilt, "Please, Glen, tell me one more time why you're throwing all this away."

Moments later, a final farewell embrace in an airport hotel parking lot permanently ripped two hearts in half. While staring deeply one last time into her trusting chestnut eyes, I could see only a flaming bridge behind me as I selfishly sabotaged what could have been lifelong happiness. Will she remember our life together with pleasant recollections or regret our losing love affair? At times wanderlust is a curse.

Even my departure is awkward — an around-the-world motorcycle ride that begins by flying on a jet to Japan? For a mission so well planned, I am already a month behind schedule, needing to beat seasonal turbulence of monsoon rains, frozen mountain passes and fiery desert heat. July is the warmest time of year to navigate Siberia, but there will be winter snows in November crossing into Iran from Turkey's rugged Anatolian Plateau. That's if the Iranian government grants me a transit visa. Because of an unpopular foreign policy and the seemingly endless war in Iraq, Americans are suspect in the Middle East for now, but who knows, maybe peace will break out by then.

To cross some international borders with a private vehicle, a special legal document is required to guarantee the vehicle will not be sold there to circumvent local import tariffs. For a fee backed by a credit card, the Canadian Automobile Association (CAA) issues a *carnet de passage* that guarantees, if the vehicle is not exported on time, they are responsible for taxes owed. When forwarding this motorcycle-passport, the CAA included a warning list of countries to avoid because of civil unrest, human rights violations, or imminent evacuation of U.S. citizens. Most of those on the list are ones I want to visit or at least will need to cross. But my optimistic belief is that people will differentiate between citizens and governments. I am betting my life on that.

The odds favor disaster on a journey this long, but the most relentless threat is traffic. Poorly maintained roads, if they even exist, are plagued with unskilled hordes of kamikaze drivers convinced that size does matter, and two-wheeled vehicles don't. ABS brakes, a bright yellow helmet and a shiny red riding suit help balance the scales. The word "reliability" takes on new meaning, knowing that mechanical failure during a mountain snowstorm or running out of fuel in a remote desert carry dire consequences.

Selecting the ultimate motorized companion involved a series of careful tradeoffs. American built, powerful Harley-Davidsons are too bulky and heavy, so the critical decision came down to proven Japanese performance and dependability versus German engineering for better handling. For its endurance record, both in on- and off-road riding, BMW's dual-sport 650 Dakar reigned supreme. My judo students, Jimmy, Paul and Donal, were also the dedicated team of mechanics who spent a hundred shop hours prepping the two-wheeled Blue Beast. Half the bike had to be disassembled to install Touratech long-range gas tanks and off-road suspension, but now there is a 700-mile fuel range and proper maneuverability for an overloaded motorcycle. Every upgrade counts, from wider foot pegs for stand-up riding in rough terrain to powerful auxiliary driving lights for when I'm caught out after dark. Modified electronics will accommodate an electrically heated vest, GPS and Jimmy's secret security gear.

Nothing works the first time. Just changing the handlebars and installing risers for better reach meant hours of machine work to make aftermarket aluminum hand-guards fit. You can't take a ride this long without going down — the bike and the rider must be able to contend with varying degrees of impact. In most regions ahead, there are no motorcycle repair shops or medical trauma centers serviced by emergency helicopters. One of the downsides to traveling alone is that I am on my own during a crisis. There is no margin for error.

My equipment is new, but road-testing was limited to scenarios I could only imagine from studying *National Geographic* photographs — there are bound to be failures. My padded riding suit is made with space-age plastic fabrics that glow in the dark and melt slower during high-speed slides across asphalt. Knee, elbow and spinal areas have built-in shock-absorbing rubber pads for crash-related collisions. The problem is that it's uncomfortable to wear in warm temperatures, but I've made a promise to myself not to ride without it, even when crossing deserts.

THE FAR EAST

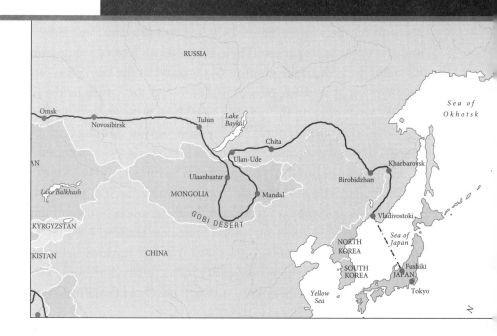

Home to Japan
July 5, 2004
Over the Pacific
● ● ● ● ● ● ● ● ● ●

At 30,000 feet, it is hard to doze inside a humming aluminum missile hurtling across the sky at an even 550 miles per hour. As cheap
plastic headphones blare along with a synchronized overhead video,
flight attendants pass out Japanese newspapers. Although the Asian
dancers lack rhythm, they attempt American musical ghetto talk in
comical accents while awkwardly mimicking street-gangster hand
gestures. I wonder what their conservative family elders think about
these popular Western antics that conflict with their ancient belief in
restrained and disciplined behavior.

On the horizon, Mount Fuji slowly protrudes like a massive cone-shaped sentinel guarding an elongated, overcrowded island. Japan is my spiritual home. For 25 years, I've studied martial arts refined by devout Japanese masters who wrote the rules centuries ago. Their images tumble within my consciousness as distant gongs reverberate with recollections of harsh discipline and spiritual awakening. I am one with the Japanese. Their methods and creeds ring true. Bushido, the code of the samurai — the Ways of the Warrior — are laws of integrity and discipline as well as respect for nature. In love or war, it's total focus on the task at hand. There is no gray area; either you have honor or you don't. Emotionless years of training through blood and sweat are tributes to the *sensei*. Nothing less is expected.

Flashbacks of polished wooden floors as tight as the surface of a drum appear. The only sounds then were pivoting feet squeaking while bodies gracefully spun through the air upside down, slamming onto mats of straw. Judo, karate and jujitsu are studies of redirected force — techniques that become a way of living. Intricate ballets of battle honed through hand-to-hand combat, broken bones and torn cartilage all form our disciplined dance of life. The martial arts command my spirit; there is no other way.

In a few hours, I'll roll across the surface of this gentle land for a pilgrimage into my past. I feel welcome here. Whether they like you or not, the Japanese are always polite. If lost, travelers don't need to ask for directions. While you're bumbling around deciphering maps, someone wanting to practice English invariably comes to the rescue, pointing the way. Fellow bikers are even more accommodating. Interesting news travels fast. Internet-savvy Japanese world riders heard reports of an invading American wanderer, and, even before my arriving in Tokyo, they had emailed me an invitation to a weekend outing. They are waiting to tempt me with countryside cruising and bottles of sinus-clearing sake.

Japanese friends who had also ridden motorcycles around the world

The Vikings Arrive
July 10, 2004
Tokyo, Japan

● ● ● ● ● ● ● ●

After a long, annoying wait at airport immigration, clearing myself and the motorcycle was simple. Having paid a customs broker 50 bucks to handle the complex importation procedure, my only job was to uncrate the Blue Beast and reinstall the windshield and front wheel. Within two hours, I was navigating a sophisticated maze of modern concrete roadways toward a particular hotel in downtown Tokyo. Despite driving after dark on the opposite side of the road and with few signs in English, I rendezvoused with my cousin Kjell from Norway who arrived on business the same day. We both feel better having said goodbye face-to-face.

My first call home to Jodie temporarily relieves an aching loneliness that is certain to grow worse. Her sweet voice pours like honey through the phone as we reassure each other that our planned reunion in India is only eight months away. Soothed but not convinced, I know that every mile deeper into this journey will push me emotionally farther away from this woman I love. Keeping busy by looking forward makes me forget about the burning bridge.

This afternoon, I'll meet with Japanese bikers for a weekend of camping and sightseeing. After many phone calls, I manage to obtain a transit reservation on a boat leaving for Russia this Friday from the other side of the island. Vladivostok, Siberia, is a mere two-day sail but a civilization away, and I twitch under the anticipation of actually beginning this adventure. Lounging in a modern hotel with TV and running water has, so far, made this journey seem awkward. I can't stop thinking of what lies ahead.

Temperatures have been a hundred degrees with high humidity all week, a test of my pledge to wear the heavy-duty riding suit. All my equipment checked out, but the rear mono-shock required adjustments to balance the excessive load I was carrying. Still, that was not enough, so I dumped 10 pounds of extra supplies that weren't worth hauling at the cost of stability. To keep weight low, the spare drive chain fits perfectly between the engine bottom and skid plate. Since traffic is the biggest safety threat in foreign lands, better bike handling is critical, but practice begins in the most organized city on earth.

The streets and walkways of Tokyo morph into scenes out of science fiction. Surrealistic streams of short, black-haired men dressed in identical business suits clutching brown leather briefcases file from tall, faceless concrete buildings and underground tunnels with slender, ivory-skinned women clad in tight-fitting dark slacks sprinkled in as reminders of how they reproduce. Every act is prearranged with Japanese logic. Japan is a spotless, pragmatic island where everything makes sense. There're no used cars, old clothes or people dressed out of fashion. Supermarket fruit is the ideal color, never under- or overripe. With no apparent time for relaxation, there is purpose in every step of the people's overstressed lives. Business dominates, and the Japanese communicate so fanatically that there are now signs in subway cars ordering people not to use cell phones. Never mind — those sitting are busy on their laptops.

Japanese live for planning and discipline — theirs is an orderly, near crimeless society in which, at least superficially, they respect everyone. Enter foreigners — *gaijin*, the barbarians. Many wealthy Japanese businessmen will not socialize with inferior gaijin and there are signs posted at upscale nightclub entrances — Japanese Only. Being born here will not make you Japanese either, not even if you're Asian. Recently, a 60-year-old former Japanese man had his citizenship revoked by the courts after his father, a Korean, admitted to fathering him with a Japanese woman.

Gaijin
July 11, 2004
Atsugi, Japan
• • • • • • • •

After riding in circles exiting the labyrinth of high-tech Tokyo, I was an hour late for my meeting at a designated entrance to the Toumei Expressway. I'd guessed that reaching the toll plaza 40 miles outside Tokyo by 3:00 p.m. was a long shot. Fellow world riders would surely be waiting for their blundering American counterpart. As in Mexico, expressways here are expensive but convenient and hard to get lost on. Destinations are noted in English below Japanese characters, so if you're paying attention it's easy to determine where you are.

After I apologized for being late, my host assured me it was *"No ploblem,"* and we rode into miles of steaming gridlock to pick up Kiki's wife and her bike and head for the campground. Once past rows of soaring futuristic skyscrapers, the countryside blooms into mountains of rich pine forests and meandering mountain streams. A narrow, swirling asphalt road flows through still villages of blue-tile-roofed houses shaped with traditional upturned corners. Finely crafted wooden structures architecturally designed with nature in mind blend into hillsides and stunning green meadows. The marvel of Asia never falters.

A dozen globe-riding veterans gathered at this crystal clear river for a weekend of camaraderie and inspirational tale-swapping. The first question: "So Glen-San, do you miss your ranch?" A respectful signal that they had done their homework and read my website journals. Most of them speak some English, but I recall only a few phrases in Japanese. Since we'd all toured Latin America, our common tongue was Spanish. Around a smoky campfire, we sampled dried fruits, salted fish and sizzling, sweet chicken teriyaki sticks. As the sake flowed, late-night conversations drifted between languages, punctuated by *"Ah so!"* There is little to say that we don't already feel — a kinship of adventurers born to follow our spirits.

Close to midnight the sake bites hard and, combined with jet lag, I fade early before my mild spins turn to wild spins. Yet my energetic hosts ramble until dawn, mixing beer and "Japanese whiskey" with wild tales of their common passion — motorcycling.

At sunrise the anxious crew is awake and planning the day. *"Ah Glen-San, you like-a see Mount Fuji and take mineral bath? We musta go wery soon."* While trying to appear ready for anything, I stumble toward the cement-block bathroom with an aching head and strained neck muscles after passing out and using my boots as a pillow. Once outside Tokyo there are few foreigners and only Japanese is understood. Bleary-eyed in a bulky nylon riding suit and towering above curious black-headed natives, they peek out from vans and trailers gawking as though a Martian has landed in their orderly midst. A startled audience hears me bellow, *"Koh neechy wah!"* (Good day!) with a failed attempt to conceal a belch. The unruly barbarian has arrived.

Snags
July 13, 2004
Outside Tokyo, Japan
● ● ● ● ● ● ● ● ● ● ● ● ●

After only a week on the road, my first casualty is a broken kickstand. For increased ground clearance, this motorcycle was designed without a center stand, a handy tool for raising the bike to change tires and lube the chain. Normally it's easy to tilt the bike over onto the kickstand high enough to sweep a rock underneath and then pull it upright to balance the rear wheel off the ground. It's a simple move on lighter bikes, but with 200 pounds of extra equipment and fuel, today the hollow support tube buckled.

A loud crack before the kickstand bent in half afforded the split-second needed to catch the bike before it tipped over. Now what? Even simple problems in Japan are community affairs that require lengthy discussion considering all options. After leaning the motorcycle against a tree, a conference begins, prompting the first of several long winded telephone calls. After the third, I ask, "So what did they say?" The answer: "Wrong number."

Hours of conversation with BMW representatives reveals the best solution is to order a new kickstand from a local dealer. This means a two-day wait for something that takes five minutes to install. Yet such delays can be part of the adventure, and once we find a decent hotel my companions depart for home, leaving me to sort out communications. Whomever I ask insists that there are no Internet cafes outside major cities, but the motorcycle shop owner lets me use his computer to check email and upload a website journal. After nine days in Japan, I am finally alone.

After showering and donning a button-down shirt, I peer into a 10-seater sushi bar. At 8:00 p.m., it's packed with a raucous crowd, but the beer-guzzling diners call to come in anyway, they will make room for an alien. *Gaijin* is welcome for entertainment. In an attempt to be casual, I nod with a smile, mumbling *"Kon bon wah."* (Good evening.) Curious looks erupt into broad grins and friendly laughter as the interrogation begins. They know as much English as I do Japanese, but while I pantomime the story of my adventure, their jabbering amazement subsides into solemn appreciation. Japanese respect ambition.

Next comes the ritual of exchange of business cards — a serious moment in Japan. They don't take them to quickly stuff in their pocket, that would be rude. Instead, cards are accepted with both hands as a sign of respect and then studied. After discovering I teach

Japanese martial arts, they offer enthusiastic applause as though I am expected to demonstrate. Without ordering, the chef produces a sushi plate reserved for guests of honor. He *"maka special for Gren Sensei."* Later the owner, with both hands, presents a gift wrapped in rice paper — a porcelain cup with painted pictures of different sushi. It should last a day bouncing inside the aluminum saddlebags, but I accept it with both hands and a bow.

Getting Naked
July 14, 2004
Kanazawa, Japan
● ● ● ● ● ● ● ● ● ●

On weekends, on the backcountry roads of Japan, motorcycles outnumber cars, spinning through the curves of narrow lanes that slice across gentle farmland. Sporadic squalls have little effect as motorists continue puttering across narrow wooden bridges that only allow one yielding vehicle at a time. This is two-wheeled heaven. Outside cities, the mountains are too steep to build houses or roads, so much of this island remains pristine wilderness. But determined drivers are able to reach distant destinations quickly if they're willing to spend the money. Tokyo toll roads can deliver a fast-moving rider anywhere on the island in one long day. Hotels, although more expensive than in Latin America, offer great services. Internet costs five dollars an hour, most hotels provide free DSL you can access if you have your own laptop, television and air-conditioning. In the mornings, they offer opulent buffet breakfasts simply called "Viking." Space is scarce in Japan so rooms are low-ceilinged cubicles with barely enough room to step by my bags, and most doorways require stooping to pass.

Japanese are the ultimate gadget freaks, with the edge on everyone. Their latest technology will not reach the outside world for another year while it's test-marketed here. Rejuvenating electronic foot massagers deliver divine bliss, while automated toilets shoot warm streams of water wherever desired. Bathroom mirrors contain heating elements at face level so after showering there is always a clear spot. For those wanting to see naked girls, there are pay-per-view dirty movies with subservient Japanese babes being violated by well-endowed, burly black men.

Red-light districts awaken at sundown with flashing pictures of what goes on behind thick-curtained, black velvet entrances. Doormen in shiny black business suits with slicked-back hair utter warnings behind mirrored sunglasses — no gaijin allowed. Working in front of nightclubs, tall, blue-eyed Eastern European blondes in long sparkling gowns turn their backs as I approach. These slender young beauties can't risk conversation with gaijin because disapproving Japanese clients will think they also service white men.

Japanese politeness is accented with an air of understandable superiority. In this nearly crime-free country, there is no need to watch your back or guard your belongings. I've seen only one cop since arriving. Everyone is civil and tolerant whether they like you or not, while they adhere to similar philosophy without betraying emotion. They are famously honest, with a penchant for curiosity, and I have the constant feeling that in this society so well planned, nothing can go wrong. Could the world learn from Japanese culture?

Yesterday, my biker friends took me to a Japanese bathhouse where stone pools of naturally heated spring water relieve aching bodies with inner-earth mystic powers. The polished wooden building was divided into two tiled rooms, male and female, as bathing is done without clothes. But a nagging question reverberated: "Why am I dipping into steaming pools of water with naked men when right next door there are steaming pools of naked women?"

Last Days in Japan
July 15, 2004
Kanazawa, Japan
● ● ● ● ● ● ● ● ● ●

While en route to the ferryboat seaport, an overnight visit in Kanazawa becomes a step through history, into feudal Japan, when martial arts were developed as tools of war. Wandering ancient temples rekindles a familiar spirit similar to modern traditional dojos, where training is a dedicated religious affair. The serenity of orchestrated hand-to-hand combat pervades the cool morning air like an imposing mist, commanding respect. Pausing in the silence of meticulously manicured gardens, you feel the presence of masters other warriors wrote books about. Did Musashi engage opponents on this hallowed ground? Were these mystical courtyards early classrooms of Kano or Funakashi? But even lost in my imagination, all thoughts eventually drift to Russia.

In 24 hours, an aging converted passenger ship destined for Siberia will steam from the port city of Fushiki to deliver me towards my elusive vision.

A One-Way Ticket to Siberia
July 16, 2004
M/V RUS on the Sea of Japan
● ● ● ● ● ● ● ● ● ● ● ● ● ● ● ● ● ●

If a journey of a thousand miles begins with a first step, what's considered the first step? Since life is a continuous journey, maybe it began at 16 when I read Jack Kerouac's novel *On the Road*. Afterwards, so overwhelmed with images of purposeful wandering, I immediately stuck out my thumb, hitchhiking from California to New Orleans. Or was it at the age of 10 when an aging uncle took me out of school a semester early for a trip to Norway to discover my roots? Forty years and 50 countries later, arriving in the east Siberian seaport of Vladivostok, I stand on the threshold of another major step.

The ship was my first encounter with Russians on their turf. It's different meeting them in their own environment rather than through televised images or otherwise distorted reports. After approaching a team of workers near the *M/V RUS*, for a moment we just stopped and gaped at each other's similar features. As children, my generation grew up fearing the "Red Menace." We were taught in school how to crouch beneath desks for when the USSR launched its inevitable nuclear attack to conquer the USA. Then there were scenes of Premier Nikita Khrushchev at a United Nations meeting pounding his shoe on the table: "We will bury you!" Sputnik — the Soviets had beaten us into space — more reason to fear them. The Cuban missile crisis — when the world was breathless and on the brink of destruction, one nervous finger away from launching humanity into oblivion.

The Cold War. American citizens once blacklisted and ostracized if even suspected of sympathizing with dreaded communists had careers ruined and lives destroyed on rumor and innuendo. Then came the pawns, people's armies versus freedom fighters. Murderous battles for hearts and minds waged throughout the Third World. Clad in rags, surrogate warriors were manipulated by military dictators supported by opposing superpowers. But growing up in a Norwegian household included a different version of world history than that taught in California schools. My father explained that Russians were not really monsters and also had their own story.

Briefly accustomed to towering over the little, black-haired Japanese, it's startling to discover how much these Russians and I resemble each other. It doesn't require a DNA test to prove my roaming ancestors made it this far. Muscular, blond, blue-eyed youngsters wearing shorts and sandals casually slinging cargo onto the ship's decks could easily be descendants of Olav or Erik the Red. In a moment of clarity I realize these inquisitive men from the "Evil Empire" are likely my relatives.

Once aboard ship I am directed to the captain's quarters to pay for passage. *"You havk Ahmerdikan dohlars?"*

"Da."

"Chew musta pay two hahdred tventy for da pahssenger un von hahdred for da motorcyclick."

The port city of Vladivostok, once so secret it was off limits even to Russians, is now the gateway to forbidden lands infamous for mass starvation and Stalin's gulags. During long, dark winters, the Russian Far East has one of the harshest environments on earth. Yet here I stand, peeling off fresh, crisp Ben Franklins for a former enemy, giddy with the notion that I just purchased a one-way ticket to Siberia.

Since being released from Colombian rebels, it's been my goal to not only finish riding to the tip of South America but also to complete a world tour, with phase two beginning in Vladivostok. I wasn't sure when because of the time I needed to recuperate. Two years later, I am peeking out a porthole, straining to spot what I've seen only in my dreams. From the edge of the Sea of Japan, our rusting old groaning vessel pitches and rolls over bubbly swells in a monotonous motion not meant for land-based mammals. It's good that meager portions of the mediocre food are only served three times a day. Who could eat anyway? Beleaguered cooks and bored waiters offer only boiled cabbage soups, foul-smelling hot dogs and eggs packed with onions. I hate onions. But my guidebooks warn that most meals in Russia are served with onions. Canvas gas-tank panniers stuffed with 20 pounds of chocolate-flavored protein bars are likely my last familiar meals.

In spite of the pervading seasickness, it's time to practice communicating and swap gifts with my shipmates. I have only the protein bars, but Russians are polite enough to eat them, thinking they must be American candy. Being notorious drinkers, an offer comes quick. *"You vil drik Rahshin wahdkah vees hus?"* As a teenager, my first time drunk and violently ill was on a full pint of vodka, and it's been nauseating to smell that foul fragrance ever since. Moaning under my breath as the ship pitches and rolls, memories of the sickening spins return, and my rich Viking blood turns as green as the churning sea.

Second Thoughts?
July 18, 2004
Vladivostok, Siberia
● ● ● ● ● ● ● ● ● ● ●

It's the people you encounter along the way that enhance the experience of adventure travel. When trapped on planes, boats or trains, there are always like-minded voyagers from foreign lands available for swapping inspirational tales of life on the road from other perspectives. Those whom you meet while wandering make the discomfort of travel worthwhile, especially those who've also ventured down unbeaten paths. All the crew and most of the passengers aboard ship are Russian except for half a dozen Japanese. But there is enough limited common language between us at mealtimes on plastic benches to discover an interesting variety of missions.

The Russians have bought used cars in Japan and are taking them home to sell for profit. Depending on the scam, each family member is permitted three to ten cars, so they bring relatives to increase their quotas. If the cars are missing certain major parts there is only a few hundred dollars duty owed; otherwise it's several thousand. The whole process is lucrative enough that they've drained the ship's decaying swimming pool to accommodate additional vehicles. Even rust-scaled decks are packed with secondhand speedboats and shiny cars missing wheels and engines, to be reassembled later in Moscow. Lenin must turn pinwheels in his grave as capitalism thrives in the land of the Bolsheviks. While former Soviets shed the remnants of restricted economies, the "Red Menace" grows green with the currency of choice, U.S. dollars. And as our ship docked in Vladivostok, the rush to process importation documents erupted into a frenzy of pushing and shoving at customs offices.

Yet the few foreigner passengers without such issues were guided through without incident, and I was temporarily delayed with the Russians to ponder the dreaded complications of processing a temporary vehicle permit. According to local reports, approval requires several days of waiting in long lines to comply with regulations that few understand. This is also a moment to revisit lingering health issues and a last chance to reconsider.

That incomplete kidney-stone surgical procedure now haunts me. What if something goes wrong? The curled ends of eight-inch-long soft plastic stents the diameter of a coat hanger continue to cause internal bleeding. Postponing that time-consuming treatment in California might cause me a regrettable difficulty in Russia. Although my urologist admitted that it was possible to travel by car with the stents, riding a motorcycle radically increased any risk and would be extremely uncomfortable. Rejecting further delays in California, Plan B became waiting for medical care in the nearest Western country — Germany. But the advantage there is being treated at the Munich hospital where the ultrasound procedure (lithotripsy) was invented.

Previously not caring how bad further kidney problems would be, I now sit guessing if it's too late. When I walk a few blocks, the internal grating makes me pee blood. The further I go, the more blood there is. I have a constant urge to urinate whether I need to or not, and when I do it's a grimacing, hold-on-to-the-wall experience. Pain is manageable, but when the doctor advised that there is a chance the stents could slip into another organ, I forced myself to believe that this just couldn't happen. With the current discomfort, I am more conscious of what could go wrong. In Japan, I brooded over my decision every second. Bite the bullet by taking a jet ride back to Los Angeles, get treated and return to the road in a few weeks, or roll the dice on reaching the German doctors?

If something does go wrong, there is no competent medical care before Munich, 8,000 miles and seven times zones away. Barring further incident, that's three months from today. In the meantime Western-style emergency services don't exist. Once I enter Russia, strict importation laws make exiting without the motorcycle illegal. The next country is Mongolia, without hospitals outside the capital. If it was all asphalt to Germany this would be easy, but there are 3,000 miles of off-road riding between here and the first autobahns of Bavaria.

The Vikings Have Landed
July 19, 2004
Vladivostok, Primorye *(Pree more e ah)*
● ●

Tales from fellow overlanders praising Russian hospitality were understated. Since arriving in Vladivostok, there has constantly been one of the local riders either whisking me about the city sightseeing, patiently haggling in long lines at customs or bringing me to an apartment for traditional Russian meals. *"Eef you lak vee gan went my house for zee food."* Since it's unusual for travelers to import motorcycles, the locals want to entertain me and government officials don't know what to do with me. Previous riders posted Internet warnings on horizonsunlimited.com, describing the exhausting process of bouncing around the city obtaining new documents and stamping old ones. I hoped this was an exaggeration, but so far it's been sillier and worse than I'd imagined.

In addition to hotel receipts, fictitious business letters of invitation and detailed currency exchange forms, sworn statements by a local resident are needed to assure the bike will leave Russia when I do. If not, my cosigne will have to pay an exorbitant import tax or go to jail. After all that, those handwritten statements must be authenticated and stamped by another agency to be forwarded to yet another. Triple copies are required to study and store so the government can be sure foreigners don't spend thousands of dollars hauling a bike here to sell for a few hundred dollars profit. One bureaucracy oversees another that exists to keep public employees seemingly busy. Most don't want to work, all find excuses to get in your way and none are as important as they think they are. It's like dealing with city hall when applying for a building permit in California.

Tomorrow morning we'll receive our 37 pages of documents restamped by the same bored officials and then find a customs inspector to bribe for a drive across town to verify the bike's engine serial numbers. There are dozens of different strings of numbers handwritten on all the documents; if one was copied incorrectly we must start over. For the last two days, my Russian hosts have hauled me across Vladivostok from 8:00 a.m. to 6:00 p.m., trying to sort out a procedure that confuses even them. But at least it's a whirlwind city tour and a taste of the notorious bureaucracy Russians must endure. Without the connections of "Biker King" Sinus and tireless help from his friends Vitali and Elena, this task would have taken weeks.

Notwithstanding the difficulties, it feels good to finally plant my feet on Russian soil. During early evenings, I wander about the city, booming one of 10 memorized Russian words, "*Pryviat!*" (Hello!) Surprised locals only stare back at the grinning lunatic until my California accent registers that I am American. Russians love Americans, and, once you're past your protective shell of paranoia, they let it be known with welcoming smiles and hearty handshakes. There is no time to accept all the dinner invitations and places to stay; besides, it's too risky sleeping in large apartment complexes without adequate bike security.

In the morning, if we've filed our papers correctly, by sundown officials should release my bike. Yet then, a new dilemma arises — where to park it. The safest place at the moment is where it has been stored, padlocked behind the giant wooden doors of the customs warehouse. Since Russian mafia and local thugs control the streets, whatever is unsecured in their domain is a reasonable target. Natives warn that unguarded motorcycles in particular don't last more than minutes. Last night, two Czech travelers staying at the clubhouse of local motorcyclists were robbed at gunpoint. Masked bandits stole everything — cameras, cash and motorcycles — a bold move even by Russian standards.

On the ferry ride over from Japan, two burly young Siberian men sporting homemade tattoos were asking about my journey. Feeling lucky to meet real Russians, I gave them my business card with website information. Before realizing it, I had answered questions about my equipment and told them I would be staying in Vladivostok with local riders. Red flags didn't flash until they commented that my laptop and cameras looked expensive and that, to support my journey, I must carry a lot of cash. This didn't seem significant until I heard today's news report. Yet, for now, a basic 20-dollar-per-night tourist hotel is home, with two no-neck security men dressed in expensive business suits who don't respond to my greetings lurking in the lobby. The hotel owner probably pays for protection, but there's no knowing if that covers bikes parked on the street. I'm anxious to pay security bribes when necessary, but clearly it's best to hire the toughest guys.

Situated directly on the Pacific Ocean, Vladivostok's climate is warm and humid, leaving my clothes constantly damp. There is a short break in the mornings for cooling squalls that dry up quickly but not much to do afternoons except wait in customs lines counting the seconds until I roll. A young Japanese rider, who I met on the ship, and I have joined forces to tackle the importation process together. A short but stocky young factory worker from Saitama, Yasutomo appears undeterred by any of the ridiculous paperwork hassles, and, after noting his stout-hearted determination, I nick-named him Little Samurai.

Vladivostok
July 21, 2004
Vladivostok, Russia
● ● ● ● ● ● ● ● ● ● ●

Because Japanese demand the latest technology, they don't buy secondhand goods. This means that there is no market for used cars in Japan, and since Japanese cars are right-hand drive they are useless in neighboring countries unless offered at a substantial discount. This is a dream come true for nearby Russians, with their voracious appetites for affordable transportation with which to cover the wide expanses of Siberia. It makes little difference to them if cars have steering wheels on the right or left, so most vehicles here are used Japanese versions. A perfect match — Japan unloads what's junk to them and hardworking everyday Ruskies menace the roadways in affordable, luxurious SUVs.

Russian motorists are widely known for aggressive driving

maneuvers. As our hosts blast Little Samurai and me around the city in terror rides from hell, it's scary to think about soon being in the crosshairs of these copycat racecar drivers out on the open road. While crisscrossing the city to various government offices, I sit nervously in what would normally be the driver's side of a 20-year-old Japanese car, while, to my right, Vitali plays Indianapolis 500. I can't help automatically reaching for a steering wheel or fumbling for a brake. The truth is, I am terrified. With one near miss after another, it requires steady nerves just being a passenger in a vehicle operating in such substandard safety conditions. Vitali's bald tires don't screech when he stomps on the brakes, they hiss while sliding across crumbling asphalt, forcing him to stop every 20 minutes to reinflate them after the air has seeped past exposed cord. There are no rules of the road. The craziest driver is king, and the vying contestants are fearless.

Pedestrians crossing the road know their safety doesn't matter, and getting from one side to the other intact requires the courage and grace of a matador avoiding angry bulls. It's like pedestrians are invisible. I want to ask Vitali if he saw that woman we may have just clipped, but I am afraid of the answer. Although there wasn't a thunk, it seemed like we at least grazed her. Not wanting to know, none of us looked back. More effort is put into dodging potholes than avoiding humans.

Still, the citizens of Vladivostok endure their chaotic situation with fewer wrecks than would be expected. But noting the danger is enough to make anyone rethink driving a motorcycle across Russia. In a few hours, I'll be unprotected, riding alone on a bumper-car exploration of the city. Bored from the long, lonely rural roads of Siberia, ambitious truckers roaming the main highways will likely relish the prospect of fresh foreigner prey. But to remain positive, I balance the precarious prospects ahead with a breathless anthropological study of native females.

Long-legged Russian blondes with aquamarine eyes strut about the city in daring miniskirts and bare midriffs. Imagination-stirring panty lines should be outlawed. I admire statuesque women covered in flawless pale skin decorated with shades of pastel makeup. Departing for jobs as waitresses, store clerks or prostitutes, they dress like runway models in fashionable high heels while nonchalantly stepping over smelly sewage outside of dilapidated two-room tenements.

Despite the continuing hardships of a difficult past, the dignity of Russians is remarkable and unmistakable. Long ruled by oppressive tsars and communist dictators, human tragedy has become an accepted way of life. Death tolls in the thousands don't alarm Russians; anguished peasants measure their dead in millions. Because of terror-induced secrecy, the dozens of millions who died or disappeared under Stalin will never be known. Threatened by the infamous tentacles of the KGB, Russians grew accustomed to remaining quiet about what ails them. Even now, Russians are still cautious about being reported for saying something illegal and are reluctant to speak with strangers. Between suffering at the hands of foreign invaders and being persecuted by their own leaders, Russian history seems to justify their paranoia.

Freed
July 22, 2004
Vladivostok, Russia
● ● ● ● ● ● ● ● ● ● ●

If the first obligations of government are to maintain order amongst the people and to provide for the common defense, then an overly cautious Russian bureaucracy is doing its job. They maintain absolute order when it comes to defending against foreign travelers importing motorcycles and secure the nation's future by burying us in piles of senseless paperwork. Although still not sure if I am a spy or a motorcycle smuggler, officials finally decide to grant my critical temporary importation documents — all 37 of them. At the 30th hour of waiting in long lines while employees drank coffee and looked important, the long-awaited moment arrived.

It was time to enter all the numbers, statements and photographs into the computer, which would hopefully spit out a three-page, perfectly printed pink form authorizing them to free the bike from impound and permit me to cross Russia. Except in the U.S., it's common to drive next year's model vehicle in the current year; in Russia it is not. On my California DMV-issued certificate of title, it states that the bike is a 2005 version of the BMW 650 Dakar, but the Russian computer refuses to accept this data in 2004. Importation permit fees vary according to the year built and the horsepower, so the indicated model-year data locked up their computer hard drive and no one knew what to do. Solving the crisis required three additional hours, two supervisors and desperately creative program manipulation, but we finally arrived at the correct amount due: 150 rubles as opposed to 180. There are 30 rubles to the dollar.

Such complications are all part of the experience of adventure travel, and, fortunately for me, only a taste of what local people endure. Long, depressing lines of forlorn citizens surrendering to frustration from government overload are standard in Russia. The result is a stifled economy and massive corruption. The cycle is endless and the masses suffer. Experiencing the poverty while visiting my new friends gives me a small taste of the misery, but only living in it can make it real.

But it's the same all over. People wanting to build things, people wanting to sell things and people wanting to buy things. What stands in the way is usually government. Foreigners spending several thousand dollars converted into rubles traveling across Russia is insignificant to bureaucrats following petty rulebooks. Most travelers avoid Russia because, between the ridiculous visa process and strict regulations regarding registering your whereabouts every 72 hours, few find it worth the hassle. But my patience had been rewarded.

All that remained was a return to the pier where my bike was off-loaded last week to lay claim to the iron steed that I'd almost forgotten what was like to ride. After paying 20 dollars a day storage fee and 20 dollars for wheeling it 100 feet into a shed, we were led to a musty old warehouse where my magic carpet to adventure was waiting. The Blue Beast was unharmed and ready to ride — as long as I carry my private, personal pink documents. Officials warn with grim expressions that if I'm stopped without them, I will be jailed and the bike will be confiscated.

It's compulsory to produce these documents to law enforcement on demand, which will likely be every 50 miles for the next two months. Imagine losing them and trying to obtain new ones. But between concealing cash from both crooks and cops or guessing the safest place to park, there will be plenty of other details to monitor. Through it all, for the next four continents, I'll keep my electronics safe, take lots of pictures and post a journal when possible.

Adios Vladivostok
July 24, 2004
The Russian Far East
● ● ● ● ● ● ● ● ● ● ● ● ●

For me, taking on a riding partner is rare. It's nice to have someone around if you're sick or need to notify next of kin; still, the minuses outweigh the plusses. Who wants to teach someone how to watch their back, prepare their equipment or behave in a tight situation? Getting into and out of trouble alone is easier, without a companion to worry about. It's better to wake up and hit the road on a whim or change plans at a moment's notice without worrying if someone else thinks it's okay. And a traveler is more inclined to connect with locals and blend with local culture when there is no one familiar to spend time with. But what the heck?

Yasutomo Ogihara is a 28-year-old factory worker from Saitama, Japan. He's a shy but always-smiling, ready-for-anything youngster headed for a turnaround in Spain via Estonia and Western Europe. We listened together when the TV news broadcast covered the two Czech riders who were beaten and robbed. That report concluded with a horrendous account of the radical rise in vehicle theft and carjacking across the country — a sobering thought for anyone about to ride alone over an unfamiliar landscape with no knowledge of the customs or language. But for a mild mannered young man from a nation where you can leave your keys in your bike with your wallet on the seat and everything is still there when you return, this is a real shock.

Yasutomo tried hard to conceal his alarm as Vitali burned up the city in a madcap race of bumper cars, but we were both on edge. Yasutomo has moto-toured Australia and Canada before, but this is his first foray into the stark chaos of a developing nation and his nervousness shows.

Because the Japanese are so polite, it's easy to mistake them for timid, not a good persona in a tense situation that calls for a positive attitude. But from meeting them in the ring, I know that Japanese are polite like coyotes and as timid as wolverines. You can also learn things by inspecting a rider's equipment. His bike, of course, is high tech and new. It's a 400cc Honda Enduro, about half the weight of my Dakar and far better able to contend with rough terrain — a plus if he has the skills that go with it. Enduros are proven machines for dirt, but because of low gearing they're slow on long stretches of asphalt. He's installed long-range fuel tanks and big knobby tires for off-roading. Still, it's hard to decide if he'll be a plus or a minus crossing one of the toughest routes in the world in the middle of a crime wave.

He has questions of his own. How fast will we ride and how often will we rest? At least he knows to be cautious. We review hand signals for silent traffic messages and, most importantly, the crossed-finger gesture that means we are in danger with the person in front of us and to be on guard. We ride tomorrow at 10.

With typical Russian hospitality, our friends came to see us off in force. The surly security men in the lobby had become inquisitive friends, and it was soon impossible to pass them without answering questions in sign language about our journey or demonstrating a judo joint-lock. After posing for pictures together, the moment had come to swap the madness of the city for an escort into the adventure of the countryside. In a small motorcade of cars and bikes, with those who befriended us in the lead, we wove our way past Vladivostok's crumbling rows of Soviet-era tenements to a lumpy but paved road to Khabarovsk, the jump-off point into rural Siberia. Hillsides layered with multilayered brick enclaves similar to "the projects" in American inner cities were final reminders of the hard lives of Russia's middle class. Half of the two-room flats lacked running water or indoor toilets, a nasty drawback during winter.

Although the constant assistance from our hosts was appreciated, it felt good to finally be on our own, bursting onto the open road while sensing a rush of enthusiasm, watching the smoggy metropolis diminishing in the mirror. Vladivostok, sister city to San Francisco and close enough to the North Korean border to make a Geiger counter click, will quickly be a distant memory.

Kicking into high gear, thick traffic thins to a trickle, and we are absorbed into a Russian countryside blooming with vast waist-high green meadows sprinkled with splotches of purple wildflowers. Yasutomo returns my thumbs-up gesture with a smile as the gentle thunks of raindrops tap out warnings of squalls ahead. In a moment of complete satisfaction, a darkening sky draws us to the horizon, and finally the Viking and Little Samurai become one with Mother Russia.

Khabarovsk
July 26, 2004
Khabarovsk, Russia
● ● ● ● ● ● ● ● ● ● ●

It's only 500 miles north to Khabarovsk, where the pavement ends, but we decided to enjoy the scenery and take two days. Aggressive truckers and obnoxious motorists passing too close kept us alert and hugging the shoulder. Yasutomo's Enduro bike is geared so low that top speed is only 50 miles per hour. That's fine, he'll fly when we hit the dirt.

Driving slow allows a 650-mile fuel range. At the first gas stop, we're confronted with a matronly monster even more grotesque than the customs women in Vladivostok. Perched high in a cramped bulletproof enclosure packed with cartons of cigarettes and oilcans, she slobbered over a plastic microphone, shrieking orders over a piercing outdoor loudspeaker. This alone was deafening. It wasn't necessary to shout, but she did so anyway, as though commanding an army for battle. All Yasutomo meekly requested was a few liters of fuel. He speaks no Russian, just Japanese and broken English, but the wretched troll not only continues to scream at him, she will not take a breath or pause long enough for a reply. I try not to laugh while sneaking in, *"Nyet Ruskie!"* (No Russian spoken.)

She ignores this and continues to berate Little Samurai as if she thinks shouting louder will eventually make him understand. Finally, she storms from her glass cubicle to breathe in his face while ranting up close through a porthole of gold teeth and spittle forming on the corners of her mouth. On top of her flabby legs, covered in leopard-skin spandex, an enormous potbelly supports a hideous pair of watermelon breasts oozing from the top of her blouse. A bleached-blonde, sixties-style beehive do matches her bright red lipstick that looks like it has been applied with a stamp slightly off-center on two pounds of pale pancake batter makeup. At every word, a protruding mole on her upper lip the size of a large pea with a hair growing out of the center quivers up and down.

In Japan, female employees speak to male customers accompanied by bowing in a polite display of appreciation. My poor little pal's narrow eyes turned round as his jaw dropped. She will not relent as she grabs his hand while continuing to screech out a lecture and marches him back toward our bikes. With a clenched fist she pounds the top of the pump and wiggles the rusty lever, and suddenly an electric motor whirrs on while the hose grows taut with fuel under pressure. She holds up her hands and waves them through the air in gestures of "How could you have been so stupid?"

Until today, I had kept a handheld video camera ready, but since we were back rolling it was stashed in the top-box for security. Too bad we missed this one and a few more to come.

Guidebooks warn about the peculiar way Russians respond to greetings, so we considered ourselves prepared for the blank stares and noncooperation. It was still a shock when encountering hollow expressions in return for a hearty *"Privyet!"* (Hello!) When calling out greetings in countryside restaurants, it's as though no one has spoken, and patrons simply keep eating in silence, not speaking even with each other. Half the time, we're in the Twilight Zone surrounded by empty-eyed zombies.

Most people, without a common tongue, can communicate with sign language or pantomime. Often, the inflection in articulated speech accompanied by hand gestures conveys an idea even in a different language. Anyone needing to communicate can. In small, smoke-filled roadside cafes where everything is spoken and written in Russian, cooperation is difficult. I point to my mouth after using a fork and knife cutting motion and then tuck my fists into my armpits muttering *"Boc boc boc, boc boc."* With a little imagination this should be easy to figure out, but the waitresses turn around and go back to what they were doing; talking to each other and smoking cigarettes. Not even a blank stare — a blank back.

When someone does talk to us, they shout as though that makes things clearer. Today we've found a broken-down but tidy little wooden hotel typical in Russia — two miniature beds, but with clean sheets and a bathroom a short walk down the hall over creaking, yellowed linoleum floors. Of course there're windows with torn screens to let the mosquitoes out.

Nothing in Russia is easy; you're either waiting in lines or filling out forms, even for parking a motorcycle. Today, a wretched old-woman innkeeper wants more than our passports for identification. She also needs papers for the bikes so she can fill out the necessary forms for us to sleep there. She studies our documents while silently mouthing the words as though scanning for an error so she can deny us our rest. Disappointed everything is in order, she holds out her palm and screams more long-winded orders. In short, she has asked for 200 rubles each — about six bucks.

Just as we settle in and swat the last of the horseflies, there is a sharp knocking on the door like rapping with chunks of wood. They were, with billy clubs, two large but friendly young country cops in frayed blue uniforms, wanting to inspect our passports so they can fill out more forms. They asked to see the page our visas were glued in, which made me suspect that they had never seen one before and were going through these motions more out of curiosity than official procedure. Between hand gestures and reference to our dictionaries, they want to know what we intend to do with our bikes at night.

Since this was a small town, we felt safe and decided to use my one heavy-duty cable lock and Yasutomo's two chain locks to secure them to a tree outside our window. Not possible the cop declares, followed by motions indicating they would be stolen. They take us outside to show how other hotel visitors secured their vehicles at night, even removing their windshield wiper blades. They pointed to our mirrors and seat cushions and flicked open their hands demonstrating how they would disappear. So far, everywhere in Russia we've been warned that our bikes or equipment would be in instant jeopardy if left unattended. It's nice to think the best of people, but we are finally convinced into wrangling our bikes down a narrow hallway to park them outside our room. It's been a long day in friendly Russia.

The Trans-Siberian Highway
July 28, 2004
Eastern Siberia
● ● ● ● ● ● ● ● ●

One day in any major city is too much, so by the third night in Khabarovsk we were ready to roll. Last night, Little Samurai crushed his big toe when trying to drag his bike down the hotel corridor barefoot — that cost us time waiting for the toenail to finish falling off so he could get a boot on.

Escaping from Khabarovsk on the road west into Siberia wasn't so bad — two hours of riding in circles using hand-drawn maps by taxi drivers dumped us on the waterfront. Our final farewell stretched over a mile-long bridge spanning the sprawling Amur River, which borders on and reaches into China. The next town is Birobidzhan, capital of the once-autonomous region for Jews to live in after World War II. But the deteriorated conditions of faded wooden cottages and dilapidated buildings reveal another failed Soviet plan.

After a short run of asphalt, for the next 1,300 miles it's mud and gravel until we emerge in the Siberian city of Chita for a possible detour to Mongolia. Barring extreme weather, this could take a week at a reasonable pace. It's the roughest stretch of the Trans-Siberian Highway, so bad most riders put their bikes on the train between Khabarovsk and Chita. An up-on-the-pegs motorcycle ride in these conditions is an event to look forward to, but if there is a place between here and the hospital in Germany where my plastic stents or that renegade stone are going to jerk loose, it's here.

Between the anticipated slipping and sliding and jarring and jolting, this will be a significant test of what our equipment and bodies can stand. The reports are all the same — this may possibly be the worst road in the world. Small villages are a hundred miles apart and signs along the roadway warn not to camp because of robbery. At night, we plan to find trails through the mosquito-infested swamps and head deep into the forest to pitch tents. We're hauling enough bread, water and smoked fish to last a week, and we'll likely find fresh fruit along the way.

One of the common issues for motorcycling anywhere is foul weather. Here in the outback, crossing unknown terrain, random summer storms are a constant concern. Bikers learn to keep one eye on the road and the other on the sky, sorting the dark from the light clouds and calculating where the load is coming down. Because it's a hassle climbing into rain gear at the roadside, it's normal to procrastinate when it first starts to drizzle. Too often, it takes a soaking to become fully convinced. Still, when entering a storm, there is often a shot at riding it out. The rain must eventually end, and when it does the wind will dry us off, and we will not have to stop. At least that's what we thought nine hours ago when enough of the first pellets of water persuaded us it was time to suit up. And there was no break coming, just a deeper plunge into darker clouds of driving rain.

Bad weather requires study and an evaluation of the terrain for traction. Bare ground reacts differently to moisture. Sand gets firmer, dirt gets softer and red clay becomes slippery. Red clay when dry is hard as concrete; today, it's slick like ice, and even knobby tires have no effect. There is a persistent fear of tires sliding out from underneath my overloaded motorcycle, resulting in a jolt that might dislodge those plastic stents precariously placed directly behind my belly button. To remain upright, our pace is constrained to a first gear crawl.

We started at 10:00 a.m., and even now, at 10:00 p.m., there's enough remaining daylight to ride more as we roll up to the only hotel within a hundred miles. Not a hotel by Western standards, but rather a three-story decaying cement-block building that was formerly military dorms. The first two floors are uninhabitable, only the third has space to accommodate us in a cramped four-bed cubicle. The bathroom at the end of the hall is a mangled mass of cracked porcelain and rusted pipe. None of the power outlets work, but there is a flickering fluorescent-tube light in the hallway. Moments later, four policemen come to inspect our documents and recommend that we chain the bikes up inside their gates. Even that, they warn, is no guarantee against theft during the night.

Once bedded down, it is difficult to rest as my irritating stents compel stumbling down the sticky linoleum corridor for hourly relief. But even in between bathroom calls, there is too much sinister history to ignore. After all, this is the land of infamous gulags and mass starvation. Aware of the ghostly evil, I wonder who built this rotting structure? Was it the millions sentenced to slave-labor camps? Maybe those who died of disease and starvation? Tormented lost souls are moaning for remembrance, forcing me to review my history lessons.

First it was the tsars, then the Communists. In ships and in boxcars — hollow-eyed humans frozen in horror were condemned into a wasteland of waiting death. Soviet Gulags. Initially constructed for exiled criminals, then political prisoners and finally whomever Stalin felt like sending — he picked up where Hitler left off. Ghastly images of bones and chains rattle and howl inside my head, and, no matter how I turn, blood dripping from rafters haunts my dreams. After a night of clenched fists and grinding teeth, I awake more exhausted than when I'd gone to bed. Little Samurai is ready to ride at sunup.

Food
July 29, 2004
Somewhere in Siberia
● ● ● ● ● ● ● ● ● ● ● ●

As warned, the further west we travel, the rougher the road. Strips of asphalt deteriorate between miles of rutted gravel grabbing our tires. The temperature has dropped into the comfortable 50s, and we're dressed for a storm that doesn't appear. When traveling without an itinerary, it's best to not expect much, that way you're seldom disappointed. It's as fun to sleep in a tent as in a hotel, and as long as there are eggs in the morning the rest of the day's hassles don't matter. In the empty expanses of heavily forested Siberia, when we can find

A roadside cafe in Siberia

someone to ask for directions it still takes hours to locate run-down roadside cafés with limited menus. Eggs come only one way boiled, cut in half and smothered under globs of mayonnaise. At least they are eggs. Russians also make thin, sweet crepes called *bliny*, and I order enough of them to make the waitress gag. "Four?"

"Yes, four." I insist by holding up four fingers.

I meant four pancakes — she thought four orders of four. Too embarrassed to acknowledge the error, Yasutomo and I gobbled them down as though that's what we wanted in the first place. The bill — breakfast for two is less than five bucks.

At the local post office/telephone company, we found the only Internet terminal in the region. This is the last stop before jumping off into what is arguably the roughest part of the journey. As we could be out of touch for a while, we send final emails home. Jodie is growing impatient with what she considers a lack of communication on my part, and efforts to console her with weekly love letters are clearly insufficient. It appears as though she expected me to call her nightly. On the one hand, I don't want her to worry about some of the difficulties on the road, but, then again, if she knew how hard it was to find Internet in these remote areas, she might understand.

Trans-Siberian 1000
July 30, 2004
BFE, Russia
● ● ● ● ● ● ● ●

My temporary travel buddy has been holding his own, but today he stands gasping at the challenge ahead. The Trans-Siberian Highway is everything it was reputed to be. Boldly beautiful, wet, muddy, littered with obstacles and dotted with unpredictable locals who respond to us in unusual ways. One minute Russian villagers are cold, ignoring our repeated requests for directions; the next they are friendly to a fault and reeking of alcohol. Where the vodka flows like water, most are wildly intoxicated by noon. We ponder a maze of side streets and dead-end back alleys in the morning — far too difficult without street signs or a guide. After signing autographs at the hotel, a young man in a business suit asks in a British accent if there is anything he can do for us. "Yes, please show us how to get out of here." We agree he'll pick us up at the Internet post in 30 minutes for an escort to the main road.

Exactly a half-hour later he appears with his private driver carrying a hardbound Russian road atlas. "A present for you my friends." Then he leads us back to the dirt-surfaced Trans-Siberian-Highway, and we're off, kicking up pea gravel with spinning tires. We've only had to stop for document checks three times a day, including when caught on radar for speeding. Each time we end up humoring the cops and posing for pictures.

The road is actually a raised gravel levy dividing thousands of square miles of swampland meadows. Long dark clouds of mosquitoes hover overhead, waiting for victims. At hourly pee-stops, huge horseflies instantly coat our riding suits. We only expose as much as we dare.

The vastness of the Russian Far East lowers the lid of a graying overcast sky, stretching the empty horizon almost wider than we can see without turning our heads. Flat, without a rise in any direction, the only interruption is thick, towering stands of white birch trees clumped together in between marshes. Tall silver poles with crowns of furry green flicker in the morning sunlight. Four-fifths of Russians live on one-quarter of the land on the opposite side of the country, west of the Urals. Most of Siberia is a powerful, peaceful land devoid of humans, except for those we encounter wandering drunk or huddled by fires along the road selling fruit and mushrooms. Living in dilapidated villages with ancient wooden cottages crumbling under their own weight, Siberians are sometimes rude beyond belief. Although there is only one main road, in small towns it feeds into an illogical crisscross of muddy alleys devoid of signs. When we stop to ask directions, the drunks scream and wave their arms, other times they just mumble in unintelligible one-sided dialogues.

By early afternoon, the highway has turned pure motocross. Deep gullies sever the road every 20 feet, but the earth is damp and firm. Unlike on the Bolivian altiplano, this time I am set up properly, with correct suspension and proper training. For three months before departure, I'd practiced with a heavier bike, working hard on mountain trails and long, drifting sand dunes. After Jimmy Lewis's off-road riding school, I had a better idea of how to handle what lay ahead. And here it is.

After standing on the pegs for miles of gullies and bumps, my legs burn with fatigue. Yet it's hard to stop grinning. Bring it on! Rising to the challenge, my dual-sport workhorse comes alive, never skipping a beat. Although weighted down with 200 pounds of extra equipment and fuel, it performs well enough to leave Little Samurai in the dust. After increasing the compression dampening, the suspension sweet spot appears to tame the terrain — as long as it remains dry.

Weather patterns have been established. Freezing afternoon storms blow in at 4:00 p.m., but to get our 12 hours in, we must ride until 10:00. Preparing for this early, I zippered into my rain suit before starting out in the morning. No matter what they claim though, no riding apparel is perfectly watertight. Strong winds eventually push tiny streams of icy water through the neck and cuffs. The Savanna II crash suit holds the misery at bay for hours until, finally, even the electric vest can't stave off numbing chills. But if you continue to ride wet, hyperthermia is a risk. We need relief.

Our maps indicate only emptiness ahead for another 65 miles, three more hours at this pace. Little Samurai's riding suit is not waterproof, and his case of the shivers arrived long before mine. I'm unsure how long he can last. Finding immediate shelter is critical. It's solid swamp on either side of the road so it's impossible to pull off and set up camp. The tree branches would be too wet to burn anyway. Afternoon fun turns survival test as we are forced to ride even slower by the mud. The remote Trans-Siberian Highway often follows a parallel path to the Trans-Siberian Railroad, the longest tracks in the world. Vladivostok to Moscow is just under 4,000 miles hrough mostly remote wilderness — a transcontinental challenge by any standard.

Occasionally we pass directly next to it, and, for a moment, catch glimpses of comfortable passengers in lighted railcars. I imagine them sipping wine and nibbling French cheeses in their steamy, warm carriages. Yasutomo must hate me at the moment. Before we left together, he'd asked about taking the train to Chita instead of riding. My bellowing reply was, "Are we motorcyclists or what?"

I wonder now — as we ride into the night, blue with uncontrolled shivering — if he regrets his decision. Humming loudly inside my helmet is Willie Nelson's "On the Road Again," and I tell myself once more that it's good to be here.

Chilling in Siberia
July 31, 2004
The Road to Chita
● ● ● ● ● ● ● ● ● ● ●

Our guidebooks say that in this region, wintertime temperatures drop to 40 below zero but in summers we can expect anything from light snow up to a balmy 60 degrees. It was so cold this morning that we've opted to remain in our sleeping bags until a hazy morning sun warms the air. There was no shelter available last night, and after the "Let's just ride another 50 miles" routine, we wound up wet-camping in the woods. We soon discover a massive public works project.

Taking advantage of extended daylight at higher latitude, Russian road construction crews work double shifts to finish surfacing their infamous highway. In such a hostile wintertime environment, it's an engineering feat already, but they still have a long way to go. Although most of the steel-girder bridges are half-built, it will be five more years before motorists can roll from Vladivostok to Moscow on uninterrupted asphalt. For the last two hours, the mangled road has miraculously smoothed to four lanes of graded loose gravel trafficked by rolling heavy equipment shaking the ground beneath us.

Intimidating, futuristic 16-wheel dump trucks with hubs higher than my head pound forward in mile-long convoys kicking up long, choking clouds of cement dust. The way it spreads in solid gray swirls expanding into the sky, it's like a detonating atomic bomb. Gritty dust clouds are so thick we can neither breathe nor see 50 feet beyond our windshields. I imagine that the lead monster-wagon is piloted by a cloaked Darth Vader sadistically enjoying his mischief. And there is no stopping and resting to let them get ahead; there are more convoys following behind.

Gravel roads, although firmer than mud, cause mild wheel-wobbling, making the bike sway as though riding on flat tires. Cognizant of variances in surface conditions, especially when the front wheel twists off in unintended directions, we lack proper control and have to resist the urge to fight the handlebars. Like flying an aircraft, good motorcycling requires delicate steering. To stay relaxed, it's best to control the handlebars by pinching the handgrips with your outside two fingers and use the other two for brakes and clutch. Caution is critical. If we slow abruptly the weight shifts forward, loading the front end and digging the front tire into the gravel instead of rolling over it. This plowing effect can send the bike sideways into a horizontal slide.

Our best hope is to speed ahead of the pack during lumpy detours around uncompleted bridges where the speeding trucks need to slow down. Standing on the foot pegs, we bound over knee-high bumps like riding bucking stallions. Every inch is a spine-banging struggle with menacing grin. We're winning.

Minutes later, we head the merciless procession but don't dare stop and rest or the madness begins again. At 11:00 p.m., the sun is setting and we find a trail leading into a clearing through tall, pungent pines. Recalling warnings, we camp out of sight to avoid unwanted midnight visitors. Zipped in tight, not even the grumbling roar of the Trans-Siberian Railroad cars or the hoarse blast of the train whistle can disturb me now. The moment I'm tucked into my bag, exhausted from the day's struggle, I tumble into comatose sleep.

An hour past sunup, the tents should be dried from the evening's condensation, but an early morning freezing fog rolls in to delay the process. I holler to Little Samurai, "We can go now or wait for the sun to dry out our gear." He thinks it's best to wait also. Neither of us wants to admit we lack the strength. There is still half a liter of water and a dozen protein bars — I can hold out for a while, curled up in this mummy bag, so I am going back to sleep.

From Russia with Love
August 1, 2004
Final Stretch to Chita
● ● ● ● ● ● ● ● ● ● ● ●

The weather turns colder each morning, requiring layers of full foul-weather gear — sweaters, thermal underwear, electric vest and rain suit. Even then it's hard to get warm. Last week, temperatures were in the 60s; now it's the high 30s but the rain has subsided. Yasutomo was ill-prepared for this and is constantly shivering.

Back on the road, we battle for lead position against teams of Russian professional drivers racing to deliver imported Japanese cars from Vladivostok to Moscow. We only get ahead when the road returns to motocross and they slow to creep over massive bumps and gullies. It's a friendly race we can't win whether we're ahead or not. When we grab the lead, to maintain it we ride a reckless pace with no time for photos. If the string of daunting daredevils takes over, we eat their dust. It's either ride like madmen or suck dirt.

My jarred kidneys piped with plastic stents feel like they've been used as punching bags, and I must stop every hour to pee. To measure the internal bleeding, I monitor urine color. It varies from pink Chablis to Burgundy when the terrain gets extra rough. When it hits a 50/50 mix, we'll stop to rest. Until then, we push on to Chita for promised hot showers and Internet. Encrusted in white cement dust, our voices crack from parched throats and nasal passages caked with dried powder. But the equipment is more important.

Abrasive granite dust has invaded every opening. Switches, wiring harnesses, levers and even the sealed aluminum panniers produce little puffs of powder when flicked. The air filtration system is so clogged the bikes will not idle. There is also a gritty sound when I twist the dials on the digital camera, but the video gear was triple-sealed and has survived. Between the extreme beating and intensive dusting, our motorcycles have aged 20,000 miles.

At 9:00 p.m., we arrive at the last village before Chita, a mere hundred miles away — three hours if we push it. Since we're no longer in a hurry, riding fatigued on a road this bad is foolish. We receive mixed responses from locals when we ask about hotels. *"Gde gastinitza?"* (Where's a hotel?) Finding a place to sleep seems to be an unsolvable riddle until a red-faced old man behind a crooked wooden fence eyes us suspiciously through a missing slat. But soon he breaks into jolly shouting, swinging open two large wooden gates and motioning us in. We're not sure what he wants, but he's so close I can smell the fresh vodka on his breath. Everyone shouts here so we were not alarmed, but I try to determine what he's saying. Yasutomo points to his wooden cabin, *"Gastinitza?"* (Hotel?)

"Nyet gastinitza!" But he continues to flail, waving us in.

What the heck, we're out of choices, so we roll into a small pine-planked courtyard as he shut the gates behind us, still smiling and shouting. He points to himself declaring, *"Pavio!"* With finger gestures he indicates his age is 72 and then points to us. Next, the farmer's wife rushes forward cradling a baby in her arms, and she, too, is laughing and shouting. Pavio, still waving, cups his armpits with massive hands, roaring, *"Banya, banya!"* (Bath, bath!) None of the cottages we've seen so far has running water or indoor plumbing, so we have visions of being handed buckets of ice water and told to clean up.

In the meantime, the hugging has started as we're led to a smaller cabin inside the courtyard. Like everywhere here, I must stoop to enter. By local standards, it's a studio apartment, complete with ancient wood-burning stove, broken black-and-white TV and lopsided kitchen table. There are two tiny beds with an overhead lightbulb — if there is an electrical outlet to charge batteries we'll take it.

Within minutes, Pavio's wife, Luba, is setting the table with mismatched plastic plates and cups then brings out an electric frying pan full of wallet-sized river fish. Pavio continues his tirade in Russian as though we're engaged in deep conversation. We smile back repeating, *"Spahcebo, spahcebo."* (Thank you, thank you.) He responds with long-ago memorized English, *"Goot mornig, von, tvo tree."* Luba keeps loading the table — crackers, bread and a giant jar of ice-cold milk. Real milk, with a layer of thick cream floating on the top.

While we eat, from the small, smudged kitchen window, we can see Pavio carrying armloads of wood and tubs of water to another smaller shack behind ours. *"Banya, sauna!"* he shouts as he grabs Yasutomo by the hand and drags him into the shed. Ten minutes later Samurai emerges grinning. "Very hot, very good. You try."

Opening the door to the darkened 10-by-10 room, a burst of dry heat sucks away my breath. There is a wood-burning kettle mounted on a pile of bricks in the corner with a cast-iron valve to drain water. A 20-gallon tub of cold water, for dipping and mixing into a smaller one, is used to adjust to the perfect temperature for a traditional European sponge bath. Since it's been four days without a wash, this is welcome relief.

Later, we shoot video and stills for playback on the computer. Our hosts are amazed and want to continue, but it's late and time to sleep. No longer fazed by the shouting, Little Samurai and I doze while Pavio sits on the end of my bed continuing to laugh and rave in a drunken stupor.

In the morning, while the roosters crow, a creaky wooden door bangs open as Pavio barges in with a skillet of sizzling eggs and thick squares of extra-fat bacon. More milk and crackers are followed by cutlets of fried pork. We politely decline to eat more, but our requests are ignored as Luba hands us more plates of bread and cheese.

While packing our gear, we are aware that we have likely eaten the last of their food and ask our hosts, *"Skol Kah?"* (How much?) This earns us an instant stunned response, like "How dare you!" Yasutomo insists, handing forth a wad of Russian rubles. Suddenly, they grow angry, vigorously slapping their hearts, indicating hospitality comes from there and cannot be bought. With this, I consider the irony that, at this very moment, our respective governments have targeted each other's cities with thermonuclear weapons. And one can't help but ask what is wrong with this picture?

Storm clouds are rolling in early, so there is no hurry to get moving — we prefer to savor the final road into Chita dry. The Trans-Siberian Highway doesn't end there, just the roughest section. The rest of the route to the Baltic Sea is coated with potholed asphalt and aging steel-girder bridges. From Ulaan Ude I'll detour south into Mongolia for a few weeks and maybe ride the Gobi Desert. Then, it's onward to German doctors via Moscow and Poland.

Whew!
August 3, 2004
Petrogorovsk, Russia
● ● ● ● ● ● ● ● ● ● ●

The Lonely Planet guidebook speaks of "the Russian's famous love of suffering." The same might be said of those attempting the Trans-Siberian Highway from Khabarovsk to Chita. Gluttons for punishment we are, but we're also fulfilled ones. The road after Chita returns to deep swells of asphalt, wavy enough that if you exceed 65 miles per hour the bike becomes airborne. But compared to the miserable route behind, it's now an easy flow on a long strand of licorice whipped cream under a crystal blue sky. Stow the rain gear and sail into nirvana, there is nothing left to block the way. Russian truck drivers still slide into turns, but there are fewer of them. Next stop Ulaan Ude, gateway to Mongolia.

Between language barriers and contending with remnants of a stale Soviet bureaucracy, traveling Russia is unnecessarily complicated. Just parking overnight requires finding a garage, usually blocks away, to lockdown until dawn. Because of a reported high rate of theft, it's a hassle but worth the effort. Rolling west, gingerbread villages of rough-sawn wooden cottages puff streams of blue smoke from tilting red brick chimneys. Baking aromas from fireside meals permeate the cool forest air as if beckoning us to the source. Connected by ribbons of orange dirt wrapping around hillsides of yellowing wheat fields, little has changed in the last hundred years. In a Siberian summer breeze, Russian cowboys tend cattle grazing in the afternoon sun, assisted by packs of yapping long-haired dogs. This could be a back road across Montana except the isolated cafés are further apart and there are still no road signs.

Local restaurant food is substandard, but it's tolerable if you're hungry enough. When traveling, it's a struggle to schedule meals anywhere; in empty Siberia, it's even more difficult. You eat when and what you can. We've figured out the standard fare in roadside cafés and are accustomed to tiny portions of bland protein. Yasutomo doesn't eat much — mostly Cokes and candy bars after cigarette breaks. To stay healthy, it's best to stop and eat every three hours, but that never happens. He rides painfully slowly, so I blast ahead and wait for him at restaurants. We miscalculated today, and he's been gone since I passed the last road fork this afternoon. That's okay, he was continuing west to Moscow when tomorrow I head south into Mongolia.

Even good travel partners can be a hassle, and being alone delivers me deeper into adventure bliss. The effect is immediate. Locals are friendlier to lone strangers, and when you stroll into restaurants the welcomes are heartier and there's instant conversation. We've been offered vodka at every stop in Russia, and "no" was not an acceptable answer. But guzzlers back off with knowing nods when I tap my kidneys and say, "Sick."

Communicating gets easier when there is time to sit and talk. If you're able to count and ask who, what, when and where, at least basic information can be exchanged. It's not enough to debate politics, but we figure out where we're all from, how many are in the family and where we're going.

This afternoon, on a dinner break at a roadside café, four mid-30s men slap an empty chair next to them and offer me one of the shot glasses of vodka on their table. My explanation for declining their hospitality is accepted on the booze, but they've already ordered an extra a plate of dumplings — hamburger meat packed with onions. Even if I was okay with the onions, they don't mix with my sugared pancakes. But refusing hospitality is rude, so I have no choice but to graciously accept the coveted treats. Holding my breath, I gulp each one down without chewing and smile meekly. Too many compliments would only encourage them to order a second plate.

They are military officers, two from Russia, one from Belarus and one from Ukraine. The three captains are dressed in fatigues, and the major from Belarus wears a frayed, shiny suit. He doesn't speak or drink vodka like the others. Belarus is the last Soviet-style hold-out still controlled by a strict dictatorship. He's likely an intelligence operative, the equivalent of the KGB. They are conducting joint maneuvers, like they also do with U.S. military, proving it's better to train together than to kill each other. After posing for parking lot pictures, two tall, skinny punks approach. The way one steps in from behind me is suspicious. They speak in slurred Russian hard to understand, but by the way the military guys confronted them, their words must have been ominous. Soon an argument ensues that relates to Americans this and that. Not wanting to be part of what happens next, I shake hands farewell with the embarrassed good guys and leave a brewing brawl behind.

At 9:00 p.m., there is nothing left to do but ride west into the glare of a setting sun in search of a hotel. Excited local boys sitting in an old sedan, passing around a bottle of vodka, flag me over at the next town and lead me to a hotel — a three-story crumbling brick building with barred windows covering broken glass. Like most country hotels, it was buried far from the highway with no sign out front, appearing like just another of many abandoned factories. Again, it's a long haul up three flights of dark concrete stairs, but at last a musty room to myself.

While I'm pulling off clumsy riding boots and basking in my newfound solitude, there is a rapping on the door. A document check by the local police? No, a middle-aged man in a business suit with a leather satchel under his arm and an expectant look on his face. Another Russian pimp with a tempting portfolio of young, pretty hookers? Pointing to the empty bed, he stammers in broken English, "I, I, I, I . . . your room." Now it's understandable why they issued quarters with two cots instead of one — the 10-dollar charge was based on double occupancy. At least there was now a chance to practice speaking Russian.

MONGOLIAN DETOUR

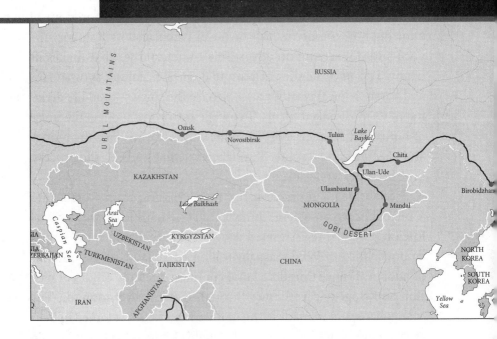

Easing into Mongolia
August 6, 2004
Khahar, Mongolia
● ● ● ● ● ● ● ● ● ● ●

On a long journey, it takes a month of adjusting to erratic routines to find the rhythm of the road. There is a point where weary travelers either flee for the comforts of home or cross a magic line beyond which home is redefined. After four short weeks in Russia, the road is now home. Long, hard days end in rain-soaked tents, cheap hotels or on moldy couches in the tiny apartments of newfound friends — temporary shelters that reveal the starkness of how the other side lives. A month is a year when traveling, and as each day passes, swinging through a forest of adventure, I release an old tree branch to grasp a new one, often dangling in the breeze, awaiting another life lesson.

Traveling through developing nations is like an escape to reality. The developing world, the real world, un-insulated by regulations, emergency health care and insurance companies, allows wanderers to savor life's rougher edges by abandoning false safety nets that trap us within the monotonous hum of mediocrity. The boredom of knowing how tomorrow will turn out is replaced by tests for survival and not relying on advertisers to determine what makes us happy. The uncertainties of remote deserts, numbing snowstorms and harsh tropical weather also exercise the spirit — real life arriving in its most naked forms. To escape the drone and feel the pulse of humanity, I must depart from the comfort zone, take the plunge and play the hand I am dealt to wherever that leads. In the process, time becomes irrelevant.

I celebrated a month on the road crossing from Russia into Mongolia, a region where Chingas Han (Genghis Khan in the west) forcibly gathered the scattered tribes of Asia to establish the largest empire in history. While casually rolling across lands where millions of hoof beats once thundered into conquest, I felt the echoes of passion and tragedy reverberate through the still afternoon air. The Mongolians, still nomads living in the countryside yet tamed by religion and war, have immortalized Genghis Khan as the Great Uniter. Sun-scorched faces with high, broad cheekbones evoke tales of fierce courage tempered by gentle Buddhist beliefs. Now in the shadow of two mightier empires, kindness and sharing have become the way of the once-conquering hordes.

Riding west across Siberia, the footprints of history are stamped on the faces — further into Asia, blue eyes morph into narrowing brown almonds. Norsemen, Buryats, Mongols and Chinese, from enemies to allies, the threat of war never leaves. For now, there is détente concerning resources and religion, but battle lines may yet be redrawn. For the moment, pitiful poverty is accompanied by a fragile peace in the land.

The road to Ulaanbaatar — long, gentle hills of wrinkled green velvet smooth enough to ride across become the first offerings of an unforgiving land. Herds of stout, brown-sugar ponies charge the roadway at will, reminders of whose turf is actually being invaded. As I pass men huddled under the hood of a disabled car, one waves a water jug. Assuming he needed water for an overheated radiator, I returned to assist. Yet when I approached, he offered the bottle to drink from, thinking this traveler looked thirsty.

After assembling provisions and studying maps in the capital, I'll venture deep into the Gobi Desert for as long as my supplies last. It'll be nice to be out of touch again. After I've packed 10 gallons of water, bread and cheese, there is just enough room for a change of clothes, a camera and a laptop. Though my camera captures snapshots of specific moments, it's the early evening tapping on a computer that both empties and fills my mind.

Biting the Dust
August 8, 2004
Mandal Gobi, Mongolia
● ● ● ● ● ● ● ● ● ● ● ● ● ●

Solo travel can be punishing, as I discovered only eight hours past the capital's city limits. After an evening's hard rain, the dirt road to the final outpost at Mandal Gobi turned into a first-gear spin through sloppy, slippery mud. Impatient from a half-day crawl, I imagined a short dry section ahead would be solid enough to increase the pace — it was not. When an enthusiastic twist of the throttle ended with my front wheel sliding sideways, I performed a clumsy cartwheel over the handlebars while managing a decent landing.

The bike was lucky too. A busted windshield and mirror wasn't much of a problem, but the bent steel-frame supports for the aluminum saddlebags meant they couldn't be refit, at least not right away. To continue, I'd have to strap the loose one across the seat, which left no room for a rider. The last 20 miles to town were spent standing on the pegs wondering how I could repair snapped stainless-steel fasteners and realign irregular angles on precise metal fittings — a tall order in the middle of a desert.

Greeted by twenty-first century Mongolian horsemen, Gobi Desert, Mongolia

Well Drillers
August 10, 2004
Mandal Gobi, Mongolia
● ● ● ● ● ● ● ● ● ● ● ● ● ●

Soft-dirt landings can go either way — a different twist when tumbling and maybe you break some bones. Or one more rotation — tweaked handlebars. It's easy to get by without a mirror or windshield, but the snapped steel fasteners and bent steel brackets that supported my aluminum saddlebags meant an indefinite delay. It could take weeks to have replacements shipped while the last days of my non-extendable Russian visa slowly expired. On a motorcycle, riders can only carry a minimal number of tools and spare parts for the trouble that happens when least expected. Snapped clutch handles, bent shifters or broken mirrors are mere inconveniences at home, but they become small adventures chasing down replacements in foreign lands.

Mandal Gobi is the last settlement before entering the Gobi Desert. Few of the shacks have running water, and the three little shops carry only minimal dry goods. Other than a single antiquated gas pump, there are no amenities to speak of. So calculate the odds of me encountering a well-drilling team of Czech technicians on a government assignment equipped with a mobile machine shop, complete with an arc-welder. Even better, the oldest of the team had trained in Cuba during the last days of the Soviet Empire and spoke fluent Spanish. In the cramped dining room of Mandal's lone hostel, while swapping stories from Spanish into Czech and back again, it becomes apparent that no matter who you meet traveling, you will always find something in common. We talk about my judo class-mate, the Czechoslovakian national champion. They've heard of Jerry Kropechek — "You know him?"

"Yes, he is like my brother."

After they ask why I'm favoring a left shoulder, I relate the after-noon's events. They want to look at the bike; maybe they can fix it. "Have at," I say, "but there is little we can do out here without tools." At first, it confused me why they just laughed. But an hour later these surgeons from heaven were busy straightening the frame, welding steel fasteners and using superglue with duct tape to piece together the shattered windshield. Bundled metal water pipes served as a cir-cular anvil to hammer round sections of the frame back into perfect shape. Within four hours, the Blue Beast was restored to health.

After repairs, we drank warm beer over foul cigarettes until it was time to stagger up worn wooden stairs into a cubbyhole of a room with unpainted walls. I had barely crawled beneath a musty wool blanket before falling happily to sleep, dreaming of the fabled desert beyond. As barking dogs combined with an icy wind whistling through a broken window, I end another day as life passes faster than I wanted. The Gobi awaits — I roll at dawn.

Into the Gobi
August 11, 2004
Govi Gurvan Sayhan National Park

• • • • • • • • • • • • • • • • • • • •

There are memorable events that become milestones in any journey. Firing up the bike in Vladivostok was the first milestone, riding the road to Chita across Siberia was the second. Camping alone in the Gobi Desert became another. Govi Gurvan Sayhan National Park, 2,000 square miles of clay, rock and sand home to more camels than humans, is only one of nine national parks in Mongolia. A hardened clay road is chewed into deep multidirectional grooves, but at least it's dry. Once departing Mandal Gobi, the surface soon turns unpredictable, changing every 30 seconds from abrasive rocky washboard to wiggly sand. It's like riding a two-wheeled jackhammer guided by crisscrossing gouges in the road. After adjusting to one type of terrain, it abruptly changes, demanding total focus from the rider to remain upright. There is no room for daydreams. Breaking concentration means losing control, and there was little chance of running into more well-drillers with tools out here.

Only two SUVs appeared on the road today, one passing, the other oncoming, both with enthusiastic occupants leaning out of windows, waving. Vast herds of goats and camels roam the empty plain, scattering at my approach. This is where the wanderer wants to be, enveloped by thousands of square miles of gently sloping land devoid of civilization, the only companion the barren Gobi. Swallowed by the desolation of a billion years and giddy with newfound freedom, I am awed by the thundering silence.

Although the parched pink soil is coated with sharp-edged stones and small clumps of desert grasses, it's level enough to ride across. Like circular domains, white felt *Gers* of distant Mongolian nomads sprout like mushroom patches on the skyline. Waving herdsmen dressed in blue hand-woven clothing beckon me to stop, but the visits require an explanation in sign language and my accepting gulps of foul-tasting fermented mare's milk. After a few fake sips, I pass out raisins and slip back into the nothingness.

Camping in the Gobi

The road has turned into dozens of parallel tire ruts leading only in general directions. Some are deeper than others and, like driving in rush-hour traffic, the other lane always looks better. It seldom is, but still I switch back and forth anyway, hoping for fewer holes and bumps. At times, the open desert is easier to ride, but fear of punctured tires makes me return to the jolting and jarring.

I'm following no schedule. The desert is home as long as my supplies last. My laptop is wired to recharge off the bike's electrical system, and there're extra batteries for the cameras. There're no rules as a vagabond in this kingdom of nowhere. Exist as you please. Paradise is a silent desert night beneath the piercing stars, unobstructed by city lights reflecting off a polluted atmosphere. Since rain is no longer an issue, maybe all that's required is a sleeping bag laid out across a plastic tarp to absorb the celestial symphony overhead. It's August, the perfect month for viewing shooting stars at one of the clearest viewing points on the planet, 5,000 feet above sea level. Yet growing dust clouds on the horizon command pause.

After selecting the perfect knoll and focusing my camera, night-time winds kicked up. It became a fight just to pitch the tent. Like controlling a kite in a storm, I struggled with one hand to keep it from being yanked away, while using the other to feed collapsible aluminum poles through loops to form the dome. Even with all my gear inside weighing it down, I didn't step away lest it blow off across the plain.

The temperature drops with the sun, and soon I am wrapped in a mummy bag managing dinner. Containers of fruit juice beaten apart by the day's pounding still supply enough syrupy liquid to fill my cup. A can with a picture of a cow on it is the surprise of the night — a smooth-textured paste that spreads well over fresh baked bread. After dried fruit for dessert, I tumble into a deepening slumber.

During the day the road had been empty, but evening traffic increases to one truck an hour. I can see the blurs of light for miles before they grind by, inching across the sterile landscape. Here, there is a different silence. A choir of whistling and chirping surrounds me, but the singers are invisible. The desert is alive at night.

At dawn, a protein bar and what was left of the peach juice is enough to quell my morning hunger. There is no reason to rise, so I savor the horizon twisting into orange swirls of sunrise through nylon flaps of an open tent. If I continue this loop, it is possible to spend another week meandering back to Ulaanbaatar.

Fed up with jarring and bouncing, I head off-road across the desert. After entering predetermined coordinates, the GPS draws a straight line to the next destination — so with one eye on the 2-by-2 inch screen, I blast out over the plain, dodging small boulders and sharp cliff washes. Out of the frying pan, into the fire. The beating is merciless; never mind my body, I wonder how much the bike can take. Already a sub-frame bolt has sheared, the broken section lodged, threaded, in the frame. A drill will be needed to clear it before the bike bends in half. The Gobi can be an unforgiving lover.

Involuntary Wandering (Lost)
August 15, 2004
The Gobi Desert
• • • • • • • • • •

The two major manufactures of GPS units each sell a CD with down-loadable data revealing the main roads of the world. Assuming they used the same sources, it seemed logical that mine would display the same information as Brand X. It didn't. Primary roads in Mongolia are little more than frequently used tire tracks over dirt that became roads. There are thousands of these throughout the country, with countless forks dividing them in multiple directions. Brand X marks a few of these routes, mine does not. Mine is an easier unit to oper-ate, but, except for the black triangle indicating my position near the border with China, it was useless in the Gobi for identifying roads.

Asking for directions doesn't help. When nomads even under-stand my questions, they just point to a series of tracks and say, "That one." It makes no difference which track I select, a mile down the road it forks into several others making gradual enough changes that by the time the compass registers I am moving in the wrong direc-tion, it's hard to remember the way back to the original fork.

Fortunately, a friend had provided me with specific GPS coordi-nates for important landmarks in the Gobi. Since the terrain is flat with no fences, theoretically it should be possible to ride in a straight line to the intended destination. That's if there are no washes, sand dunes or low mountain ranges. And getting lost in the desert is common. Even with one eye on the GPS and the other on the hori-zon, it's easy to become disorientated enough to wonder if the GPS is malfunctioning.

On a lightweight bike with knobby tires, sand dunes are fun — but with street tires on a 400-pound motorcycle lugging 200 pounds of extra gear, it's a tiring battle. Three hours of spinning through soft sand leads me back to where I started — except now there are no nomads to consult, only herds of foul-smelling camels that hope-fully belong to somebody. Maybe following their tracks would lead to humans who can point to the right direction. Anything would be better than this.

Two hours later, the animal tracks scatter near a wash at the base of a small mountain range emptying into an alluvial plain. Loose gravel of the widening, dry riverbed is firmer to ride than rolling dunes, but according to the GPS the wash is leading in the opposite direction of my destination. It is hard to recall how long it has been since the low-fuel light blinked on, indicating 2 gallons left. That 2 gallons should last 120 miles, but there is no way to know if there is somewhere to buy fuel, even if I find a main road. Supplies are adequate — a dozen protein bars, canned sardines and three 2-liter plastic water bottles wrapped in socks. Still, the jarring has broken two of the bottles, leaving one full container and an aluminum saddlebag holding the other two. At least they are still drinkable.

Between a hand-drawn map provided by one of the nomads and the GPS, it appears that I'll eventually hit a main road I'm supposed to recognize by its tilting old telephone poles without wires. Even so, there is still another 20 miles of spinning across the desert. At this point I'm second-guessing myself, and, with sunset two hours away, I decide it's best to set up camp and tackle the situation in the morning with a clearer head. Wrangling myself into sleep with concerns over punctured tires and low fuel, the Gobi is unchanged in the morning. Unzipping the tent reveals a half-dozen camels sniffing around, looking to dine on my gear. But before they can find my protein bars, I shoo them away.

It's time for a new plan. The best solution seems to be to program the waypoint into the GPS from my current position and then add an estimated coordinate where the main road ought to be, based on the nomad's map. It should be easy to follow the thick black line drawn on the screen. Seven arduous hours later, slightly north of my programmed waypoint, tiny vertical lines appear where a blue sky meets a pink desert. This is not the home stretch though, merely where the contest begins. The orange low-fuel light is a steady reminder that the road has plenty of twists ahead.

Realizing that it can be several hours without seeing another vehicle, it's better to wait for someone to flag down and confirm that this is the right road. Halfway through a can of sardines and stale bread, I am suddenly aware of a presence at my side. Looking down, I am startled to see a four-year-old girl staring up, holding an aluminum pail and porcelain bowl. A scan of the surrounding terrain reveals no sign of nomads or their *Gers,* and it's impossible to determine from where she came.

"*Sain ban noo,*" I say. (Hello.) Her smudged face is frozen in an emotionless gaze upward at the Martian someone in her family sent her to assist. Because of their deep Buddhist belief in karma, it's in the nature of the nomads to feed and care for strangers. This is a training mission.

Accepting the pail and bowl, I pour myself a drink of hot, sweetened goat's milk. Finally, something I've been offered offer tastes good. "*Bai ar laa.*" (Thank you.) Still no response, just little brown eyes of apprehension. Nothing moves her. Funny faces and wiggling fingers in my ear changes nothing; she never flinches. After a second cup of milk, I hand back the containers, flip the bike ignition and beep the horn. Suddenly, she breaks into bright childish laughter. I see her in the mirror as she scurries back across the desert to where she came from, and when I turn to see her one last time she has disappeared. The sweet taste of goat's milk on my lips and a digital photo are my only confirmation that she ever existed.

Return to Siberia
August 20, 2004
The Russian Frontier
● ● ● ● ● ● ● ● ● ● ● ●

The rest of the ride back to Ulaanbaatar was more of the same, and I was glad to have taken this detour into Mongolia, especially the Gobi Desert. Replacement stainless-steel fasteners arrived from Al Jesse, and after a chassis lubing and steam cleaning, all critical motorcycle bolts were ready to go. After four days of restaurant hopping restoring man and machine, I suddenly had an urge to backtrack to the Russian border and finish crossing Siberia. At last the Blue Beast was ready for more. Mongolia had been such a wonder, I was sorry it wasn't closer to California. At its current state of development, Mongolia may remain unknown for a few more years. Tourism is so new the locals haven't learned to steal or gouge. Nomads still treat travelers like guests, and travelers still respect their hosts. This will change someday, but for now Mongolia remains an unspoiled adventure destination.

Rolling north along the countryside past costumed horsemen herding livestock and adjusting their *Gers*, I recall many meaningful moments spent with strangers communicating in silence. Nomads from different cultures, we are linked by our spirit to roam and share our lives. They pretended to enjoy my protein bars as much as I did fermented mare's milk, and they were as fascinated with my tent and motorcycle as I was with their camels and *Gers*. Hopefully they will remember me as I do them. It's the indomitable pragmatic spirit of Mongolians that awes travelers. The nomads understand that to survive in a brutal environment, they must work together. Long, freezing winters at 20 below zero on the wind-pummeled plains leave no room for conflict. They share or they perish. Mongolians were among the first ecologists, understanding that to preserve their lands, rotating pastures and managing livestock would become their way of life. The land feeds the animals, and the animals feed them.

In 1990, after the Russians stopped subsidizing Mongolia as a buffer against China, the country was near economic collapse. Yet the nomads, having lived the same way for a thousand years, had adequate food while the city dwellers did not. It was the nomads who rescued countrymen by bringing milk and meat into cities to prevent the people from starving. Now a wobbling new democracy, Mongolia has swung on the political pendulum from left to right and back, managing peaceful transitions of power. Wedged between the economic might of China and Russia, Mongolia is defenseless. While Moscow has relinquished its claim, Beijing has not. Mongolians are a whim away from sharing the fate of Tibet.

Although Mongolian towns were crammed with identical Soviet-era decaying prefabricated apartment complexes, the genuine warmth of the people compensated. But after the last stretch of open pastures, another numbing dose of Russian bureaucracy awaited me at the Siberian frontier. After a personal escort through Mongolian exit formalities, jaded Russian immigration officials greeted me with lengthy entry forms and the same foolish questions they knew didn't matter. Still, it was refreshing to cross another border, switching gears and looking forward to new surroundings. The road ahead sliced through rich Siberian pine forests punctuated with scattered story-book towns. A growling stomach reminded me again I need to eat. Store-bought robust Russian rye bread and creamy cheeses crowned with canned sardines became dinner and lunchtime gourmet treats.

Hungry Jack
August 24, 2004
Lake Baikal, Russia
● ● ● ● ● ● ● ● ● ● ●

As one of the scenic wonders of Russia, Lake Baikal is the largest lake in the world, holding a fifth of the planet's freshwater supply. But so far I have seen little of it through blinding summer storms. A black cloud of freezing rain requires total focus on the hazards ahead. No opportunities for sightseeing, just dodging potholes and speeding trucks. The logic of developing nations remains a mystery. No one's in a hurry until they're behind the wheel, then suddenly it's a death race.

Taking the short route, I've got 6,000 miles left to Munich and three weeks to get there to deal with my kidney stones. Three possible exit points from Russia lay ahead: Ukraine, Belarus and Latvia — the country that issues the visa quickest will determine the route. I scratched a side trip from Moscow to St. Petersburg — there can be no more side trips until I am healthy again.

Still, it's better to take advantage of the Russian countryside and interact with villagers — easy on a motorcycle as a crowd gathers whenever I stop. The splendor of Siberia dazzles even the weariest traveler, and the interactions with locals, whether positive or negative, are always interesting. For now, thick forests before me are empty, perfect for camping, except you can't pitch a tent in the rain and expect to wake up with dry gear. Cheap rustic road hostels with squeaky wood floors are the answer — tiny rooms with bomb-site toilets at the end of echoing hallways — but, most important, they have 220 volts to recharge my camera and laptop batteries. If I can find one, it's a bargain at 10 bucks a night.

Towards the end of a long day, two boys bundled in overcoats on a motorcycle wave me over to talk. I ask them, *"Gde gastinitza?"* (Where is a hotel?)

"Baikalsk." They reply, pointing down the highway.

"Skolkha kilometers?"

The driver holds up three fingers, *"Tridtsat."* (Thirty.)

"Spaceba." (Thank you.) I am on my way.

Further west, the towns become larger and the poverty less obvious. When stopping to buy fresh fruit at a Sunday market, a thick-muscled lumberjack from across the parking lot fixes his gaze on the lone *Americanski* and approaches with giant strides. He resembles the image on Hungry Jack pancake boxes right down to the broad shoulders, plaid shirt and wavy blond hair. He's shouting before I'm able to hear him, so I'm worried he's another drunk wanting to arm wrestle. Just in case, I stash the peaches and ready my motorcycle key.

Like an overgrown anxious child, he bounds up blabbering, grasping my hand with an enormous leathered paw the size of a baseball mitt. Nearly squeezing blood from my fingertips, he slaps my back with his other hand. Even as I repeat *"Nyet Ruskie,"* he continues with sign language and grunts, indicating that I should follow him somewhere to eat. Sure, why not?

A quarter-mile sprint later, me following on my bike, we reach an aging cement-block apartment complex where he pulls me by the arm upstairs, rambling out questions and answers in Russian. Hungry Jack points to himself and declares, *"Sasha!"* Once inside his 10-by-10-foot kitchen, he flings open the antique refrigerator door with one hand and pitches jars of sweetened fruit with the other. Soon a steaming pot of tea and Russian ravioli arrive, with crackers and homemade raspberry jam. He points to everything in sight, asking if I want some. After force-feeding me whatever he can, we're off to the living room for home videos and invitations to accompany him and his wife to their *dacha* for a Russian *banya*. It's already nine o'clock, and, fearing an all-nighter, I decline and instead politely request a hotel.

Back on my bike with Sasha leaping ahead like an eager puppy, we reach the only hotel in the village. While I unlock the aluminum panniers, he grabs the nylon tote bags, stuffing whatever he can under his arms. After hauling my gear inside, he surveys the room as if searching for something written on the faded wallpaper. I assure him everything's fine and that I now just want to sleep. His farewell is a Russian bear hug, picking up my 210 pounds and shaking me like a rag doll. Disappointed that we couldn't hang out more, he lopes back down the road, turning every few steps to wave. I am going to miss Russian hospitality.

Tornadas
August 26, 2004
Central Siberia, Russia
● ● ● ● ● ● ● ● ● ● ● ● ●

Siberian summer storms have intensified into what Russians call *tornadas*. Temperatures have dropped into the 30s, and it's impossible to stay dry. Roads are flooded a foot deep, but this doesn't discourage the racecar drivers heading for Moscow. They continue at high speeds, creating 6-foot brown rooster tails for me to ride through. Unlike the squalls, their wake submerges hapless motorcyclists in root beer waves of freezing water. Where once it took several hours to become drenched, now it's 15 minutes. The outside air is 20 degrees colder and nose-diving. I asked local biker Stanislav how long this weather will last. "Maybe weeks," he replies.

My timing is off. The plan was to ride the world following the sun, capturing seasons in their primes, but so far I've only followed the rain. You can ride through most summertime squalls and eventually dry out from the wind, but I hadn't anticipated this kind of weather. Reaching the Latvian border 3,500 miles away in three weeks at 30 miles an hour looks unlikely. Occasional stops to dry out and relieve the shivering provide only temporary relief. Heated grips and electric vests are ineffective in this cold, merely delaying the inevitable. Roadside cafés are warm, but it costs hours of precious daylight riding time to dry my gear over dangling lightbulbs and old, rusted radiators.

Siberian towns are not built for international travelers. The few tolerable hotels in big cities are a hundred bucks a night, with no motorcycle parking. Russian rider Stanislav lives alone and offers the couch in his one-room apartment as long as I'm not afraid of his pet rat. Sure, why not? How could a little creature disturb me when I'm this tired? After checking my email on Stanislav's computer and barely closing my eyes, I spiral into a deep slumber. Suddenly, something warm and furry slides down my leg and up around my back. Has my other half answered my midnight dreams with a surprise visit? Then a scratchy sensation like little feet marching across my face jerks me awake. Something is definitely crawling down my leg now, and it's not who I hoped it would be.

"Stanislav, your rat is in my bed!" I yell.

Flicking on the single lightbulb dangling from the ceiling he assures me, "Don't worry, he is friendly."

"Friendly? Please get this plague-dispensing rodent out of my bed immediately!"

Reluctantly, Stanislav cages the foot-long beast, only to release him in the morning in time to eat my earplugs. By now, the storm has intensified, pounding the dual-panel windows like a bass drum. Stanislav says if the humidity drops it will snow. At least that would be dry for a while.

An hour later, another biker, Pavel, arrives to guide me through the complicated side streets of Irkutsk to the main highway west.

There are no signs; without his help, it would have taken hours to ride out alone. At his turnaround, he points down the road shouting "*Pree ama.*" (Straight ahead.) Whenever someone in Russia says "*Pree ama,*" it usually means multiple forks further on. Even after the escort, I spent another hour riding figure eights around the city. Pavel forgot to mention there was a major detour that confused even the Russians. The rain is so intense, before reaching the main road I stop at a small roadside café to dry off over a cup of tea. It will take an entire night to dry out everything completely, but this will warm me enough to ride another 60 miles.

Later, back in the storm, I realize it would have been wiser to quit at the one-hour mark when the shakes first started. Now there is nothing but freezing rain and fierce winds pounding the empty Siberian plain. By nightfall, when a small village appears, the early stages of hypothermia have already hit and my thinking grows mushy. Two federal marshals driving in off the roadway find me spinning my tires through muddy streets. They know something's wrong and pull alongside, displaying hand-signs asking me to follow. Six blocks later, we arrive at a gray cement hotel without lights. Before I can step off the bike, they grab me by the arms. Shivers had turned to uncontrolled shakes, and I'm unable to walk on my own. Inside the aging hotel lobby, an overweight matronly desk clerk is bundled in sweaters and overcoats. So much for heat. I need to get warm immediately, so the marshals lead me next door to a warm, smoky café crowded with uniformed men playing cards. I'm uncertain if they are Tartars or Buryats, but they are friendly, bringing cups of steaming tea and huge metal bowls of vegetable soup. While I sit shivering, one of them pries off my helmet and motions me to remove my soggy riding suit. Siberians know the dangers of hypothermia, and they bring a heavy wool blanket and towel. After gulping down hot liquids, the shakes subside enough for me to strip off the rest of my clothes.

One of the cops knows some English. Pointing to a table of middle-aged, chubby Asian women, he says, "Those girls want you for a bath." Too miserable to care what this could entail, I think only of warmth. Hot water is nirvana. The women motion to their table, offering a bowl of Russian ravioli and shots of vodka. Alcohol is off the list, but the ravioli are hot and filling. One woman explains in broken English that they are nurses and their husbands are doctors at the regional hospital. They mention a sauna: *Russian banya.* I nod with relief, but no one heads for the door. Soon all the women depart but one, leaving me to wonder if they've changed their minds. Two hours later they return, telling me to follow their car.

Entering the confined, aromatic kitchen of a fire-warmed wooden cottage, I see women from the café busy loading the table with fruit, vegetables and smoked fish. They've spent these last few hours preparing a feast and Russian sauna. Someone has built a fire under a huge iron kettle inside a wool-insulated cedar room for what will become the ultimate Siberian treat. A towel accompanies the welcome command, *"Banya."*

It's routine now — snap some digital photos, load the laptop and seduce the crowd. The tired old and anxious young are the most amazed looking at their images on the screen. After a short slideshow, they insist that I sleep in their bed while they use the kitchen mattress. When speaking with strangers, it's always best to avoid local politics, but several times they reiterate that they are not Russians but Buryats, descendants of Genghis Khan. They continue to live in this autonomous region to retain their identity, insisting even their passports state Buryat, not Russian.

In the morning, another freezing storm pummels the landscape, bending stately birch trees like blades of grass in a breeze. The Buryats beg me to stay another day, but my visa is non-extendable and there could be trouble if I don't exit Russia on time. To slow the cold, I bundle up in thermal underwear, two wool sweaters, electric vest, waterproof liner, fleece scarf, cold-weather gloves and riding suit. Within an hour, I'll be scanning again for refuge, in need of dry clothes.

Breakdown?
August 30, 2004
Tulun, Russia
• • • • • • • •

Two straight days on a mud road appearing like it had been assaulted with cluster bombs had scrambled my thoughts. Potholes were a half-foot deep and spaced so close it caused a first-gear creep for hours. In the middle of nowhere, with the next town a hundred miles away in any direction, even the amateur racecar drivers are forced to crawl for fear of damaging their ears. It was a perfect moment for trouble.

It's always best to prepare for the worst, to develop contingency plans for things like flat tires or breakdowns in remote locations during unpredictable storms. But where there is no immediate shelter, the best option is often to pitch a tent, wrap up in a sleeping bag and try to stay warm until the weather breaks.

High-capacity fuel tanks provide extra-long-range riding when needed and can be left half-full when it's appropriate. That morning, I had deliberately filled mine only halfway, to help me maneuver through the slippery conditions ahead. Five gallons less means 40 pounds lighter, a significant plus when trying to wrangle a 600-pound bike through mud. Even when the low-fuel light blinks on, it still means that there's 120 miles left — provided the electronics are functioning.

I always stash a set of spare keys on the bike where they are easy to access in emergencies. They are wrapped in soft duct tape and tucked up underneath the rubber boot on top of the gas tank, under the seat. But constant pounding and jarring from washboard roads disturbs everything, no matter how tightly packed. Pills turn to powder and even the foam padding in the rear top-box gets beaten into gum, sticking on the instruments it's intended to protect. Most items change shape after only a few days off-road. Even knowing this, I never imagined a set of hidden keys could cause such a problem.

About the time I started looking for a place to stop and get warm, without warning the motor quit. Not with a sputter — an abrupt cutoff. After a brief inspection, it becomes apparent that repeated attempts to restart will only lead to a dead battery. Bikes with carburetors are easy to repair. If necessary, even a lawn mower could be cannibalized for enough parts to get home. New BMWs come with electronic fuel injection, a superior method of metering fuel and supposedly bulletproof, but it's also difficult to repair without tools. It's a nagging fear, wondering what to do if this system malfunctioned here or in Africa.

My brain overloads analyzing the problem. Is it a broken wire buried somewhere in the yards of electrical tubes? A burned-out circuit board? A malfunctioning computer? Chips gone haywire? How could I repair defective electronics out here? And what about that slowly expiring Russian visa? How will I ever get dry with the sun going down? The worst of my fears has arrived. But with my recently developed faith in people, I know that when I need a friend most, one appears. Short of emergency medical care, in the event of disaster, it's safer traveling through developing nations than it is in California.

The Trans-Siberian Highway is really just a lightly traveled, often barely passable, road. The forest here is far too dense to see into, yet it also provides a decent shelter from the storm. Rain still drips down, but the winds can't attack. I only have to step a few feet into the trees for relief and to wait for someone to flag down. What can they do for me anyway, take me to a town? Leaving my bike out here is not an option. I would rather freeze.

Hearing it before seeing it, a lumbering big rig bounces into view, rocking side to side over the mangled road. The truck stops before I have a chance to wave. I don't need to understand Russian to know that the driver is asking what the hell I'm doing out here in this storm. The locals are always surprised to see me riding across Siberia, but doing it alone baffles them.

The lower end of his tractor-trailer is 4 feet above the ground, but I pat my bike and point to the rear door. He considers the suggestion, and after a short conversation with his partner, they jump down from the cab, slipping on work gloves. All that's left is for the three of us to raise up 600 awkward pounds of motorcycle over our heads and shove it into their trailer.

I'm halfway through unloading my gear to ease the weight when a car stops and two muscle-bound racecar drivers step out to investigate. They recognize the situation, and before we can ask for help, they don their overcoats and head our way. With nothing to secure the bike, we wedge it against the wall between two massive spare tires and hope for the best.

The big rig is actually a new deluxe-cab Volvo with plush interior, so the driver orders me to peel off my muddy clothes before climbing in. These two men live on the road, hauling dairy products between Irkutsk and Krasnoyarsk. This truck is their home, and they want it clean. Minutes later, we're tottering westward with the radio tuned to an international rock station. The nearest BMW dealer is further than their destination, but when we arrive at their main shipping warehouse, they meet a friend driving a similar truck scheduled to drive there that afternoon. Before switching trucks, I check to see what happens if I fire the engine one last time. Bang. It pops to life as if nothing ever happened. So what does this mean? Engine failure attributable to a wet connection? Maybe a loose wire temporarily barely reconnected? Whatever the case, we unload. It's time to ride.

After a test spin around the parking lot, everything seemed fine, and a wet electrical connection seemed like it had been the culprit. It should be easy for me to reach the dealer now, but before rolling onto a newly paved stretch of road, my new friends warned that a malfunction could easily happen again. They were right. Suddenly, just when I shifted into fifth gear, the motor shut down again, sending me coasting to the curb. Now, suspecting it's a dirty filter or a faulty fuel pump, I unbutton the tank-filler to discover the real problem — no gas! Inside the lid, my set of jangling spare keys had severed the wires connecting the low-fuel light, the reason there had been no warning my fuel was about to run out.

Within minutes, another trucker stops, offering some extra gasoline reserved for his generator. After siphoning enough to reach a station, it's a massive relief to fire up the engine and be back on the road.

• •

As cowboys love their horses, riders love their motorcycles. We get to know each other through customizing and maintenance checks. From meticulous tinkering and studying specs, we memorize their features and weaknesses while constantly drooling over the latest gadgets. Forged steel and machined aluminum rolling on vulcanized rubber become sacred vehicles that we name.

My mighty Blue Beast, survivor of a rugged Tran-Siberian crossing and stained from the red clays of Mongolia, has earned its place as my faithful companion. Capable of taming the roughest terrain and gobbling up long stretches of highway, its reliability is important to the success of my journey. On top of all that, it goes fast!

At Russian police checkpoints, machine gun–toting guards stop me to point at flashing red numbers on radar guns. They don't seem angry so I laugh aloud — only 80 miles per hour? But they are more interested in where I'm going, and before the wave me on, I must recite a list of recent destinations. So far, Russian cops have been friendly to the *"Amerikanski"* from *"Calleekfornia."* Once, I'm even given the emblem off a police uniform, a souvenir from an otherwise forgotten moment in a distant land.

Finally, the muddy roads of Siberia evolve into hardened Russian speedways with room to move. On Highway M-51, I am westbound to Moscow, blasting through the countryside like a bullet through the wind. I have two weeks left on my visa, with nothing to stop me now. My exit routes into Eastern Europe are a coin toss. Left to Ukraine or straight through Latvia and Lithuania into Poland. That will be decided at the appropriate fork. My only concerns today are about dodging storms and where to camp.

A passing summer squall sets me squinting through my face shield at the glare from a setting sun glistening off slick black pavement. Twenty-one hundred miles to go — from Novosibirsk, it's a straight shot over the Urals to the onion domes of St. Basil's. After a

St. Basil's Cathedral, Red Square, Moscow

loop around the Kremlin, I'll be off to the Middle East via Europe, but for now it's a ride into rapture. With a twist of the throttle, my iron steed snorts and stretches its legs, winding through the gears in a mechanical fury, flowing through the drive train to rushing asphalt below. Captured in the euphoria of rapid acceleration, as always, I can't imagine a better state of mind.

Intercepted
September 3, 2004
Omsk, Russia
● ● ● ● ● ● ● ●

It's best to avoid big cities on long trips; there is too much traffic and confusion, and food and shelter costs triple. Further west, I run into more affluent metropolitan areas, with expensive cars driven by businessmen with cell phones clamped to their heads. Searching for bargain hotels can waste a half-day, and it's best to seek out restaurants long before you're hungry. But as in the country, the simplest tasks can still be a hassle, and there is no room to relax. Reckless drivers moving through the rain on poorly lit, flooded streets are unnerving, and because there is nothing much to do now except ride and sleep, this is the one time I miss California. Other than sluggish Internet connections in dull, gray building basements, there is little to see in Russian cities. Cheesy museums and monuments start to look the same.

In spite of wintertime temperatures of 20 below zero, Russian bikers pursue their passion with dedication. They live for their four-month riding season. As there are so few of them, they seek clubs for camaraderie. International motorcycle travelers are welcomed by such men when we're riding across their country. Through Internet chat rooms, club members monitor riders heading their way, offering assistance and friendship. Diehards are often recognized by how they greet long-riders.

Motorcyclists welcome motorcyclists on motorcycles. It's a sign of respect when I see a dozen bikes heading toward me in the rain outside a city, ready to escort me in. Actually, it's often easier to ride in alone, but it's also impressive to see the spirit of like-minded fanatics infected with the same fever.

The first question from the diehards: "Did you ride the stretch between Chita and Khabarovsk or take the train?" A cheer erupts when I tell them I rode it. Even by Siberian standards, it's one of the toughest roads in the world. They are further impressed when they hear of my anticipated trip around the planet. For most motorcyclists, this is a fantasy ride.

The Other Men, a local club from Omsk, come to greet me on motorcycles, guiding me back to their bike shop clubhouse. A few of the riders have casts on their legs, reminders of the price of our passion. No drunks either — they ride sober, in sharp contrast to the Russian truckers I met, sucking on vodka bottles at breakfast.

Until 10 years ago, the only machines available here were comical, Soviet-built Urals, unreliable copies of '40s model BMWs. Now big, meaty imported Japanese sport bikes dominate. The locals have learned how to keep them running without access to the proper parts — they make their own on old, rusty lathes. When I discover another broken sub-frame bolt from my ride in Mongolia, they machine a new one from an otherwise useless chunk of steel. Drowning me in hospitality, they've taken to calling me the Siberian Viking.

The plan was to reach Moscow quickly and head for Germany, but the pressure is on to attend a banquet this weekend. Every hour for the next three weeks is accounted for; it's critical that I see that doctor in Munich. But since this is my first and likely last ride to Russia, missing this event would be a mistake. I'll make the time up later.

Life Road, the motorcycle club from Tyumen, also greeted me on the road tonight and brought me to their favorite café to present my slideshow. Later, at a hotel they recommended, I saw the valets opening car doors for guests, and I thought I must be at the wrong place. A snotty reception clerk confirmed it, announcing the hundred-bucks-a-night room fee. That's twice my daily budget for everything and very expensive by Siberian standards. As I turn away laughing, the clerk says not to worry, the bill has already been paid by my friends. It isn't just the price; it's the attitude that comes with high-class hotels. Stuffy staff in crispy dress suits and there I am, with grimy gear slung over my shoulder and muddy boots. Country folk applaud a ragged traveler. Here, I am a pariah. Hands clasped, noses in the air, waiters in the restaurant make it clear I am not welcome. But it appears that some Russians are also angry with each other.

The country is under siege again by Chechen terrorists, with two airliners blown up last week and all televisions now tuned to a current schoolhouse hostage crisis. Paranoia abounds. There are more security men here in business suits with earphones than guests. In this oil-rich region, an expensive hotel might be the least-safe haven.

Asia to Europe
September 8, 2004
The Russian Urals
● ● ● ● ● ● ● ● ● ● ●

Separating Europe from Asia, the Ural Mountains stretch south from the Arctic Kara Sea to Kazakhstan, affecting the weather as well as the politics. But that has little relevance today. As another icy drizzle blows in while riding the summit of a geographical dividing line, I realize it's been days without sunshine. Although the countryside is cold, my favorite cowboy tunes are pumping through a set of iPod headphones, warming me with memories of sunny Midwestern rangeland. At the moment, with Waylon Jennings's beefy baritone groaning about the simple, small town life, I am ready to ride to Luckenbach, Texas. And like every day in Siberia, I prepare for battle on the highway.

While on lumpy sections of pavement, Russian truckers, likely drunk on vodka, greet me with games of chicken. Oncoming speeding cars tip side-to-side, overtaxing their suspensions enough to reveal daylight through open wheel wells, as everyone seems to be in a race for somewhere. Who backs down first? I never win, yet a stubborn streak compels me to play. Swerving to dodge potholes while locked into deep-sunken tire tracks becomes a spontaneous ballet of vehicular madness. I lose count of the close calls.

I've been warned that friendly country cops turn aggressive as you near Moscow, demanding money after flagging down speeding motorists. In preparation for foreigners, they've learned to make commands in English: pay up or else. No one wants to find out what "or else" means. The only way to know for sure would be to call their bluff. In 60, 000 miles of Third World shakedowns, the most I've surrendered is a pair of scratched-up Korean sunglasses in Peru. Despite numerous Russian speed traps, I am determined to maintain that record.

After the first straightaway, blowing off a string of lumbering big rigs, a lone highway cop holding a radar gun steps from the shoulder, pointing his red reflector paddle directly at me. I've been gambling all day, ignoring them, pretending not to notice, but my luck was sure to run out eventually. Although unarmed, the cops could have radios with them to notify comrades ahead of a belligerent speeder. This time there is no way around the man in the roadway — I rein the Beast to a halt.

As he fixates on the California license plate, I blurt out in rapid-fire English, "Howdy, how's it going? Can you tell me how to get to Poland from here?"

He goes on the defensive. *"Ni panimah."* I don't understand.

I continue sputtering nonsense until he regains his footing, demanding *"Documenkis!"*

He points to the blinking red numbers on his radar gun and then growls at me.

"You!"

Showing him my watch I say, "Oh how interesting, is that a clock like this?"

He holds out his hand. Rubbing his thumb and index fingers together, he hisses, "Muneeeee."

More babbling about Poland and pointing to the sky taxes his patience as I refuse to admit understanding a single word. Exasperated and convinced a shakedown is futile, he says in Russian, "Never mind just get out of here and slow down."

I smile and say *"Spa cee bah."* (Thank you.) His head whips around and with a glare of suspicion he says, "I thought you didn't speak Russian?"

I cover my tracks with a big stupid smile, *"Pree vee et, pree vee et, spa cee bah, spa cee bah."* (Hello, hello, thank you, thank you.)

Aware he's been had, he reluctantly lets me go. His time is better spent squeezing speeding drivers of expensive German cars.

Descending from the Urals, a sprawling rural landscape erupts across the golden plains of European Russia, and finally there is sunshine. As the highway widens to four lanes, a high-latitude lingering sunset bores through my bug-encrusted tinted visor, directly into my retinas. Half-blind from the glare, I spot the silhouette of a distant motorcyclist riding at a casual pace. Traveling bikers on Russian roads are rare; this is my first since encountering a wandering German in Mongolia. Approaching him from behind, I smile mischievously as the raspy voice of George Thorogood fills my ears with "Bad to the Bone." I slam the hammer down, spurring the Blue Beast onward, WFO. Flashing a left-handed thumbs-up, I roar past him at a hundred miles per hour, noting a Moscow numbered plate on a Honda Africa Twin, brother to the BMW Dakar.

While I roll back on the throttle, he takes the bait, tearing up the road from behind. Okay *Ruskie,* let's see whatcha got. We embark on a white-line weave, slaloming through traffic over fresh-laid asphalt that feels like a river of black velvet. We fire up the highway for a heart-pounding hour before stopping to eat. Earlier, I swore this wasn't going to happen anymore. I was going to ride sane, but it felt too good to quit. After today, I will not do it again. This time I mean it.

Eight Thousand Miles
September 10, 2004
Moscow, Russia
● ● ● ● ● ● ● ● ●

Federal Highway M-5 leads directly through rambling suburbs of triple-story gray brick apartments straight into the maze of Moscow's protruding Gothic cathedrals and looming granite office buildings. Double-wide eight-lane boulevards lined with exclusive stores are jammed tight with expensive European cars. Exasperated drivers tediously merging into the slow moving parking lot dull their senses as they tap their steering wheels, staring into space. A lone motorcycle rider in the drizzling rain can only inch along with the flow and hope it leads somewhere warm. Here, money, power and prestige throb like a spreading cancer ready to consume willing souls. Moscow, a city with more billionaires than anywhere else on the planet, devours innocent fortune-seeking country folk as though they were beluga caviar. And wandering foreign bikers on a budget don't fare much better. Posh hotels near Red Square are 500 bucks a night. Fifty buys a stinky 10-by-10 cubicle five miles out, on skid row. This city is merciless — like a fish out of water, I flop on the outskirts of a buzzing beehive of promised riches. And even the small Moscow restaurant meals cost 10 times what they do in Siberia.

Times are tough when the only welcoming sight is a McDonald's. At least the menu is familiar. Drooling with anticipation, I find the best way to order is pointing to pictures of hamburgers that never look like that when they arrive. As I stammer out a few Russian phrases, a surly waitress and impatient crowd confuse my order, and I wind up with a gooey glob of muck and cold French fries. Never mind, I'll soon be with friends.

I have a local contact number buried in my email address book that's normally easy to access. Most everywhere else in the world, Internet cafés are easy to find, but in Moscow, real estate prices have made gold shops a better value. In the country, people want to stop and talk; here, they are always in a hurry, hustling somewhere with money on their minds. It's a maddening merry-go-round with the desperately hopeful scrambling to reach for an elusive brass ring. Suddenly, I miss the muddy roads of Siberia. Russians should be careful what they wish for.

Adios Russkies
September 12, 2004
Ludza, Latvia
• • • • • • • •

Other than advertising banners, the only color I see in Moscow rises from the courtyard of Red Square. Riding into downtown, the onion domes of St. Basil's sprouted upward like candy-cane mushrooms above pea greens and mustard yellows. Against the backdrop of aging edifices, they were so bright and shiny that for a moment they seemed fake.

Yet beyond this, what was missing most in Russian cities was color. Pulsating boulevards packed with black European prestige cars muscling among dark gray Japanese suvs mirrored the somber mood of Moscow. It's rare to spot a red, and you never see yellows. This lack of color reflects the weather and amplifies the dreariness of Soviet architecture — gray blocks of stone that match the overcast skies and sunken spirits of the inhabitants. It's easy to pity their circumstance, as only a fortunate few will ever profit from the overnight fortunes, while the majority will just work harder and harder to keep pace with inflation. Seventy years of being told what to think and do by a monolithic Soviet government has left them in a creative vacuum, still reluctant to dream.

A local biker, Mikhail, had offered to show me the city by following his car. In this kind of gridlock, driving is less hassle than riding, but it still takes an hour to cover a mile because the traffic is too tight to white-line. The choice was to creep a few feet every other minute in the cold rain or creep in a warm car full of cigarette smoke. After a day of the latter, it was hard to decide which was worse.

Red Square, the focal point of the Russian ride since Vladivostok, became the finish line for this leg of the journey. It was like reaching a magic kingdom, looking for some special knowledge or enlightenment that never arrived. Still, Red Square marked the finale of a two-month ride into the mystifying wonderment of Russia's cultural and geographic diversity. Rich in history and stunning in design, from the Politburo to Lenin's Tomb, a Westerner can only stand in awe at this symbol of a once-forbidden territory.

At the Moscow BMW dealer, the Blue Beast was revived with a new chain, sprockets and brake pads. Cleaner than a hospital ward, the service department was a half-block long, and the brightly lit showrooms gleamed like upscale jewelry stores. All prices were in Euros.

Yesterday morning, while I set up for a photograph near St. Basil's, Moscow police in armored trucks had swooped in to clear traffic. A Chechen terrorist bomb threat was closing down the city. Main boulevards were sealed and vacant except for the warbling of emergency vehicle sirens echoing among the imposing granite buildings. Already packed and prepared for the road, I said goodbye to Mikhail and caught the M-9 for the Baltics.

Three nights in the capitalist enclave of Moscow was enough. Seven days ahead of an expiring visa, the steady irritation of plastic stents had turned into knee-buckling pain, pushing me toward an earlier exit. A 400-mile melancholy sprint to Latvia was all that remained of a sojourn never to be repeated. Since landing on Russian soil two months back, it had been a 6,500-mile odyssey across seven time zones and through mind-boggling extremes. Russia is not a vacation destination as much as an exercise in discovering what you can stand. As you leave your tracks across its face, it weaves its way into your soul.

Outside Moscow, modern highways are smooth and well-maintained. The westbound M-9 lacked the aggravating speed traps and annoying military checkpoints that had plagued the other side. Clearly, authorities feel security threats come from the disgruntled Far East and Southern Caucasia. Battles are brewing as mineral-rich, poverty-stricken regions tire of fattening European Russia. And it appears that greed will soon overtake common sense.

At the border, with documents in hand, there are still potential complications. A missing stamp, incorrect signature or bureaucratic snafu could delay departure for days. Trapped in an endless shuffle of paperwork for the simplest of tasks, workers still locked in a Soviet-era mentality are afraid of making decisions. Frowning border officials study my visa and importation papers, conferring with superiors by telephone. More stamping and grunting ensues, while those behind me move ahead. Meek smiles and a continuous *"Spah cee bah"* conceal my aggravation while I vacillate between fury at the nonsense and pity for the perpetuators.

EASTERN EUROPE

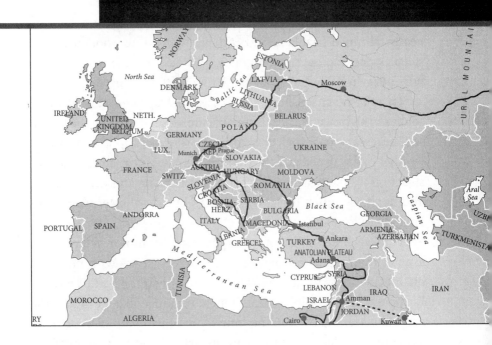

The Baltics
September 14, 2004
Czech Republic

● ● ● ● ● ● ● ● ●

Once past the last Russian border guard, Latvian immigration officials stood ready with welcoming smiles and polite requests for my
passport and insurance card. Thirty seconds later, after a souvenir
stamp that I requested, they waved me on. Once in the EU, for U.S.
citizens, visas or importation documents are no longer necessary.
From here to Turkey, at every frontier, it's just a flash of a passport
while only slowing down. Meanwhile, on the Latvian side, there was
a line of parked commercial trucks stretching six exasperating miles,
awaiting entry into Russia.

Cultures and conditions varied greatly across Russia, but former Soviet republics are like different worlds. Freed from the bruising yoke of communism, the standard of living has risen as national identities have been restored. The Baltics offer a quaint orderliness with a Scandinavian flavor. Meandering country roads wrap around neatly trimmed farmland and cottages with white wooden church steeples peeking over green grassy hillsides. In timeless harmony, horse-drawn hay wagons share the road with modern diesel rigs.

There're no speed-limit signs or radar traps and nary a cop or soldier in sight. Latvia and Lithuania are so small that by the time it was necessary to refuel, the Polish border had appeared. As the weather had warmed and the traffic on single-lane roads under construction was so heavy, it was better to sleep late and ride all night. You don't see much traveling like this, but it's a faster way across Poland to Germany.

The Czech Republic is a well-kept secret for motorcycling. Fresh asphalt roads slice through thick-forested scenery with plenty of quaint café stops for delicious local food at half the cost of most of Europe. Czechs cook like the French, organize like Germans and greet like Mexicans. Avoiding touristy Prague, I stop in a medieval stone block village just on the outskirts. Podebrady, population 15,000, is an orderly town plucked straight from the last century, with prices to match. Twenty bucks a night for a mini-suite, color TV and a desktop computer with free high-speed Internet. I have tomorrow slated for my hospital checkup in Munich; otherwise, this would have been a nice place to linger.

It's hard to miss the rigors of traveling in Russia but easy to miss the Russians. Who can ever forget Russian hospitality and those unique translations? *"Glan vot do you call zee fly zat dreenks blahd?"*

Temporary Downtime
September 21, 2004
Stadtisches Hospital, Munich, Germany
● ●

Arriving in Munich on Friday too late to see the doctor, I'm just in time for the Munich Motorcycle Show, the largest of its kind in the world. A hundred thousand riders from around Europe converge on the International Trade Center to view the latest motorcycles and high-tech gadgetry. Nearby campgrounds for bikers include hot showers and tent restaurants with overhead pipelines to giant containers of stout German beer. But swelling kidneys make it hard to walk, and it is apparent time has almost run out.

Monday morning at the hospital, halfway through presurgery tests, alarmed doctors direct me immediately to bed with orders not to move. Both kidneys are congested and on the verge of shutting down, as the spaghetti-like, soft plastic stents designed as drains had formed crystals of their own, blocking the flow of urine. During the subsequent surgery, instead of being able to simply slide them out with forceps, they had become attached internally and were not responding to the doctor's pulling and tugging. When one stent nearly snapped in half, my doctor told me later that he was minutes from slicing me open to retrieve them. After the two-hour procedure, the doctors discovered more kidney stones and an infected prostate causing more backup. My simple outpatient testing morphed into a four-day hospital stay.

Assuming the first visit was only for an examination, I had left my tent setup at the city campground with three thousand drunken Australians celebrating Oktoberfest. Time was so critical, the doctors told me that all we could do was leave my bike in the parking lot with a note requesting not to tow. The good news was that this is the most advanced urological center in the world, overseen by the doctor who invented lithotripsy, the process for smashing kidney stones using ultrasound. Professor Chaussey and Dr. Hasner were surprised anyone had made it this far with two calcified stents inside them. After convincing them that there was no returning to

California, the staff began bending rules and modifying regulations to meet my hurried travel schedule.

After a second procedure of lying immobilized and semiconscious while shock waves pound at mineral deposits, I wondered how much more I could stand. While in the most humiliating posture a man can imagine, an electronic chiseling pulse jolted once a second four thousand times on each stone. The treatment was so intense that they could only work one kidney per day. But I am already fed up with needles, anesthesia and just lying here when I now feel good enough to ride. A screened urine search for stone fragments has been fruitless, signaling the need for more ultrasonic jackhammering. There were numerous blood tests to monitor infection, and it was boring being constantly connected to a bottle or machine. Yet everyone tried hard to make me comfortable, understanding how disconcerting it is to be in the hospital so far from home. Word spread about my website, so hospital staff studied my journal entries and reported back their opinions. But overhearing constant chatter in an unfamiliar language just causes more longing for California.

A few people from home considered me foolish to have attempted this journey with such questionable health, but the Palm Springs doctor never told me not to go, only that it would be difficult. Competitive athletes, especially those in the combat arena, are always injured. We're often too injured to train, let alone fight. But we do anyway. For every judo match, one or both combatants are taped up with sprained joints or cracked ribs. I figured it out once — there were only two weeks out of a year when we are not injured in some way. That's the mentality, and although there is a price, it's the only way to win. A line had to be drawn — either it was time for me to continue on this journey or become locked in a cycle of postponement. There're always reasons to procrastinate, but if you accept one excuse, you'll wind up accepting them all. Any of us could die of cancer tomorrow. But if you carry on like you have six months to live, maximizing every moment, you'll appreciate life more.

As planned back in California, my best friend Brad arrives next week for the ride across Turkey. A Canadian living in the U.S., Brad is like a brother to me. He'll rent a bike in Germany with a drop-off in southern Europe when I head east. Negative rumors from fellow travelers state Iranian visas for Americans are still questionable, so plan B may go into effect. Whether I turn right or left at the Mediterranean now depends on religion and international politics. One direction leads to Middle Eastern deserts, the other to snowy mountains on the Anatolian plateau. Either way, it'll be nice to be back on the road again.

Gypsies
September 30, 2004
Munich, Germany
● ● ● ● ● ● ● ● ● ● ●

It's been a hectic two weeks — camping three nights at the bike show, three more with Oktoberfest drunks, three in the hospital and three in a fancy hotel visiting with my cousin Kjell here on another business trip. The doctors gave up on the last 10-millimeter kidney stone because it hadn't responded to shock waves. It's now too big to move and an issue better resolved next year in California, when there is more time to deal with it. Because of internal complications, they've slipped in another temporary plastic stent and told me to find a urologist down the road to remove it in 30 days.

"What if I'm in Africa?"

"That should be okay, there're doctors there."

So the time bomb ticks, and to stretch my travel funds, I return to the more affordable medieval magic of the Czech Republic to wait for Brad. At the moment, he's likely gliding at 500 miles per hour 30,000 feet over the Atlantic, twitching with anticipation. In a few hours, we'll be jumping up and down with bear hugs in the Munich airport, then rolling for Romania.

Few people speak English in Prague, but it's easy to get by with my broken Russian and sign language. Finding out where to buy an extra set of long johns though becomes an adventure in touring smut shops. After spending a half-hour pulling on the top of my underwear and then pointing to my socks, a shopkeeper drew a detailed map showing me where to go on the other side of the city. Miles of confusing navigation led to an adult sex shop specializing in lingerie. But their fishnet nylons looked ineffective against chilling winds of the awaiting Alps.

The previous morning, when I was in a shoe store asking directions, I had left my bike only 30 feet away. Within seconds, four gypsy street-kids had snatched the GPS off the handlebars. It was designed for a one-button removal so there would never be an excuse to leave it unattended, but unsuspecting of 12-year-old boys, I had lowered my guard. A quick twist of a thumbscrew and it was in their pocket — the price for violating my own security. Yet the anger was not all mine. Residents from the neighborhood converged, outraged and embarrassed that this had happened to a traveler in their country. They ranted that gypsy children are taught by their parents how to steal. Maybe that's what happens when migrant people are ostracized from society and need to find other means to survive. Amused and thankful for the support, we sent out word that it was worth a hundred bucks to me to have it back.

Contact was established via a helpful shopkeeper, but the nervous youngsters balked during negotiations, fearing a thumping if they brought it back. Lucky for them that they never returned for the third round of talks. On a 50,000-mile world ride you know you're going down, getting sick and being robbed or ripped off more than you planned. A prearranged substitute from California arrives via express mail Sunday.

After five days in Prague, and a 12,000-mile service check at the BMW dealer, it was time to roll for Munich to meet Brad. Happy to return to the Fatherland, the Blue Beast glides over long stretches of flawless autobahn spilling out across the Bavarian Plain. Porsche drivers having far too much fun blow by at 140 miles per hour, disappearing before my eyes can determine the color of their cars. Like speeding down a greased rail, I drift into an artificial bubble of fearless exhilaration. High-performance luxury sedans soar through meticulously engineered banked turns, rocketing onto launch-pad straightaways of seamless slabs of concrete butting together without a ripple. It's worth a trip here just for an unrestrained foray down a thousand-mile racetrack.

Deutschland — the arrogant brain-trust for a confused planet. Cold intelligence shines with incredible brilliance. It was World War II German rocket scientists that put Russians and Americans into space. Subtle superiority pervades the land of reasonable perfection and passion for law. Culturally programmed to obey the rules in a mechanized tidiness, this is the occidental version of Japan. Unconcerned with what doesn't make sense, Germans are friendly because it's logical. Still recuperating from the maddening silliness of Russian bureaucracy, there is a healing confidence that accompanies traveling here, convinced that those in charge use a familiar common sense.

Eastern Europe
October 9, 2004
Budapest, Hungary
● ● ● ● ● ● ● ● ● ● ●

Since landing in Vladivostok last July, it's been an interesting passage through varying types of forests broken up by one desert, and now a series of capital cities crowned with Gothic grandeur. Medieval Europe's striking remnants of castles and cathedrals reflect stories of its warring past. Cruising the cobblestone roads dividing ancient architecture draws me into European history, and it's a relief to be able to daydream without dodging potholes. Early morning breakfasts in city center cafés and evenings spent catching up on televised world news almost make me forget the hard life of Siberia.

And time spent coming in out of the cold also makes a man lose his edge. After a day or two, I resent the comfort and long for the developing world's unpredictability. It's the only way left to feel like I am still in the ring.

With the advancement of the EU, most of the continent is now economically unified, with the best roads in the world laid out

Riding into Budapest over the Danube

across open borders. Brad picked up his rental bike in Munich, and after two days tracking down the new GPS, we rode for Hungary. The faster the better, we thought, as we raced over the autobahn through Austria directly into Budapest, stopping only once, for a Hungarian entry stamp. With my rear shock absorber in need of rebuilding, I've notified every Ohlins distributor in the region and am waiting for a response. Planning ahead for repair work is difficult, as the lead time for spare-part deliveries can vary. Would I spend Christmas in New Delhi or Cairo? The direction to take at the upcoming fork in Istanbul — Asia or Africa — would be decided by suspicious politicians displeased with my government.

The Iranians were friendly enough at the consulate in Budapest, assuring me a tourist visa would be issued after they'd conferred with superiors in Tehran. Unfortunately, that would take two weeks. In the meantime, I submit two photos along with the application, while Brad and I drift around Eastern Europe in limbo. Either continent will be covered eventually, but for my follow-the-sun timing, it was best to ride Asia first. It's been a week of early fall sunshine since Brad arrived, but I haven't forgotten the freezing rains of Siberia and I've had my fill of daily submersion. To tour Pakistan and India during dry season, I'll still need to cross the high-altitude mountain passes of northern Turkey into Iran before November. But after that, I'd be ahead of the rain for the next year through the Himalayas of Nepal and jungles of Southeast Asia. Africa was as enticing as India, but reversing my route meant a half-year of monsoon storms on muddy savanna roads. All I can do now is take everything one day at a time.

I've surrendered the guidebook to Brad, telling him, "This is your five weeks so pick your adventure." His only restriction is delivering the rental bike in Athens in time to catch a flight back to the role of Corporate Guy in California. Today, we'll follow the banks of the Danube River south into Croatia, Bosnia and Serbia for an easy ride south along the Mediterranean coast. Somewhere on our itinerary is Romania, Bulgaria and Turkey, but since we can be anywhere within the region in two long days, we'll choose our next destinations on whims and weather.

Roamin' Ruins
October 12, 2004
Croatian Coast
● ● ● ● ● ● ● ● ●

In an effort to outrun a massive storm moving down from the Baltic, we depart early from Hungary, before the rains engulfed all of south-eastern Europe. God bless satellite weather forecasting. Rolling through the countryside, there is no escape from the forerunning squalls, but we'll edge closer to warmer rain on the Mediterranean coast. Crossing from Croatia to Bosnia with signs and menus in Cyrillic marks the transition from West to East. After the dissolution of Yugoslavia, cultural differences have become more pronounced and old vendettas renewed. News stories of ethic cleansing and genocide stick in my head as we pass bombed-out villages and bullet-riddled farmhouses. It's hard not to wonder what became of those huddled behind shattered brick walls and hidden deep inside dank cellars.

Wandering the earth, history books and stone fortresses feed my imagination with tales of wars and conquest. But these fresh fingerprints of terror serve as reminders of what otherwise decent people can do to each other. It's always about God and gold. As we follow behind in restless monotony, long olive-drab convoys of SKFOR peace-keeping forces chug through sharp mountain curves. Filthy trails of thick black smoke taint the rain-fresh air, making us gag as we weave between giant troop carriers and military police vehicles with flashing blue lights. Civilians lining the streets wave and flash peace signs; others turn their backs. Why do you have to put a gun to someone's head to stop them from killing their neighbors? Who will be held to account? Separate perspectives mean different versions of history, with whoever wins the war writing the book.

Italian tourists from across the sea spill from ferryboats moored in the yacht-filled harbor. With credit cards in hand, they eagerly fan out through stone corridors of Roman ruins now lined with glittering jewelry shops and expensive shoe stores. If not for the constant fleecing, this would be a nice place to visit. Our muddy motorcycles and stained riding suits clash with impeccably fashioned, chain-smoking tourists sipping cappuccinos in sidewalk cafés. Sunburned college students buzz the beachfront on bright yellow rented scooters as we mull over guidebooks, plotting a course to Albania. For now, we're content to realize there is nowhere we have to be.

Albanian Holiday
October 17, 2004
Macedonia
• • • • • • •

The Mediterranean coast south from Croatia to Albania meant a return to torrential downpours through more quick border crossings than we can remember. The former Yugoslavia is still dividing into smaller nations. Narrow cliff side roads winding over tiny strips of oceanfront real estate made us lose track of which country we were passing through. Centuries-old ethnic communities and antiquated fortresses are redefining new countries faster than mapmakers can record. Because the names and alliances were changing every few months, two border police were laughing when they realized that we did not know the name of the new country we were about to enter.

Finally, we cross into Albania, a land once ruled by one of the most repressive communist dictatorships. Now a democracy free from Soviet domination, it's also one of the poorest but friendliest countries in the region. Although there's been little positive news for their economy, we were surprised to discover that amidst such pronounced poverty, the hotels and restaurants are remarkably modern and clean. Albanians are kind. If we slow for a moment passing through small towns, we're mobbed by locals baffled by invading alien bikers, and everyone has a question about our journey. When we ask for directions, a dozen men answer at once.

There is only one highway connecting the countryside to the capital, Tirana, but there is nothing to do when we arrive in the middle of another storm. Traffic is a slow-moving mass of honking horns and worn-out suspensions banging over deep holes filled with water. The rain is so dense, taillights from other vehicles disappear in the gray.

To complete our intended loop back to Hungary, we entered through Montenegro to exit through the mountains into Macedonia. On a sunny day, this route would be paradise, spiraling into the hillside forest. Instead, navigating precarious switchbacks through the freezing fog, we catch only glimpses of distant farmland patchwork. It's taken six hours to cover 150 miles of twisted mountain roads, half on crumbling asphalt, the rest in mud. These are standard conditions on a world ride, but Brad is here for five weeks, and I wanted him to have a good experience.

Soaked to our flesh at halftime, we arrive at the Macedonian border only to be informed that Canadian citizens need visas. Don't worry, just backtrack to Tirana and apply? This was distressing news to hear, shivering at nightfall with a shrinking travel window.

Brad is sick of the rain and opts to detour south into a reportedly sunny Greece, while I must continue riding back north to Budapest in hopes of receiving better news from Tehran. Being separated from Brad is a bad idea. Disappearing into the chilling mountain night air, our final uneasy words were to ride for another day and then connect through email to schedule another rendezvous again in Istanbul. This was not how I'd planned to show my brother the world, but perhaps he was about to discover that the adventure begins when things stop going as planned.

Progress Report
October 20, 2004
Back in Budapest
● ● ● ● ● ● ● ● ● ● ●

After three days, Brad finally sent me an email indicating he was enjoying a calm ride across Bulgaria. Frantic for the past two days, I was 30 minutes from alerting the Canadian embassy in Albania and beginning to backtrack his route.

There is still no Iranian visa news, not surprising considering the rising levels of political tension. The shock would be if Tehran cooperated in the midst of the current saber rattling. On top of everything, it's Ramadan and the next two days are holidays, so embassy staff tell me to return next week, when maybe there would be an answer. Maybe. Am I supposed to wait in Budapest for weeks to see if maybe they grant one?

In the meantime, I've applied for the Pakistani visa, which as of January 1, 2004, because of security measures to inhibit the movements of international terrorists, they no longer issue outside of home countries. This means that Americans must apply in Washington, DC. "There has to be a way," I plead over the phone. "Is it possible to speak directly with the ambassador?"

"Well, you can try."

It was a pleasant surprise when the ambassador himself invited me into his office for tea to discuss my trip. After hearing my story, there are few in the world who would deny someone trying so hard to see it through. Time and again, when people hear what I am up to, they want to help in some way. It hasn't failed yet — just pointing to the Blue Beast and explaining how, by riding through storms, deserts and lonely nights, I hope to meet the people of the planet on their home ground, look them in the eye and shake their hand. Hesitant officials become instant believers and eager allies. No matter their religion or political beliefs, the best in them usually surfaces.

It took four trips to the embassy and a lengthy interview with a reluctant ambassador, but, in the end, he not only issued a transit visa but handed over gifts of maps and guidebooks. My first official contact with Pakistanis ended with a photo together next to my bike.

Autumn in Romania
October 23, 2004
Romanian Countryside
• • • • • • • • • • • • •

The closer we get to the Middle East, the more frustrating the delay on visa news becomes. After rescheduling a rendezvous point twice via email, Brad and I decide to meet in Bulgaria, at Varna, on the Black Sea. From there, it's 300 miles to Istanbul, where he heads west and I head east.

Another farewell to Budapest begins a leg going deeper into Eastern Europe, with only a passport stamp from jovial Romanian border officials standing guard with nothing to do. Answering all of their questions about my motorcycle's performance would have taken an hour, so I politely cut them off to take advantage of the last of the afternoon sun. Within a mile, the countryside opens into yellowing agricultural fields littered with rusted farm machines and scattered piles of golden wheat stacked in perfect triangles. Boring stretches of flatlands are interrupted by drab villages of aging blockhouses and the occasional Soviet-era small city.

Most cobblestone streets were jammed with too many vehicles contending with broken traffic lights, but that didn't discourage determined old farmers following their daily routines. Rickety horse-drawn carts with warped wooden frames and wobbling, bald car tires are reminders that nothing goes to waste in poverty. It's a maddening allocation of road space, between these primitive vehicles and the slow-moving semitrucks lumbering through mountains while impatient businessmen en route to Bucharest compete to pass through the curves.

Tired old men bundled in frayed woolen overcoats sit hunched over the reins. Forlorn expressions are hidden beneath short-brimmed caps pulled low over bushy gray eyebrows, as they mope, unconcerned with the impending hustle. Worn-out ponies trudging methodical paces have long given up freedom and stare mindlessly into memory. Farmer's wives, fighting the cold, hunker down, wrapped in thick horsehair blankets, riding in back, perched atop piles of corn and potatoes. With heads hung low, enormous noses poke from bulky plaid scarves concealing craggy, lined clay faces that speak of labor and struggle. Anxious Western executives in luxury cars back up for miles in traffic, waiting their turn to weave to the front. In the war of opportunity, these hungry soldiers race for the spoils of an ailing post communist world. Undisturbed by the scene around him, for a moment, the farmer has forced the world to follow his terms.

In the mountains, like an enormous watercolor painting, sections of fresh green forests explode with splotches of auburn and mustard along the banks of still rivers. Their reflections on the mirror surface announce autumn in Romania. Mentally replaying my recent conversations with Jodie stands in stark contrast to my surroundings. My poor communication skills have made her furious, leaving me more reluctant to call. The gap between us widens daily, now filling with bitterness. She feels neglected as I continue with my selfish journey, and, finally, in a clumsy attempt to dodge the inevitable, I refuse to even send more emails. How can I properly explain that what's happening here, in this moment, has become more important to me than what has been?

A darkening overcast sky cools the landscape with mist as early evening fog creeps in mischievously to alter the odds for motorcycle riders. Against piercing headlight glare, streams of water droplets form sparkling cobwebs on my face shield, making me drowsy. Mesmerized by blinding smoky white, the second I forget caution, the looming back end of a big rig instantly zooms into view.

Stomping the brake and squeezing the hand lever almost hard enough to snap, the ABS kicks on with a klickety-klickety abrasive motion. Bright red lights approaching too fast is a familiar panic scenario for unfortunate motorcyclists in the sphincter-puckering moment before we know we're going down. Regrets flash as blazing neon — what was I doing out here at night? The rain-slicked road loses the battle of friction as the front wheel of the Blue Beast bites into the asphalt, barely tapping the steel fangs of the truck's undercarriage bar. Spared without reason, I release a breath, fighting the shakes as the sinister square ghost chugs eerily back into the night. With a shakey smile, I acknowledge the mercy of the Travel Gods once more and search for somewhere to sleep.

THE MIDDLE EAST

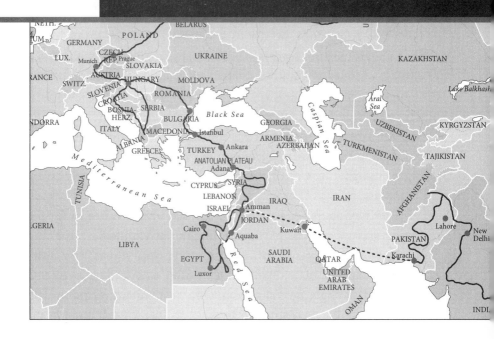

The Infidels Arrive!
October 25, 2004
Turkey

• • • •

Although it had only been a few days since we'd parted company, it was a great relief to find Brad waiting in Varna. Taking advantage of the delicious sunshine, we enjoyed a two-day rest along city beaches before heading south to Istanbul. On our early morning departure, a thick fog burned off quickly as we soared among rising foothills past dried-out vineyards to the west and a sparkling Black Sea to the east. Wide-banked turns leading back through the Bulgarian mountains provided a welcome contrast to crowded cities and freezing rain. A warm afternoon sun ignited passion for adventure and a feeling that it's never going to be cold again. After three months bundled in foul-weather gear, it's a relief to shed layers of thermals and sweaters and switch from bulky cold-weather gloves to thinner, lighter versions. In this newfound freedom of movement, it's easier to feel the road.

Down to his last eight days, Brad has only three left with me before he rides alone to Athens and I zigzag Turkey toward Iran. Running into winter storms over the Anatolian plateau is still a possibility, so I closely monitor current weather conditions and study topography maps in hopes of finding an overlooked alternate route. There is none. My main concern is the 8,000-foot summits icing over, making two-wheeled travel impossible. Yet none of this seems real during an unseasonably warm day nearing the Mediterranean. Soon enough, one way or another, I'll be looking at a winter crossing in Turkey.

After paying 45 bucks for a border visa and another 10 for the bikes, we cross an invisible threshold into the Middle East. Istanbul is where Europe meets Asia in a subtle departure from Christianity into the world of Islam. Had we kept riding, we could have reached the famed city by nine o'clock, but with daylight fading and us still wanting to enjoy the countryside, we opted for a small hotel in the first village across the border. Weaving our way among single-story stone houses, it was as though the martians had landed, with giggling black-haired Turkish children dancing out to greet us. Toothy grins from unshaven faces of town elders looking out from open doorways assure us that we're welcome. For Muslims, this is the equivalent of Christmas season.

During Ramadan, a month of daily fasting is followed by elaborate evening feasts, where entire families gather at single elongated tables. The locals are delighted to celebrate with hungry foreigners. After piling our table with fresh garden salads, fluffy flatbreads and plates of barbecued meats, an anxious restaurateur steps back with folded arms, waiting for our approval. There was far more food than we could eat, but we felt as though we should, just to be polite. Unaccustomed to the bizarre exchange rate, we are shaken then relieved to discover that our 20-million-lira meal really only amounts to

15 dollars. It's a constant mathematical riddle, learning to compute currency values when crossing new borders, but today we make a cultural leap as well. Entering Turkey marks our first major shift in civilization-hopping.

The religious transition is immediate. In European cities, to solicit the faithful, gonging church bells reverberate in waves from imposing granite towers. Here, stately stone-domed mosques are centers for broadcasting inspiring calls to prayer. Ancient Arabic verses, the same throughout the Muslim world, are sung over loud-speakers by unseen imams in wobbling off-key tunes. The echoing moan reaches deep into the mind. Whatever their meaning, it's an eerie yet intriguing song, impossible to forget. In one spine-tingling moment, I am drawn into the embrace of Islam.

Constantinople
October 29, 2004
Istanbul, Turkey
• • • • • • • • • •

As the one-month mark passed for Brad, he was already mentally back in the office, anxious to reach Athens. But after a few days in the U.S., he will be certain to miss the call of the road and start planning our February rendezvous in Southeast Asia. At least that's the plan. In the meantime, we make the most of our last days touring museums and exploring mysterious back alleys.

With 15 million people crammed into 50 square miles, Istanbul is the most congested city I've seen yet. Confusing highways bottle-necking in downtown traffic make it more logical to walk than drive. With Europe on one side and Asia on the other, the Bosphorus channel feeds from the Black Sea into the Aegean. Bridges and ferryboats keep Istanbul connected to the surrounding mainland and are the quickest way to get anywhere.

It's been tricky coordinating the shock absorber rebuilding process. A repair kit had to be mailed from Sweden to the local

Ohlins distributor, now a bike shop with tools was needed to remove the shock. After that it had to go out to another shop for rebuilding and yet another for spring compression. But because of days off for Ramadan, a half-day job stretched into two days. Strangers wrenching on my bike to access the shock was nerve-racking to watch, especially when the mechanic who reassembled it was different than the one who initially disassembled it. Finally, after bolting the Beast back together with pliers and vice-grips, the wires were reconnected and sealed with masking tape. Life is laid-back here, and nothing stops Turks from chain-smoking, not even gasoline pouring out onto the floor from severed fuel lines.

No one else speaks English, but we all become quick friends after the Turkish motocross champion who owns the bike shop offers dinner and a place to sleep. The bike handles better than ever now, and I can't wait to get back on the road. Sunday morning, early, I'll head south to Izmir and cruise the beaches until the Iranian embassy personnel approve my visit.

After reapplying for another visa, this time in Istanbul, and paying 65 dollars, they told me to return in two weeks for their answer, a common procedure that almost always extends into a month. The first snows in eastern Turkey are falling at this moment, and two more weeks might exceed the acceptable danger zone. KEEP SMILING is the mantra for successful travelers. When this fails, you head for home. As I no longer have a home, I continue to chant.

Ephesus
November 2, 2004
Selcuk, Turkey
● ● ● ● ● ● ● ● ●

To be a happy traveler in Istanbul you need a sense of humor. Visitors are under constant siege by friendly but persistent businessmen trying to sell something or coax you into stores where they receive commissions. Because of terrorism, tourism is down more than usual in the winter low season. Teams of hungry touts outnumber customers ten to one. From the back of dingy, smoke-filled cafés to second-story balconies, the world's most proficient high-pressure salesmen are lurking, constantly at work. Shake one off and another attacks, and, like schools of circling piranha, all of them are somehow related. And the system is rigged. No matter if you're buying a soda, dinner or a hand-woven carpet, you're going to get beat out of 20 percent, either on a price change or last-minute product swap.

"I thought you said dinner was eight dollars?"

"Ah yes, but you used the ketchup and that costs another two."

With SUCKER stamped on my forehead, I wander alleyways of souvenir shops only to be attacked by aggressive hordes of conmen competing to shake my hand. *"Hello my fren, where you cone fron? Please come in and try a coffee or look at my beauteeful rugs. I has somesing special just for you."* (Never trust anyone who calls you "my fren.") There is no escape — every tourist attraction worth seeing including the legendary Blue Mosque of Istanbul, is ringed by legions of fast-talking street vendors.

Having meditated in remote Tibetan monasteries and peered through more towering stone cathedrals than I can clearly recall, nothing rivals the aura of the Muslim mosque. Maybe it's the architectural simplicity of the semi-sphere or the laidback atmosphere, but in the dozens of simultaneous murmuring conversations, a powerful silence conveys spirituality and communion with self. Soft silk carpet floors under enormous dome ceilings of hand-painted tiles evoke a stillness devoid of human images. There are no statues. Just as Buddha requested on his deathbed, the prophet Mohammad commanded that his likeness never be recreated. These great spirituals figures wanted their words immortalized, not themselves. The Blue Mosque is a place to savor so much that you don't want to leave. Hungry for another moment of internal calm after the sensory experience, a peaceful euphoria accompanies you back into the throng of annoying hustlers and daily realities.

The Iranians continue to tell me to "Come back tomorrow," but another night in the smoggy chaos of Istanbul is more than I can bear.

Three flights down from my tiny hotel room, the Blue Beast waits patiently for the order to ride. The destination is not important. Today, I'll settle for anywhere, as long as I am traveling on two wheels.

At last, a warm autumn wind and rushing asphalt transmit the soothing relief of the open road as I roll beyond the Istanbul city limits, heading south. After crossing the channel to Bandirma, reaching the ancient Roman city of Ephesus is a four-hour sprint over the opposite mainland and into a thousand years of history. It's hot enough to ride without a jacket, but I recall my pledge, enjoying the sweltering heat. I imagine I'm absorbing the sun's energy like a recharging battery, storing it for the upcoming mountains. After a short search, I find a cozy hostel in Selcuk, a tree-shaded village nearly two miles beyond the best-preserved classical Roman city on the eastern Mediterranean. It's here where the apostle Paul is said to have written his profound epistle to the Ephesians.

Under the constant threat of terrorism, the few tourists still in Turkey are avoiding famous historical sites. The once lively capital of Asia, second only to Athens, is now deserted on a bright November afternoon. And there is nothing to do but doze in the pleasing sunshine and drift through time. Over the ages sacked by conquerors and rebuilt by rulers, Ephesus still presents the magnificence of ancient Roman architecture with captivating images of early life. Ornate stone carvings and polished marble columns evoke foggy images in my head, until suddenly a velvet-cloaked Byzantine emperor is addressing a roaring crowd in the 25,000-seat granite amphitheater. Chronologically disoriented, I sit alone, daydreaming through history until suddenly the hollow grating of wooden-wheeled carts and dancing minstrels fades into the chill of an approaching sunset. I awaken to discover I have been resting on this rock for the last three hours.

Parts and Visas
November 7, 2004
Istanbul, Turkey
● ● ● ● ● ● ● ● ● ●

Maybe the mechanic's assistant in Prague thought he was being help-ful when he adjusted my rear drive chain far more than was necessary. Since he'd been supervised by an experienced technician, I didn't double-check his work when it would have been wise to do so. When a drive chain is stretched too tight, it stresses the transmission shaft bearing. After 3,000 miles, a faint grating noise sporadically surfaces but, of course, never when anyone else is listening.

Odd noises can be deceiving when traveling through metal. Even when you use a stethoscope to pinpoint them, diagnosis is difficult. We couldn't hear the lower-end-whine at the repair center, but the BMW service manager in Istanbul decided it could be the water pump and installed a new one to be safe. Then, when the sound persisted, a new generator, hydraulic cam chain tensioner and starter were replaced. More shots in the dark. Because the grating was inconsis-tent and barely audible, mechanics had to regularly test ride the bike, attempting to identify the noise. After a final checkup at the shop, we determined the problem to be the small bearing in the transmission that wears prematurely when the chain is too tight.

Only the bearing needed replacing, but the entire engine had to be disassembled — a three-day process. The good news was that since the bike had a record of maintenance by authorized dealers across Europe, BMW assumed responsibility and covered the cost under warranty.

In the meantime, I return to daily check-ins for my visa at the Iranian embassy. Peering out through an inch of bullet proof glass, a bearded young man wearing wire-frame glasses states in a British accent, "I'm sorry Mr. Heggstad, but at this time you must consider your application to have been denied." But I am certain if we can speak face to face, we can reason together, we just need the oppor-tunity. It was time to push.

"So we will let the media's image of Iranians prevail?"

With a cocked eyebrow, he turns to ask, "So you do not think bad of us?"

"Why do you suppose I am struggling so hard to enter your country? I want to see for myself."

"Give me your passport and wait here."

Five minutes later he returns to the window and says, "Please take a seat and I'll be out to talk with you."

After an intense 20 minutes, tiptoeing around precarious political territory, he requests a number to reach me, but there is no phone at the hostel. We agree that I'll return Monday and bring a copy of my travel diary pasted together as a gift. After a long handshake, he assures me that he will do all he can with the officials in Tehran. If these efforts fail, my only option is the unthinkable sin of airfreighting over Iran into Pakistan. Overland border crossings with a motorcycle into developing nations can be all-day affairs, but clearing customs through airports can take weeks. And an Internet search for the Karachi procedures proves fruitless, leaving only apprehension about the unknown complications ahead.

The Cup Is Filling
November 9, 2004
Sultan Ahmet
● ● ● ● ● ● ● ●

Although the Iranians have denied the visa again, here in the Middle East, persistence counts and it's acceptable to tell them I'll be back next week. A phone call to the consulate in Budapest was also fruitless. "I'm sorry Mr. Heggstad, nothing has been approved yet; maybe tomorrow." These men are making it hard for me to like them. In the meantime, the Iranian national legislature continues to chant "Death to America" while the U.S. State Department issues ominous warnings about nuclear issues and an "Axis of Evil." I still believe that while governments may differ, people don't, and all I ask is an opportunity to prove that.

Even though crossing Iran might still be possible, the time has come for plans B and C. There is a shot at visas for Syria and Jordan, but Saudi Arabia is the wild card needed for catching a ship out of Oman for Karachi. The absolute last resort is the unthinkable air-freighting to India, with its dreaded importation procedures. But even worse, failure to convince the Iranians means that extremists from all sides will win again. And at the moment, nothing else is working out for me.

Relations with Jodie have come to a standoff, with neither of us budging. To save the relationship, she demands that I return immediately to California, but I say the same, she must meet me here at once, in Turkey. Maybe this is the best way to end matters, taking positions that we both know are impossible. Realizing that our romance has deteriorated beyond the point of no return, in a final, sad conversation, we agree to disagree.

Languishing in Limbo
November 14, 2004
Istanbul, Turkey
● ● ● ● ● ● ● ● ● ●

Three weeks trapped in any capital city will drive a traveler mad. It's worse for motorcyclists, as we constantly crave the soothing winds of the open road, with an alternating landscape to ignite our passions. Waiting with nothing to do only strangles our spirits. My motorcycle parts, ordered through Turkish distributors, are somewhere between the BMW warehouse in Munich and a complicated local customs procedure that is rife with delays. Even if they arrive next week, it will take three days to rebuild the machine, which means I'll be lucky to escape Istanbul by December. Fellow overlanders come and go, exchanging information and confirming or denying rumors. Ensnared within the tentacles of Third World regulations, I covet their freedom. At least the religious holidays are over.

Ramadan has finally ended, but not before the one last impediment of a three-day shutdown for the entire Muslim world. Embassies for Middle Eastern countries, which would likely convey bad news anyway, are closed until Wednesday. According to official reports, Syria and Jordan will still grant visas to Americans — my most likely plan B. UAE and Oman might do so as well but will not confirm this over the phone, so to find out would require a maddening shuffle across Istanbul. A three-day transit visa is rumored to be available from the Saudis, but no one knows the procedure or even at which consulate it is best to apply. Some say the frontier at Jordan, but that would mean riding across two countries to receive a yes or no at the embassy in Amman. No officials respond to my emails or answer their telephones.

Without Saudi cooperation, my options are shipping from the southern Jordanian seaport of Aqaba or crossing into Egypt by ferry. Evidence of travelers' visits to Israel provokes automatic visa denials in Arab countries down the road. And the Israelis will be equally wary of people who have passed through Arab lands. The wrong entry stamp brands a traveler and poisons a passport. Suspicion runs deep in the Middle East.

Exiting Egypt again by air or sea is reportedly a nightmare of confusion and bribes equal to what's ahead in Karachi. At this point, I'll settle for any direction other than backward. Autumn storms and city traffic have me pinned down to a comfortable hostel room with a TV that receives CNN World News. Now I can keep track of international weather and the Middle East body count while cringing at the ignorant obstinacy of world leaders. Maybe it's time to get healthy.

During the first three months of this journey, plastic stents in my organs prevented me from exercising. Even walking was difficult. But since Brad appeared last month, strutting around shirtless, flashing his washboard stomach, I've been plotting a comeback. Lately, I spend afternoons sprinting up and down narrow cement stairwells and practicing martial art drills. Stress-relieving yoga sessions followed by meditation balance the madness of waiting. Without an event to train for, it's hard to generate fire into workouts, but at least the evidence of too many chocolate bars is diminishing. Istanbul is safe and clean, and although there are no beggars, armies of slick vendors continue to lurk outside any areas worth visiting.

Built upon the rubble of Middle East history, the modern buildings of the Sultan Ahmet district cast shadows over the skeletons of antiquity. Crumbling Roman archways, Greek pillars and sealed stone caverns are tucked behind backstreets full of hustling merchants and sidewalk cafés. Languishing in limbo, there is nowhere left for me to go.

After visiting all the famous mosques, sultans' palaces, Roman ruins, Ottoman fortresses and European castles, I've given up trying to memorize which civilizations defeated which. Muslim invaders, Christian crusaders versus barbarian conquerors — you need a scorecard to keep track of the sacking and rebuilding. It's amazing how long these structures last. Three-thousand-year-old columns built on top of thousand-year-old remains. Scattered triumphantly across the Middle East, architectural wonders of granite and marble have been stacked together by forgotten civilizations at the whims of kings, sultans and emperors. And now, curious tourists marvel at the dubious grandeur of excess created on the backs of slave labor and human suffering. Monuments of slaughter and exploitation were created in the name of religion and to control resources. Struggles for God and gold. And I wonder if the next 5,000 years will be the same as the last.

Into the Cold
November 26, 2004
The Anatolian Plateau, Turkey
● ● ● ● ● ● ● ● ● ● ● ● ● ● ● ● ●

This morning is a new day and an anxiously awaited email finally arrives from BMW; my motorcycle has recovered from surgery and is ready to ride. A constantly monitored CNN weather report predicts snow flurries and below zero temperatures on the 280-mile stretch to Ankara. The alternate route, south along the coast, will be covered in freezing rain for the next three days. Since it's dryer, I opt for snow, hoping the asphalt holds heat long enough to keep the slippery ice at bay.

Istanbul, a temporary home but one to escape from, sends me off with an elegant goodbye fitting Marco Polo. Sunday morning departure jubilation — a traffic-free ride along the Bosphorus channel separating Europe from Asia, gliding through miles of green lights. Saluting waves slap the shoreline rocks and send sprays of seawater upwards as a final farewell; within the blink of an eye, the gaping Autobahn E80 spills out to the horizon.

An empty, jagged mountainside of the rising Anatolian plateau turns into an eerie moonscape of frozen forests and white, powdery plains. As the altimeter climbs, temperatures plummet until chilling pain turns to numbness from my fingertips to my shoulders. An electric vest maintains my core heat but has no effect on a runny nose freezing to the inside of my helmet liner. It's going to be a long two days through a high-altitude glacial odyssey.

Savage headwinds bite through thick nylon and five layers of thermals, gnawing their way from my legs to my lower torso. The Pillsbury Doughboy under siege. Icy elements relentlessly hammer and tear, chipping away barriers to hypothermia. If I can keep my organs warm, another hundred miles is possible, but with the sun behind the clouds, odds shift. At 45-minute intervals I must stop to stomp my feet and let the heated vest chase away shivers. Uncertainty reemerges like a long-lost nemesis. The volatility of nature reinforces the idea of fate, I think to myself, as the ferocity of adventure returns, like plunging into a raging sea. With a wry smile, once again I hum Willie's tune "On the Road Again."

The Anatolian Plateau
November 29, 2004
Adana, Turkey
• • • • • • • • •

At 4,000 feet, a deep inhale of prickly morning air is cold and dry enough to make a set of lungs flutter. After such a deep freeze last night, a pair of fresh apples left in my tank bag turned into baseballs of red rock, brittle enough to shatter if dropped. For relief, I'll ride 300 miles of varying summits across the rugged Anatolian plateau to the mild temperatures of sea level. Far colder than yesterday, the sky is a pale steel blue, minus threats of shadowing clouds. But violent weather in this region can dominate as quickly as a scene in fast-forward video. To best use the heat of the sun, luck and departure timing are critical.

Along with the planet's major roads, my *World Basemap* CD also contains vital topographical details. My laptop becomes a command center for strategic planning. In Topo mode, when clicking on a specific road, a chart pops up, displaying elevations and distances, graphically correlating with a sliding ball on the route selected. This permits me to schedule high summits for the warmer parts of the day. I fear to guess the temperature at 7,000 feet, but, whatever it is, I'll be tackling it at 2:00 p.m. If the road remains dry, the cold is manageable.

Local long-riders in Istanbul, with furrowed brows, advised against a winter crossing; "If the snow doesn't get you, the ice will." But when asked about alternatives, they only shrugged their shoulders, "It's much prettier in the spring." Yet waiting out the winter in western Turkey means enduring humid heat and monsoon storms in the chaos of Asia. If I can reach India by Christmas, that means ideal conditions for the next year. A short section of road ice, at the very best, promises a guaranteed high-impact fall and a grinding slide. I must constantly strain to scan for slick sections ahead, guessing which are frozen water and which are just wet asphalt. Yet today all is clear.

Turkish toll roads are equal to Europe's, with autobahn-quality surfaces stretching out across the west. It's as though they were created with a distant future in mind because for the last two days most roads have been deserted. Built wide enough to handle big city rush-hour traffic, the triple-lane highways are empty, and there are no cities. It's hard to imagine what road-planners had in mind. To remind myself that better times are coming, I continue to zoom in and out on the GPS screen to glimpse the approaching Mediterranean Sea. Warmth ahead provides something positive to focus on.

I've been riding between mountain peaks and dormant volcanoes, so the sun sets early, instantly forcing the temperature down another 10 degrees. Just in time, an abrupt, rapid descent lies ahead. The highway suddenly spirals downward in a steep, dizzying decline to the sea. Within 20 minutes, the winking lights of Adana, the last stopover before Syria, come into in view. Traveling in Westernized Turkey is comfortable and safe. Wanderers are treated well. Yet the religious enigmas of the Middle East continue to beckon me deeper into a world where Islam is law and the very roots of civilization have been buried and reborn a thousand times. In the morning, another chapter of the adventure begins, as I am drawn into the scented mysteries of an ancient world.

Arabs
December 4, 2004
Palmyra, Syria
• • • • • • • • •

Third World border crossings can be lengthy hassles, but my processing from Turkey to Syria today only takes two hours. The cost is 40 dollars for insurance and road tax and 10 more to bribe fake immigration inspectors before being released into a flowing demolition derby. Turks are timid drivers compared to Syrians — the 30-mile terror ride in the dark to Aleppo is only a peek at what else is in store. There are too many near-death experiences to consider recounting.

Anxious to meet the Arabs, I've been practicing the language. Spoken Arabic isn't hard to learn, but, with the flowing symbols written backward, it's tough to read. So far, Arabs are extremely polite when greeting everyone, with an extensive predetermined dialogue to recite before real conversation begins. But questions about health and family are too much to remember, so foreigners are forgiven for their ignorance and applauded when they try. Translated into English, *"Ahlan wa sahlan"* literally means welcome, so, when addressing strangers, they reverse it into one of the few words everyone knows in English — "Welcome!"

Hearing this a hundred times a day, I clasp my heart in return, saying, *"Ahlan bik."*

Arab hospitality includes gracious offers to guide me around Aleppo, invitations for tea or help to carry my baggage. In other countries, such gestures are given for tips or they lead into scams. But Syrians do it to be nice. You'd think since everyone is so pleasant, I could relax and trust them. Taught well by the smiles of thieving Gypsy kids in Prague, I keep my guard up and don't leave anything of value on the bike or in the tank bags. Apparently, whatever is not bolted down is fair game.

At a downtown restaurant, locals crowding around my table exchanging small talk was normal. And who would have suspected a diversion to block a line of sight to my bike, which was quietly being stripped of its vital driving lights? Because the danger factor increases tenfold after dark, I try not to ride at night. When poor timing dictates the need, auxiliary lights brighten inky nights, making a significant safety difference. But as I said yesterday when someone stole my water bottles and this morning when the chain lube disappeared — what the heck, turn the page. Let's only count the good times.

Other than a famous castle and some extraordinarily well-preserved Roman ruins, there is little to experience in Syria except endless deserts and its ever-so-curious, friendly people. Being a desert lover, I take a day trip east toward the Iraqi border intent on returning off-road to the Mediterranean. While traveling the dual-lane highway, warnings of insurgents infiltrating through Syria make me uneasy about my California license plate — it'll be safer leaving the pavement.

My electric vest remains on high, and, riding due west, a glaring afternoon sun has no effect on the cold. The desert is powerfully empty yet alive with intrigue, a pleasant reminder of being lonesome in crowded cities and at home embracing desolation. Barren plains tug and nurse my restless spirit with long-lost recollections and journeys back in time — loneliness is at the center of my metamorphosis. Crossing a country buried in 3,000 years of history further expands the imagery.

The pebble-crusted, flattened landscape is sprinkled with peculiar beehive-shaped houses built from clay blocks. Isolated Bedouin camps are interesting stops. A bearded man in long, pale robes waves me in with invitations for bread and tea. Allies without borders.

Abdu Mahan, an Arab sheepherder, shares his pot of tea with a stranger as have his ancestors for the last 3,000 years. His closest neighbors are beyond the horizon; the world to him is infinite. A thick black woolen tent lined with rich, colorful carpets covering the hard-packed dirt floor subtly enhances a lifestyle as ancient as the desert itself. His wife and two daughters scurry, covering their faces, hiding at my approach. We're close enough to the Iraqi border to hear American fighter jets ominously roaring overhead, muffling the bawling of his sheep. They have no electricity or TV, but a pained look in his eyes is evidence that he is aware of the war a hundred miles away. Abdu carries no weapons, only a walking stick for tending his flocks. A man of peace, it's unlikely he hates anyone, and neither of us understands why men continue to butcher each other in the name of God and money. Nomads from different worlds, we sip in silence, knowing that we are of the same spirit and will depart this world as we entered it — alone.

Damascus, the oldest continuously inhabited city on earth, with its elaborate restaurant goat feasts and cheap accommodation, was becoming an easy place to linger — but getting lazy means getting stuck. The main city mosque was one of the few in Syria that admitted non-Muslims, but after my morning visit, all that remained for me was to schedule a departure for Jordan. If your itinerary depends on politics, it's possible to find yourself stuck in the Middle East all winter just trying to leave. The decision to move on is often determined by the moods of restrictive governments or by the fact that your pocketful of local currency has run out. Spend it while you can; money changers at border crossings always cheat travelers. Turkey had offered gas at six bucks a gallon, but Syria's engine-pinging super was only two — so after saddling up, I spent the last of my wrinkled pounds on fuel.

Exiting Syria took five minutes. The Jordanian side was reminiscent of Central American frontiers — you wait in long lines at numerous tiny one-way-mirrored windows only to discover that you are at the wrong one. Even Arabic speakers were confused and annoyed. I was lucky to buy a visa in Damascus for 11 dollars; they were 50 at the border.

Riding south toward Amman on a modern highway with road signs written in English under the Arabic was relaxing. Thirty miles in, an empty desert abruptly sprouts sand-colored, square houses with rooftop satellite dishes, which silhouette as mushrooms on boxes against the pale evening glow. When robed Arabs see me stop to check directions, their first words are "Welcome, welcome."

"Yes my friend, I know that place. You must turn here, then turn there and then go that way and then go some more and you will find it!"

"Yeah, okay, thanks, that should be easy from here. *Sulcran, sulcran, Allah maak.*"

Jordan and Syria offer little in the way of tourism — combine that with terrorist fears in the region and a war going on next door and it's understandable why there are so few foreigners. The tourist hotels are empty, but the business hotels are full. This ten-dollar-a-night cement-block building is heated by a hot water system that the manager refuses to turn on for only one guest. An appointment is needed for showers, but to remove frosty air from my sparse cubicle, a small portable gas heater was provided by a friendly doorman. "There is no ventilation Mr. Glen, so you must leave the window open when you use it." Not bad considering it's colder inside than out. There is, however, a television in the downstairs lobby.

Tired of the Western media bias against them, enterprising Arabs have created their own version of CNN. Now, they have their own biased news coverage against the West. Al Jazeera televises graphic scenes of wars in Iraq and Afghanistan, carefully minimizing the violence that Arabs commit against each other. Even though various sects of Islam feud among themselves, they feel that their often violent struggles should not include outsiders. For situations like this they say, "The enemy of my enemy is my brother." In hotels and restaurants, TVs are tuned to Al Jazeera, and even with the volume down, when blood and guts start flowing, crowded rooms fall silent. When I ask local people about their worldview, they all want to know why Christian armies are stationed in Muslim lands and not the other way around.

As an American, I am the political white elephant wherever I travel, but unless I ask for opinions, Arabs are too polite to comment. Most of the world is angry about America's Middle East policy; the Islamic world is furious. Americans are seen as meddlers pumping billions into an Israeli war machine that is operating against the Arab world. Conversations begin friendly and often end in bitter remarks. It's interesting how people of God in the Middle East, often the same race — Christians, Muslims and Jews — hate one another. You love the wrong God, therefore you must die. I wrestle myself to sleep at night, troubled by the day's disturbing dialogue.

The Syrians had questions. "So Glen, what's the difference

between chopping men's heads off and dropping bombs where civilians die?"

"Tell me Glen, what's the difference between a Palestinian suicide bomber and Israeli helicopter gunships attacking refugee camps and killing children?" Both sides seek blood revenge. An Arab man in a business suits states, "U.S. tax money kills my brothers, so America sponsors terrorism." Even though I had many questions, most of the time I was sorry for asking.

The Saudis are another story. In efforts to preserve strict Islamic values, they prefer to keep foreigners out. Unless you are a Muslim attending hajj or a businessman generating income for the kingdom, you're not welcome. In any case, don't bring your wife; she will not be permitted to drive or venture into public alone. There is no tourism in Saudi Arabia, not even a three-day transit visa for a determined Western motorcyclist out to meet the people of the world. Embassy staff this morning were curt. "Why don't you just put your motorbike on a plane Mr. Heggstad?" Even with persistent efforts from a supporter in the U.S. haggling with Saudi officials in Washington, they will not budge or offer assistance.

The options narrow. Ride southwest to the port of Aqaba and take the ferry across the Red Sea to Egypt and attempt airfreighting from Cairo or continue on the forbidden route to Israel and try it from Tel Aviv. Transport out of Egypt would involve several weeks of unknown bureaucratic nonsense, and since Pakistan will not allow Israeli citizens to even change planes in their country, they will not accept their cargo. After a short ride to the ruins at Petra tomorrow, Amman to Karachi is the new plan.

Intimidated?
December 11, 2004
Petra, Jordan
● ● ● ● ● ● ● ●

When continually asked which country was the most impressive, my reply is always Mongolia. But my opinion of which holds the most alluring sites constantly changes — the castles of Europe, the mosques of Islam or the splendors of Siberia? Today it's Jordan, with its ancient city of Petra, built in the third century BC by industrious Nabataeans to control the trade route from Damascus to Arabia. Caravans of silk, spices and slaves enriched the inhabitants long enough for them to master metals, sculpture and hydraulic engineering. Carved into the sheer walls of rocky crevices, the city met its ultimate demise in a massive earthquake in 555 AD.

And like so many man-made wonders of the world, all that remains to stoke the imagination are the hollow structures of a lost civilization. Other than advances in science, how much has really changed in the last thousand years? Olive-skin Bedouin men with flowing headdresses atop trotting camels send gaping tourists' imaginations back into history through a land forever in turmoil. Is it possible to ever know peace in a region of religious hostilities? Or will fanatics from colliding cultures take the world down with them? The Middle East, still seething like a puffing volcano, is today the center of world conflict, preparing for the next eruption. No matter where you're traveling in the land of devout, it's hard to escape wondering whose God will prevail.

Riding closer to the Red Sea, my uneasiness grows as I think about crossing the Holy Land. I'm so close to Egypt and Israel but deterred by illicit bureaucracy or fear of a poisoning passport stamp — it feels like I'm succumbing to political intimidation, surrendering because it's too hard or cowering before government buffaloing. But if I don't cross, it means extremists have their way. For the last several weeks, a bad taste has been developing; it appears each country will hassle me for visiting the others. Before embarking on this journey, most everyone I know declared this the wrong time to tour the world. "Glen, what about terrorists?"

My answer was: "Now more than ever is the time to travel." Terrorists want to make us afraid to venture from our homes and lead normal lives. They provoke us into turning on one another and seeking safety by strangling our hard-earned freedoms through repressive new legislation. Citizens of the world should never be intimidated by terrorists or obstinate governments.

There are nations that I harbor deep disagreement with and initially considered boycotting. But if I expect to be free of political branding, I must not do it myself. To prove my belief that although governments don't get along people do requires changing my own thinking. In the beginning, when asked which countries were on my itinerary, the answer was easy: "Whichever issues a visa." But now some of those countries want to punish those who visit their enemies. Sudan, a country necessary to later transit North Africa, is known to reject visa applications showing evidence of visits to Israel. In turn, I can expect trouble in Israel with a Syrian passport stamp.

The southern Jordanian seaport of Aqaba is two hours from here, and with a short ferryboat ride to Egypt, it's possible to reach Cairo in two days. A week of museums and pyramids would allow time for a crossing to Israel and Christmas in Jerusalem. It's going to be tight, but the 14-day Pakistani visa is good until mid-January. This requires doubling back through Jordan and hoping they are quick on their export procedures. In the spirit of adventure travel, though, I'll worry about crossing those bridges later.

Bedouins
December 13, 2004
Wadi Rum, Jordan
• • • • • • • • • • •

When it comes to adventure travel, you can't take a wrong turn — a thought shared simultaneously by both parties when I meet a young backpacking British woman touring the ruins of Petra. She, weary of advances from optimistic teenage Arab boys, and I, lonesome for a woman's touch, seem a good match. Neither of us requires convincing. Doubling-up on a motorcycle can be crowded, but Barbara's warm, little body fits perfectly between the small of my back and her rucksack strapped to the motorcycle tail rack. Because the load is awkward, it is understood that when we encounter pockets of deep sand she will climb off and walk while I spin through, wrestling to the other side.

Once off main roads, street signs, if they exist, are in Arabic only, and no one speaks English. Not only were Barbara and I unsure of how to find our way, we weren't certain what we were looking for, except it had to be something not in guidebooks.

Southern Jordan comprises thousands of square miles of sandy desert divided by steep ravines (wadis) with powdery dunes piled high against sheer rocky cliffs reaching toward the sky. Scenes from *Lawrence of Arabia* were filmed here. Bypassing signs that say Tourist Road, we continue another 10 miles until we find a suitable photo op for an empty panorama. We didn't realize how close we were to people until noticing a half-dozen children running toward us yelling, "Welcome, welcome!" Sipping and waving with invisible cups, they continued shouting and beckoning, "Tea, tea."

Their excitement seemed sincere, and since the bike was now buried in blow sand, we had little choice other than to be led by the hand back to waiting Bedouin elders. In a strict Islamic culture, to sleep together without problems, Barbara and I decide to wear wedding rings and declare ourselves married. Once the Bedouin are satisfied that we are legitimate, negotiations begin for a spouse-trade. The men are allowed four wives, who can be bartered for the right price. But after seeing the toothless-wonder one old man had to offer, it was clear who'd be getting the best of the deal.

Bedouin don't recognize international borders, and those still living as nomads roam with little interference. Renowned for their hospitality, they insist we stay. At night, the village women bake large flat disks of bread tossed directly in the fire coals to be dusted off before eating with spicy tomato paste. The dirt-floor shack is too smoky to see across but warm enough to hold off a biting desert breeze. Cold dry air sucks moisture from our skin, leaving gritty lips of paper.

Mysterious young women covered in beige veils wait silently in the shadows until it's determined we're safe to approach. Within moments of a mixture of our English and Arabic, the Bedouin girls bond with Barbara and coax her to dress in their traditional clothing. I am ordered to remain outside their home as the giggling entourage drapes her in fancy full-length black linens. And when I donned a Bedouin headdress, we became members of the clan. She later said that once behind closed doors, the cloaks and veils came off to reveal chatty teenaged girls in jeans and colorful blouses. They told Barbara that they love wearing the headscarf (hijab) and that beauty should be revealed through the eyes.

It's made an enormous difference traveling together — Barbara is no longer hassled and groped by Arab men, and we gain immediate acceptance with locals as a married couple. When dreaming of adventure, it's times like these that travelers live for — camping beneath a blackened canopy of shooting stars amongst strangers who treat us like family. Journeying into simplicity with the Bedouin reminds us of how we all should live. A special room is prepared for us, with bedding of thick, soft carpets and piles of heavy wool blankets.

In the morning, the women teach Barbara how to prepare breakfast; more fresh bread with dishes of olive oil and fresh herbs. They are deeply moved when seeing my copy of the Koran with English translations next to Arabic script and seem pleased to think there was hope for Westerners yet. It is hard to decline pleadings that we stay, as the women cry and give presents of bracelets to Barbara. After farewell photos, we are back in the desert wind for a short ride south to Aqaba. Tomorrow is our ferryboat crossing to Egypt. The Sinai awaits.

Forks
December 16, 2004
Sharm el Sheik, Egypt
• • • • • • • • • • • •

Next to Russian, Egyptian customs procedures are the most complex. But as the ferry landed, a special tourist police officer boarded the ship, whose sole mission was to assist me and another rider through the mindless series of dozens of document stampings and dizzying numbers of vehicle inspections. Five hours of formalities later, we were legalized with Egyptian license plates to go with new Egyptian driver's licenses. Odd men on the road.

It's always interesting to note the unique items travelers choose to bring. Folding lawn chairs, favorite hats and laptops have become the norm. Mark from England hopes to ride into Africa loaded down with 50 pounds of paragliding gear. Freed from the customs compound, we race a setting sun for the nearest coastal shelter.

Because of scattered stretches of five-star resorts and restaurants, the Sinai is known as the Red Sea Riviera. For the best diving on earth, there're hundreds of water-sport shops where you can rent everything from Jet Skis to scuba gear. Local Bedouins own half the land, with some becoming overnight millionaires on revenues from land leases and building booms. Cancun, Mexico, is to the U.S. what the Red Sea Riviera is to Europe: a year-round sunny playground with all the comforts of home.

It's also a target ripe for another al-Qaeda bombing attack like the one in Taba earlier this year. Military roadblocks are manned by nervous young soldiers fingering triggers on submachine guns, but after the first passport check, we're waved through the rest. Traveling under such tight security is unnerving, especially knowing this is not the real Egypt.

This artificial paradise of extravagance and opulence beckons, but it's better to learn about real Egyptians, not sterile colonies of Western affluence surrounded by golf courses. Continuing past sprawling gated luxury resorts and alluring tourist traps, I am reminded of what to avoid. A disappointing lap around touristy Sharm el Sheik alleviated any further curiosity.

As the time dwindled before Barbara had to return to London, we had less to say yet more to consider. She must finish her MBA and go back to travel writing as I sail solo again across the Gulf of Suez. After the ferry from Sharm el Sheik to Hurghada, I'll ride on to Luxor and the Valley of the Kings. Due to violent rebel groups infesting the countryside, sections of the Central Nile Valley are closed to travelers. For the return leg, maybe I'll catch a riverboat down the Nile to Cairo.

Wandering with Barbara was a dream, yet I knew nothing about her. We spoke little of our lives. Of course, through my website, mine is an open book; all but the most intimate details are there for readers to judge — and later, even those will be revealed. I keep my life's darkest moments of hurt and anger to myself, honoring a pledge to write only of the good and let the media report the rest.

Although Barbara and I reached a fork in the road that would separate us, up until the final moment there were silent hopes that something might change. A flight delay? A lost ticket? Reflecting back to our last fireside dinner on sandy floors of a seaside café, I try to imagine the grandeur of pyramids or memorable photos by the Great Sphinx. Upriver scenery should be exciting, and the Egyptian experience overwhelming. Yet why such dreariness? Perhaps it was the empty roadside farewell as she waited for a bus to the airport and I rode south.

The swelling sea is rough enough now for seatbelts as this speeding hydrofoil ferry bobs and tumbles among the waves, yet I am oblivious to the surrounding groans. My eyes are open to the future, yet they see only a fading past. Through a crack in my heart, a desert wind whistles a hollow tune while recollections of Barbara and the Bedouin evaporate into the bleakness of solitude.

Deserted Deserts
December 17, 2004
The Eastern Arabian Desert, Egypt
● ● ● ● ● ● ● ● ● ● ● ● ● ● ● ● ● ● ● ●

When we land in Hurghada, an Egyptian rider I met on the hydrofoil shows me to a cheap hotel, with an invitation to join him later for a night at the local disco. "I can pick you up at midnight." If I didn't normally fall asleep at 11 that might be a good idea. But he persists, "I have a safari company, you can join 30 of us tomorrow for a visit to an authentic Bedouin village for authentic Bedouin tea. I'll make a special price for you my friend, only 30 dollars."

"Thanks, but it's better I get an early start for Luxor in the morning."

Fifty miles down the coast of the eastern Arabian Desert was supposed to be an open road leading west toward the Nile River and Luxor. But the turnoff is blocked by heavily armed military forces under sandbag barricades. Islamic extremists are at work in the countryside so the road is closed to foreigners — the commander directs me to another possibility 40 miles south.

That's okay, the highway along the Red Sea is a stunning scene of aquamarine waters separated from a booming surf by hundreds of miles of coral reefs. Yet it's the same story at the second checkpoint — foreigners are forbidden for safety reasons. I gesture a rifle with my hands, "You mean, boom, boom, boom?"

"No, no. The road just has too many trucks on it today and there could be some rough spots." The first commander told the truth, but this one doesn't want to admit that they don't control the countryside. They, too, send me further south, seeking another road that leads directly to Aswan. If this keeps up, I'll be in Sudan by midnight.

The entire coastal region is under construction, with so many new projects that companies have built cement factories every 10 miles. Yet it's empty of people. Friday is the Islamic day of rest, so it wasn't unusual for job sites to be vacant, but there were no tourists either. The roads are as bare as the hundreds of ghost town construction projects littering the coast. Half-built shopping malls, shells of half-finished condominiums and massive unpainted resort compounds were all deserted. It's as though a year ago they all began at once and abruptly stopped together.

Even at the few functioning five-star hotels, the only humans were guards at the gates. For a traveler, living in constant crud gets old. So once a month, I stretch the budget and splurge on a bug-free room with clean sheets, satellite TV and hot water. Anxious to see if the low-season crisis could be exploited, I stop to check prices. In the marble-coated reception area of a posh resort, an optimistic manager offers a special deal — an all-inclusive package for 100 U.S. dollars. "Sorry, my budget is 50 a day for hotel, food and gas."

"That's okay, we'll accept 40 and include a gourmet breakfast, lunch and dinner." Because of recent car-bombings, parking in front of hotels is prohibited, but they provide a spacious suite overlooking the Red Sea on one side and a football field–sized lagoon-style swimming pool on the other. At dinner, in a resort for 600 there are 25 well-dressed Italians and one shabby Yankee motorcyclist wearing big, clunky riding boots. After a sumptuous scampi feast, one at a time they approach to shake my hand, "Bravo, bravo!" Later, we clink wine glasses poolside under a crescent moon serenaded with singsong Egyptian love tunes. Yes, I think to myself, the Viking be livin' large.

Unescorted
December 19, 2004
Luxor, Egypt
• • • • • • • •

Tired of debating issues with checkpoint police at the final westbound road to the Nile, I am determined to continue, with or without their permission. If I can't reason with them, I'll find a way to cross off-road, but there will be no backtracking up the coast to be told no all over again. We're at a polite standoff, but a patient police major agrees to hear my case back at headquarters.

It's an encouraging moment as I enter the compound and am immediately surrounded by cops extending their hands, "Welcome, welcome!" In the major's office, he offers tea and sympathy but still insists the road is closed to foreigners.

"I appreciate the concerns of police, but if there is a chance, I would like to try."

He understands only the word "police" and asks, "You are American police?"

Seeing an opening and recalling that there are cops in my judo school, I assure him, "Better than that, I am teacher of police."

He reconsiders. "You understand there are no fuel stations and there is much danger?"

"That's fine," I state, pointing out the window, "that motorcycle can go 600 miles on one tank."

For the next 20 minutes, from his rattletrap, severely dented police truck, he transmits a series of queries over two separate sets of VHF radios with 10-foot whip antennas. The relayed messages are likely monitored. If the insurgents didn't know a foreigner was coming before, they know now. With a final shrugging of shoulders and wave of his hand, the crazy American is permitted to pass, yet I suspect that, in view of the lull in violence, he also thinks that there is little risk.

Egyptian Islamic extremists connected to al-Qaeda are linked to several terrorist attacks against tourists a year ago, which destroyed an already paranoid travel industry. Murdered tourists have cost the country millions, and the government takes no chances, sealing off the entire Nile River Valley and refusing civilian traffic unless escorted by the military. This is clearly an overreaction, still I heed his final warning, "Don't stop for any reason."

Long stretches of the newly constructed highway are devoid of life, not even a tree. It is a ride across Mars — low-level, parched, rocky mountains with broad, sweeping curves, but even in the hot dry air, it was a motorcyclist's delight. With the throttle wide open, 150 miles passes in two hours, until I am teased by balmy breezes off the Nile blowing through countless rows of towering date palm groves.

Distant from the tourist strip of the Red Sea, Egyptian life emerges through the sweet smell of fresh fruit stands and camel dung. Donkey carts on the highway are smothered beneath bulging loads of sugarcane, followed by throngs of children shouting and waving. "Welcome, welcome!" Street-corner greasy food stalls made my stomach gurgle just looking, but after an hour, a traveler's favorite meal appears — roast chicken. It's the most consistent protein source on the road — five bucks a piece in every country on earth.

Decisions — do I head to the laid-back city of Aswan, which is an hour south, or go two more to the north for the legendary time-capsule of Luxor? With sufficient daylight remaining, Luxor wins. But it's a route with even more police checkpoints. Fortunately, the cops are lazy, sitting in trucks, cradling assault rifles. From seated positions they wave me to stop. But I look straight ahead, easing over speed bumps and pretending not to see. They will certainly demand that I wait until tomorrow's military escort. I watch my mirrors, checking for soldiers leveling firearms, but no one gets excited enough to pursue.

Cops 'n' Dodgers
December 22, 2004
Cairo, Egypt
• • • • • • •

It takes four hours to fill out the necessary paperwork in the crowded military office to satisfy apprehensive Egyptian tourist police that I want to travel to Cairo alone — with no police escort or in a slow-moving convoy among dozens of stinky tour buses. To relieve government liability, a reluctant commander demands a handwritten statement declaring the condition and ability of my equipment, along with an acknowledgement of unspecified dangers that everyone denies exist. To seal formalities, copies are faxed to provincial authorities further north.

Finally, shortly before sundown, I am directed to the nearby highway and instructed to have each military checkpoint radio ahead to the next one; advising that I had arrived and would continue until reaching Cairo. Anticipating misunderstandings along the way, I request a written document authorizing solo travel. "Don't worry Mr. Glen, everyone knows you're coming."

At the first roadblock out of Luxor, a friendly federal police lieutenant checks my papers and scribbles in flowing Arabic on his clipboard that American motorcyclist Glen Heggstad, bearing Sinai plate number 52, is officially on his way. If a few Europeans got shot in New York and Boston, would the U.S. government use this as an excuse to declare martial law on the entire East Coast? Worse than that, I assume that if the bad guys are seeking targets, it's likely they'd choose whoever is locked in a convoy.

Each of the first 10 checkpoints are five miles apart and require delays while soldiers radio behind and ahead, confirming I am continuing north. But the further from Luxor I get, the less authorities understand the situation. Finally, one soldier flatly insists I accept a military escort. It's useless to argue as armed men clamber aboard sputtering old pickup trucks, eager to protect me from whatever happened a few years ago.

A long-dreamed-about sunset on the Nile is reduced to a muddy glow through a translucent glaze of bug guts on my visor while I'm in a 30 mile-per-hour procession of wailing sirens and flashing blue lights. An hour later, I am delivered to a local hotel sealed off by soldiers and ordered not to leave. This time they are serious.

"Can I at least go out for Internet?"

An overcautious captain worries for my safety. "No, the manager has agreed to let you use his."

At sunrise, a new game ensues. At their pace, it will take days to reach Cairo, so when they assign new escorts at checkpoints, I quickly ditch them at traffic snarls. Freedom is brief but delicious. Annoyed by my antics but friendly to a fault, soldiers at the following roadblocks patiently plead that I wait for new escorts. Recognizing the overkill, still, no one wants to accept responsiblility for mishaps, so they all do as they are told. But even when they sometimes catch up with me, the sternest commanders break into toothy smiles when I pull off my helmet, laughing.

Gawking crowds in small-town traffic jams wave and cheer, welcoming the alien vagabond. Fleeing the appointed entourage through side streets and alleys, I find a dingy roast chicken stand. Curious locals peer through smudgy windows at the traveler from Mars, with questions about his strange machine. I explain in sign language while demonstrating GPS functions, and soon I have them stroking their beards with satisfying nods.

A stop for oranges in a crowded market draws an instant throng of giggling schoolchildren reaching to shake hands and pose for pictures. "We want you to stay with us!" they shout.

"Is there a hotel here?"

"No, no. You may stay with any of us."

An alarming surge of bodies intensifies as I am nearly shoved off my feet, being almost killed with kindness. Everyone wants to shake hands. Dozens turn into a hundred before plainclothes police arrive to disperse them and order me on my way. Turbaned men in bell-shaped gowns shout goodbye as children sprint beside me, and finally I return to the highway.

Weaving through chaos, I compete for road space with camels beneath enormous loads of sugarcane and strings of housewives returning from the riverbanks with laundry loads balanced atop their heads. A 450-mile ride tediously stretches into fascinating days snaking along the Nile until delivering me into the pulsating streets of Cairo well after dark. My first thoughts when entering the confusion of cities are when to leave, yet with so much to see, decisions of where to spend Christmas and New Years are left to whatever unfolds.

Christmas in Giza
December 26, 2004
Suez Canal, Egypt
● ● ● ● ● ● ● ● ● ● ●

Everyone has a fantasy to-do list. Travel the world, date a movie star or visit the pyramids of Giza are a few dreams that come to mind. Life wouldn't be complete without fulfilling the latter, and what better time than Christmas? Most people won't lose sleep pondering when they'll see the pyramids, but if the opportunity arises, they'll know what's been missing. After the grandeur of sultans' palaces, the majesty of conquerors' castles and ruins of Roman empires, these sacred tombs of the pharaohs exceed the other ancient marvels combined. And choosing a hotel with a panoramic sunset view of the imposing majesty beyond guaranteed a restless night.

An early doze with hopes that I'd awaken early failed to happen. Images of mythical triangles at sunrise tugged me from slumber at halftime, and the more I insisted on sleep, the brighter they glowed. I was groggy and hungry, but there was no time to eat. After guzzling two liters of water, I was off into the brisk predawn air, ahead of eager crowds.

Unfortunately, it seems many had the idea of photographing legendary antiquities before the tourist invasion. Daybreak revealed a glaring, polluted haze in a cacophony of snorting camels, honking taxis and black-smoking tour buses, all converging on ticket booths scheduled to open at eight. To maintain minimum historical dignity, the pyramids are fenced off for miles except for a busy paved entrance-and-exit for tourists — with the ever-watchful military outnumbering visitors. There has got to be a better way.

Bedouin teenagers offer long, monotonous camel rides to circle in from the rear for unobstructed approaches through the open desert. Unfortunately, the sand is too soft for a loaded-down motorcycle with street tires. But who's going to let common sense get in the way now? An hour later, sweating with desire and furiously paddling to remain upright, I am still searching for the Bedouin secret entry through the fence. I spent more time buried than riding while spinning over drifting dunes along the wire barrier. Recalling admonishments from my riding coach to relax my arms temporarily staved off fatigue — but, all the while, I knew I must return the same way.

With an overheated engine, a final sand-flinging moment occurs at the summit of a dune that has more determination than I do. At first, I am too exhausted to comprehend stumbling into the majestic gaze of history — yet soon enough, a stately serenity of 5,000 years commands me into submission. Big enough to see from the moon, these holiest shrines of civilization shrink the horizon, solemnly shimmering in the desert landscape.

The lure intensifies. What powers dwell within? Should I join the masses on an official tour? Four hours later, bent in half with my spine grazing the rough-chiseled ceiling, 150 of us panting gawkers scurry down through a narrow granite tunnel into the steamy depths of Cheops, the biggest and oldest pyramid. Once nearly 500 feet high and 13½ acres at the base, it's honeycombed with hidden passageways. Jammed together, stooped over shoulder-to-shoulder with other tourists, if you don't start with claustrophobia, you develop it quickly. Declining wooden ramps with rungs to slow a steep descent are barely wide enough for one, yet the line stretches two abreast, coming and going. Though cameras are forbidden in the burial chamber, I find an empty corner for a moment of contemplation and to burn into memory that which I feel.

Study the walls, sense the air and slow the mind. Zazen, the sitting or kneeling meditation posture in Japanese Buddhism, comfortably aligns the spine. Like sinking into a soft leather chair after a long, hard run, I plunge — deeper — seeking, listening, hearing. The energy of the pyramids gently reverberates, dangling images of geometric shapes and mathematical equations. Is this warm, humid softness of the dark a key to universal knowledge? Is it here where the ancients gathered science and wisdom? Is this altar a gateway to the stars? A unified shuffling of shoes on stone indicates it's time to make room for the next tour group — I'll have to ponder the pyramids another day.

Sunrise on Mount Sinai
December 28, 2004
St. Catherine Village, Egypt
● ● ● ● ● ● ● ● ● ● ● ● ● ● ● ● ●

Still undecided about visiting Israel, I head east from Giza, back toward the Sinai, where the first major city is a major contrast to the rest of Egypt. Miles of smoking oil refineries and storage tanks line the approach to Suez, as the canal itself is clogged with idle freighters and giant supertankers waiting to pass. There is little worth stopping for, but I decide to stay overnight to get an early start. From this stinky industrial center, it's a full day's ride south to St. Catherine village along a sparkling gulf that's prettier in the light.

Since my best female friend, Sharon, has ordered me to climb Mt. Sinai, there is no choice. So that I experience the most incredible sunrise on the planet, my fierce little Israeli pal has insisted that the 6,800-foot ascent must begin at two in the morning. For 25 years, since we were pen pals while she worked on a kibbutz, Sharon and I have spoken of doing this together. But trekking into the night up a mountain on foot when there is a perfectly good motorcycle to ride has little appeal for me. Now she knows how much I love her.

Picturing deserts usually conjures images of vast, empty wastelands of soft sand, but it can also be boulder-strewn, hard-packed, and perfect for motorcycling. Today, my ride off-road across short stretches of the Sinai desert leads to sheer, shiny mountains of barren, wrinkled granite. Sometimes you just have to go and find out for yourself. I could easily blow the day cruising to nowhere in search of more friendly Bedouins, but to reach my destination before dark requires that I return to asphalt and follow the route on my GPS.

A lone police checkpoint marks the turnoff from the coast to St. Catherine with no indication of what lies ahead. Often, the desert lulls you into boredom, but other times it smacks you in the face with sensuous splendor. As an eagle, I soar into an early afternoon darkness between sharp, rising mountainsides and silent Arab villages. The Sinai comes alive. Gliding among dark canyon walls so high that they block the sun, the temperature plummets to zero. In minutes, I zip into an electric vest and double thermals.

Here is where God spoke to Moses from the burning bush, leading him up Mt. Sinai to receive the Ten Commandments. At dusk, dozens of packed tour buses roar into dusty hotel parking lots and spew out hordes of weary Christian pilgrims. Organized by nationality, they march obediently to designated quarters, where they stay until embarking on a predawn climb to the peak. Sunrise on Mt. Sinai is said to be a spiritual awakening, but events begin poorly.

A crowd of angry Nigerians argue with their guide, "But this is not a four-star resort."

Later, at dinner, another group passes our table, asking what religion we are. Beneath elegantly framed scrolls of Arabic scripted

Muslim prayers, Egyptian staff are tolerant when asked, "How about you, do you have Jesus in your life?"

The hotel manager smiles, "Sorry sir, I don't speak English."

Sharon has provided me with the names of Bedouin friends to visit. A long, sandy road into the desert leads to the cement-block homes of Ahmed and Saad. Ahmed speaks English. "Your are brother of Sharon, you are brother of mine."

Political discussions in the Middle East have previously left me sleepless, but temptations to know Ahmed's thoughts overcome all.

"Ahmed, how was life under Israeli occupation?"

With a smile, he stares into the cackling fire, uttering, "Paradise."

He continues: "Israel man give work to Bedouin. When Bedouin sick, Israel man bring doctor. Bedouin work, Israel man pay money, Bedouin no work, Israel man no pay."

"What about your laws, what if a Bedouin kills?"

"We put him in the sand with only head outside — family of dead man shoot with gun three times from a hundred meters. If no kill, he can be free. Allah must decide."

On matrimony, he explains that Bedouin can marry non-Muslims if they both live under Islamic law, adding that if there is no mosque nearby, Muslims may pray in churches.

"What if Bedouin man wants to divorce his wife?"

"He can divorce but must give her house and all his camels."

"Tell me of your camels."

"The camel is life of Bedouin. We start to train at six months and work them at three years. Camel good for Bedouin mind. When I angry or sad, I ride camel for long time in desert and come back happy. At 35, camel mean and bite — when 30, we eat."

As tea is served with chicken and rice, the sky darkens into a diamond-sprinkled canopy of coal dust, while the evening chill stings my eyes. Returning to the hotel, I consider how a short visit with the Bedouin means we are brothers for life.

The Lonely Planet guidebook says it's a three-hour trek to the freezing summit of Mt. Sinai, but I assume that's for tourists and oversleep an hour, deciding I can do it in less time by eliminating rest stops. It's 3 a.m. as I leave the motorcycle resting in the twilight shadows of St. Catherine Monastery, home to 22 Greek Orthodox monks. A fleet of double-decker tour buses lines the foothills with dozing drivers awaiting the return of exhausted passengers.

Ten minutes of hiking renders me drenched in sweat, stuffing my thermals and jacket into a plastic bag. A moonlit trail reveals ghostly images of robed Bedouin guides floating beside lumbering camels. Two backpacking British girls stride past, snickering at a wheezing out-of-shape motorcyclist. To stave off humiliation, I kick it up to cardiac-arrest mode. Their pace is what I would jog a mile. Mountain climbing hags from hell tarnishing my pride. The final 750 stone steps are too steep, and I have to take breathers every 20. Barely out of breath, the witches wait at the top. "Need some help Glen?"

Chilling gales howl across ice-patched peaks as hundreds of pilgrims huddle beneath wool blankets spread over massive slabs of granite. Cold from the stone penetrates our bones. As hundreds of videos whirl and cameras click, a tiny spark of distant light grows brighter, reaching out across the early morning sky. Soon a bursting ball of blazing orange ignites the mountainsides into radiant hues of glowing beige. In the grip of the universe, a befuddled planet hurtles in a furious spin toward the horizon. A narrowing rocky landscape eerily stretches wider, and suddenly I begin to feel the rotation of the earth.

While the daylight grows, as if on cue, awestruck masses stand, waiting a turn to file back down the mountainside past legions of Bedouins hawking camel rides to the busses. A mile-long snake of shivering tourists pausing and stumbling is incentive to linger. Alone on the summit, I call out to the wind, but there is only the echo of my thoughts with the question arising like so often before — "How can it ever get any better than this?"

Silver Linings
December 31, 2004
Egyptian-Israeli Border
● ● ● ● ● ● ● ● ● ● ● ● ●

As frustrating as it was at the time, the best turn of events yet was being denied the Iranian visa. Had it been granted, I wouldn't have detoured deeper into the Middle East and met the Arabs. A five-day transit visa meant sprinting across Iran to Pakistan with no time for much else. The trade-off was a rush across one country for a leisurely tour of four.

While it's important to heed danger warnings, traveling without preconceived notions allows one a broader perspective. Most people use their own judgment, balancing safety and freedom, yet travelers soon discover that, usually, dire warnings are overreactions based on rumor. But this was not so clear when dealing with the Middle East. Even automatically discounting the evening news, over the years, negative images of Arabs are hard to erase. They've always been the villains or fools in the cinema or on TV, acting as chanting crowds of religious fanatics applauding terrorist acts against the West. But is this true? As Fidel Castro manages to rally tens of thousands in a country where only a minority support him, a few fanatical Middle Eastern governments similarly misrepresent their populations. Meeting them face-to-face on their turf, I realized that Arabs were angry with the U.S. government, not Americans. And if U.S. polls are accurate, 50 percent of American citizens, and perhaps more, feel the same.

It is true that in the Middle East religion dominates the lives and behavior of devout Muslims, Christians and Jews to a degree that is shocking to outsiders. But that doesn't mean they are dangerous or dislike Westerners. Extremists in most religions have demonstrated a desire to kill in the name of their God; when it comes to Islam, that's who the media focuses on. Yet from peasants to professionals, the Muslims I encountered were warm and generous people, anxious to learn about others. Peaceful people are the stories of buildings that didn't burn.

Jaded by high-pressure touts in the tourist sections of Istanbul, I

Following Israeli military vehicles along the Lebanese border

found it hard at first to accept Arab hospitality as genuine — assuming it must be a lead into a hustle. After a while it was evident that they want to know your name and where you are from because they are curious. If you encounter them again, they remember what you told them when you first met. Who can resist their greetings? "Welcome, welcome. What is your name? Where do you come from? Would you like some tea?"

Like Orthodox Jews and Christian fundamentalists, Middle Eastern Muslims abide by religious law. For adult Westerners, such restrictions are unthinkable, but it's normal if you are raised that way. Similar to strict Christians and Jews, Muslims are forbidden to consume alcohol, yet they don't want to either. Radios are tuned to Islamic prayers as much as we turn to rock 'n' roll in the West, and it's common to wait for shopkeepers to finish praying before dealing with customers. You'll hear "*In sh'Allah*" in Damascus, as much as "praise the lord" in Mississippi. They also practice what they preach.

Men and women decline sex outside of marriage and think that, to keep hormones in check, women should dress conservatively in public. Muslim women I spoke to believe this as deeply as the men. You never realize how sexy hair is until it's covered. But Bedouin women have shown how beauty can be revealed through the eyes, and they can tease as effectively with a veil as with a plunging neckline.

Growing up in politically correct California, I found my first glimpses of veiled women appalling. Although only Iran and Saudi Arabia mandate by law that women wear headscarves in public, it's a popular tradition throughout the Middle East. For some, it's a fashion statement. Store-window mannequins display varieties of styles from laced to see-through. When asking a college student in Jordan why she was not wearing a headscarf, she replied, "Oh, I might tomorrow, it depends on how I feel like dressing."

Every society has its own code of which body parts can legally be exposed in public, with the roots of these decisions being based on religion. In the West, women can expose as much breast as they dare, but if they are in public, a nipple displayed could land them in jail. This type of conservatism can be shocking to South Pacific Islanders visiting Western nations. Men bare their breast but women can't?

Religion is everywhere. It's stamped on U.S. currency, "In God We Trust." Some people declare that America is a Christian nation or that America is based on Judeo-Christian values. If the Pledge of Allegiance was changed to "One nation under Buddha," there would be a revolution. Yet liberalism appears in strange places. Turkey, Israel, Pakistan and India all had female prime ministers long before a woman ran and lost for vice president of the U.S. Trying to make sense of the world is a job for far greater thinkers than me.

Travelers venturing into developing nations soon discover that it's those with the least who are the quickest to share, while the simplest of all teach the deepest lessons. Arab hospitality is contagious, but so is Mongolian and Siberian. It feels good being around nice people.

Secularism expands with prosperity. Two color TVs and a new car makes us forget more important things like how to treat one another. Have we become lost along the way? Maybe Jesus had it right — it's as easy for a rich man to enter heaven as for a camel to pass through the eye of a needle.

The Middle East is not the land of milk and honey, but it is the land of black gold. Engage locals on politics and you'll hear more than you want. Just as North Americans would be upset if Islamic nations established a military presence here to stabilize lumber prices, so are Middle Easterners proprietorial about their resources. Muslim troops in the West propping up dictators would be greeted with bullets. Locals don't speak freely, but most don't like their sheiks, princes, or shahs and don't appreciate foreign intervention supporting them.

There is often public discussion about a collision of civilizations with Islam and the West, but so far all I've experienced is friendship. My original plan was to speed through the Middle East, thinking "Why bother with people and places where I'm not welcome?" — but all the Arabs have shown is that they want to be friends. Even when talking about their blood enemy, Israel, they said, "Israel government bad, Israel people good." I'll soon be relaying that message in Jerusalem.

Shalom
January 3, 2005
Tel Aviv, Israel
● ● ● ● ● ● ● ● ●

The charred skeleton of the bombed-out Hilton Hotel in Taba, a resort town on the Egyptian side of Sinai, instantly focuses the reality of war and, in particular, terrorism. Last year, to be certain those of all ages could experience his terrorism, bin Laden's thugs also blew up a nearby backpacker's lodge catering to the young. Islamic extremists are equal-opportunity mass murderers. No doubt tight security lies ahead at the Israeli border.

European students in Cairo who, like me, had visited Arab countries spoke bitterly of experiences in the Tel Aviv airport — hours of interrogation at immigration points and arrogant Israeli soldiers at checkpoints throughout the country. I wondered what else to expect from a second generation growing up in bloody conflict, never knowing where the next bomb would detonate — a crowded Tel Aviv nightclub or a Palestinian refugee camp? Whatever the excuse, women and children are crippled and slaughtered daily.

In Israel, both sexes are drafted into the army. Every Israeli child knows they will have some experience with death before college — theirs, the enemy's or that of someone they love. The same for Palestinians, who have as good a chance of being cut down by Israeli bullets as going to college. There is no maybe: during nearly 60 years of armed conflict with neighbors, two generations of Israelis and Palestinians have grown up in bitter bloodshed over issues a thousand years old.

It is confusing at first because I don't realize that the kids dressed in civilian clothes at the border are soldiers. A muscle-bound, clean-cut youngster wearing an earring and two teenage girls wielding automatic weapons request my passport. I fire back an aggressive defense, using the biggest smile I can muster with an outstretched hand — "Howdy, my name's Glen Heggstad and I am out to meet the people of the world. What's your name?"

The first girl takes over, "Please tell me which countries you have been to before Israel."

"This trip or the last one?"

"Let's start from the beginning."

It's hard not to laugh when being interrogated by a 19-year-old girl who is a solid 10, even with an automatic weapon. She eyes me as a suspect as I imagine her without clothes. But she is very serious.

Assuming they'll know my life history within seconds of a passport scan, I begin with the ride to South America three years ago and events in Colombia. I've learned that it's best to not mention being a writer because people suddenly act differently. There is always a good response handing over a card from my judo school, but during a search they'll likely find my mangled copy of *Two Wheels Through Terror*, a title sure to raise more questions. After citing visited countries, they stop me when mentioning Syria, an

Islamic nation the Jewish state is still technically at war with.

"Syria? Why were you in Syria?"

"Well, I was in Istanbul and couldn't get a visa for Iran."

Now ever more alert, she asks, "Why would you travel to Iran?"

"In order to get to Pakistan."

Even more astounded she dares ask, "Why did you want to go to Pakistan?"

"In order to get to Afghanistan . . ."

As though this has gone beyond her comprehension and rank, she orders, "Please proceed to the white building and enter through the rear door."

Inside, the first adult of the day explains that because of a Syrian visit, further questioning is necessary. Fine with me, there is plenty of time until sundown and this could be interesting. They direct me to an office where another 18-year-old supermodel in uniform begins with a checklist.

"What was the purpose of your trip to Syria? Who do you know in Syria? Where did you go in Syria and what were the exact dates of your visit there? Did anyone in Egypt give you a package to deliver in Israel?"

I tell her that I wound up in Syria because of an involuntary diversion and the only person I met there was a very dangerous Bedouin camped in the desert, whom I forget the name of.

Seeming satisfied with my answers, she continues, "Where do you intend to stay while in Israel?"

"Actually, I was kind of hoping your house."

We laugh and banter until she says that because of my answers, she must deny me entry into Israel and send me back to Egypt. This is a problem, I tell her, because I have an already used single-entry visa. "I need to refer this to my supervisor," she says.

Suddenly, it's apparent to me how suspicious my travels appear to paranoid border officials who expect a car bomb to blow them up any second. A thorough search will net further problems. A gift from an Iranian friend in California — the plastic case sealing my AAA international driver's license stamped on the cover "Islamic

The wall across Jerusalem

Republic of Iran" in Farsi and English. If they find this, the fun is over. What if they examine my laptop?

Moments later, the supermodel returns smiling and hands back my documents. "Enjoy your stay in Israel, Glen." I pitch once more to lure her on the back of my bike. It could be just my imagination, but while riding past the final concrete barricades, it seemed like she paused and considered before shaking her head once more.

Compared to the Sinai, there is not much to see in southern Israel, except empty desert and miles of barbed-wire fencing with signs posted: "Military Area, Do Not Stop, Do Not Photograph." Gun towers and remote TV cameras underscore the seriousness. Sophisticated microwave antennae line distant hilltops, while enormous satellite dishes confirm this is major communications corridor. The weather report is sunny for the Negev desert but predicts storming north on the road to Tel Aviv.

Breaking for dinner at a major bus stop, I find a roadside cafeteria that is crowded with young Israeli soldiers lugging bulky backpacks and M16 machine guns. The troops are sullen and stone-faced — most are talking in Russian on cell phones or listening to CD players. The room needs a Viking assault to break the ice. "Howdy, how ya' doin'?" No reply.

I repeat this to each of them, but from two feet away, sitting at the same table, I receive an identical response from a half-dozen soldiers. They turn their heads as if no one had spoken, a few sneer. There is no conversation among them, and all make it clear from bored gazes that they would rather be somewhere and someone else.

As youngsters trapped in involuntary military service, it's impossible for them not to wonder about the freedom of a roaming biker, but they are determined not to acknowledge me by showing interest. As a gathering storm appears overhead, outside in the parking lot, I make a show of adjusting equipment and zipping into foul-weather gear. While cycling through a GPS check, they abandon their indifference and crowd to the doorway. Rolling onto a rain-slicked highway, I turn to see young soldiers' forlorn eyes and more faces fogging the windows — I wave goodbye, continuing north for Gaza to see what the Palestinians have to say.

Palestine
January 4, 2005
Erez Checkpoint, Gaza Strip
• • • • • • • • • • • • • • • • •

By all accounts no one should have got this far, but here I sit at the last Israeli checkpoint to enter the Gaza Strip — the infamous Erez checkpoint. It's now a restricted military area on the edge of a war zone. Using homemade rockets, Palestinians have recently blown up a power line. Approaching, I meet the crew erecting a new wooden pole. The workmen are confident. "We don't worry though, our men will kill them."

As I type this journal, attack helicopters flying overhead fire strings of missiles amid sporadic ground gunfire a few hundred feet away. A body count is being generated for the evening news as military office personnel and a few Jordanian diplomats silently complete entry applications. I had started eating some boiled eggs, but picturing humans at the receiving end of those explosions eliminates any appetite.

The field major here has faxed to central command in Jerusalem, requesting special permission for me to enter the occupied city. At the moment, this is the only way in or out of Gaza, a 25-by-8-mile strip along the Mediterranean Sea, home to Palestinian families imprisoned in their own cities. Militants resisting the occupation are their only hope. Since the intifada began four years ago, it's been sealed to civilians. Palestinians are not allowed in or out; the area is only open to UN representatives and approved members of the press.

UN workers in the lobby of the checkpoint said they've been waiting here for the last three days, but because of steady fighting have not been allowed through. There is a no-man's-land to cross, where Israeli Defense Forces drop those wanting to enter and Palestinian authorities take over, escorting them to the other side. From there, you're on your own. It's like the movie *Escape from New York*, except this is real.

When the hotel clerk in Tel Aviv heard I wanted to see Gaza, he tried to direct me to somewhere more touristy. "Why don't you go to the beach instead? We also have nice parks here." It was sure to be a hassle, but Sharon has told me that if I wanted to understand the conflict, it's essential to visit both Gaza and the Golan Heights.

After four hours waiting for authorization to enter, officials say that in the event permission is granted, it's impossible to drive a private vehicle. If I go in, it's on foot and alone. Assuming food would be in short supply, I brought boiled eggs, fresh bread and canned sardines, along with my laptop. Internet access is unlikely, but it's the first stop if I get in and out.

Everyone waiting in the checkpoint lobby is curious about what I am up to, but they also guard their comments. Misspoken words keep you out or make trouble inside. An Israeli TV news support person tells me she is in favor of withdrawing from Gaza. "What's five kilometers, if you can have peace in exchange?" I ask UN workers who live in Gaza if they ever feel threatened or in danger — a simultaneous whispered reply, "Yes, but not from the Palestinians."

Four hours later, an extremely polite young Israeli soldier announces my request has been denied by central command but will be reviewed. He provides a telephone number to call every day in case someone changes their mind. His superior also requests that the photos their security cameras caught me uploading to my laptop be deleted. Sometimes data automatically saves to a second separate file — I'll check later.

Jericho
January 5, 2005
The West Bank, Palestine
• • • • • • • • • • • • • • •

Foul weather kept me pinned down for two days in Tel Aviv, but with only 10 more appropriated for Israel, I couldn't wait. Israel is so small that if you were up high enough in the center, you could see all the borders. Departing early in the morning, I should have easily reached the Golan Heights by sundown, but steady storming forced me to overnight at the Sea of Galilee. Like everywhere else in the Middle East, low season and the threat of terrorism meant empty hotels and restaurants.

If it weren't for signs in Hebrew and Arabic, it'd be hard to believe this isn't California. Same scenery, road system and architecture — you can even drink the tap water. Since crossing the border last week, my travel costs have doubled — a McDonald's hamburger costs the equivalent of nine U.S. dollars. The ride to Golan is uneventful, with road signs in English and modern freeways. International boundaries are disputed throughout the region, and, for the last 10 minutes heading north, my GPS indicates that I am in southern Lebanon.

But when I reach the disputed border, it is closed and unmanned, with triple, electrified barbed wire in front of a tractor-plowed corridor between another set of fences. Gun towers and communication outposts are the only signs of life among bombed-out commercial buildings. Heavily defended Israeli settlements are built within a hundred feet of the line.

Equally unsure of the Syrian border when heading directly through the Golan Heights, I stop in a Druze village for directions. "Hello. Can you please tell me where I am?"

One of two elderly men playing cards dressed in frayed sport coats in a sidewalk café replies, "That depends on who you're asking. To some, it's Israel; to others, it's Syria."

"What do you call it?"

"First you must come and have tea." Once we're sitting together in the bright mountain sunshine, he continues. "We are Syrians, but since 1967, residents of Israel."

"Okay, if you were to travel to England, what passport would you use?"

"We are not provided passports because we're Syrians living in Israel. Israel issues a travel card."

"What countries can you travel to with that card?"

"Only Jordan, to visit our families from Syria."

"Why don't you go from Jordan into Syria?"

"Because our travel card says we are from Israel and no one from Israel is allowed into Syria. But our children go to college in Syria and are allowed to cross from here twice a year."

"How is life under the Israelis?"

"Life is good with Israelis, very nice people. But we are still treated as Arabs, and we want to be with Syria again."

I noticed a sign nearby that said "Area of Heightened Surveillance." Everyone is aware of Israel's intelligence-gathering capabilities, so no one can be certain of who they are really talking to or who is listening.

As I head back south toward Jerusalem, sundown appears sooner than expected. The Jericho exit off the highway leads only to rows of five-foot-high cement barricades placed across the off-ramp. Assuming this is due to a washed-out road, I return to the highway, seeking another entrance along several miles of barbed-wire fences leading to gun towers and massive steel gates. Israeli troops step into the road, waving machine guns, indicating that I should turn around and enter from somewhere else.

Five miles later, I find there is a long line of cars waiting to enter the city and more cement barricades with armed soldiers checking paperwork. When I'm next for interrogation, they carefully inspect my passport. Curt soldiers enquire, "Why do you want to go into this area?"

"I need to find a hotel."

"Why not continue to Jerusalem?"

"Because I'm here now. Is it unsafe inside?"

"There is no police force to protect you and there is an election coming Sunday. The Arabs may kill you because you are American."

"Thank you, I appreciate your concern but if it's okay with you, I'll take my chances." Shrugging their shoulders, they wave goodbye and good luck as I roll forward into the dark, dusty streets of Jericho for my first encounter with Palestinians.

Palestinians
January 7, 2005
Jericho, The West Bank
● ● ● ● ● ● ● ● ● ● ● ● ●

A mile-long empty corridor of bullet-ridden cement-block buildings and broken streetlights leads deeper into central Jericho, until suddenly I am back in the developing world. Arab life is casual and laid-back, with hookah-smoking men playing cards in sidewalk cafés — women don't venture out at night. After a loop around the city center, the first stop is for fresh baked bread and roast chicken at half the price of Tel Aviv. Unsure of the new stranger, they still greet me with warm smiles, "Welcome, welcome."

Three Italian civilians posted as election observers point out a decent hotel up the street, and they extend a smug question. "Isn't traveling for Americans a problem these days?"

Pushing the last of the chicken bones away signals to my neighbors at the café an opportunity for questions. "Hello, welcome. Where you come from?"

Holding out a hand, "My name is Glen and I'm from California, traveling the world by motorcycle to meet the people."

"Ah, you are American? Why are you not afraid of us?"

"Should I be?"

"Don't worry, you are safe here unless you are Palestinian."

As word of a visiting American spreads through the 15,000-member community, a small crowd forms outside the chicken restaurant. They are more curious than intimidating, with a few kids peeking out from between their fathers' legs. To get their attention, I take a moment for a maintenance check and chain adjustment. Spreading tools on the sidewalk, I give one to each of the gathering children to hold until needing it. I suddenly have a team of anxious apprentice mechanics.

An older man steps forward, "Hello, welcome, I am Salah Ali. I love American people but hate American government." (And during the course of the evening, those sentiments echoed from all who approached.)

My reply was the same each time also, looking them dead in the eye. "I have traveled a long way to meet you, where do we go from here?"

Soon, 60-year-old Salah Ali reaches to take my hand. "You must come with me for tea."

"Thank you, I'm tired and would rather find a hotel; maybe later."

"No, you must come with me first for tea."

Arab hospitality means that there is no such thing as refusing, so hooking his arm in mine, we stroll down the alley to his favorite café for a traditional herbal brew.

Like most of the others, his English is good. "For why have you come to Jericho?"

"Up until two hours ago, I had never met a Palestinian but had always wanted to."

"We know what your news says about us, why are you not afraid?"

"Maybe I don't believe everything on TV."

"You must come to the election rally, hurry and finish your tea. We must go now. Dr. Mustafa Al Barghudi is running for president and he is coming to speak with us."

With Salah Ali on the back of the Blue Beast, we thread our way through throngs of gawking young Palestinians milling beneath election banners in Arabic. I am the only foreigner. There are no police or press, but with Arabic music blaring from tinny loudspeakers, the crowd is festive. Lines form to shake my hand with the previous greeting.

A ragged man of 30 continues his handshake longer than comfortable, shouting with wild eyes, "Osama bin Laden is my savior, he helps Palestinians. Americans only kill us. I hope he kills your cities." Still refusing to let go of my hand, he breaks into sobs. "I am sorry, I am sorry, I do not mean this but what can we do? Look at our lives. I was 10 years in Israeli prison that your government built." A disturbing reality check — was I staring into the eyes of a future suicide bomber?

Throughout this uncomfortable encounter, no one intervenes, and I wonder what else is in store. Once we move inside a crowded lecture hall, if events go awry, there will be no escape. Like it or not, this situation could turn ugly. The candidate coming to speak may have made comments earlier, angering a militant group. In the West Bank, political debate can end in gunfire. Government crowd control using lethal force is another possibility. If this meeting became unruly, Israeli soldiers may enter the city, firing into mobs.

Before considerations turn to paranoia, men on either side whisk me inside to a row of folding chairs in front of the podium. "From here you may take pictures." Past the point of no return, I am in the middle of a situation that could go either way. Rumor spreads that Dr. Barghudi was detained at the checkpoint, and I recall recently televised scenes of him dressed in a business suit, being roughed up and dragged around by Israeli soldiers.

As I ponder the outcome of political enthusiasm evolving into hostility, a five-car motorcade of honking taxis arrives. The excited town-hall crowd parts barely wide enough for Dr. Barghudi to be carried in on the shoulders of shouting supporters.

To make sure I understand what is happening, two young Palestinians translate the words of the introductory speakers. They address democracy, fighting corruption and standing up to the Israelis. I peg only one security man behind the candidate, next to satin-vested high school kids passing out flyers. I still haven't seen a cop, and it appears that Palestinians police their own and may have finally come to the realization that this is their big chance for democracy. Sealing off Palestinian cities, the Israelis have made it difficult for candidates to campaign freely, but maybe that has kept the potential chaos in check.

Later, after bringing me to his home for the night, Salah troubles me once more. "It's now four years since Israelis have closed our cities. We are prisoners in our own country. What is left for us anymore? How can we live like this? What if this happened to you in your country?"

Sometimes adventure travelers seeking what's restricted or off the beaten path can find more than they are able to stomach. We need to be careful of what we wish for. At times, it's a struggle to remain on topic and avoid the politics of the suffering we encounter. We often fail in our attempts to balance tales of our journeys with what affects our conscience. This is a wanderer's diary concerning adventure, not a critique of international issues or an evaluation of how others choose to govern themselves. But to feel a man's pulse, you must take his hand — and then determine for yourself how close to the fire you can stand to be.

Brothers
January 10, 2005
Tel Aviv, Israel
• • • • • • • • •

The quickest way to meet fellow motorcyclists when you're traveling is to experience a problem. It seldom takes more than minutes for local riders on bikes or in cars to spot a brother down and stop to offer assistance. Flat tires and empty fuel tanks can occur anywhere, but bikers in distress don't wait long.

Drive chains and rear-wheel sprockets are high-wear items that eventually need replacement. If we pay attention, half-worn sprockets can be unbolted and reversed to extend their life. For unknown reasons, the teeth on mine went from starting-to-wear to full-blown fishhook-shapes in 100 miles. Complications never occur when convenient — only in the rain or on a desert road after dark. In this case, it was both. Motorcyclists learn to constantly listen for unusual clinks, sputters or metallic grating noises that alert us to impending mechanical failure. There is usually a warning just prior to a final snap. So when my engine RPMs abruptly increased and the bike immediately slowed, it was obvious the rear chain had jumped off the worn-out sprocket teeth.

When mechanical failure strikes while we are in motion, even before stopping, experienced bikers are calculating damages, worst-case scenarios and resolutions. Months before, I had stashed a spare chain and front sprocket but no rear — in Turkey, local dealers seldom stock new ones. With 130 percent taxes in Israel, motorcycles cost twice as much as they do in the U.S., so expensive BMWs, and spare parts for them, are scarce.

Within minutes of coasting as far as possible and wrangling the Blue Beast under a bus stop roof, the first car arrives. Me with no Hebrew and Uri with no English, we manage in sign language to determine that we'll need a wrench bigger than I have — but he will go get one and be back in 20 minutes. In the meantime, another car stops, whose driver insists on returning home to retrieve a light. Soon, a mini-workshop is underway on the outskirts of Jericho. With the help of total strangers, in less than an hour, I am back on the road, easing cautiously toward Jerusalem.

As in Russia, local Israeli and American riders have been tracking me via the Internet, and when reading my posted report, they contact me with directions and information about the only town with a dealer in the region — Tel Aviv. Feeling safe in Israel, I violate my own security procedures and reveal the name and location of my hotel. Members from the local off-road riding club were quickly on the phone with offers for escorts to the workshop. Upon arriving at the dealership, even before I shut down the engine, I see Nadav, the BMW service manager, come walking up — "Hi, you must be Glen, we've been expecting you, your parts are ready."

Even with a discount on the brake pads and rear sprocket, the prices are outrageous. But Nadav says, "Don't worry, we'll handle maintenance on the house." With that, two technicians spend the next hour inspecting my bike for other potential problems. There are another 6,000 miles ahead through Pakistan, India and Nepal, where there are no parts or mechanics familiar with BMW. Nadav, concerned about this, gives me personal contact information in case I need help. Although long-riders don't take this kind of hospitality for granted, we're accustomed to the brotherhood of motorcycle riders.

We may be from different countries and cultures, but when it comes to our passion, we all speak the same language. As others in the world bicker among themselves, those in the biking community are anxious to meet and lend a hand. One more reason to believe there is no better way to experience the world than on two wheels.

Gaza
January 11, 2005
Gaza City, The West Bank
● ● ● ● ● ● ● ● ● ● ● ● ● ●

My original plan included only Christmas in Jerusalem and a short ride back to Jordan for air-transit to Pakistan. But after I also visited the Golan Heights, Sharon insisted on expanding my itinerary to include Gaza. The truth is, it didn't interest me until I discovered that it was a closed military zone. For the last four years, without special permits, almost no one was allowed in or out.

The term Occupied Territory is used so often that the meaning is lost. Besides, the issues are clear; Arabs are dangerous terrorists who should be separated from the rest of humanity. But the more military officials tried to discourage me from visiting, the more important it felt. Like in Egypt, I became suspicious when I saw authorities trying to control what foreigners see.

It took five days of telephone interviews to get approved for a special unescorted entry, without a private vehicle and alone. After working my way up through the ranks, my last phone call was a direct plea to the general of the regional Israeli Defense Forces, whose subordinates had obviously thoroughly researched my name and U.S. records. Somehow, presumably to determine my politics, they had even managed to read my book. Yet, once I reached the infamous Erez checkpoint with a green light from central command, the crossing still involved two more hours of last-minute questioning before I began the half-mile walk through an intimidating tunnel of 20-foot-high cement barricades and slamming security gates. From security personnel watching on closed circuit TVs and inaudible loudspeakers barking scratchy orders to remove my jacket and empty my pockets, I went through buzzing steel gates feeding into electronically operated bull pens and rows of human cages. Scanning cameras and abrupt commands from heavily armed and nervous young soldiers left no doubt: a careless mistake could mean a bullet in the back. And I was an ally.

Sacrificing moral high ground for security, Israel disregards world opinion. This is little comfort for an imprisoned Palestinian populace fenced in by a foreign army. Even knowing I could leave, halfway through the dehumanizing transfer process, my stomach still churned — one can only imagine what it's like to live here.

At the end of a dreary concrete corridor ripped open in places from car bombs, indifferent Palestinian guards sign me in for the

The no-man's-land corridor entering Gaza via Erez Checkpoint, Gaza City, The West Bank

final thousand-foot walk through open space manned by Red Crescent workers. Once I clear, I find only an idling beat-up taxi awaiting. If it was the army's intent to spook me by delaying entry until dusk, it worked.

This is election day in Gaza, and Palestinians are determined to peacefully choose a replacement for Yassar Arafat under the suffocating yoke of a humiliating occupation. It's a life-threatening economic disaster for humans entombed at gunpoint within electrified barbed wire and checkpoints manned by soldiers who don't hesitate to fire their weapons with deadly accuracy. With radical Palestinians refusing to participate in the election and a general fear of the unknown, the challenge of an orderly transition of power is immeasurable.

In response to attacks by militants, daily Israeli army incursions to arrest suspects and bulldoze homes have become a way of life. Revenge. It's a circle of violence that amounts to last-tags of murder and mayhem. The horror is unfathomable and mostly hidden from the world, even from Israelis.

To a certain extent, I trust Palestinians but not enough to venture out tonight — U.S. government financing of their tormenters might affect their judgment, and all it takes is one hothead to create an international incident. Divisions on both sides run deep. But today it's irrelevant who slaughtered the first civilians; everyone is involved now. As Israelis load helicopters with sophisticated heat-seeking missiles, and Palestinians strap explosives on teenagers, each knows the outcome. At the receiving end, women and children are going to die. Yet, amidst the killing, life goes on.

Central Gaza in the daylight was a typical Arab city — strings of honking taxis backed up in traffic and crowded, fragrant markets scouted by veiled housewives bartering for fruits and vegetables. Busy streets were lined with groups of friendly old men huddled around small plastic tables, beckoning strangers to stop for tea. "Hallo, escuse me, ara you Germany man?" If accepting all the offers, it'd take a day to reach the end of the block.

Israeli commanders had only issued me a 24-hour pass. Unsure how to spend that time, I opt to wander the crowd. A third of the men here are unemployed, which has left groups of disgruntled young men idling on crumbling street corners, ripe for recruiting by militant leaders. Futures as gunmen or suicide bombers are more certain than college. These are the kids on TV throwing stones at Israeli tanks — if they survive the hail of gunfire; scars from bullets become badges of honor.

Abruptly aware of being forcefully prodded and nudged through a tightly packed throng of shoppers, I suddenly find myself in a garbage-strewn alley, facing an informal tribunal. Clearly the local tough guys, they still remembered to smile. A 20-something leader offers a strong handshake with a menacing grin. He issues sharp commands to his inquisitive lackeys who have surrounded me to back away. Pointing to one of two folding chairs, he orders, "You sit."

Revealing my creeping fear would only ensure his upper hand. I point to the other chair, "We sit."

"*Verdee goot, verdee goot.*" Pounding his chest with a fist he declares, "I mafia king!"

I resist gulping and reply, "It's very nice to meet a mafia king."

Eyeing my camera, he asks, *"You telebison man?"*

"No, I am *motorsickle* man from California." Looping an index finger in circles, "I go around the world on *motorsickle*." Knowing Arabs like being photographed, I ask, "Can we take a picture together?"

Waving his hand, *"No peetchur, beeg problam."*

It's understood that these young men likely don't pose without face-hoods. I also noted that none of them had the indelibly inked-stained thumbs that officials used as proof for having voted in the election. As his questions continue, my discomfort increases.

"You Amerdica man. You like Eesralee man or you like Hamas?"

Merely hearing the name Hamas suggests that my feet are touching the fire. It's underscored with the pocketknife he's now unfolding. *"This for Eesralee man. You like Hamas knife?"*

Maintaining eye contact while attempting to control a rapidly increasing heart rate, I roll up my right sleeve while raising a tattooed forearm bearing a nine-inch scar. "This is from Mexican machete, a much bigger knife."

"Ah haw! You verdee goot, verdee goot Amerdica man."

Certain to lose a game of can-you-top-this with militant foot soldiers, I rise, tapping my watch. "Time to go now, Israeli soldiers have my motorsickle, maybe they don't give it back. Where is the bus to Erez?"

Slapping the back of one of his obedient young henchmen, he says, *"My fren take you to verdee goot taxee."*

Just before entering the no-man's-land strip to Erez, an International Red Cross ambulance monitors the last stretch of dirt road leading to the first Palestinian Authority checkpoint. UN workers block my path, stating that no one is allowed to pass until Israeli commanders give the okay. There has been another shooting at the border, and soldiers are edgy. It could be several hours.

Much to my relief, 30 tense minutes later, cell phones ring and walkie-talkies crackle with permission to let people pass, but only one at a time. With a camera tucked inside my jacket, I click off as many photos as I dare until again intercepted by bullhorns and scanning closed-circuit TV cameras. Shamed for my complicity, departing Gaza is like shoving a manhole cover aside to climb from a sewer that I have escaped, with others left behind.

Jerusalem
January 12, 2005
Jordanian Border
● ● ● ● ● ● ● ● ● ●

Since it's claimed to be the holiest city in history, you'll be either drawn or repelled by what you see in Jerusalem. This is ground zero for the Arab-Israeli conflict, today's biggest obstacle to peace. With biblical justifications, religious extremists risk world war over this hallowed ground. True believers are not just dangerous to themselves — in this case, they are willing to take us all down in a quest for domination over the hottest chunk of real estate on the planet, their pipeline to God.

Travelers can get into trouble discussing religion, so we'll just say it confounds me. But my opinions don't matter; this is about meeting the people of the world to find out what they think. Seeing the world through my own eyes is insufficient. It's better to feel it through the thoughts of those living there. To experience their life, it's important to speak, eat and sleep with natives in their environment. To be invited home with the locals is the traveler's dream, yet if those opportunities don't arise, we're content with street corner tea breaks or restaurant chat. Words are not the only way; ideas can be exchanged with gestures. At times, we communicate with sign language, facial expressions and drawing diagrams in the dirt. There is never enough time, but we reach some understandings. A soiled spaceman riding suit and helmet in hand draws the curious for instant engagement.

The Wailing Wall, the Temple Mount and the right to worship are discussed at length. I spent two entire days wandering East and West Jerusalem talking to whoever would take the time. I learned

The Viking and the rabbi, Wailing Wall, Jerusalem

about Hasidic Jews, Orthodox Jews, Muslim clerics and holy shrines. At the Wailing Wall, I wore a skullcap out of respect for the Jews; on the other side, for Palestinians, I donned a black-and-white kaffiyeh. When asked what I thought, I told them that it didn't matter. What didn't vary was the ending of dialogue. Jews asked whom I supported. "I support world peace."

"Very clever, Glen."

Raising their arms with tears in their eyes, Palestinians asked, "What can we do?"

I had no answer. To an outsider, the solutions may seem simple, but they are not. A good start is to focus on what people have in common. What unites us is more important than what makes us different. Like Muslim women, many married Jewish women must cover their real hair, and instead of *hijabs* they wear wigs. Men of both religions feel that the hair of their women should only be seen by their husbands. Both places of worship have separate entrances for men and women and segregated prayer sections. Jews explained the logic — it's too hard to concentrate on God with the opposite sex nearby. Shaking hands between unmarried men and women when greeting was also forbidden — "It feels too good."

Devout Muslims and Jews both spend long hours in daily prayer and participate in arranged marriages for the primary purpose of reproduction rather than for love. Sex outside marriage is forbidden. According to their respective holy books, for countless centuries, both Jews and Muslims expected a savior to appear. Life is for worshipping God. They pray on street corners, in businesses or while walking. But when I point out the myriad of similarities among them, conversations abruptly terminate. For me, it became a struggle to keep silent. The more they spoke of their differences, the more frustrating it became.

Without visiting the Middle East, it's impossible for Westerners to comprehend the depth and control of religion here. Everyone is convinced that they are right, and those on the fringe are wielding disproportionate influence on moderates. Liberals are silent.

So today I ride from Jerusalem across the desert toward Jordan more unsettled than when I arrived. Thousands of miles of electrified barbed wire and imposing cement walls separating humans scar the landscape. Even if the complacent don't care who dies, the economics are sobering. Everyone is broke. As I reflect on Middle Eastern cities with empty restaurants and hotels manned by forlorn owners, I wonder if they've finally had enough.

WESTERN ASIA

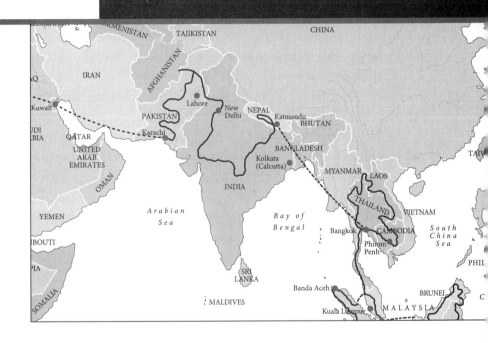

In Transit
January 15, 2005
Karachi, Pakistan
● ● ● ● ● ● ● ● ● ● ●

On a world ride, a motorcyclist will eventually reach a dead end at the edge of a large enough body of water that in order to cross, he will need either an oceangoing vessel or an airplane. In my first such case, it was international politics based on religion that compelled air transport. Despite five weeks of face-to-face haggling, Iranian and Saudi embassy officials refused to budge on granting me visas. It's more than just a hassle or unnecessary expense; for moto-adventurers, it's a sin to fly when you should be able to ride. It's also an uncomfortable experience, like being a fish out of water and trying to breathe.

Airports are cold-water plunges back into a world that long-riders try to avoid — long, polished marble corridors of glittering arcades with a pace that jolts us back into the fast lane of civilization. Worst of all, we become separated from our machines, only to plunder a month's travel budget on a few miserable hours crammed aboard an aircraft. Draining my financial resources this soon certainly limits other activities down the road — potentially cutting short my entire journey.

When considering time factors, port charges and shipping mishaps, hemisphere-hopping is still more economical by air than by sea. The quickest and most reliable process that reconnects us to our machines is to pack them inside wooden crates for loading into the giant holds of cargo planes. But since civilian passengers are not allowed on these types of flights, coordinating simultaneous arrival times is tricky. Because much can go wrong with last-minute mix-ups, it's best to make sure that the bike is airborne first. If it's still waiting to move from an airport freight terminal while you reach your new destination and there are complications with legal documents, remedying the issue from another country is nearly impossible. One signature missing, a forgotten fee or a technical violation of company policy can leave you stranded with only one solution — return to straighten it out personally. Backward bureaucracies buried in senseless regulations don't allow for creative solutions like, "Go ahead and just sign my damn name, and I'll wire you the seven-dollar fee."

While traveling through the Middle East, I had been communicating daily with Seven Seas Shipping in Jordan for a month. When I finally met them last week, we were like long-lost friends, and in keeping with Arab tradition, they immediately took me to dinner. Everyone wanted to put me at ease by assuring me that they knew their job — except that according to my Internet research, this is a first for any shipper in Jordan or Karachi.

Although the base of a wooden crate that a local carpenter built was strong enough to carry the weight of solid machinery, it felt far too flimsy for tying down a balance-sensitive motorcycle. It was a delicate, ego-saving challenge for me to convince workers that motorcycle suspensions need to be compressed by tightly strapping them down for stabilizing. No one understood why we couldn't cinch their thin nylon cord over plastic turn signals to the flexing wooden base. "Don't worry Glen, we are professionals." But at that particular moment, time was a significant factor.

My Pakistan visa was valid for only two weeks, and no one reading the handwritten date-of-use knew if that meant I had to arrive by January 19th or be out of Pakistan by January 19th. Hoping to be able to play the stupid foreigner, I figured I'd get to Karachi first and then beg from there. The new snag was that every airline in the Middle East was booked solid for the annual Muslim pilgrimage of hajj in Saudi Arabia, and there were no seats available, connecting or otherwise, for two weeks. But while spending the afternoon working with travel agents, a last-minute cancellation popped up on Qatar Air, with one budget-busting business-class seat available that with two transfers would still stretch an otherwise three-hour flight into 12. Since I'd also reentered Jordan on a three-day transit visa, choices were limited.

Even counting my medical bills in Germany, for the last six months I've stayed just within a 50-dollar-a-day budget. But transport costs of 700 bucks for me and another 1,000 for the Blue Beast mean a return to fleabag two-dollar hotels for the next three months. That's all tolerable if Mr. Murphy stays out of the way. But since the next available shipping date for the bike was two days after my scheduled flight out of Jordan, I now sit in downtown Karachi trying to shake a miserable case of the flu while my enquiry emails to the shipper are being returned as undeliverable. And so we wait.

Sadar
January 20, 2005
Karachi, Pakistan
●●●●●●●●●●●

Overland travelers heading to or from India usually sprint across politically unstable Pakistan, spending little time investigating the country. Bloody regional conflicts, ethnic strife and, in certain places, nonexistent law enforcement suggest it's wise to cross quickly. Western embassies long ago evacuated nonessential personnel and live under stringent security. But I also wonder, is the world getting more dangerous? Or are we merely more aware of what always existed? According to Uncle Sam, we should all stay home and prepare for the next terrorist attack. Nothing would make Osama bin Laden happier.

Yet half the countries in the world carry U.S. State Department Travel Warnings — even Israel made the list. Foreigners may have bull's-eyes on their backs, but it's hard to hit moving targets. My plan was to land in Karachi, clear the Beast through customs and be gone in two days. Then, hopefully a few weeks riding south to north, with maybe a quick detour into Afghanistan to satisfy a wanderer's curiosity. Considering the high number of recent bombings in Karachi, Kabul is likely safer than it is here in Sadar District. Besides, much like Iran, Afghan hospitality is legendary. And since the allied invasion, Taliban and al-Qaeda thugs have reportedly fled to Iraq and Pakistan. But total safety anywhere in this region is impossible; even among themselves, government intelligence agencies don't know who's who, so it's hard to define what is safe.

The worst city in Pakistan to be stranded in is Karachi. With 12 million people jammed into a stinking, sweltering seaport on the shores of the Indian Ocean, it's a hotbed of conflicting cultures. The pollution is so bad, I seal my hotel windows to keep out lung-searing gray. The sour fragrance of human misery and rotting garbage leaves a film on my clothes that will not wash off. Here in Sadar, there're no police, not even military patrols. Although driving should be on the left, vehicles travel in any lane with an opening, no matter the proper direction.

Preparing for the final day of Ramadan by butchering livestock to feed the poor in Karachi, Pakistan

Crumbling boulevards carry bumper-car traffic jams flowing in grimy rivers of choking congestion then swirling into intersections of coughing chaos. Somehow, severely battered vehicles manage to scrape and nudge their way to the next stoplight that most will ignore anyway. Passive disorder is the law of the land. Three-wheeled motorcycle taxis fare best, piercing downtown gridlock with pointed front ends and drivers determined to win. Crossing streets on foot means sprinting slightly ahead through the sliding sludge. Eventually, I master the daredevil leaps between broken-down, elaborately decorated buses farting vile black smoke. Pedestrians must also watch for deep holes in the sidewalk lest they step into raw sewage.

Tomorrow is the final day of Ramadan — like the Christian Christmas, *Eid* is a major Muslim holiday marked by family gatherings and the butchering of livestock to feed the poor. "Glen, have you ever seen a camel slaughtered? Come with us tomorrow and bring your camera." An ancient civilization prepares. Painted cattle tied to car bumpers twitch and shake their heads while stomping the pavement. It's unclear if this is mad cow disease or pre-execution jitters. By noon, I am sure to become a vegetarian.

There is still no email response from the shippers in Amman, but a garbled cell phone message indicated the bike would be on a flight Thursday that Royal Jordanian Air says doesn't exist. Since *Eid* is a serious religious holiday, the Islamic world is about to shut down for three days. Even if the bike arrives as promised, a backlogged customs department won't reopen until Monday. But it's not all bad news.

What Karachi lacks in hygiene, it makes up for in friendliness. Where the least of the least struggle to survive, there is a disarming calm instilled by Islam. Even with the warnings about attacks on foreigners, Pakistanis, smothering under widespread poverty, still offer smiles and hospitality. Hotel staff, wherever I stay, constantly ask me if everything is okay. "Mr. Glen, your television is good?" Actually, it probably broke in 1970, right about the time they quit cleaning and painting. If they want to repair something, they should start with the hot-water system.

Anticipating a complicated importation process, I contacted a recommended Freight Forwarding company. They should know who to bribe. But after spending a half-day finding them, Mr. Mohammad tells me their services are not necessary and that it's better to deal with Customs directly. "They will treat a white man better." He even orders his personal driver to take me to the airport and familiarizes me with the process. Later, he is offended when I offer to pay him for his help. "Please, Mr. Glen, it's our pleasure."

I am back to learning a new language. Communication with the locals is hit and miss. Sentences begin in English and end in Ordu. Students approach me on street corners, "From where do you come Mister?"

I could easily cover up in my Kaffiyeh, Arab style, and claim Jordan, but pride gets in the way. "I'm traveling the world on a motorbike from California . . ."

So far, anywhere in the world, when locals hear me say I am from California, their invariable, enthusiastic response is a shouted, "Arnold!" Pakistanis, like those others I've met, love the California governor but express only rage for President Bush.

As evening temperatures plummet, by local standards, to 70 degrees, street merchants dressed in long cotton gowns shiver and ask, "Is it this cold in America?"

For personal security reasons, in case lone militants are looking to make a political statement with a bullet or a bomb, I change hotels every other day. There are premiums on the rooms in the back. It's common knowledge that detonating car bombs do more damage up front. Currently, the price for a city view might be absorbing the blast. Despite combing seething Sadar district, I find no other westerners. Just to be safe, I finally called the U.S. Embassy for advice. "You're in Sadar? That's definitely the wrong place for Americans," they say. "Let me see what we can to do to get you out of there. Today's a holiday but we'll phone you next week." My only remaining concern is food.

In an effort to pinpoint what's making me sick, I'm continually switching restaurants. It does no good. Food everywhere is cooked in vats of smelly grease. Eating the local tortilla-like flatbread with oil dripping down my hands may be messy, but it's too delicious to stop. At makeshift street stalls, I feast on chili-pasted meats of questionable origin — at least it's easy to see *what* they are cooking.

Home is still just ahead of my front tire, and I couldn't be further away from the sterile world from which I've ventured. At this instant, those whom I love are resting comfortably with maybe the nagging worry if I am doing okay. At times, I also wonder how bad I need to see this; but there is no rest until I do. Amidst the jabbering beggars and sputtering taxis, I pause to absorb the intensity of the moment. For all my trouble, I am still happy to be here.

Highway to Hell
January 28, 2005
North from Karachi

• • • • • • • • • • • •

After two weeks, once the Blue Beast finally arrived and cleared customs, it was like meeting an old friend — almost like a first ride. It was a thrill to be on the road again, and I quickly forgot all the recent hassles. Last night, feeling weak, I dozed off early while reorganizing my gear, only to awake with a rising fever. It's been a double whammy the last two weeks — respiratory flu accompanied by stomach disorder. Total exhaustion had finally set in. After popping the last of the Immodiums and first of the Ciprols, I closed my eyes for a minute and opened them 12 hours later — more time wasted on a dwindling 14-day visa. With two days left before it expires and no possibility of renewal, I needed to make a hard choice.

It's a 30-hour ride to the border of either India or Afghanistan. If I choose the latter and I reach their embassy in Islamabad, what do I do if they deny a visa? And once in Kabul, would Pakistan issue me another in order to cross back to India? There're 800 miles until a fork in the road where that decision must be made — a right-hand turn to sunny India or a hard left upwards into the winter mountains of Afghanistan.

While visiting the U.S. embassy in Karachi to obtain additional passport pages, a skeleton staff invited me to the American Club, the compound's only restaurant, pool hall and media room. Karachi is so dodgy, none venture outside the embassy walls without armed guards and chase vehicles. Embassy personnel advised against traveling anywhere in Pakistan. Actually, the regional security officer (RSO) suggested a return to California, as this was not the right political climate for international travel: "If you get by the robbing cops, the villagers will kill you. This country is way more treacherous than you understand." But was this rational advice coming from those who'd lived barricaded under guard for the last year? I understood the tension in cities, but the countryside in every country was always different.

Finally back on the road, Pakistan highway police stop me seven times in one day for riding in the wrong lane. Pronounced well, their English is spoken in unfamiliar phrases. "I am sorry to recommend to you that you must to drive in the next position." Each time, I prepared for intimations for bribes, but conversations ended with "We are service to you. You are guest in our country, how can we be of assistance to your journey?" And of course, "Would you please to accompany us to a restaurant for to take tea?" Declining such offers is an offense that's only overlooked after my request that we take pictures together instead.

At the first gas stop entering Punjab province from Sindh, I met a motorcycle character straight from a Cheech and Chong movie. So stoned his bloodshot eyes could barely open, he claimed, in perfect California slang, that as one biker to another it was his duty to show me a good time. "Dude, you wanna' smoke some killer hash?" Not wanting to experience the marvels of Pakistani prison for consorting with druggies, I thanked him but continued north solo.

His final reminder was to "watch out in Southern Punjab man, people sometimes don't dig foreigners. But if you're cool, they're cool." As another note of caution, he adds, "Yeah and the road gets real fucked-up ahead." What else is new?

Successful travelers learn early not to stare down at a man when it's better to look him in the eye. Often, I walk away having looked up to the simplest of people. Wary crowds are best handled by first selecting a child to talk to. Coax a curious youngster to smile and move on to a better-dressed elder, then greet him in his language while offering a hand. Win him over, and the rest are easy.

With seven Islamic countries to cover, the most effective tool in my arsenal is my translated copy of the *Koran*. One way to better understand this region of the planet is to study Islam. The response from Muslims when we discussed the Five Pillars or the early life of Mohammad was encouraging. They are pleasantly surprised when a Westerner is interested in their culture. But nothing can save me from the perils of traffic.

Although India is supposed to be worse, there's no way to

describe how bad driving is in southern Pakistan. At dusk, the road transforms from semi-organized double-lane pavement to a death-wish bumper-car ride to hell on a single strip of dirt and mud traveled in both directions simultaneously — with no one using their brakes. It's hard to believe what's happening. Riding on the out-skirts of Karachi had put me on edge, but now I can only gasp in apprehension. The last four hours have turned into a suicide ride by collision-seeking demons determined to meet Allah.

Truckers are bad, but bus drivers rule. They seem to have been recruited from asylums and selected and graded according to their lunacy. Everyone backs down from them, and they fear only each other. My reflexes develop quickly after cringing from earsplitting trumpet horns followed by the intimidating roar of an accelerating diesel coming straight from behind. Fishtailing buses spin through mud and rock side to side, making me think each time that, for certain, this time he's going to roll. Since commercial cargo is more valuable than human life, truckers cower onto shoulders, letting the thundering busses pass. Terrified motorcyclists and the men cautiously managing overloaded camel carts hauling piles of sugarcane can only pray. When able to catch up to ornately decorated buses, I draft in behind them, safe inside a wake bored through masses of bullied motorists.

Reflected particles of road dust and black soot turn headlight beams into swirling opaque clouds of sinister gray. It's like trying to see through wrinkled wax paper. Four hours later, my lungs clogged from the grime, my nerves are frazzled and my eyes burn so badly I can't see. As I pass through a small, isolated village, someone calls out from the roadside, "Hello!" Warnings from all were to sleep only in major cities, but weary from the strain of riding, another electrify-ing drive through a city is unthinkable. Disregarding the potential consequences, I stop to acknowledge the familiar greeting.

The Western-dressed Pakistani youngsters are English students excited to meet a foreigner. Few pass this way. "Please wait, we will bring our teacher to speak with you." On top of the national lan-guage of Ordu, three different dialects are spoken locally, while business is conducted in English. Anxious to offer hospitality, they pool their money, insisting on buying me dinner and setting up a room in the town's only guesthouse for an evening of language lessons and tales from the road.

We laugh about our lives from other worlds until exhaustion takes over and I fall asleep mid-conversation. The last I recall is the teacher silently latching the door on his way out. In the morning, the students return to guide me to breakfast and provide valuable information about the road north.

Cop Shops
January 29, 2005
The Fork at Highway M-2, Pakistan
• •

Two 500-mile days of strained riding is taking its toll, but relief is timed for sundown at the T-junction in the road where I'll make a critical decision. For the past three hours, reassuring taxi drivers have been insisting better times are ahead. "In one hundred miles further you will encounter a luxury road." There were frequent signs indicating the M-2 Freeway was near, but none told me how far, so when finally appeased, the relief was instant and welcome.

To this point, motorcycles have been exempt from road tolls and permitted to pass the toll booths without stopping. But these cement shacks are different, with signs on the sides listing rules. One of them is a motorcycle symbol with an X over it. For 12 nerve-racking hours, I had fixated on the ecstasy of a quality asphalt autobahn as a sweet relief from the punishing madness. There is no turning back now, and as authority figures so far have been passive, I don't fear an aggressive reaction, and I break just this one little rule.

Ignoring shouts from soldiers waving their arms, I rocket past flashing blue lights, looking straight ahead. Aware that capture is inevitable, nothing matters except this joyous dash from the chaos. I unleash the ponies anyway and soar onto the seamless tarmac of heaven, followed by crying sirens and highway police in hot pursuit. Two miles later they catch up. Polite and proper, apologetic Pakistani troopers approach. "From which country do you travel?"

"Hello my name is Glen, how are you? I come from California."

After accepting stupid-foreigner excuses for not seeing them, we engage in amiable debate why it's unsafe for motorcycles on a super-highway. "We are responsible for your safety Mr. Glen and you must return to the small road." Realizing the flaws in their argument, we reach a compromise. "We will please to honor you for tonight at our camp. You can sleep there. And as you wish, you may demand our service to you. We will prepare meals according to your satisfaction."

Thirty minutes later, chicken and rice is served in a chilly but empty 20-bed dormitory, followed by photos and tea with the commander. In the morning, there is a timid knock at sunrise. The soft-eyed police sergeant from last night is holding a tray. "We have prepared for you these boiled eggs and hope they are to your acceptance." The recital continues. "It gives us pleasure that you restored your sleep and we have prepared to escort you to the small road."

As for me, I am almost to the place to which I am going.

Complications
February 1, 2005
Peshawar, Northwest Frontier Province, Pakistan
• •

As promised, I've been checking in with the American embassy RSOs in major cities while traveling Pakistan. The agent in Peshawar warned me that having an Afghan visa might not be enough to even get me to the border. "Be prepared to be turned back, because they could require a permit to cross the autonomous Northwest Frontier Province tribal region."

"How hard is that to get?"

"You may want to reconsider then, because even if granted, it takes 15 days of bureaucratic runaround."

The borders of western Pakistan have been in dispute for decades. Afghani brothers on one side visiting Pakistani cousins on the other don't consider themselves under either nation's rule. As stateless tribes, they cross back and forth, recognizing only tribal boundaries. With rugged terrain an ally, they do as they please, earning fierce reputations for effectively using sophisticated weapons to answer challenges to their independence. They are the law, and even the military doesn't dispute this.

So far, Pakistanis I've encountered in other provinces have been polite and peaceful with a childlike innocence, even the patrolling soldiers. In other lands, I've learned some authority figures can be friendly to strangers while mistreating their own. Still, it's difficult to imagine them at their worst. Whether in the city or the country, handshakes and smiles are always followed by their humble insistence that we have tea. Pakistanis are never too busy to talk and have always taken me in hand when I am lost.

Arriving at the border of Northwest Frontier Province confirmed the worst reports. Thugs in shabby green uniforms at the tribal outpost were neither accommodating nor amused by my presence. In a region of lawlessness, this heavily armed militia answers only to itself. I surmised a request for photos together would likely result in a confiscated camera and a beating. There is no pretending here; the friendliness is gone — foreigners are unwelcome in this no-man's-land plagued by warlords, bandits and drug smugglers. Draped in local garb, Taliban and al-Qaeda warriors blend together well, in sharp contrast to a wandering biker in a space-age plastic riding suit on a shiny blue motorcycle. As frowning guards approach, I take a deep breath.

Next to a sign stating "No Foreigners Beyond This Point," a sneering, bearded soldier in a tattered woolen sweater fiercely barks his only English: "Permit, permit!"

Holding up my passport, "No, but I have Afghan visa."

His patience already gone, he seems more likely to use his gun than reason. "Permit, permit!" His tone makes it clear; violence is the next step, and he and his friends are ready to demonstrate. I begin to wonder how far it is to the nearest hospital.

From a decrepit wooden building, a better-dressed commander steps to the rescue. He's firm but polite. "You must have a permit to proceed to the border. If you want to cross tribal areas, go back to Peshawar and apply."

As he retreats into his shack, I follow. "Can you please tell me where to get this permit?"

After scribbling "Khyber House, Bara Road" on a slip of paper, I am dismissed as he points to the road. "Now go."

It was just five miles to Khyber House, but still time for a lot of second-guessing. There were so many variables ahead . . . or was I just spooked? Was it a weather forecast calling for snow in Afghanistan or uncertainty over getting another Pakistani visa? And what about the overall security situation? Obstacles are what we see when we lose sight of our goals, but then again, what of omens?

Despite what I'd been told, the Tribal Passage Permit took only a few hours of office-hopping downtown, but it was accompanied by strong warnings. "Yes, the people are nice but anything can happen. Just remember, don't stop. Keep going no matter what." Whenever I've hear such things before, I've found things very different inside so-called danger zones. Still, a precedent is being set here. No one here can remember the last time a Westerner requested to drive into tribal lands or Afghanistan, and on a motorcycle was beyond their comprehension. The only way they'd permit the 45-kilometer crossing was if I trucked my bike, using armed local bodyguards to deliver me to the border. "After that, we unload and you will be on your own."

But I am not alone in my interest. Most embassy workers to whom I spoke, despite all the warnings, admitted, if given the opportunity, they might attempt the trek also. "It's not so crazy then, to want to see Afghanistan?"

"No, someday I will try also, but for now, my job, my family, my . . ."

As of this moment, I have 12 hours to think this over. A wiser man would turn and bolt for India. Who would blame me? But am

I just whining over a few obstacles or really stepping into the lion's den? Where was the fine line between adventurous and foolhardy? The only real threat was the first 27 miles, right? After that, it was smooth sailing all the way to Kabul and back. When making decisions like this, I always ask myself, how will I feel about this later? Will I kick myself someday in California for missing this opportunity or be grateful that I'd had more sense?

Deviations
February 3, 2005
GT Road, Eastbound Across Pakistan

As though escaping breathless from a bad dream, I awoke wide-eyed at dawn, jolting upright with piercing mental alarms jabbing my consciousness. This was rare. In the past, my intuitive warnings had usually been far more subtle — twitches in the stomach telling me to slow before the next curve, and moments later discovering a rock slide or an oil spill. Motorcyclists recognize such sensations; it's what keeps us alive in a high-stakes game with unfavorable odds. Experienced riders realize that a simple roll-back on the throttles never hurts and, sometimes not knowing exactly why, do it subconsciously.

This morning, a signal flashes unmistakably — DON'T GO. It wasn't merely the logistics of a fogged-in Khyber Pass or the frozen roads leading to Kabul. I still had an even shot at beating approaching winter snowstorms, while the threat of bandits has existed before, in other countries. Every developing nation on my itinerary is in some type of turmoil underscored by stern warnings that have thus far been overstated. What about the civil unrest in Nepal next month? Maybe I would just flee for the comforts of cozy California. It should be easy enough to store unfinished business in a wanderer's cross-that-bridge-later file.

To justify my wounded pride and self-doubt, I needed facts to confirm my misgivings. My phone call to the RSO provided a troubling list. After numerous murders and kidnappings, Western workers in Pakistan were no longer permitted to bring their families. For political reasons, Americans were primary targets. If terrorists can establish our patterns, they kill us. "Glen, there was a slight possibility you could have made it yesterday unannounced," the RSO tells me. "Today you have no chance. Never mind the bandits — Taliban and al-Qaeda fighters know an American is coming."

To establish a baseline, I examine the man's background and reasoning. He's ex-military and an experienced adventure traveler who's not just warning me, he's pleading, one man to another, for me not to go. In fact, he tells me to avoid the designated rendezvous point altogether — don't even bother canceling. Get on your bike and ride while you can.

Experience with a terrorist army alters a man's perspective, as I learned from my encounter with the ELN rebels in Colombia. But it's not all for the negative; it also inspires deeper understanding. Yet, in moments of fear, there is still the question, "Is this just ELN-induced paranoia?" It takes an effort not to let those events affect my future decisions, and, sometimes, risky moves are necessary to vanquish them. Terrorists thrive on instilling fear. Every time anyone crosses an international border or shakes hands with a foe, it's a collective middle-finger-message to those who terrorize — we control our lives. But today, I am afraid. Perhaps I am fortunate that the fear meter went off early instead of after the fact. But the question for me will always be, who won here today?

It was an easy one-day ride on the Grand Trunk Road from Peshawar to Amritsar, just across the Indian border. But without a schedule and foul weather behind me, there was no reason to hustle. The mighty wings and steady beat of a faithful Blue Beast become a magic carpet ride into the promised marvels ahead.

Halfway Around the World
February 4, 2005
New Delhi, India
● ● ● ● ● ● ● ● ● ●

The hardest thing about crossing the Indian border was getting there. From Lahore, it was a 18-mile two-hour weave between rickety donkey carts, unwieldy camel caravans and suicidal bus drivers. Yawning Pakistani customs and immigration officials didn't care about my expired visa, stamping me out in minutes. It would have been the same from the Indians if anyone was awake. Just minutes after stirring from his midday nap, a mildly annoyed border guard helps me fill in an entry questionnaire then points the way out. My guidebook tells me there is an elaborate drum-and-bugle corps border-closing ceremony scheduled at sundown, but it was too long of a wait.

After three weeks in Pakistan, the vibrancy of India blossoms in vivid reds and blues. More welcome than that is the appearance of females. Islamic culture provided few glimpses of women, let alone of their hair. Here, nose-ringed Indian girls in dazzling green saris buzz about on purring motor-scooters, while bearded men in bright orange turbans tend roadside food stalls.

Jangling music and pungent smells enhance the imagery, gripping the senses in an exotic dance of spiritual intrigue. From roadside restaurants, scent, of eye-watering spices and frying meats mix with the smell of diesel fumes and fresh-cut fields. It's a long 12-hour ride to Delhi in new territory with much to see. Sikhism, a blend of Islam and Hinduism, is rooted in Punjab, with Amritsar home to its holiest shrine. The stately majesty of the Golden Temple alone is worth a trip to India. Non-Sikhs are discouraged from visiting, but if you remove your shoes and cover your head in cloth wraps, outsiders are tolerated. Entering the massive stone courtyard, you're met with the captivating repetitious background music, as visitors are drawn into a trance intensified by burning incense and skin-prickling vibrations.

Like a floating island attached by a granite catwalk, the gold-leafed temple shimmers in the center of a marble pool, mirroring the surrounding walls. In reverence to the founders, strings of silent pilgrims sink to their knees, kissing the final steps. Sitars whine out tingling tunes while tabla drums tap out repeating beats, reverberating somewhere in the back of my mind. It's an experience that transports listeners from one consciousness to another. My first dose of India blossoms like a wild orchid in a polluted swamp.

The roads are as terrifying as promised but not as death-defying as the ride from Karachi. Warned of the touts and thieves in Delhi's motorcycle district, I've prepared for the worst. Bargaining down prices for new driving lights from 10 dollars to nine was easy, witnessing the installation was priceless. Preferring my own hands, no one other than Jimmy or white-smocked BMW techs should touch the Beast. But how bad could someone err bolting on lights and attaching two wires? Determined to impress the foreigner, 10 pairs of oily hands compete to tape connections and reroute electronics until neither the horn nor ignition function.

Finally, one light shines up and the other straight down — "That's okay Mr. Glen, better to see the trees and watch the front tire." It was useless trying to explain why wiring should be tucked away neatly; they were far too proud to be corrected. Everything could be reassembled later when no one was looking. When finally ready to ride, this time it was locals who aimed cameras at me. It took an hour to escape the series of one-more-shots.

Next on the list was a visa for Nepal and an extension for India, finding a laptop repair station and a store to stock up on canned sardines. Local hotels were fully booked, but there was an empty little guesthouse on a side street with cable TV and a shower. Local fiery curries are delicious despite my knowing that within moments this could lead to all-night trots to the bathroom. Thursday morning is slated for Agra and a visit to the Taj Majal. After that, it's up to the gods.

Visas
February 9, 2005
New Delhi, India
• • • • • • • • • •

Indian immigration officials are as abrupt and unaccommodating as their American counterparts and behave in stark contrast to the friendly citizens. But without a visa extension, I must leave the country in 10 days. Accustomed to the welcoming locals, the scowling, I'm-too-busy-reading-the-paper government employees are a suprise. Time was their ally, not mine. India should be relieved such arrogant bureaucrats are not in charge of tourism. It wasn't just that my 50-dollar-per-day road trip didn't impress them, neither did the French businessman in his three-piece suit. Even after he'd finished informing all who would listen how long he had been waiting, the scowling officials were unmoved. "You will take a seat there."

Completing the extension application process wasted two solid days, waiting in lobbies and running to find copy machines to print more documents to sign. And that was just to get the approval letter to apply at the office across town, which required a life-threatening navigation through the treacherous crush of Delhi rush-hour traffic. But the pacing Frenchman in the business suit kept us entertained with his comments about how, since he had more documents, we were sure to be denied. Officials made certain he was last in line.

Indians are the most curious people yet. Within moments of stopping, mobs of inquisitive black-haired natives gather for a lengthy interrogation. "From which country are you?" "What is your good name sir?" Scooter riders flatter, "Your motorbike is looking very graceful today." While testing the throttle and brakes, all the switches must be flipped by the crowd as they take turns trying on my helmet. The rest is standard talk about cost, speed, mileage, the number of gears and how long I've been on the road. None understand ABS brakes or a bike with electronic fuel injection. Strict protectionist Indian legislation prohibits imported cars. Foreign brands must be manufactured in India, so they are unaware of the latest technology. Few have even heard of BMW automobiles, let alone seen intergalactic-looking motorcycles with big aluminum boxes packed with unimagined items.

It takes an hour to break free, making parking downtown more trouble than it's worth. At times, I am the rude American in too much of a hurry to chat. But later, feeling guilty, I return with bags of peanuts to reestablish relations. Even when I find secluded spots on highways to park and adjust my gear, one at a time local motorcyclists stop to offer aid. "May I instruct you to the place to where you are going?"

Relaxing in my luxurious 10-dollar-a-night guesthouse, an anxious staff continues to dote, asking about my itinerary. "Allow me to show you that proper location on this map." For a buck and a half, including a generous tip, they deliver four fried eggs every morning while I study world weather forecasts on CNN. Between the ridiculously lengthy stories of an upcoming British royal wedding, poofy-haired newscasters offer brief reports of genocide in Darfur. A dutiful receptionist confirms all's well with the Beast three times a day, with assurances there are no thieves in this neighborhood. A week is like a month of building relationships, and there is sure to be sadness about my leaving. But after a few days of relaxing, once again the road beckons.

The Taj
February 12, 2005
Uttar Pradesh, India
● ● ● ● ● ● ● ● ● ● ● ●

Today's white-knuckle ride from Delhi to Agra was another six-hour suicide run through 120 miles of black-soot-gulping raving lunacy on wheels. Fortunately, there was mostly gridlock, so when cars bumped my hand-guards with their mirrors, it wasn't so unnerving. As long as it's not trucks or buses, I should survive.

After the snowy-white domes of Jaigurudeo Temple popped up from the cluttered landscape of ramshackle buildings and semicultivated farmland, it was only another hour before reaching the first of the tombs from India's feudal past. A tour of the surviving palaces begins in the countryside at Sikander, where a stately blend of white marble and red sandstone encase the burial chamber of Akbar the Great, noblest of Mogul rulers. Remembered as a fair and just man, he retained power by acknowledging and respecting all religions.

Reaching Agra after sunset meant combing torch-lit, smelly alley-ways in search of cheap hotels with safe parking. Choices were limited. The power was out, and narrow, winding stone passageways were packed with bicycle rickshaws, sacred cows and babbling souvenir peddlers circling like sharks. The equivalent of $3.50 U.S. buys a damp but tidy cubicle with a weak promise of hot-water-buckets for bathing in the morning. There is a possibility of electricity if the aging generator fires. Not bad, considering directly next door is roast chicken and an Internet café.

It was early to bed, early to rise for that ultimate predawn photo, but as the sun ignited the sky into a pale gray dome, the mighty Taj Mahal was shrouded in an annoying smoggy mist. When the confluence of choking hydrocarbons and early-dawn haze eventually clears, a blinding glare from an imposing white marble mausoleum blazes above the surrounding tropical green gardens. Four outward tilting minarets mark the corners of this astonishing display of obsessive romance. Multicolored stone inlays and semiprecious jewels adorn polished walls and patterned columns of this seventh wonder of the world. Carved into rows of translucent stone, ribbons of Arabic script citing Koranic verses flow over windows and archways.

Dark-skinned women in dazzling saris of brilliant fluorescent pinks and limes burst across the backdrop of opulent, palatial magnificence. Designed to capture winds from the river, forceful breezes flow through honeycomb marble screens, producing cooling drafts, while the brightness can't be tamed. Unobstructed sunlight reflecting off slabs of sparkling white stone is unbearable for the naked human eye.

Built in 1653 by Emperor Shah Jahan in honor of his beloved wife who died bearing his 15th child, this is history's most spectacular testament to love. So distraught at her passing, he commissioned the finest Persian architects and 20,000 craftsmen to spend the next 22 years constructing this monument to her memory. Later, Jahan was overthrown by his son and imprisoned across the river so he could spend his dying days gazing in remembrance. Such images are consciousness-stilling visions that last a lifetime. As with the pyramids, neither prose nor poetry can adequately describe what you feel when seeing the Taj.

Rajasthan
February 16, 2005
Jaipur, India
● ● ● ● ● ● ● ●

The trouble with India is with so much to see and experience, there can never be enough time. Including my one-month visa extension, I have just six weeks, barely enough to visit the north.

Delhi consumed a week, organizing travel docs and minor bike repairs. I stopped in Agra to visit the Taj Mahal and in Jaipur to inspect old forts and palaces. Next comes Pushkar, a small religious village surrounding a sacred lake, one of the holiest sites for Hindus. Bathing in the hallowed waters represents a spiritual cleansing for Indian pilgrims.

My motorcycle continues to draw crowds, providing opportunities to meet the locals and hear what they have to say. Determining where to eat and sleep could be challenging. India can be confusing and frustrating at times, especially if you're fending off predators and hustlers. It takes a lot of conversation, but occasionally it's possible to break through the scams and make friends. Bikers are treated better than backpackers, still you're never certain if you'll be asked for rupees after someone has done you what you thought was a favor.

With its billion people, occupying 2.4 percent of the earth's surface, India is the world's biggest democracy, with six major religions and a different culture appearing every 50 miles. There're 18 official

Awed by the Taj Mahal in Agra, India

languages, with nearly a thousand dialects. English is the medium for business, so most people in the cities speak a familiar tongue, but out in the countryside, it's back to hand gestures. The minimum wage has risen to a dollar a day, yet 65 percent of the population is literate. Small roadside restaurants are too risky to consider. Even in cities, unless the restaurants are crowded, with rapid food turnover, it's wise to avoid them. The best may have bathrooms but no soap or toilet paper for customers or employees.

But India is paradise for bargain traveling. In Jaipur, three nights, hotel, three deep-fried-egg breakfasts and hand-washed laundry comes to 20 bucks. A classical dinner in a decent restaurant sets you back five. Gas is three dollars per gallon and climbing, but riding so slowly on the overcrowded roads has increased my fuel efficiency to nearly 700 miles per tank. By the end of the month, I'll be back on budget.

Midwinter weather is perfect for riding, warm and sunny with no clouds or rain. With a little luck, I might not need my foul-weather gear again until June, when crossing Australia. My faithful Blue Beast still fires on the first spark, but due to the constant hard braking, the tires are wearing fast. The odometer reads 24,493 miles, with the next major service due in Thailand, April 2.

Hucksters and Holy Men
February 19, 2005
Pushkar, India
• • • • • • • • •

Traveling in India, there is a photo-op on every corner. But the best ones often appear at the worst times. The day you forget your camera, you are certain to encounter a wedding procession with grooms in elaborate costumes astride gold-decorated, prancing white horses. Even with the thousands of digital photographs stored on my laptop, I only capture 10 percent. All I have are memories of camel caravans in downtown Karachi or elephants humping in hotel parking lots.

On the road from Jaipur I encounter a typical sight throughout India — stonemasons at work assisted by streams of graceful women laborers. Men stand around smoking hand-rolled cigarettes as younger boys help stack heavy rocks on top of the women's heads. Dressed in traditional elegant saris and smiling through a grimace, they accept their plight as second- and third-generation slaves. Their futures are determined by caste; even when they are paid, it will not be much.

There is no second-guessing in Pushkar, where the most colorful people of Asia provide endless opportunities for shutterbugs. According to Hindus, Pushkar Lake was formed at the desert's edge when Lord Brahma slew a demon with a lotus flower. Ever since, it's been a site for religious pilgrimage. Now, sadly, it's a colony of lazy, pseudo-spiritual wannabes who take themselves far too seriously. But they can also be entertaining. Last night, there was a decent '60s-style benefit concert for street children, featuring turbaned white boys from France dressed in authentic local garb. Groups of "recently converted" musicians strummed and banged under the stars using native instruments while aging, scraggly hippies tried unsuccessfully to dance to the music.

I have finally figured out why all the women in Israel are beautiful. They've exported the homely to India, where the population is rife with space-cases wandering about in Indian garb with matted dreadlocks and bloodshot eyes. Most are just out of the military, recuperating from the stress and unpopular politics, so they seldom speak to other foreigners. Curiosity wins out, and I ask a weathered young woman, "So, how come there are so many Israelis here?"

"Hash, man. It's a tenth of the price in Tel Aviv and if you bargain, you can live on two dollars a day."

"What about the spiritual aspects?"

"Oh yeah, that too."

The hundred-acre Lake Pushkar is lined with cement block steps leading down into formed pools for bathing pilgrims. Colorfully costumed, scamming pimps on the street above lure the unsuspecting with handfuls of flower petals to toss into stagnant sacred waters as tributes to Hindu gods. But spirituality is not free. Holy men await lakeside, ready with rehearsed prayers and demands for rupees. While those who've ignored Lonely Planet guidebook warnings naively fling petals at sunrise, prayer-mumbling priests in dirty robes circle like vultures.

After the chanting, whichever way they turn, the hapless face a grinning old man with painted skin and open hands. "As you like . . ."

"What?"

Humble smiles accompany meek bows with outstretched palms. "As you like, rupees."

Twenties and 50s are handed back with sterner requests, "As you like — more rupees."

At sunset, I find some secluded steps free of gawkers and hawkers for a moment of meditation. Settled into a balanced lotus posture, the relentless tapping of tabla drums merge with fluctuating whines of Indian string instruments echoing inward, drawing me deeper. I'm half-expecting a miracle or brief glimpse of nirvana, but none arrives.

Friends gather around to see the Blue Beast

No holy man approaches to slap my forehead and reel me into enlightenment, but I surface in time to stop mischievous monkeys from scampering away with my helmet. Still, the show is endless.

Juggling musicians and clever beggars compete at the water's edge, each plying their trades. A cunning old man with a bamboo violin and his tiny daughter are the winners. While sawing out off-key Indian folk songs, his ragged little girl sings at the top of her lungs, with smudged face and twinkling brown eyes. No matter which way you turn, she scurries around to face you, belting out verses while staring deep into your eyes. Even the most hardened tightwads buckle, surrendering crinkled bills.

Back on the street, animal dung dumped from cows, pigeons and monkeys is trampled into clouds of stinking dust. Some of the more experienced beggars don't even bother to rise. They merely sit in family circles, sipping tea next to plates of cash. Retorts of "Sorry no small money" are met with wads of bills waved in the air and replies of "No problem, I can make change."

Despite the circus of hucksters, there are many excuses to stay another day. Time on an Indian road is time in hell. If the buses and trucks don't get you, a heart attack will. There was a new triple-lane freeway stretching down from Jaipur that was even separated by a raised concrete median. Still, every 10th vehicle hurtling through the traffic was a bus with blaring horns, roaring directly into my lane. The only option was to grab the brakes and head into a field. In Turkey, I stopped frequently to recover from the cold; here, I halt to slow my pulse and wait for the shakes to pass.

Everyone has their weak points; for me, it's giggling street children skipping circles around my motorcycle, begging for rides. I agree to a lap of Main Street; soon, three excited youngsters pile on back, urging for horn beeps and wheelies. As the word spreads, a crowd grows. I don't give them money, but a few bucks buys enough oranges to appease my army.

Indian pilgrims, also tired of shams and hustles, consume my afternoons asking questions of "Which are the places from which you have come?" Reciting a list of countries, I end by shouting, "And then, INDIA!" After applause, I ask questions about their lives and professions. Shopkeepers, doctors and factory workers all have their stories of family and religion, and they are delighted a foreigner wants to hear them. Soon they shove handfuls of scribbled addresses my way, with invitations to visit their towns. As Pushkar is a Hindu holy city, animal protein is forbidden. But someone has taught the locals the art of Italian cooking and basic hygiene. Too bad I can only eat a limited amount of pizza and ravioli for breakfast. The overcooked flesh of unfortunate chickens tempts me onward. In the morning, I'll repack freshly river-laundered riding clothes and head southeast to "determine the direction for which will be the location of my approaching destination."

Detours
February 21, 2005
Kota, India
● ● ● ● ● ● ●

Even using two computers simultaneously, their sluggish dial-up speeds consumed four hours at the Internet café just to upload 10 photos and answer email, extending an already late departure to 2:00 p.m. Although it would be tight, five hours should be enough to cover 120 miles before sundown. Dodging herds of donkeys and camels, if I am cautious and keep moving, it's possible to average 25 miles every hour.

Since it was Sunday, commercial vehicles would be scarce, making an easier ride from Pushkar to Kota. The shortest route shown on the map, a secondary road through farmland, provides an opportunity to absorb India's country life. For a change, traffic is light and the patchwork of deteriorated asphalt tolerable — if taking breaks standing up on the foot pegs.

Road signs are written in Hindi, so at forks I stop and wait for opinions. Young Sikhs on scooters stop to help, but today even a bus driver parks mid-road to check. Lost travelers never wait long for assistance in India. But outside the cities, no one speaks English, and even single words can be misunderstood. It's quicker to hold up pieces of paper with scribbled city names and shrug my shoulders. From there, an arm-waving spiel in unfamiliar dialects suggest a general direction. On changes in direction, I tap a right or left arm and enquire, with a rising inflection, "Kilometer?" then hold up my hand pointing to my fingers one at a time. They get the idea and smudge the appropriate number on my dusty gas tank.

Most country folk have never driven cars and have little knowledge of what lies two villages ahead, so I take it one fork at a time. The road has been slowly worsening, until soon, the surrounding mesquite was encroaching from the sides. That should have been the first indication that few travel this way.

My GPS tells me I have 50 miles left to Kota when another reason to turn back appears — a flooded road. There was no way to gauge its depth, but the water in front of me was slow moving and barely 100 yards to the other side. It's usually best to wade in first with a long probing stick, but sunset was fast approaching. Tired of waiting for someone to appear who might know exactly where to cross, I rolled the dice.

Halfway across, the bottom was still visible until I abruptly hit a pothole, sinking the Blue Beast instantly to mid-tank level and over the top of the seat. A wet body is manageable; a wet intake manifold is not. Engine air snorkels on BMW Dakars are purposely set high for this reason, to facilitate river crossings in up to three feet of slow-moving water. Turning around midstream was not an option, and with 50 feet left, there was no way for me to tell if the bottom dropped further or sloped up to a welcome climb out.

As chilly water gushed into my boots, I nudged the bike fast enough to stay upright yet slow enough to keep fluid from flowing into the snorkel. The strategy was complicated by the need to stay prepared to squeeze the clutch if the motor coughed. Sucking water into a running engine is a bad idea under any circumstances, but out here in the boondocks at sunset — it could be a big issue. To my relief, a gradual incline led to higher ground.

Without further delays, it was still possible to reach Kota just after dusk. But Mr. Murphy had other plans. Twenty minutes later, a fading sun provided enough light to show me why the road was no longer used — the deteriorated asphalt only led to another deeper flooded valley, this time stretching for miles, forming a lake.

While considering my options, a half-dozen field workers approached. Yes, there was a detour — 30 miles back. This would not only mean adding another five hours but recrossing the first flooded road. Then Lady Luck intervened. After studying a wading old man piggyback his child, I memorized his zigzagging path and made it my own.

On the other side, a car had sat idling while the driver evaluated his chances while I crossed. Satisfied he would fail, he called out to me to follow him to the detour for Kota. This new road was a maze of dips and potholes, often felt before seen. Without a guide and now in the dark, there was little chance of finding the way alone.

We race into blackness, bouncing and bumping at unsafe speeds. Back on the main road, the driver's confidence exceeds mine, and he soon disappears through a frightening surge of oncoming buses. The ride offered one extreme or another. Either the buses ran with lights switched eye-level-bright or not on at all. With aching eyes and splintered nerves, I rolled into Kota at midnight, 10 hours after I'd started out this afternoon.

Orchha
February 23, 2005
Madhya Pradesh, India
• • • • • • • • • • • • •

The further I venture from oversized, congested Indian cities, the more pleasant life becomes. Out in the country, the midday air is clear and dry, with wide open spaces of golden agricultural fields touching the edges of a pale blue sky. In small towns with packed-dirt roads and ramshackle marketplaces, you become less wary of what people are really up to. That's what eventually drives travelers from India — the incessant hustle and trickery.

Unfortunately, there is no escaping the poverty and filth, and it takes half the day to find a semi-clean café to eat in. I always carry water and canned fish just in case, but, still, the abundance of animal dung and raw sewage is a constant reminder disease is never far away. My GPS memory chip only stores coordinates and waypoints for interprovincial highways and major cities, so the best places to visit seldom appear on the screen. Much is left to chance.

Orchha is an out-of-the-way village with more decaying palaces than hotels, and unless you know where to look, difficult to find. To those on their way to somewhere more important, it's just another detour on a deteriorated asphalt road, but to Hindu pilgrims it's home to the sacred Ram Raja Temple. There's no sign at the turnoff, in the midst of a dry woodland forest; the isolated outskirts of

Orchha appear without warning. By Indian standards, its two-story run down hostels are overpriced. Even then, nine bucks rents a sparse room with an ancient TV pulling in BBC News and a bucket of hot water in the morning. As elsewhere, there is a dusty blanket and bottom sheet that gets changed once a week regardless of how many guests have used the room. But it's been awhile since I've woken up itching, so I'm okay with it.

Instead of another evening of fending off hustlers and rickshaw drivers, tonight, amiable locals provide a chair on the hostel porch to sit and watch a show. As rows of mobile food stalls and wooden souvenir stands button up for the night, a variety of wandering animals converge. Leftover rice, vegetables and rotting fruit are tossed into the street for strays and sacred cows to scrounge and feast on. Irate Brahma bulls with broad, convincing horns poke and moan at barking dogs while wily alley cats sneak scraps from behind. It's like a scene from a show on Animal Planet.

Up until now, I've had regular access to money; even small cities have ATMs to spit out a few days' worth of rupees when needed. So while Orchha is out of the way, I assumed there would be at least one in town. There wasn't. With travel so cheap in India, your money tends to last. It's easy to forget to resupply. After pre-paying my hotel bill, I discover I am nearly broke. Being cashless in India is a dodgy proposition. An old wooden building with a broken-down metal door serves as both post office and village bank. An ancient rotary-dial telephone connects them to Delhi. From behind a paper-strewn desk, an apologetic manager tells me the nearest cash machine is 10 miles back, in Jhansi. I can either spend an hour backtracking at sundown or eat my last can of tuna for dinner and have enough rupees for bottled water on a morning ride to my next destination of Khajuraho. As a precaution, I always keep hundred-dollar bill folded in the back of my wallet or emergency traveler's checks glued behind my helmet lining, but this situation hardly warrants pillaging that stash.

For now, it's a full moon, and the muddy backstreets of Orchha are lined with two-room stone-tile houses leaking wafts of incense and sinus-burning spices — pleasant confirmations of how far I have come and have yet to go. With my senses buzzing, it's time to wander strange neighborhoods and see who invites me for tea.

Sex in the Shrines
February 26, 2005
Khajuraho, India
• • • • • • • • • •

By avoiding cities the ride has become more pleasant, but I'm still not sure how to reach Thailand. During the last 20 years, Burma has been officially closed for overland crossings, by the military. In Nepal, since the king suspended democracy and fired the government they are nearing all-out civil war. Outraged Maoist rebels have blocked the roads in protest, and there have been numerous bombings and shootings. According to recent reports, truckers and bus drivers defying the rebels have had their tires shot out and hands severed. It's difficult to imagine the ever-gentle Nepalese caught up in such nastiness, but as of today, 11,000 people have been killed, most of them civilians.

Shipping a bike from India requires weeks of paperwork and unknown quantities of baksheesh. The next best option is choosing Bangladesh for airfreighting from Dhaka to Bangkok. I arrived in Khajuraho yesterday to temple-hop and weigh the options while awaiting news from Katmandu. Speculation on travel websites is that the blockade may be lifted, but even if that's true, it's still best to wait long enough for the word to get out to all the rebels. For now, the embattled king of Nepal has shut down the cell phone connections the rebels require to communicate. What if I run into guerillas who haven't heard the blockade has ended?

With my Indian visa expiring March 18, my destination choices in India are limited to the northern provinces close to the Nepali border. If I ride any further south, there will be no time to stop and get to know a place. Besides, 10 years exploring India would only scratch the surface. The more I see, the less I understand, and two straight days of lunatic driving is plenty, considering it takes four to calm down afterwards.

In the meantime, I'll linger in Khajuraho, investigating the puzzling legacies of the Chandela dynasty. Historians are uncertain how, in just a hundred years, the limited population in a remote location mustered the manpower to construct their massive, multi-story, intricately carved sandstone shrines depicting daily life. Most intriguing and confusing are the erotic hand-chiseled stone sculptures depicting unusually creative lovemaking. Equally interesting is noting who, when no one is looking, snaps discreet photos of the explicit sex scenes: Everyone.

Off the main rail lines and bus routes, Khajuraho is as much out of the way now as it was a thousand years ago, which is what likely saved it from invading Moguls. Although reduced to a village, the dusty streets sprout boxy hotels and tatty European restaurants touting authentic lasagna and pizza. The double cheese is great. Electricity comes and goes while snail-paced Internet fails just when you're about to send a long email. Guidebooks warn about the hustlers, but considering locals survive on so little, the amusing barking of street vendors doesn't annoy me. A marble-coated hotel room with ceramic tub costs 16 bucks a night, but splitting the cost with a budgeting female Canadian-Bengali backpacker enhances the bargain.

At first she caught me off guard, suggesting that since we were both sleeping in the same hotel we should share a room. While unpacking our gear she turned and smiled, "By the way, my name is Sheila." In other circumstances, a woman offering to share a hotel room with a stranger would have explicit implications, but among shoestring travelers it's common. Still, she is alone and so am I, and her adventurous spirit as a solo woman traveler in India is impressive — especially watching her sparkling eyes grow wide as I described the thrills of motorcycling the earth. And she seems to understand when I also mention the accompanying loneliness.

A Good Woman
March 3, 2005
Varanassi, India
• • • • • • • • • •

Despite warnings of how difficult motorcycling India can be, Sheila has abandoned common sense and accepted my offer for a ride to Varanassi. "Since we're both headed that way, you're welcome to hop on the back . . ." Sheila agrees without a second thought. What made her so eager? Was it yesterday's country cruise with the warm wind in her hair? Or our discovering hidden brick shrines near villages along the riverside? Or was it puttering through the woods trailing giant deer? Either way, her enthusiasm matches mine.

Moving from backpacking to motorcycling is a significant jump, but what she lacks in experience she makes up for with zeal. If I would just show her how, she is willing to change the oil for a ride to Varanassi. Without blinking, Sheila gobbled up instructions on how to lean with the turns and now knows not to squirm when we slow to white-line between cars. An hour after my list of terms and conditions, she arrives with a helmet and riding shoes. "What's next Glen?" She's already begun jettisoning non-essential items to compress her pack.

Still, other conditions apply. "Sheila, you ever listen to Willie Nelson?"

"Yeah, sometimes."

"Good, every morning at sunrise we sing 'On the Road Again.'" To be certain she understands what I mean, I pinch my nose to imitate Willie's nasal twang and mumble-hum the pertinent verses.

Overnight buses and two-day train rides are as taxing in their own way as highway riding, so Sheila is ready for a change. Yet tucked away in my worry file is the responsibility for a passenger's safety. Her well-being and safety depend on my judgment. Motorcycling is always a numbers game, and no matter how hard we try to change them, the odds never favor the riders.

While shipping from Jordan, the Blue Beast without fuel weighed-in at 260 kilos. With aftermarket equipment and luggage, that's a 60-kilo gain over original motorcycle specs. While additional weight negatively affects maneuvering, the beefed-up suspension has made it a reasonable load to handle, but that's without a passenger. The travel dynamics are about to change.

An energetic Canadian-Bengali girl traveling alone, Sheila is in search of her roots. Bristling at my teasings that she's a wandering half-breed, she reminds me her father was of the Brahman caste. A good description of Sheila would include her adventurous spirit and sense of humor — and she was a solid nine with her hair down. An avid reader lugging a personal library, she and her book, upset the tolerance by another 70 kilos.

To carry additional weight, Ohlin's mono–shock absorbers are designed with adjustment knobs just below the fuel tank. When twisted clockwise, an aluminum collar hydraulically compresses the heavy-duty spring to stiffen the ride, making it possible to reset the sag and raise the rear end. In case this system failed, mechanics in Istanbul had spent a day fine-tuning other parts of the bike to handle precisely my weight and my gear at the minimum position. Sheila's additional mass would seriously affect handling, but a simple twist of that knob should rebalance the bike.

I'm not sure if it was air trapped in the line or simply that there was not enough internal fluid, but when I was getting it ready to ride, that easy twist of the knob had no effect. Inadequate suspension to compensate for the load changes the situation from possible to risky. Yet hints of the problem don't deter my passenger as she only impatiently wonders what's holding us up. Enthusiasm like hers is hard to ignore, but even under ideal conditions, this is a question-able situation.

According to many travelers, Siberia is home to the world's meanest excuse for a roadway. And while that's true in terms of length, today, that intensity is matched by the road to Varanassi. Two hundred fifty miles on the map becomes two long days of treacherous wrangling. While temperatures climbed into the 90s, humidity dou-bled, making inching through congested small-town dusty streets sticky experiences hard to forget.

On the open road, where there was asphalt, it was so chewed and mangled that riding through the boulders of adjoining fields looked easier. Off we bounce and jolt toward Varanassi in a first gear crawl over lumps and ditches, and even at 10 miles per hour, the suspension slams shut. At every spine-snapping shock, I wonder if the sub-frame bolts will last. Yet through it all, Sheila never flinches.

Late afternoon, we break for the night, and Savera Hotel becomes our refuge from the encroaching hordes and hassles. Riding the world gets lonely, and it's nice to have someone around at night to laugh about the day. A visit from Brad and rare encounters with other riders break the monotony, but there are times when the friendship of a woman is what you really need. And the same goes for single female travelers.

Backpacking women are a breed of their own, but those who venture alone give new meaning to the word courage. From all directions, they endure constant harassment for sex or for their money. Finding a man who requests neither can be a boon for both. It's not just the travel expenses suddenly divided, there is now someone to share the sunset with and reflect upon the day's lunacy.

For partnerships of convenience, there are no established rules of conduct. Satisfying arrangements can be either ruined or enhanced by crossing certain lines. It's a balance hard to maintain. But then again, difficult days on the bike with a woman's arms wrapped around my torso can also plant seeds. So we'll just have to see how long our comfortable friendship remains pleasantly platonic.

The City of Lights
March 5, 2005
Varanassi, Uttar Pradesh
● ● ● ● ● ● ● ● ● ● ● ● ● ●

The intensity of India is remarkable — depending on the day's events, travelers are consistently either cursing or loving this colorful menagerie of ancient human civilization. There is no in between, you're either retching or savoring; while reeling through its mystical layers of celebration and suffering. How you view the country depends on whether current cultural jolts move your spirit or turn your stomach. The Hindus are far more accepting of the extremes in life; living and dying are set on a course beyond man's control. Among the deeply religious, little effort is made to affect the future.

Although the major cities are thought of as the real India, Varanassi instantly lives up to its legend as the best and the worst. On the western banks of the hideously polluted Ganges lies this fabled City of Lights, the most sacred of sites for Hindu pilgrims. On the massive granite steps of holy ghats, the devoted come to bathe away sin or sip the magic waters. To expire in Varanassi is believed to free the soul; cremation on the riverbank is the ultimate burial rite. Aged cripples and the incurably sick arriving to die are housed in riverside ashrams, waiting to transcend. By the time melted snow from the northern Himalayas reaches Varanassi, it has become an oxygen-free sludge of poisonous bacteria and dangerous microbes. Upriver cities, with their 15 million people, pump untreated raw sewage and chemical waste directly downstream towards the highest concentration of humans in Uttar Pradesh. Those further south are even less fortunate.

From bankside sunset religious ceremonies to cremating the dead, life along the Ganges rocks the senses of wandering Westerners here to bend their minds. From the water's edge, centuries-old red brick temples hum with mesmerizing songs and harmonious chanting, while bells and gongs permeate the soggy stench of muggy evening air. While the thumping beats of rock 'n' roll urge you to move your body, repetitious Indian chords tug at your mind, changing directions just at the moment you seem to identify one. Repeating taps of tabla drums lull the consciousness so it's slow enough for softly plucked strings of twanging sitars to sweetly penetrate your mind. Gently guiding listeners inward, in unfamiliar keys, soothing voices moan of myths and legends millenniums old. Varanassi becomes an irresistible spiritual seduction.

The Indian experience is tough to describe — tourists and travelers seldom agree on what draws them back. Still, a lure overshadows the exasperation, and no one visits India just once. Everyone returns.

Is it the twisting of our souls in painful reminders of how simple life should be? Or is it the realization of the insignificance of all that surrounds us, including ourselves? From cheap hash to meditation and yoga, whatever entices you to India is sure to change your life. Emaciated foreigners in local costume, some sincerely converted and others just striving to be cool, saunter in stately poses speaking only to each other. Everything is real, yet nothing is as it seems. And in the steady spinning of your thoughts, you never know what's next.

BFE
March 10, 2005
Aurangabad, Bihar
● ● ● ● ● ● ● ● ● ● ●

All good things must come to an end and so it is with romance on the road. Sheila's short journey was over as mine was only half-finished, and we both tried to dodge the awkwardness of returning to being strangers. Packing our gear and reviewing guidebooks, it was a peculiar feeling parting ways with a woman I'd only shared great times with. We might exchange a few emails down the road, but it's a virtual certainty that we'll never see each other again. In the past, arguments or strong disagreements on values had ended relationships with women I once cared for. But maybe this way was the best of the best, knowing only Sheila's good sides.

Still, despite my suggestions that she quit her job in Canada and ride with me to Nepal, Sheila was heading for the airport, and I toward Katmandu. With a brief hug and a benign kiss farewell, I silently thanked the gods for the magic of Indian whiskey and the hotel receptionist who I generously tipped last week for announcing that the only room they had left had a double bed. While watching her taxi disappear down a crowded side street, I knew someone important was leaving my life forever — and I would surely miss awaking to silky black hair on crisp white pillows. But at least I was still in magical India.

As a wobbly-kneed democracy a half-century old, India struggles hard to hold together its differing factions and cultures. Due to separatist rebellions and inter-caste violence, entire regions remain closed to outsiders or require special entry permits. Controlled mainly by bandits and local mafia, according to news accounts, the treacherous northeastern state of Bihar is the most corrupt of the nation. The most immediate threats come from muggers; even buses in convoys don't travel past sundown. Train robbery was common when engineers used to stop at small towns. Known as an outlaw haven, the Rough Guide manual states that several executive legislators are wanted for murder. And for overland crossings, my Lonely Planet book advises hiring armed escorts.

The Grand Trunk Road, stretching from Peshawar to Calcutta, is the Indian subcontinent's version of America's Route 66. Although the section from Varanassi east was described as "good," reaching Nepal still required passage across forbidding Bihar. As always, "good" meant barely passable on an eight-and-a-half-hour stand-up ride of 110 miles on a decimated dirt road under construction. For now, I am just anxious to cross the next border.

Once in Nepal, there are several roads leading to Katmandu, but all pass through areas beyond the army's control, and local truckers I talked to offered little information on the safest route. As with all civil conflicts, with 11,000 dead, the war has mostly affected Nepalese civilians. My emails to shippers in Katmandu confirmed cargo flights were available to Thailand, but reaching that airport by motorcycle is still questionable. There was an unsettling trade I could make — the least dangerous road through Nepal connects from the most hazardous route across India, due north from Raxual, Bihar.

Ironically, Bihar is the land where Buddha spent most of his life. International pilgrims flock to Bodhgaya, a subdued, tree-shaded village like a tranquil island in the center of Bihar. This is where the young Indian prince sat in meditation beneath a Banyan tree patiently reaching nirvana. Having had my fill of Hindu culture, a smooth buzz of gentle Buddhism was in order. With a week left on my Indian visa, Bodhgaya would be the perfect stopover to monitor the situation in the Himalayan kingdom further north.

Traveling east, the sun drops before a city appears, and traffic instantly diminishes to the occasional stragglers hurrying home before we're swallowed in total darkness. Soon, I am alone, again violating my common-sense pledge never to ride at night. Finally, after pantomiming my immediate needs, some villagers direct me to a dirt road leading to Aurangabad, a grimy out-of-the-way city drowning in poverty. As elsewhere in India, its dust-clouded streets are congested with swollen rivers of pedestrians and rickshaws with barely room to pass. Crowds part only for a slow-moving military jeep inching forward with blaring siren. I follow it as closely as possible in the all-consuming gap of rushing humanity.

During momentary breaks for directions, I am nearly crushed by throngs of gawking natives. Pointing to the bike, they shout in unison, "How much, how much?" Getting on my way again is difficult, as nobody wants to be the first to move. At the first of Aurangabad's two decrepit hotels, the manager merely points back to the door stating, "No." This was not a good sign.

Back on the street, a frail little man in neat civilian clothes steps forward to my aid, and after some haggling, takes me by the hand over to my bike. Pointing to himself he says, "Police. We go other hotel." Assuming he's another tout hustling a commission, I agree anyway; there was nowhere left to go. Before I can stop him, he climbs on the back of the Beast, and we ride, him shouting to the crowd to get them out of our way.

The second hotel was worse than the first — red spittle-stained walls with no running water and more mosquitoes than a Siberian campsite — but there was a vacancy. Certain a finder's-fee is about to be announced, I prepare to bargain. Instead, the kindly old man merely shakes my hand while kissing my fingers. "You are my guest." Warning me not to venture outside, he brings me a strange meal of stringy meat on unfamiliar bones cooked in a greasy sauce. The source of this mysterious feast may have been recently swinging from trees, but considering I had had no food since morning, any food was welcome relief.

In a wobbling twilight hum, the ceiling fan functions long

enough to dry my sweaty filth to a crust, and once barricaded inside, I climb into my laptop to record today's events. Like a flashing disco light, the power flickers and mercifully ends at about the time my computer battery dies. Tossing and turning with an open pocket-knife in one hand and an oil-stained blanket pulled over my head, I drift into sleep dreaming of Nepal.

In the morning, I am awakened by persistent knocking. With a bleary-eyed stagger, I pull the chair from the door to discover two smiling cops in uniform, one of them the man from last night. Using a mixture of Hindi and English, I confirm that my evening had been uneventful and that after a breakfast of four fried eggs, I'll be back on the road. After instructing the manager to report when I leave, we pose for a photo before I have to sprint for the bathroom. Monkey meat does it every time.

Impressions
March 14, 2005
Bodhgaya, Bihar
● ● ● ● ● ● ● ● ● ●

No matter your first impressions of a country, it's the last ones that linger in your memory. There're so many highs and lows in India that even when rereading my diary, my emotions are scrambled. One day the Indian manner of speaking with their faces uncomfortably close has me ready to leave; the next I'm overcome with gratitude when a stranger selflessly offers me aid.

This was my second journey to India. The first was in 1989, when I rented a jeep and drove the cease-fire line with Pakistan along the Indus River into the northern province of Ladakh. There had been an ugly situation brewing in Kashmir, with fighting breaking out between Muslim separatists and Indian troops. Bus station explosions and random acts of terrorism against civilians eventually became routine. That senseless religious violence had been disturbing enough to make me move from Asia back to California. At that

Elegant Indian women in traditional dress

time, I had no intention of ever returning, and if India hadn't stood between Pakistan and Nepal, I wouldn't be here now.

It takes years to understand the shock of what travelers experience in India, and time is always in the way. Difficult choices of what to see are made after studying guidebooks and talking with fellow wanderers.

"Glen, you really need to hit the beaches of Goa and Kerala."

"What would I do there?"

"Nothing. You just relax and drink beer."

At this stage of my journey, the notion of idling in paradise was appealing, but the 12 days it would take to get there and back might be misused time. Bodhgaya lacked the circus-like hustle of other Indian holy towns, mainly because this mecca for Buddhists is so far out of the way and the tourist season is over. The daily temperature is rising quickly, and devastating monsoon storms are just weeks away. Even the ever-persistent touts are too lazy to annoy the few remaining temple-hopping backpackers.

This is where Buddha is said to have reached enlightenment, and Buddhist countries have built temples and monuments here to honor the sanctified land. Even the sacred Bodhi tree outside the Mahabodhi temple has been grown from four generations of saplings cut from the original. Streams of peaceful pilgrims pay silent homage with meaningful, slow garden walks and offerings of fragrant garlands. With the obnoxious hawkers walled out, sunrise meditations under the Bodhi's canopy are moving experiences that touch the soul.

Although each sacred site holds unique significance, I find it's the people of India who leave the deepest impressions. When asked by the natives why so many foreigners visit their country, I explain, "It's because your peculiar beliefs and ways twist our minds. To free our own thinking, we seek that which is furthest from our own." Ideas that confound us also deepen our thoughts; India is as far from the West as you can get without leaving the planet.

Maintaining a sense of humor is the only way to enjoy Indians. With a rapidly growing middle class, overnight there has been a proliferation of new vehicles on already gridlocked roads. Four million motor-scooters alone appeared this year, with few of the drivers licensed or skilled. Anyone of any age who can afford a scooter is allowed to drive one, carrying however many passengers they can fit. This makes for constant light collisions and numerous near-death experiences.

But Indian men are always around when you need them and often when you don't. If stopped by the side of the road, it never takes long before an inquisitive man approaches, offering assistance. The women are more reserved. Like Arab females, for whatever reason, Indian women are quiet in public. Although much more visible, they hardly acknowledge a foreigner's greeting. Typical of developing nations, India is undoubtedly a man's world. As women toil in fields, jabbering men stand by, smoking cigarettes.

From festivals to palaces, even considering the Taj, my most moving impressions of the country were of the remarkable grace of the enduring Indian women. Whether laboring in agriculture fields or stepping from luxury cars in uptown Delhi, Indian women have a unique style. Draped in brilliantly colored saris, their compelling composure suggests histories of royalty, no matter the reality. In cities and villages, emerging through choking clouds of blackened exhaust fumes, they casually step over cow dung, fluid as fabled princesses. Peeking through transparent veils of silks and chiffons, whatever their caste, they convey mythical elegance.

Giddy with the Gods
March 16, 2005
Chittawan Royale Park, Nepal
● ● ● ● ● ● ● ● ● ● ● ● ● ● ● ● ● ●

News of escalating violence in Nepal would not deter me. Since trekking the Himalayas in 1981, before it became trendy, I'd yearned to return and rekindle my fading memories of these authentically spiritual people. Witnessing firsthand the sincere humility of the people in this sacred landscape had provoked a profound internal awakening, prompting me to question my Western materialism. Over the centuries, many a wandering foreigner has been stunned by the generosity of Nepali mountain tribes. In those days, money had little meaning as long as everyone had food and their particular religion.

From its ancient prayer wheels to manicured thousand-mile trails lined with hand-chiseled boulders, Nepal was far too intense to absorb in one visit. After learning the wonders of Buddhist culture in the guiding hands of intensely loyal mountain sherpa, California had never been the same, and for the last nine months I'd been counting the days. As was my habit, my itinerary remained vague until reaching the border — I didn't even have a Nepal guidebook until swapping for one with an outbound traveler this morning. Yet as long as monsoon storms are trailing, anywhere in Asia can be home.

Crossing from India into Nepal was the usual developing nation congested mess of old, groaning buses and broken-down trucks vying for limited road space. But because foreign motorcyclists are in a class of our own, we're usually bumped to the front of customs lines while the officials scramble to determine what to do with us. Three hours later, after the last of the reviewing and stamping, I'm permitted to enter with a glide into bliss on better roads and without aggressive, suicidal Indian drivers. The first step across the border brings a relieving warmth from the heart and soul of the Nepalese people.

Trapped between giants — much as Mongolia languishes in poverty between Russia and China — Nepal trembles under the twin pressure of Beijing and Delhi. An ethnic blend of Indo-Aryan and Tibeto-Burmese, Hindus occupy the lowlands, while in the mountains, descendants of Tibetan Buddhists subsist as they have for a thousand years. Lack of natural resources or an industrial base makes those living in the land where Buddha was born some of the poorest on earth. Twenty percent of their income comes from tourism that war has now brought to an agonizing standstill.

Halfway to Katmandu lies a cutoff for the Royal Chitwan National Park and a convenient stopover in my nine-hour ride to the capital. After reveling in a day ride of relative calm, I tumble into sleep on a saggy, smelly hostel mattress, with dreams of hunting rhino from an elephant's back and awake to the tantalizing call of the mighty Himalayas. Formed by colliding tectonic plates 60 million years ago, the windswept, icy peaks are still on the rise, six inches a year. That notion alone has me giddy with anticipation of soaring through mountain curves until sundown. The asphalt is wavy but smooth, and at long last empty straightaways provide welcome room for the Blue Beast to stretch its legs. Once I've overtaken convoys of tanker trucks, a steady spiral upwards from the Indian plains leads into the forested foothills of Everest. Boasting some of the best scenery in Asia, Nepal is home to 10 of the 14 highest mountains on earth.

Since it's the end of the dry season, lowland jungle terrain is parched and golden. Seasonally lush, green rice fields are now multi-acre patchwork squares flattened into cracked cakes of mud. A mountain fire burns somewhere unchecked, enshrouding distant hillsides in a brown haze. Busy battling the rebels, the government lacks adequate resources to fight fires, and so they rage on unchecked. Cement-barrel Checkpoint Charlies are manned by friendly young soldiers waving me past. The only agreement that exists between warring factions is that foreigners will not be intentionally targeted. Leaders on both sides understand that without the flow of tourist dollars, their deteriorating economy will collapse further, to the point where everyone starves — which is happening anyway.

Even as they shake down trekkers for money, gun-toting Maoist rebels politely issue receipts so reluctant donors will not be taxed twice by another patrol. While Nepali warriors will butcher each other, they still smile at tourists, and, so far, none have been shot. Yet the suffering inflicted on these people by their own has broken the heart of many a visitor. A kinder people have never existed, and if anyone's ever behaved in the image of God, it's the simple folk who dwell within these mountains.

With tourism quickly collapsing, competing businessmen forlornly accept whatever you'll pay. Just outside Chitwan, three bucks a night rents thatched huts on the riverbank, including breakfast in the morning. The water level is down but so are the mosquitoes, and my ears have almost stopped ringing from the bloodcurdling screams of trumpeting Indian truck horns. Cold-sweat awakenings at midnight with images of converging headlights are replaced by the serenity of the southern Nepali jungle.

For recharging my fading batteries, there are electrical outlets back by the road, right next to an impossibly slow Internet terminal. Chunks of just-caught river fish fried in garlic sauce complement an already glorious sunset, while another 15 bucks books me a predawn elephant ride and half-day trek to spot crocodiles. Guidebooks warn against hiking, as park rhinos have been known to charge — they can trot at 30 miles per hour and sprint even faster. It remains to be seen if Vikings can snap photos while climbing backwards up trees.

"Yeah, I'm to Goin' to Katmandu . . ."
March 20, 2005
Thamel District, Katmandu, Nepal
● ● ● ● ● ● ● ● ● ● ● ● ● ● ● ● ● ● ●

An off-season storm raging through the night swelled the dwindling Rapti River to flood levels, washing out the last road leading to the highway to Katmandu. By morning, the river had risen three feet, swallowing sections of an already decimated dirt track to a shorter route through the mountains. Buses can't enter or exit the village at Sauraha, but bicycles and motorcycles have access to a tilting wooden bridge across a slow-moving stream.

The day is cloudy and threatening, but torrential downpours aren't expected until late afternoon. Under normal conditions, it's a five-hour ride to the capital, but with landslides and missing sections of shoulder, it is best to start early. With the roosters still crowing and an insistent morning sun still trying to burn through the fog, I'm content to be bouncing and sliding through mud and water-filled potholes — at last en route to Katmandu! A disaster for local farmers has left surrounding jungle refreshed and teeming with new life. The predawn tropical air is sweet enough to taste.

Even at gunpoint, traffic never stops in Asia. Sputtering motor-scooters blaze the first after-storm trails as minivans are followed by lumbering commercial trucks and crowded country buses pounding new pathways over the storm-altered terrain. From the days of the Silk Road, a halt in traffic has meant a halt in life. Accustomed to disaster, from wars to tsunamis, and the encroaching jungle land-scape, stricken Asians eventually find ways to reclaim their lives.

The contrasts to India are a relief. It's strange to no longer cringe on rural roadways. Drivers here see me sliding and slow to make way. I'm grateful enough just for a passable road, even without guardrails separating dangerous slips from thousand-foot drops. Although at the mercy of Mother Nature, my journey has returned to an adventure ride rather than a death race. When pausing for cliff-side sardine breaks, no one stops to stare. Instead, while passing, they offer only a gentle wave with shouts of *"Namaste."*

Covering a 30-mile shortcut to the main highway consumes four hours, but, from that junction, riding becomes an eardrum-popping soar into the mountainous mist of the towering Himalayas. Commercial traffic is confined to tightly packed, chugging convoys of diesel trucks, while speeding local motorcyclists haul colorfully dressed Nepali women sitting sidesaddle. Corroded electrical connections have rendered my GPS useless, and there is no English on the road signs. But after concerns that I'll be traveling past dark, the rust-tiled rooftops of Katmandu soon poke upwards into the radiant skyline.

Guidebook tales of maddening congestion and filthy streets fail to materialize, and just after feasting on fresh roast chicken, a guesthouse conveniently appears down the first side street. A transfer point for river expeditions and mountain climbing adventures, enterprising Thamel District merchants cater to homesick Westerners with goodies from brightly lit mini-markets to upscale restaurants. This whole section of town is a comfortable blend of history and decadent earthly pleasures. Yet the most welcome site for a road-beaten biker was a bustling alleyway lined with pretty Nepali girls under signs advertising Trekkers Massage.

Thoughts on the Road
March 22, 2005
Katmandu, Nepal
● ● ● ● ● ● ● ● ● ● ●

Although it's only been nine months and 24,000 miles, the intensity of this experience continues to distort time. If it wasn't for dating these journals, I might not know the year or even remember much of the past decade. If you've ever wondered how the world would appear to visiting aliens, take a ride around the planet — you'll feel like one. Disconnected from daily routine, a stark reality jolts you into an awareness you don't hear of in the Western media. Life remains a mystery, but you can discover much about your own life

Nepali girl on the route from Katmandu to Tibetan border

once you step outside the party and look back through a very different window. This is as close as I've come to walking in another man's shoes.

Wandering the dampened backstreets of Katmandu is a walk back into time. Ancient Buddhist temples and red brick stupas in the shadows of Hindu shrines represent ancient beliefs and a constant celebration of life. The roots of these religions reach back long before Jesus. The dedicated spirituality of the mountains that initially attracts travelers, whatever their faith, is as potent as ever. Even the corrosive influence of tourism seems to have no effect on the hearts of the natives. Despite the recent temptations of Western materialism, they remain as humble and tolerant as I recall them being 25 years ago.

Travelers in Nepal are unique. From the thrill-seeking mountain-climbers to simple trekkers to those out taming wild rivers, few wander about without purpose. Environmentally conscious explorers concerned over Nepal's future show a sincere respect for its natural beauty and conduct themselves as world citizens. The penny-pinching dope-smoking parasites prefer India.

The rain that's fallen every day since I arrived has given me a great excuse to do nothing but eat and relax. The stress of thousands of miles on difficult roads now unravels in the pure pleasure of hanging out with curious young men on street corners and weight-training in a primitive gym. Locals want to know how it was possible for me to just pack up and leave California. So far, that's a hard question to answer because what happens after this journey will determine its success or failure.

Reshuffling the deck with life half over has been as risky as it has been rewarding. But what happens at journey's end? Is this the beginning of the end of an otherwise satisfying life? What lies ahead — the fruits of metamorphosis or the seeds of decay?

Through the miracle of technology, thousands from around the world have logged onto the Internet and followed my journey in real time. Reading my biweekly journals, with a little imagination, readers can sense the uninsulated glory of a tumultuous world as discovered by a wandering biker. As word spreads and my readership grows, some folks check in just to see if I am still alive, while critics wait for disaster so they can say I-told-you-so. Although my goal is to live free of safety nets, that's never entirely possible. Western passport holders are only 20-hour plane rides from the comforts of home, those living here are the ones really sinking or swimming . . .

As long as ATMs spew currency, in most countries I can find clean sheets and a shower accompanied by tolerable food. The same can't be said for the half of the world living on a dollar a day. It's only by the grace of someone's God go those more fortunate. Travelers eventually learn how to cope with witnessing the misery of grinding poverty, yet it's still awkward when meeting desperate people concealing their misfortune behind a pleasant demeanor. One can feel rather foolish smiling back and asking, "How's it going today?"

Tibet, So Near and Yet . . .
March 28, 2005
Kodari, Nepal
● ● ● ● ● ● ●˙●

Western-style food, relative cleanliness and bargains at every street corner make the Thamel District of Katmandu a convenient place to be stranded. Twenty bucks a day buys three Western meals and a clean-by-Asian-standards hotel room with satellite TV that even receives American sitcoms — making it easy for me to remember what I don't miss. Reports of trivial nonsense on the national news provides another eye-rolling cure for temporary homesickness.

Dreading the next airfreight scenario, my dream of crossing overland to Thailand is barely a false hope. A ride through Tibet and down into China for access to Southeast Asia via Laos would be blazing a trail world riders have only fantasized about. But there're reasons why such objectives are out of reach. Governments.

China is growing more lax about tourism, but they're still picky about who visits Tibet. All tours involving lands under their rule are processed through the government-owned China Travel Service (CTS). Most international journalists are forbidden to tour Tibet for fear they will expose what's happening to the inhabitants. Unless travelers are willing to pay the exorbitant salaries of military escorts, entering with private vehicles is illegal. Even short stays cost thousands. Yet in a land and bureaucracy as vast as China's, the left hand is often unaware of the right. Scattered reports from motorcycling websites mention lone motorcyclists appearing at borders and fast-talking their way in. Getting out can be another story.

In any case, entering requires a visa, and to obtain one in Nepal, travelers must go through local agents. Even after a week of telephone haggling with officials in Tibet's capital, Lhasa, the best-connected guides can only promise a five-day road trip packed in a minivan with a return flight back in 10.

A river-rafting company advertising a tropical base-camp of canvas tents on the banks of the Bhote Kosi River near the Tibetan border was my next best option. A four-hour sprint from Katmandu, the Last Resort is only accessible from the road by crossing a massive boulder-sprinkled gorge on a swaying aluminum footbridge suspended over foaming river waters. Five hundred feet from one end to the other and the same distance looking down from the center makes me dizzy enough to wonder about walking across — let alone diving off it headfirst attached only by a reinforced elastic strap. Designed by Swiss engineers, this dual-purpose bridge has become the world's second highest bungee jump. Posters showing the deluxe campsites nestled in seductive jungle surroundings closed the deal.

As of today, Maoist rebels have still not killed a tourist, and they've officially agreed to halt further blockades until university students have finished exams. But a call to the American embassy RSO is unsettling. Because of continued U.S. support of the embattled king, as of last week, rural insurgents have ordered the arrest of any American. Several have been detained and required to make war-tax payments while being lectured on the ills of Uncle Sam's foreign policy. So far, they have been scared but not harmed. With the midday sun finally burning away enough of the clouds to dry the muddy roads, I am off on a 60-mile ride along the Arniko Highway to the Tibetan border.

When the asphalt ends, sporadic mountain squalls lasting just long enough to settle the dust make half-buried river rocks more slippery than desirable for worn street rubber. The Blue Beast's spinning tires kick up enough golf ball–sized stones to make hardened riding boots essential. The long climb up a narrow, bumpy track requires steady standing on the pegs and rest stops every half hour. Set against gaping mountain ravines, this is one of the best dirt rides since Siberia.

Stopping in small mountain towns for directions, I realize the only English phrase spoken is "20 kilometers." Whatever destination I ask about, villagers claim it's 20 kilometers away. Just before sunset, through a misty drizzle, the last Nepali army outpost before Chinese customs comes into view. My guidebook's assertions that it was possible to proceed past the outpost to the bridge dividing countries proved incorrect. After a token photo, armed Chinese soldiers point to the road, insisting I immediately turn around. The path back down, sliding over wet rocks at sunset, proves to be tedious work. But the Blue Beast holds its ground, and just as pale, ghostly moonbeams reveal the skeletal silhouette of the suspension bridge, a teenage mountain porter appears to assist the lost Americano.

Known as a rebel stronghold, the entire region is empty of travelers, and the Last Resort has been without guests for weeks. That's a disaster for hapless staff working for tips. Beneath surrounding mountains terraced in neat agricultural rows lies the finest river rafting and waterfall-rapelling in Asia. It's eerie being alone in such a delicious paradise, but my sweet-natured hosts promise to make my stay worthwhile. Dozing while the river roars with baritone croaking bullfrogs and awaking to honking geese makes it hard to want to be anywhere else. Quiet nights at the Last Resort became the ultimate blend of modern and rustic as I tap out journals by lantern light. There are no phone lines or Internet, and power comes from solar panels. But after yesterday morning's accidental gulp of untreated water, the most critical convenience is a sit-down commode.

Oarin' Around Asia
March 30, 2005
Bhote Kosi River, Nepal
● ● ● ● ● ● ● ● ● ● ● ● ●

Since my one and only previous whitewater-rafting excursion was spent upside-down, it's hard to claim I have experience. As luck would have it, just as I'm preparing to pack for a return to Katmandu, a tourist minibus rolls in, hauling a rambunctious crew of eager young Europeans heading for a tumble down the gushing Bhote Kosi. A glance down at the churning river, and my pleading look made my question obvious. And yes, they had room for one more. Budget constraints also mean a choice has to be made. It's an easy decision — 30 bucks will either buy me a 45-second bungee jump or a whole day slicing through boiling rapids on one of the steepest rivers in Asia.

Ten years ago, while riding across Idaho, out of curiosity, Brad and I wound up following signs pointing to Hell's Canyon on the Snake River. Seeing a 20-person expedition loading supplies and equipment, we asked if we could tag along. "Sorry guys — not a chance, these people booked this trip months ago and there is no room."

Pointing to two empty inflatable kayaks tied behind the rubber rafts, Brad asked "What about those?"

A skeptical boat-master replied, "Do you know anything about kayaking?"

"Hell, I'm Canadian. Kayak is my middle name. I've been kayaking my whole life."

"Well if you're sure you can handle them, we can have your bikes trucked downstream to be picked up at the final landing. But the river is at record level, and there have been five drownings this month. Tomorrow will be mostly class three and four rapids."

Despite Brad's confidence, neither of us was sure which end of the kayak was which, and as we began rotating underwater at the first ripples in the swift-moving current, everyone was soon aware that we were cherry. Though the bulk of our time was spent submerged, our first rafting experience was still the best three days we've ever spent together.

The Lonely Planet guidebook does have a small write-up about rafting in Nepal. Of all the rivers, this was rated among the best, and Ultimate Adventures was listed in the top-five rafting companies. Safety is critical, so we spend an hour before departure with cautious guides teaching us how to rescue each other and ourselves. Commands were next. "Right-side forward" meant those on the right of the raft dug in their paddles to change directions. "Right-side back" meant paddle backwards, and so forth. "Jump right" meant those on the left dove to the right to keep the raft from hanging up on submerged boulders. "Get down" was the order to drop to our knees in the center of the boat because capsizing was likely.

Rapids are graded on a universal scale of one to six, where one indicates easy-moving water with few obstacles and six means life-threatening rapids and nearly impossible rafting. Fours require significant experience, and fives are white-knuckled leaps beyond reasonable risk. For the first hour, everyone confused right from left, and despite a patient boat-master shouting sharp commands, we spun backwards through most of the twos and threes. But shortly before lunch break, we'd developed a coordinated cadence that roughly corresponded with hollered directives. We were gaining our river legs.

The class four rapids required boat landings and scouting ahead, climbing over giant boulders to look for routes through the exploding current. Shooting the rapids while feverishly digging deep with our paddles called for teamwork. Lulls in the action were filled with sporadic water fights and a strategic dunking.

At the end of the day, grins sunburned on our faces, the Danes and the Canadians, along with our faithful, smirking Nepali guides, all bussed down to Katmandu while I hitched a ride back to the Last Resort for one last night of heaven. It's sad to realize that time is dwindling in Nepal. Brad arrives in Bangkok in two weeks, and 11 days later, we will be saying goodbye at the Laotian border, as he'll return to the U.S. while I drift deeper into Southeast Asia.

It's the People You Meet
April 5, 2005
Katmandu, Nepal
● ● ● ● ● ● ● ● ● ● ●

My first encounter with real adventurers was beneath flickering neon on the dark, steamy backstreets of Hong Kong. In 1981, China had only been open to the West for a year, and the line of visitors to be first at anything was growing. Striding through swarming crowds of five-foot-tall Chinese were a dozen broad-shouldered mid-30s American athletes sporting bright yellow T-shirts with purple lettering on the back — Upper Yangtze River Expedition. With bulging biceps tearing at their sleeves and the disproportionately enlarged lat muscles of oarsmen, they were out to define what made them men.

As a competitive martial artist, I was there to match skills with local kung-fu fighters, but while witnessing such audacious legends in the making, I could only stare and dream. Mere mortals were left to envy and fantasize about slicing through crashing rapids of uncharted mountain gorges. Images of those adventurers never vanished.

Similar legends appear in Nepal. In the polished wooden lobby of the Katmandu Guesthouse, an American team of stouthearted mountaineers carefully stow climbing gear into idling minibuses for transportation to an airfield. Soon, a twin-engine Sea Otter will drop them halfway into the Himalayas for an ascent of Mount Everest. Vibrant spirits permeate cold morning air as they methodically test and repack equipment that their lives will depend on. Each man knows his job, and they silently mingle only with each other in somber understanding of the task ahead. It's almost too late in the season for decent visibility without a cloudy mist, but they are taking the shot anyway; rearranging their lives for a future opportunity is unlikely. It's mind-boggling to consider that, if they're lucky, in a few weeks they'll be fighting blizzards at the lung-searing summit of a 29,000-foot peak.

And there is no forgetting the 20-year-old Dutch girl who had been backpacking solo across southern India when it struck her that two-wheels was more challenging. Nine riding lessons later, she was en route to Katmandu on her first motorcycle — alone. The last I saw of her, in a Thamel District backstreet hostel, she was double-checking her saddlebags, heading for Tibet.

World motorcycle travel is nothing new. Swilling down Indian beers in a Chitwan Park café, an 82-year-old Scotsman recounted his adventure of 1956, riding from Sri Lanka to London on a German-built 49cc one-half horsepower scooter — cruising at a thumping 22 miles per hour. His mesmerizing tale prompted obvious questions: "Tell me sir, do you ever miss the two-wheeled thrill?"

"Aye, that I do, I do. That's why I've rode 'ere now on me bicycle."

Wherever you travel in Nepal, when you're not basking in local hospitality, you're meeting people coming or going somewhere with purpose in their lives. Off to India, back from Africa or beginning a multiweek high-altitude trek into the Himalayas. Other Westerners here are aid workers — soldiers on missions of peace battling ignorance with olive branches of care and personal sacrifice. From UN personnel here to negotiate ceasefires to Red Cross workers caring for war victims, the world community loves Nepal.

In the meantime, civil conflict flares in the countryside with strikes, blockades and blood revenge. The toll on civilians is brutal as the death rate soars with random shootings and planned bombings. The result is worse than economic deterioration; it's about starvation and the demise of human dignity. As Maoist rebels continue to punish nonsupporters, their moral high-ground erodes. When the military can't capture rebels, they shoot civilians and claim them as the enemy. Extremism grows, and children robbed of their innocence grow up amidst the mindless savagery of war.

Soon I'll be swallowed in Bangkok, leaving behind memories pleasant and troubling. The disturbing intensity of Nepal makes it hard to move on to other countries, as none can match the sincerity of the human experience here. Either stumbling through cities or wandering the countryside, the endearing Nepali people willingly give travelers their aching hearts and souls.

Yesterday morning, in the chaotic cargo department at Katmandu airport, the Blue Beast was crated and X-rayed, and, as promised, had arrived safely in Bangkok last night. Crossing international borders is always a hassle, but after a few dozen, shuffling paperwork has become routine, and I'm resigned to the realities. Continuing on the plan-of-no-plan, my general direction will be north into Laos and back down through Cambodia into Southern Thailand. Monsoon season is approaching, so the main concern is to stay ahead of squalls on chewed-up dirt roads. It's time to fly east.

Memories flicker into flames aboard a modern aircraft as petite Thai stewardesses in shiny silk gowns clasp their palms together in traditional greetings of respect. Except for ordering meals in Thai restaurants, I haven't spoken this language in 15 years. But after hearing familiar words, mispronounced phrases tumble out from buried files in the back of my mind. Trivial jabbering fills an otherwise boring flight as the ever-polite Thais respond to my kindergarten level speech with, *"Poot Thai gheng!"* (You speak good Thai!)

The robotic voice of our former military pilot announces it's a seething 95 degrees on the sultry boulevards of downtown Bangkok. Seriously congested, with the air polluted by clouds of noxious black fumes, face masks have become standard attire.

Problems in Nepal and recent terror bombings in Southern Thailand have intensified security to unprecedented levels. All bags and purses are triple X-rayed and passengers pat-searched a dozen times before boarding. Aware of the reasons why, no one complains. Except for Australia, every country left on my itinerary is in some type of violent turmoil. Worse yet — terrorism now seems like an acceptable risk.

Nine weeks late, Brad arrives tomorrow. Our dream of riding together for a month out of every three has been derailed by his erratic company schedules and deadlines. He's as addicted to business as I am to adventure. After 11 days, he'll be sucked back into the arena of corporate America, dodging and dueling the sharks seeking the upper hand. I haven't abandoned my quest to lure him from a suffocating workload. I've got a week and a half to change his mind.

SOUTHEAST ASIA

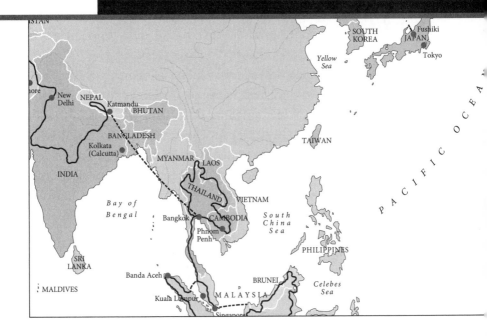

Riding North
April 9, 2005
On the Road in Northern Thailand
● ● ● ● ● ● ● ● ● ● ● ● ● ● ● ● ● ● ● ●

Like stepping into a sauna of steamy tropical flavors, the first thing you sense when the aircraft door unseals is an overpowering gulp of fragrant, waterlogged air. Throughout the city, massive air conditioners pump around the clock, sucking out tons of moisture while changing the atmospheres of contemporary office buildings and multilevel shopping malls. When you return outside, trying to inhale is like trying to breathe underwater.

Welcome to Bangkok, capital of Thailand — the City of Angels in the Land of a Thousand Smiles. Silently communicating using practiced facial gestures, depending on preceding events, a smile can mean hello, goodbye, go to hell or let's make love. Following ancient traditions of saving face, Thais would rather yield than risk conflict and humiliation. In the West, traffic mishaps often end in road rage, or at least venting with jabbing middle fingers. Here, negative energy is redirected and confrontation is avoided — also fundamental to Asian martial arts.

Thousands of makeshift alleyway food stalls conveniently appear wherever humans congregate. From outside government offices to busy street corners, sweet-smelling fresh fruit stands and sizzling mini-barbecues tease the senses for closer inspections. No need to pack a lunch when going to work. At factory entrances, lines of vendors peddle the same food listed on menus of expensive Thai restaurants and dish out delightful bargain meals on rickety curbside tables from improvised kitchens.

Piercing scents of fresh-cut vegetables and sinus-clearing spices permeate thick, humid air, while skilled street chefs deftly combine ingredients to produce the flaming flavors soon to explode inside your mouth. Sizzling woks with boiling meats and stir-fried noodles send up clouds of scorching vapors strong enough to burn your eyes. None sit idle, and there is always a line of drooling patrons.

Bangkok, the capital of Siam, is also a world capital for foreign intrigue and international espionage. From black market weapons brokers to hedonistic pleasure palaces, you can purchase either a shoulder-fired rocket or sexual favors from well-trained, perfectly formed women or men of any age. Hidden down smog-choked alleyways, discreet signs promise to satisfy every need and to massage whatever body parts ache for relief. Yet, spirituality dominates this culture with ancient beliefs and sacred rites. Reclining Buddha statues and elaborate temples corral the faithful in a spectacular display of religious conviction.

But Bangkok is a brutally overcrowded city and a biker's frightmare of clogged traffic arteries and stifling heat. Yesterday afternoon, the Blue Beast was serviced and given fresh tires, so by the time Brad arrived we were chomping at the grips to ride north into the cooler, less-populated tribal highlands. After four hours of confusing attempts to escape the city, the elongated dual-lane highway empties, and we twist our throttles for a blast into the haze of a fiery sunset.

Bangkok bustle gives way to meandering country roads and smiling rice paddy workers strolling home from their labor. Herds of hulking water buffalo lounge roadside, ominous reminders to remain alert. Speeding motorcyclists would have better luck colliding with brick walls.

The weeklong holiday of *Song Khran* marks the beginning of the Thai new year with festivals of water wars and painted faces. To wash away sins, mini-trucks packed with giggling teens scoop buckets of water from 50-gallon drums to fling at one another and anyone who gets in the way. With cameras zipped inside our jackets, we white-line between cars, ducking sprays and the gleeful shouts of pearly toothed, laughing children.

Once again, time is our biggest concern. In nine days, Brad reluctantly returns to corporate America, so we'll milk the most from every moment.

Northern Thailand
April 18, 2005
Doi Ang Kong, Thailand
● ● ● ● ● ● ● ● ● ● ● ● ●

When I recall the better moments in life, times when I've thought, "Today can't get any better than this," I realize that they've all been spent rolling somewhere on two wheels. But the next best thing to traveling the world is spending quality time with my brother. Showing Brad a real taste of the country and culture would take months, so we settle for covering as much ground as possible, off-road. The section of highway we had been seeking finally appears outside the last small town — the end of pavement. Ahead are long days of riding ridgelines and stopping wherever we like to overnight in jungle villages.

A thick, overcast sky protects us from a blazing tropical sun as we spiral upwards, spinning our tires over dizzying mountain dirt tracks while kicking up layers of powdery orange clay. Hugging the Burmese border as close as we dare, we're careful not to drift too far. Refugee tribesmen have directed us to trails not shown on maps, but the black triangle on my GPS indicates we're nearing the forbidden line. With the chaos of ethnic feuding in the heart of opium country, it's unlikely either army patrols or drug warlord mercenaries would accept our explanations for stumbling over the border.

Boiled-noodle breaks and rest stops with inquisitive natives prove as rewarding as they were when I visited 20 years ago. Villagers are shy at first, but after breaking the ice practicing my slowly returning Thai phrases, talkative elders approach us to investigate. Soon we're surrounded by quacking youngsters eager to talk and pose for pictures. Brad is captivated by the sincerity and simplicity of strangers offering such friendship. This is just a hint of what's ahead, but already the stress lines on his face are fading.

And the fascination is constant. The border regions of Thailand are safe havens for persecuted victims fleeing neighboring massacres and inter-tribal violence. In Doi Ang Kong, we visited a government-sponsored agricultural project where refugee hill-tribe people are taught how to grow plants other than opium poppies. At nearly 6,000 feet, experimental fruit orchards mature alongside bonsai gardens and hydroponic greenhouses. The climate here is typical of a tribal natural habitat, and the program directors are hopeful their current students will someday return to teach others.

Dampness from early morning fog settles the sticky orange dust thrown from grinding tires, and the air is cool enough to require we zip up our nylon riding suits. A parched jungle lies further north as our heads fill with growing scents of pungent green. As we corkscrew up and down the steepest roads in Asia, the foliage alters from broad-leafed banana trees to towering pines. It's the end of the dry season, and soon nourishing monsoon rains will return the land to the vibrancy of pulsating tropical cycles.

The only bike available to rent in Bangkok was a 1,300cc heavyweight street Honda, but Brad manages to wrestle it over yawning ruts and washed-out ravines. By the end of the day we've seen only two trucks, packed with natives chugging their way south. Outside the tribal villages, the jungle belongs to us and billions of roaring insects. Exhausted by nightfall, directly after a dinner of chicken and rice, we plunge into comatose sleep until crowing roosters inspecting our bikes rouse us with a start.

There're only three more days before our parting in Chiang Mai. I tempt him with dreams of quiet nights in Laotian villages slurping on fresh diced mango and sweet sticky rice. The first of his corporate meetings are scheduled within hours of landing in Los Angeles, while my life here continues to be about flipping coins to decide the next alluring destination. Soon enough, summer rains and meandering side roads will once again guide me softly past the equator, into another hemisphere of unfamiliar pleasures.

Brad
April 21, 2005
Chiang Mai, Thailand
● ● ● ● ● ● ● ● ● ● ● ●

Planning our limited time down to the minute, Brad and I are meeting our goals and hitting our intended targets like well-behaved, seasoned adventure travelers. Seven days of jungle trails, remote villages and Tribal peoples have hardly been sufficient, but we're accomplishing more than we initially thought possible. Despite our gentle rush, we're enjoying a decent balance of twisting tarmac and up-on-the-pegs dirt tracking with balmy afternoons and chilly mountain evenings. Built by the U.S. Army Corp of Engineers, the Friendship Highway loops around Northern Thailand's jungle peaks with racetrack-quality banked curves carving through mind-blowing forested terrain. Riding on- or off-road anywhere in this rural region is motorcycle bliss — because the metropolitan areas also have their allure.

Karen tribal woman hitching a motorcycle ride in Northern Thailand

After roaming Southeast Asia in the '80s, I returned to California with stories of the best motorcycling roads on earth and an undefeatable style of kickboxing that was far superior to anything seen in the West. Skeptical road dogs and martial arts buddies rolled their eyes at my wild tales of drifting across Southeast Asia encountering lethal Muay Thai boxers. Theses days, Muay Thai dominates the televised no-holds-barred fighting events and a proliferation of motorcycle rental shops in Chaing Mai cater to adventure riders. We're using the same guidebook I bought 18 years ago to select and explore old routes. Most of the dirt is now paved, but the steep hairpins and scenic landscape remain unchanged.

Every day, new tribal villagers welcome us in unfamiliar tongues as the men from Mars in space-age plastic clothing, while inquisitive youngsters surround us. Graceful, long-necked women eye us with suspicion, and, no matter our efforts, can't be coaxed into a ride. Each year, Kayan tribal women add additional solid-brass collar rings below their jawbones in an effort to create a longer neck. But in reality, the metal tubes merely push their shoulders down, creating a visual effect. Having sung the praises of Asia for years, it's a dream fulfilled to share these scenes with Brad. Northern Thailand provides the ultimate contrast in a provocative cultural buffet with spicy aftertastes that lasts a lifetime. Crossing worlds plants the deepest seeds.

Brad flies home from Bangkok in two days, and this morning I reluctantly sent him riding south to the airport alone. The new highway is a straight shot with signs marked in English, but there is always the chance of a mishap. Having counted the minutes until he arrived, now, after less than two weeks, he's moving from dirt-floor noodle stands to the helm of his empire as the world's biggest franchisee of Gold's Gyms. I urge him to stay: "Damn the business Bro, let's ride." But in the tug-of-war between running off into wanderland and corporate responsibilities, I lose.

Art
May 1, 2005
Mae Sai, Thailand
● ● ● ● ● ● ● ● ● ● ●

When I rode through Southeast Asia in the '80s, there was never any fanfare over international motorcycle travel. A few anxious friends waited patiently at home for letters that often got lost in cluttered mail rooms or primitive postal systems. There was no Internet for uploading daily journals, checking weather reports or managing affairs at home. When I was able to find a machine, I faxed intended routes to a friend in California. If he didn't hear from me within a few months, he would know approximately where I'd disappeared. Back then GPS was restricted to military use, yet I still eventually managed to find the next unmarked turnoff or realize when I had passed it altogether.

At that time, big-bore bikes were illegal in Thailand, so I shipped a 1985 Yamaha V-Max from California to Penang, Malaysia, to sneak across the border along a notorious smuggling route. Off I rode, using gas station maps written in unfamiliar languages while gawking at road signs trying to memorize their mystifying symbols. A purple metal-flake helmet kept most of the wicked monsoon rains at bay, and a small set of throw-over nylon saddlebags held an extra set of dry clothes and canned food. Spare parts were unavailable.

Fast forward into the cyber-age, where long-riders can remain in constant contact with each other — ahead or behind, with hardly a week passing without an exchange of message of some kind. Using Internet connections in major cities, we can update each other on border problems, road conditions and civil disturbances. Yet even with the high-tech advantages, there're still enough unknowns to keep the journey challenging. Almost every developing nation is in turmoil and subject to sudden violence from rebels or governments. Bridges and roads still wash out, while earthquakes, typhoons or equipment failures always arrive when least expected. Still, alien cultures and fascinating traditions continue to dazzle even the most experienced wanderer.

For the last several weeks, I had been exchanging email, with a Canadian rider touring Viet Nam and heading for Thailand via Laos. Art Kernaghan began writing to me after reading my website and discovering we were traveling the same region. Gradually, we modified our routes to rendezvous near the Thai border. He told me he was riding an aging Belarus-built Minsk, but other than envisioning just another off-brand motorbike, I couldn't picture it.

Several days past our last communication, while cutting through an arcade parking lot, a long-haired man with a Canadian accent steps in front of my bike. "Glen Heggstad! Striking Viking! It's me — Art Kernaghan!" We spent the next few hours like old friends, ranting about recent routes and adventures.

I tried hard not laugh when I saw the $150 clanker he'd been riding from Saigon. Guided by the sympathetic hands of fate, this young man from Toronto had somehow passed through the twisting mountains of Laos into the Land of Smiles. Grinning with pride, he stood chest-out, displaying his smoking two-stroke 12 horsepower 125cc sputtering weed-whacker on two wheels. Motorcyclists call these wheezing rattletraps Rat Bikes.

On one side of the bike, village-made steel racks supported a plastic beer crate packed with tools and spare parts, while on the other, a backpack was held firm with overstretched bungee cords. Oil seeped from gaskets, a red taillight lens was taped on and a dimly lit headlight only functioned some of the time. He explained that most of the flickering electronics on the bike had been "sorted out" and that the dubiously thin cables should hold. In a grimy Vietnamese bike shop, one American dollar bought a new clutch, a few more to straighten bent forks and purchase two locally manufactured tires that might last if he kept the speed down.

Now that Art is an official adventure traveler, he's also better informed about wolves in sheeps' clothing. Southeast Asian tourist areas are populated by varieties of destitute expatriates just waiting for the inexperienced to arrive from the West. Most had originally been seduced by the easygoing lifestyle and ready access to cheap sex with young women. After discovering that their new girlfriends were still married to their pimps, they often turned to alcohol and drank themselves into early graves. Constantly on the lookout for new hustles, these loser parasites sucker newcomers into buying failing bars, investing in bogus building projects or promise to save people money by showing them around. Most are skillful enough to secure temporary loans from the trusting, never to be repaid.

Shortly after departing Ho Chi Minh City, Art at least had the presence of mind to dump his new best friend expat tour guide before being soaked too much. Depressed and alone, he'd throw up his arms in defeat. And until stopping to speak with other Western travelers, he'd been headed back to Viet Nam to fly home. But roving Australian strangers had provided much-needed inspiration. "Never give up mate — keep riding. You don't need anyone but yourself."

Art's destination is south and mine north, but we're having so much fun exploring the spices of Thai nightlife, we opt to zigzag together for a while. Side by side, we growl and sputter amid blue plumes of *wing-ding-ding-ding* through bustling city streets at a rampaging 20 miles per hour.

Last night, a midnight monsoon shower had pinned us down in a roadside noodle stand, recounting our failed attempts to coax two lean-bodied Burmese girls into all-night massage lessons. Using sign language and pigeon Thai, we made decent headway until making the mistake of mentioning that we were only passing through, a flashing red light to security-seeking local babes. Within moments, our sure-things in tight jeans and bulging blouses faded into tasty kisses goodbye. Vagabonds on the prowl bite the dust. For the last few days we've been the Asian 21st-century version of *Easy Rider* and *Route 66*, but tomorrow Art rides the dirt toward Burma while I find the windiest road to Laos.

The fact that he made it this far is astounding; that he's continuing, oblivious to the potential mishaps is admirable. To Art Kernaghan, the glass is always half full. Defying the laws of physics, he bobs and weaves across Thailand with inspired determination and blind faith. He can make it because he believes he can.

Down the Mae Khong
May 7, 2005
Huay Xai, Laos
• • • • • • • • •

The only way I could leave the comforting fantasy that is Thailand was by vowing to return later via Cambodia on my way to Malaysia. For the last month, Thailand has been the proverbial port in the storm lone travelers crave — the communication in a familiar tongue, the endless smorgasbord of exotic cuisine and the swapping of smiles with a steady stream of accommodating women. World famous traditional Thai massage was even available on side street corners in every small town. For two bucks an hour, shriveled women with steel sinew fingers will poke and press my aching back muscles back into their original shape. And no matter their mood, everyone smiles.

The more you reach out to Thais, the warmer their return

embrace. Life is about *sanuk* — having fun — and enjoying the moment is ingrained in the national conscience. A stress-free pace of life and the wide availability of basic pleasures often seduces wanderers to linger. Everywhere sex is for sale. But eventually, the lure of the open road overrides my hedonistic lollygagging.

The docile pace of Thailand is still the fast lane when compared to Laos, where life reverts to a passive shuffle backwards. Clearing Thai customs involved 20 minutes of stamping and joking followed by a short ferryboat ride across the Mae Khong River. On the other side, the lone Lao customs official had left for lunch. The old man left sweeping the floor advised me to return tomorrow for clearance. The immigration office was a few miles into town, down a nondescript alleyway. A talkative middle-aged woman dressed in frayed military fatigues issued a visa-on-arrival then forgot to stamp my passport.

From the riverside town of Huay Xai, there're two ways to reach the interior: via a chewed-up mountainous adobe track or on a slow, chugging riverboat. Experienced motorcyclists from Thailand had already warned me not to attempt the steep, rutted road after it rained — soggy, softened clay becomes like ice during storms. No matter his skill or equipment, every rider loses in mud. Even in dry weather, it takes eight hours to ride the 150-mile stretch. Anxious for either a waterway adventure or an up-on-the-pegs thrill ride, the steady all-night rain showers made the decision easy for me. Anyway, any trip to Asia is incomplete without a river cruise.

Of the two government-contracted boats designated to haul tourists and supplies downstream, the first was full. The second, beached on the bank, had to sail anyway to pick up passengers at the other end. But being the only customer for the second boat, the skipper's wife insisted I pay for the unoccupied seats. After an hour of haggling and bluffing, we settled on a triple ticket fee based on weight.

When I was ready to roll aboard across a flexing wooden plank, three lounging dockworkers offered to help lift the Beast over a foot-high step-rail — for 12 dollars each. For the two-minute job, I countered with a day's wages apiece. Sticking with their screw-the-foreigner attitude, they declined and walked away. But seeing my predicament, four muscular young European backpackers from the first boat lent a hand. Once the motorcycle was securely settled, we sailed downriver for Pak Beng, the nearest landing with a link to a passable road.

After accumulating moisture further north, the churning, muddy Mae Khong flows down from the skyscraping Himalayas in a billion-gallon gush of whatever trickles off those massive granite shoulders. At the end of dry season, the water level is so low, expert captains and alert crews must carefully navigate the shallow sandbars. Alone we drift, propelled by a monotonous, moaning diesel, nudging us slightly faster than the current.

The river ride is more like a two-day float to the final stop at Luang Prabang, but I'll disembark after reaching the nearest strip of all-weather road. Six hours should be enough of sitting still and letting someone else steer. The hypnotic rocking and rolling with river swells past thatched roof villages offers an opportunity to relax. Jutting jungle peaks are concealed behind swirling morning mist enveloping the green towers above. With carefree laughter, small brown children splash naked in the shallows with little notice of the passing aliens. To feed their villages, scrawny, old, shirtless fishermen cast hand-strung nets from splintering wooden canoes, dragging in flopping catches of tiny silver fishes. Except for the variation in invading armies, little has changed for Laotians in the last thousand years.

With Laos still in the grip of a communist dictatorship, we must stop every three hours for police checks. A scowling clipboard-wielding official breaks into a smile when I invite him to sit on my bike for a photo. Old war wounds and political dischord can still color the moment, but desperately needed tourist dollars offer welcome relief for a stifled economy.

Downshifting into the bleakness of rural poverty means another rollercoaster ride concerning my nutrition and health. Tasty meals with protein are difficult to find even when you agree to pay more for extra chicken. My growling stomach is pacified with bags of flavorless cookies and stale potato chips chased by lukewarm bottled water. But as long as there are eggs in the morning, the day begins right. Further inland, I should find vendors peddling grilled river fish and fresh diced mango with sticky rice in coconut milk.

Off-loading the bike in Pak Beng is a replay of the same hassle again. Ridiculous demands for money from natives before an international crew comes to the rescue, as six of us wrangle the Beast onto a rocky beach with a steep, soft sand climb to the road above. Disappointed locals stand idle as I spin my tires, sending up rooster tails of fine sand, while panting backpackers push from behind. At last, I'm on solid, level ground!

Gliding on a ribbon of graying asphalt into the vibrant Lao countryside is a plunge into moto-ecstasy. As monsoon gloom turns into sheets of flooding rain, villagers invite me into their huts for a taste of rice whiskey and leafy aromatic greens I thought only cows would eat. Within minutes, inquisitive schoolchildren crowd inside carrying tattered English books, requesting proper pronunciations. Outside the crudely built shelter, darkened skies erupt with a crackling thunder deafening enough to shake the uneven brick walls and set the porch dogs howling. Content to find what I had been seeking, we settle onto bamboo mats for an evening of swapping languages and life lessons.

Soldiers
May 13, 2005
Vang Vieng, Laos
● ● ● ● ● ● ● ● ● ●

Monsoon season in the tropics means that whether it is raining or not, a suffocating humidity constantly soaks your skin. For a motorcyclist, the only thing to do is to keep moving. Spinning up and over jungle mountain passes, villages of bamboo huts and flooded rice paddies color the landscape. Roving broad-horned water buffalo and frantically waving, giggling black-haired children set the pace of the day. As I putter by, puzzled toothless elders can only gape in wonder.

Jungle temperatures, sizzling hot climbing one side of the empty mountain summits, become smothering black fists of storm clouds on the other. Like the ticking hands of a wind-up clock, raindrops plunking on my helmet warn me seconds before torrential downpours send me fleeing for cover. With storms thundering in so quickly, there is seldom time for rain suits, but there is usually shelter somewhere nearby. In the midst of the pummeling liquid onslaught, people are temporarily stranded in whatever dry spot they can sprint to. In this afternoon's downpour, a wooden shed under an overhanging corroded tin roof affords sufficient relief for the front end of the Beast and me if I stay plastered against the sides.

Barefoot teenagers in ragged olive shorts indicate this is a military outpost, while a pudgy female commander wags her finger at my camera. No photos. Propped in the corner as if holding up the rough, sawn hardwood wall, the only symbol of authority is a rusted old carbine. Both weary and wary of foreigners, Lao people lack the giddy warmth of Thais. After suffering at the hands of various intruding foreigners, older natives recall only fear and domination.

For a hundred years, from the colonizing French to the brutalizing Japanese, to the persistent French again, tribes of forlorn peasants watched bewildered as invaders re-carved their boundaries and mismanaged their future. In a final affront, American forces weeding out Vietnamese soldiers in Laos had pulverized the pristine countryside with the largest sustained aerial bombing campaign in history. During 580,000 sorties, two million tons of ordinance tumbled from the skies — one-third of it never detonating. Once rich, eastern farmland is now useless. Laotians are still waiting for someone to clean up the mess.

Indifferent to political ideologies, patient country farmers struggle to feed desperate families. Seldom further than a drought-year from starvation, commerce to these people is trading sacks of rice for cooking oil. Today, under communist military rule, laborers stand and stare as the outside world zooms ahead. Yet, traces of a fledgling

A Siberian Welcoming from Internet connected motorcycle riders.

A Mongolian nomad girl sent by her family to care for a stranger in the Gobi Desert.

Comparing transportation with modern nomads in the Gobi Desert, Mongolia.

En route from Turkey to Syria during a mid-winter crossing of the Anatolian Plateau at 8,000 feet.

Taking a tea break at the invitation of a Bedouin nomad camped in the Syrian desert near the Iraqi border.

A Jordanian Bedouin woman making breakfast in a rare photo without her veil.

A difficult pyramids shot captured by entering from
the open desert through the Bedouin's secret hole in the security fence.

In a small village along the Nile River, eager Egyptian Arabs swarm forward with shouts of "Welcome! Welcome!"

Dining on roasted chicken with curious Egyptian Arabs.

A Palestinian man, forbidden entry to visit his family for nearly five years, prays at the entrance to Erez Checkpoint.

Election day during Palestine's first presidential race.
Gaza City, The West Bank.

Chatting with friendly Palestinians in Gaza City.

A crowd gathers to help when a traveler stops for directions. Islamabad, Pakistan.

The front of a typically decorated Pakistani bus.

A very creative, multi-handed beggar in Pushkar, Rajastan, India.

Female slaves laboring outside of Pushkar.

Mother and daughter portrait in Varanasi, Uttar Pradesh, India.

While defying a Maoist rebel blockade, a Nepali driver's hand was severed and his bus burned. En route to Katmandu, Nepal.

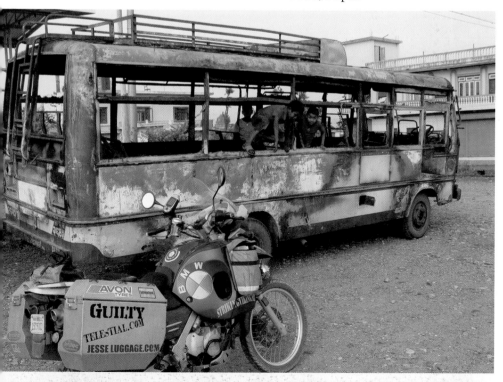

Everyone's sins are washed away during
the week-long Songkran water festival in Chiang Mai, Thailand.

Thai language lessons in the remote mountains of Northern Thailand.

Long-neck Pa Dong tribeswomen in Northern Thailand.

Hill-tribal women in Northern Thailand
with teeth blackened from chewing the betel nut.

Sinking in the sucking mud of the Borneo jungle, Sarawak, East Malaysia.

Orphans from the Tsunami still manage a smile, Banda Aceh, Sumatra, Indonesia.

The only entry into Borneo's murky interior was upriver by a small fishing boat.
Simanggaris, Kalimantan, Indonesia.

Enthusiastic Dayak tribal villagers greeting an alien vagabond
in Borneo, Kalimantan.

The result of riding with a burned-out headlight in the jungles of Borneo, Kalimantan, Indonesia.

Boxing lessons for Dayak village youngsters under the watchful eye of their father, the chief. Borneo.

Camping in the Namib Desert, Namibia, Africa.

Curious Masai tribal youngsters look on as I take their photo in Tanzania, Africa.

Hamer tribal girls saluting the world, Omo Valley, Ethiopia.

Masai tribal women evaluating a motorcycling alien, Tanzania, Africa.

An afternoon encounter while off-roading on the open savanna, Omo Valley.

Volunteers gather to assist changing a tire after a dozen blowouts in one day, Omo Valley.

entrepreneurial Asian spirit seeps in. Along the tourist trail, innovative villagers cautiously welcome hordes of marauding travelers trekking in the daylight and guzzling Lao beer by night. In backpacker ghettos of bamboo-hut bars and Internet cafés, Western college kids stumble drunkenly through the dark.

Foreigners occupy Laos again, but this time they're sightseers and businessmen whose affluence tempts the natives into gouging. Prices vary according to the seller's mood and whatever they can get away with.

Alone among the soldiers, my time waiting out the storm passes in awkward silence. Normally locals congregate, filled with questions; today, it's just eyeing from a distance. The mission of this particular stranger is unimportant; they know only that he's a foreigner heading for Vang Vieng. My uneasy moments with the soldiers ends, and before the squall subsides, we bid a meek farewell. As the Blue Beast growls to life, startled chickens scurry from the roadway, seemingly happy the alien is leaving. Passing the last curve out of town, in my rearview mirror the settlement returns to normal, with watchful residents likely wondering what the next invaders will bring.

Vientiane
May 16, 2005
Vientiane, Laos
● ● ● ● ● ● ● ● ●

With no industrial base and little traffic to speak of, travelers have the fresh open spaces of Laos to themselves. When I rode a bicycle through Vientiane in 1987, there was only one paved road; now, concrete suburbs and pop-up businesses fan inland from the edge of the Mae Khong River like the fingers of an expanding delta. By Asian standards, the capital is barely a village, with a population of 162,000 people.

Beside the Soviet architecture, a variety of colorful, gold-fringed Buddhist temples and snow-white stupas blend with budget hotels and Internet cafés. Along with their recipes for baking bread, the French left behind a reasonable tradition in gourmet cooking — the restaurants are good as long as you don't bring too big an appetite.

Even a liberalized communist bureaucracy can't stop limited free enterprise — evidence of prosperity is slowly beginning to appear across town. Not counting three-wheeled rickshaw taxis, rush-hour traffic means a dozen automobiles per block. In poorer countries, motorcycles are the equivalent of family cars, and sales here are booming. Mom and dad buzz out for an afternoon with children dozing on their laps while teenagers team up for cruising. With one hand on the throttle and the other clutching decorated parasols of pinks and yellows, petite Lao girls on step-through scooters cruise the tree-lined boulevards. Shaded from the penetrating tropical sun, dainty girlfriend passengers sit sidesaddle, with cell phones pressed against their ears.

Yet it's still a city of accelerating lifestyles. A simpler version of country culture awaits me further south. After a day of quick-scanning city temples, completing Internet business and doubling up on meals, there is not much else to do.

It's Saturday night in Vientiane, and as prowling travelers fill the crowded bars below, I spend the evening alone. In a colorful gleam reflected off the timeless Mae Khong River, the psychological sanctuary of Thailand beckons just a half mile away. Drifting through snapshots of mangled memories, from the riverside rooftop of the Orchid Guesthouse it's possible to see everywhere I have been or ever hope to go.

But even the euphoric solitude of paradise has its price. As a fluorescent silver moon slips among the monsoon clouds, from somewhere down an echoing brick-cased alley, Willie Nelson and Julio Iglesias croon about lost romance. Long after lyrics from "To All the Girls I've Loved Before" fade into folded chairs and locking doors, I chug the last of my warm beer while lamenting the one girl I loved. And in the stillness of this melancholy haze, it becomes painfully apparent how far away home will always be.

The Bolaven Plateau
May 18, 2005
Pakse, Laos

●●●●●●●

A visa is required to travel from Laos to Cambodia, but local embassies are closed for a four-day weekend, and waiting is not an option. At Thai borders, visas are issued on arrival, so plan B means riding as far south as possible, to Pakse, before crossing back through Thailand to reach the bone-jarring route across Cambodia to the ancient temples at Angkor Wat.

From Vientiane on, the road straightens into flat rural farmland beset with swarms of waterborne insects. Restaurant stops become bug-slapping massacres between gulps of spicy noodles. But it's worth it because the next best thing to a lazy riverboat cruise is a lazy motorcycle ride next to one. Here, the graceful life along the water is unhurried. The slow, contagious flow of the Mae Khong sets the meandering pace of the nation. Laos is not so much a destination but is a quiet place you pass through on your way to somewhere else. With just one main highway running its length, moving from one end to the other is simple enough, unless you want an unfiltered peek into the lives of its people. Yet as monsoon storms continue to arrive, the minor roads must be reevaluated daily. Are the bridges washed out or have landslides blocked the way? The only way to be certain is to ride them.

With three days left on my visa and hungry for a deeper view of Laos, I opt for a dirt track loop heading due east toward Viet Nam. As long as there're no other foreigners, the countryside should be more interesting. Spiraling upwards into dark, swirling clouds, the Bolaven plateau rises a chilly 4,500 feet above the steamy Mae Khong lowlands. In this region of lush coffee and rubber plantations, indigenous hill tribes have had little exposure to tourists.

Each village along the way offers unique markets with fruit and vegetable stands and scented arrays of specialty dishes ready to sizzle the palates of the bold. Breaks for sticky rice and sweet rambutans end in photo sessions with dazzled children anxious to see their images on my camera's digital playback screen. Eventually, teenagers join and take turns studying my GPS and grilling me about motorcycle specs. Gloomy gray skies serve as regular reminders that it's best to ride while it's dry — rain alters riding surfaces and never for the better.

The first half of my loop was paved as anticipated — after that, the locals call it the "Red Road." That means clay, and riding over clay during monsoon is an exercise in slippery frustration. The question was, did the last week of rain erode the roads enough to render them impassable? I flag down an oncoming jeep whose driver confirmed that there were some swollen rivers to ford ahead, but the road was still open.

Crossing rivers is dicey. You can study the rippling currents for shallow spots, but you're never sure about slick rocks or dips underwater. After three hesitant hours, I crossed the first hundred-meter stream twice — advancing and retreating. Once on the other side, after a fatiguing half-mile test of gooey black clay and one over-the-handlebars face-plant, I took stock. Inching along foot-paddling through more of the same meant covering the next 60 miles would likely take days. This was confirmed when some Indian aid workers stopped to help lift the Blue Beast because my feet kept sliding out from underneath. Even parked on a gentle slope, their four-wheel drive truck slipped sideways. Wet clay is difficult to walk on, let alone ride over.

Up to now, my wide-strap camera harness has worked well in avoiding neck pain and keeping my camera ready at chest level to capture those unpredictable shots. But today, plunging directly over the handlebars, a fixed position only served to guide my new Sony digital straight into the muck while sliding face-down. At least it wasn't water. It was time I retreated.

Skulking back along the Red Road left me only an hour of daylight to return to the main highway. A rustic jungle guesthouse at the mouth of Tadfane Gorge presented an inspiring scene of cliffside waterfalls and vine-tangled forest. Buzzing in deafening cycles, jungle insects were like an orchestra of high-pitched power tools competing with each other, but their anticipated twilight attacks never materialized. Perched on a stunning overlook, the spiritual serenity of a glorious morning meditation could not subdue an urgent desire to visit Cambodia.

Khmers
May 20, 2005
Siem Reap, Cambodia
● ● ● ● ● ● ● ● ● ● ● ● ●

There is little that is certain about adventure travel in developing nations — especially when factoring in political stability, changing weather and road conditions. With no pavement leading away from the borders of Thailand or Laos, those attempting to reach the Cambodian interior are subject to the whims of nature. Even if recently graded, a few days of monsoon can easily erode an otherwise tolerable dirt track and undermine its surfaces, washing out critical bridges.

There was an even split regarding information about a little-known border crossing not appearing on maps or the GPS. When I phoned ahead for advice from a friend in Thailand, who was barely audible over the roar of water cascading down on the rusted tin ceiling of a tumbledown frontier café, Robert was adamant that if it was raining, it would be best to exit Cambodia and ride further south in Thailand and find a more widely used commercial route. But tomorrow is a new day. The storm subsided at midnight, leaving the Red Road to Siem Reap dry by morning.

Winding through the jungle over deteriorated improvised bridges and rice paddy levies led me through impoverished Khmer villages and muddy unsowed fields. At my first meal stop, I understood why the locals never stray from the road to till their fields. Three of the five young men at the next table had artificial legs, presumably from stepping on one of hundreds of thousands of remaining land mines planted during 30 years of harried civil war. But everyone shares in sorrow.

Even given their own misfortune, when a hobbling old beggar woman approaches, the legless men dig deep to share a few coins. As Cambodia slowly emerges from the aftermath of genocide and famine, the bodies of the people are scarred but not their hopes. A simple gaze into the tormented eyes of docile peasants reveals a forgiving sincerity and a bashful, heartfelt smile. Like Latin American campesinos, it's always the kindest who suffer most.

Stories of Pol Pot's Killing Fields had been understated. Hearing the awful details from the survivors turned the movie into a sickening reality. A Cambodian with connections to the West, or who was suspected of higher education made them an enemy of the people and subject to arrest and interrogation. From eyeglasses to vaccination scars, evidence that you were bourgeois pre-revolution was grounds for accusations of treason. In a mindless rampage of death and destruction, the Khmer Rouge rampaged in fury from 1975 to 1979. Eventually, under the fanatical tyranny of Pol Pot, sweet-natured Cambodians turned on each other.

Today, wavering on the trembling legs of a fresh democracy, all hope for Cambodia's immediate future is found in tourism. Home to Asia's most remarkable display of early civilization, Siem Reap is a gateway to this single Cambodian cash cow — Angkor Wat. With insufficient infrastructure to support mass tourism, disoriented Cambodians trudge empty-handed into the 21st century. An enterprising elite seizes any advantages, and while shoeless village schoolchildren are introduced to computers, new hotels and restaurants appear weekly. As in Laos, ATMs are still years away, but telecommunications are on the rise. Cell phones are not permitted for foreigners, but Chinese businessmen and prostitutes imported from Viet Nam are burning up the airwaves. It's the hot rainy season, yet visitors still converge to marvel at the temples and gasp at inflated menu prices. Modern hotels with satellite TV are cheap, but most other goods and services cost twice what they do in Thailand. Angkor Wat is too vast for a one-day tour, but week-long passes cost 60 bucks.

The capital city of Phnom Penh is my next anticipated crossroads. Do I head into Viet Nam in search of a questionable route to

China or return to the certainty of Thailand? The Vietnamese government doesn't want anyone to have bigger bikes than their police, so motorcycles over 175 ccs are prohibited. Even if I'm able to schmooze my way past skeptical border guards, further north into China, private foreign vehicles are outlawed, period. A ride to Shanghai looks dodgy, and it could mean a 2,000-mile detour just to be told no. I have a lot to ask of the Travel Gods this week.

Angkor Wat
May 25, 2005
Siem Reap, Cambodia
● ● ● ● ● ● ● ● ● ● ● ●

After milking the last drop of his luck, Art Kernaghan had finally abandoned his broke-down rat bike near Bangkok. A cracked crankpin on his old Belarus-built Minsk proved too difficult to replace in Thailand. Down but not out, he continued to Siem Reap on a rented Honda to complete the Cambodian leg of his journey. We've remained in contact by email and will likely ride together until he returns to Saigon and I roll south toward Indonesia. For now, we're off to investigate a dozen square miles of fabled stone temples and palaces at Angkor Wat — Asia's Disneyland of archaeological ruins.

Constructed during the ninth 13th centuries to honor Khmer god-kings, even today, Angkor Wat is the pride of Cambodians. Once covering all of Southeast Asia, Khmer civilization was ultimately destroyed by pillaging Thai warriors. After a series of invasions and conquests from within, Angkor Wat was reclaimed by the jungle until 1860, when French naturalists stumbled upon it. Today, all that remains of the might of a fallen empire are the hand-chiseled granite walls of these decaying shrines and monuments.

Travelers often develop an idea of how famous places will appear from studying guidebooks and tourist posters. Yet when we get there, we always mumble in amazement: "I never dreamed it was like this." The history of Khmer life is written in stone. Yet, as much as the elaborate carvings are beautiful, what's so overwhelming is the sheer size and number of moss-covered buildings emerging from the forest.

An overpowering tropical heat makes lingering in one place uncomfortable, and given there's so much to see, motorcycling proves to be the ultimate way to absorb it. Leisurely cruising beneath cooling canopies of tropical foliage becomes an enchanting tour of stone temples and crumbling palaces. The encroaching tentacles of the jungle envelop the solid rock framework, providing a blissful awareness of both the natural environment and the highly developed magnificence of early Khmer architecture. With much of the ruins still half buried among roots of giant hardwood trees, Angkor Wat captivates much more than it would if it were a polished modern restoration.

S-21 Prison
May 30, 2005
Phnom Penh, Cambodia
• • • • • • • • • • • • • •

On a world tour through developing nations, travelers encounter enough gut-wrenching catastrophes to haunt their dreams for years. Will we ever get used to it? Or will we eventually yield to the psychological strain caused by our inability to affect what leaves us sleepless? This being a traveler's diary, should it exclude the immeasurable suffering caused by abusive governments, disease and natural disaster that I have witnessed?

It's impossible to separate Cambodia from its appalling past. To meekly sidestep the reality of the recent genocide is to punish the victims once more. In television news, we hear words like genocide so often the meaning gets lost — even Mr. Webster uses sterile terminology: "The deliberate and systematic destruction of a racial, political, or cultural group." He should have called it what it is, a wholesale butchering of innocent men, women and children that generally involves torture for fun. The Maoist Khmer Rouge had a

Former schoolhouse turned prison is now a museum reminding visitors that the bloody history of the Khmer Rouge regime won't soon be forgotten

special gift for inflicting such misery.

S-21 Prison was originally a Phnom Penh schoolhouse, until 1975, when bloodthirsty Khmer Rouge rebels converted it into a detention facility for interrogation — a torture center. Those who survived the horrors of questioning here were later transferred to extermination camps. Like the Nazis and other tyrannical regimes, the Khmer Rouge kept detailed records and photographs of their victims. To preserve the memory of this twisted nightmare, S-21 Prison has been converted into a museum of shocking revulsion, where the voices of the sacrificed can still be heard.

In group meditation, there is a belief in the existence and effect of collective consciousness. Focusing mental energies in monasteries and holy sites is said to intensify the power of prayer. But who is out there listening? Is there a spirit world of higher beings, gods and ghosts? Is a person without a soul a hollow vessel? Where do we go when our bodies expire?

To pass into the afterlife, Cambodians believe their dead must be cremated before burial, otherwise they languish in limbo as ghosts for all of eternity. This is a dreadful notion for relatives of those dumped in mass graves during the Khmer Rouge reign of frenzied genocide. Cambodia is a country few can pick out on a map — their holocaust is a mere footnote in history, but the lost souls of the two million murdered still demand justice.

Even your first few steps inside the S-21 Prison Museum evoke a distinctive anguish that smothers your spirit. Before you're inside the first torture chamber, tears will flow down your face, while some find it difficult to breathe. No one speaks during the tour — you merely wander through rooms in a daze of nausea. The ghosts of S-21 Prison not only cry out, but you can see their faces. Recovered mug shots of prisoners are on display so visitors can slowly walk by each one and look the victims in the eye. The innocent young, the helpless old and the seemingly average Cambodians — you study them as they study you. Suddenly your mind spins in a sickening cauldron of ghastly images — while they were being photographed were they aware of the grisly future ahead?

On their way to dank holding cells, were they marched past the gruesome gallows to witness the bodies dangling upside down? Could they hear the screams of those begging to die? What did they feel at those moments? What about when they were finally steel-bar-shackled together, lying side by side on concrete floors awaiting their turn? How long was eternity for them?

Pol Pot's regime was an efficient operation: to save bullets, executioners often bludgeoned victims to death. Enormous pits were dug by dazed prisoners who had to know this would be their next stop. "Mass grave" is another term that lacks meaning until you see one. What makes this experience more tragic is meeting the surviving Cambodians first. From the tormented families of the dead to the unlucky legless who stepped on a land mine buried in one of their fields, the gentle Buddhist Cambodians silently bear their sorrow. But the human spirit triumphs, and, after all this, they are still always first to smile.

On the Border
June 3, 2005
Chong Yeam, Cambodia
● ● ● ● ● ● ● ● ● ● ● ● ● ●

After departing Phnom Penh, I took a smooth ride to Kampot, a small country town delivering sweet riverside sunsets as well as wicked backstreets pointing like unforgiving fingers into overflowing swampland. Mosquito-infested shantytowns on stilts were reminders of how far the people here still have to come. When I pause to study the town, excited children rush to pull on my sleeves and clamor aboard the Beast. Shrieks of bright-eyed laughter draw crowds of villagers curious about the invading alien. Everyone wants to be in the picture.

Further east, the beachside city of Sihanoukville emerged as an unlikely conglomeration of sleepy Cambodians and aging expatriate businessmen trying to survive after an anticipated tourist boom never happened. Waiting out the low season, gulping down beers in empty hotels, foreign entrepreneurs have lowered their expectations. There is little for me to do here but sit sweating and wait out the sporadic squalls, answering emails under wobbling fans in Internet cafés.

With four ferryboat crossings between here and the border, torrential downpours have turned a wavy hundred-mile red road through the jungle from hard-pack adobe to knee-deep, sucking mud. Without a challenge it wouldn't be worth the effort, yet it's always a relief to find shelter at the end of the day to dry out waterlogged gear and scrub off clods of clinging clay.

Staring through the window of a riverside hotel mulling over my time in Cambodia, a familiar reluctance to leave is overwhelmed by images of what's waiting across the water. Delicious food and Thai massage: All that remained between me and Thailand were immigration formalities and document stampings. But above the rampant poverty, the soothing simplicity and basic humanity of Cambodia sticks in my mind like sweet scents of blooming orchids.

Two weeks had hardly been enough to tour an entire country,

but with seasonal rains washing away exit roads in Thailand, it was now or never.

Prospering like an Asian tiger, Thais have long forgotten their roots in Khmer civilization. Even Thai boxing combat techniques are chiseled in the decomposing granite walls of Angkor palace temples. As if in the restlessness of an infinite slumber, sweet little Cambodia endures terrible hardship and cold corruption while its neighbors march and haggle their way into prosperity. With an uneasy night ahead, tomorrow will be more than just another border crossing; it's a sad goodbye embrace for the humble hearts of a nation on its knees.

Coming Home?
June 11, 2005
Pattaya Beach, Thailand
● ● ● ● ● ● ● ● ● ● ● ● ● ● ●

Next to painting the house, changing a motorcycle tire is the least pleasurable way to spend an afternoon. Yet the Travel Gods had smiled on me once more as a blowout occurred while white-lining through stalled border-city traffic. Within seconds, a wobbling Blue Beast slowed to a graceful halt directly in front of a well-stocked motorcycle shop. Twenty minutes and four dollars later, we're back on the road with a new tube, a lubed drive chain and some new friends. Even the last hundred miles in the rain to Bangkok was uplifting.

Motorcycle maintenance is a constant. For anything not welded solid, if there is a reason for it to wear under the bike's vibration, it will. Holding out until Singapore to avoid the high-priced imported parts in Thailand wasn't going to work, and recalling a recent raping at the hands of Bangkok motorcycle dealers, mercy was unlikely. Up until now, the local's unwritten rule of two-tier pricing for taxi rides and trinkets has had minimal effect on my travel expenditures. But doubled prices for foreigners on already expensive BMW replacement parts means budget bites in the hundreds of dollars.

It took four days to coordinate what would have been an after-noon of supply shopping in California — meanwhile, the indifferent streets of the capital have grown cold. As in most countries, pretty faces and hustlers migrate to cities while the pure at heart remain in villages. Bangkok may be the center of Thailand, but its heart and soul is in the country. Returning to Siam has been the closest thing to coming home since I've left the U.S., and it's hard now to find a reason to leave. The mild climate, cheap hotels, scrumptious cuisine and great roads — is it any wonder foreigners immigrate daily by the planeload?

In the mid-80s, Pattaya Beach had a population of 20,000, mostly Thai and some foreigners. In 20 years, it's become an overdeveloped multicultural colony of two million retired white men and hopeful Thai businesspeople catering to their whims. In between Pizza Huts, 7-Elevens and McDonald's restaurants, legions of saggy-bellied Euro-pean men cruise rows of beer bars and flashy strip joints perusing thousands of catcalling young working girls. Nerdy, slump-shouldered Westerners peering through coke-bottle glasses stroll through crowds savoring their reversal of fortune. Amidst beckon-ing bargirls cooing *"Hallo sexy man I lub you too much,"* these scrawny Poindexters saunter about as rock stars fending off fans.

Just as Cairo boulevards are sprinkled with elderly Italian women clinging to teenage Egyptian boyfriends, the traffic-jammed roads of Pattaya Beach are filled with waddling drunks unlikely to get this lucky with women elsewhere. Throbbing rock music blares past mid-night as expatriates on pensions gather to drink themselves to cirrhosis. The perils of their superficial paradise can sometimes lead to suicide, as disillusioned foreigners discover the loves of their lives have more than one husband. Well coached by over-the-hill sex workers, within a few weeks, eager new service girls hone their hard-ening edges.

Outside cities, even when river-bathing, shy female Thais wouldn't dare venture out dressed in less than oversized T-shirts and baggy pants. In Pattaya Beach, at the insistence of their pimping boy-friends, once bashful country girls jiggle downtown bra-less on platform shoes in miniskirts the size of cut-off socks. Here, money rules, and temporary fortunes offer false security. Not counting free-lancers, there are a million registered hookers in a country that outlaws prostitution and bars.

The first question I am asked anywhere in Thailand is "Where is your Thai girlfriend?" More comfortable in backstreet cafés without menus in English, it requires lengthy interrogation before the jaded natives believe a foreigner could be interested in them. But soon the jabbering old women accept the wandering *Farang* and begin preparing my favorite meals the moment they hear my motorcycle engine.

Asians are superstitious as well as religious. Even downtown sky-scrapers provide exterior space for elevated platforms, with their dollhouse-sized temples supposed to house accompanying spirits. But whatever their socioeconomic status, Thais enjoy life. They smile at everyone and laugh at anything. As I explain my journey to the curious — chubby young restaurant girls enquire, *"Mai gruah bpee?"* (You are not afraid of ghosts?)

"Mai shuah." (I don't believe in them.)

They giggle in feigned fear, *"Pom gruah drah-kool-lah!"* (I am afraid of Dracula!)

Hearing stories of how life near the aqua waters of Pattaya Beach had changed, I had purposely put off my decision to visit until the last minute. There is no such thing as really going home. When I encounter an old friend, Jake, a British expat down on his luck, he reminisces about a decade of failures and heartache while dreaming optimistically of the breaks that are sure to come. Others I had known have drank themselves to death or jumped off balconies, mourning unsuccessful romances. Asia is a ruthless lover.

Seventeen years ago Khun Daeng from the MA Language Center had given me my first lessons on how to speak Thai. Wandering into the hardly changed office, I was curious if anyone would remember me. The eyes tell a lot — before I even remove my helmet, we recognize each other and rush to violate the traditionally reserved Asian behavior with giant bear hugs. Sometimes you forget how deeply someone has affected your life until you see them again.

Cruising my old neighborhood was a hesitant tour of buried emotions. Once brightly painted townhouses are now poorly maintained rows of shabby rentals. I barely recognized my old two-story home. Peeks through smudged windows revealed fine teakwood floors replaced with cheap ceramic tiles and barely latched doors on rusted metal hinges. Steel hooks still protruded from concrete beams where my boxing gear used to hang. In a moment of downhearted nostalgia, I picture a long-lost lover appearing in the doorway with dainty brown hands on her hips impatiently asking, *"Bpie nai mah Gan?"* (Where have you been Glen?)

Often troubled over the years by what her ultimate fate might have been, I silently mumble, *"Bie hah koon tee lak."* (I've gone looking for you my love.)

Jep Jai
June 27, 2005
Thailand
● ● ● ● ● ●

Whenever I'm asked for travel advice, my reply is invariably the same: "Next to 'always carry toilet paper' is learn a foreign language." Although this journey's been fascinating, a deeper knowledge of Russian and Arabic would have enhanced the experience. A few rehearsed phrases can be helpful when ordering food or seeking accommodation, but to understand the minds of the people, learning how they express ideas not only shows respect, it can provide a subtle glimpse into their ways of thinking. English speakers are surprised to discover that people in other countries share their familiar sentiment about foreigners — "As long as they're here, they should damn well speak our language."

Except for a difficult-to-master system of tones, Thai is a simple language, structured in a way that's almost the opposite of English. Because a specific tone carries the same value of a consonant in English, it must be pronounced properly. There are five to be mastered:

high, low, mid-tone, rising and falling. One word will have five different meanings according to the tone. A tongue-twister we learned in school was *"Mai mai mai mai, mai?"* — "New wood doesn't burn, does it?"

Thais don't clutter their speech with prepositions, conjunctions and adverbs, they get right to the point, and there are few variations for common sentences. In English, we say, "I am going to go home." Thais simply state, *"Glap baan."* (Return home.) *Yen* means cold. Instead of saying it is very cold, they just say the word twice: *"Yen yen."*

People are described according to their *Jai* (spirit or heart). *Jai ron* means hot-tempered spirit, *Jai yen*, cool spirit. *Jai dum* is black-hearted or dark spirit, and *Jai dee* is good spirit. Often, rude foreigners who disregard Thai customs in tourist areas are branded *Jai dum*. You know you've made points with the locals if you hear them remark, *Farang jai dee*. (The foreigner is good-hearted.)

To express emotion in public is to lose face but whatever the severity of the transgression, from the sure sign of bad manners represented by inadvertently patting someone on the head to backing a motorcycle tire over someone's foot, all is forgiven with a simple plea *"Kaw toht."* (Excuse me.) Apologies are readily accepted with smiles and a passive *"Mai pen rai"* (never mind), and then the foreigner is commended for having *"Jai dee."*

There is no such word as he or she — *Kow* denotes either. But since Thai is polite to the extreme, when addressing a superior or someone unfamiliar, a man shows respect by ending his sentences in *Khap* and a woman with *Kha*. To skip a formal ending of a sentence would be a deliberate act of rudeness — a faux pas similar to a military private addressing an officer without the accompanying "Sir."

In Pattaya Beach, Thais tolerate drunken foreigners, but they don't respect them and show it by omitting formalities. Since few foreigners speak Thai, they don't know when they are being insulted, and as long as everyone keeps smiling, they don't seem to mind. But for a traveler, to be seen as a tourist is annoying, and it requires a substantial effort — like learning the language to show the distinction.

Thirty bucks a day has bought a shiny new hotel room with satellite TV, five delightful meals, two hours of high-speed Internet and workouts at the gym. While traveling the world, three weeks in one city is long enough — but also too short when it comes time to saying goodbye to people who've been cooking your food, guarding your motorcycle and otherwise interacting to make your stay interesting.

But to reach Borneo by mid-July, I must roll for Malaysia in the morning. When recognizing the consequences of my decision, I instantly developed *jep jai* — a pained spirit. So with *sia jai*, broken heart, my baffling journey continues deeper into Asia, where, just when things seem to become clear, I discover that one and one is three, yes means no and, despite all my efforts, I'll always be a stranger in a strange land.

Loong
July 6, 2005
Sadao, Thailand
• • • • • • • • • •

From the red clay tracks of Laos and Cambodia to a four-lane highway spanning the length of Malaysia, it's been a fascinating road to travel. Originally allotting three months for the region, time has passed too quickly for a comfortable farewell. As the predominately Muslim southern provinces of Thailand plunge deeper into turmoil, the government travel warnings increase. After the brutal suppression of a peaceful uprising, the call for bloody revenge intensifies with daily assaults and, finally, beheadings.

It's been a hundred years since Britain and Thailand divvied up the south, but the inhabitants have not forgotten their identity. What was once northern Muslim Malaysia has become a troubled land of sectarian violence. Gentle Buddhist and peaceful Muslims exist in the cross fire of extremists as a struggle for independence continues.

Nearing the border, personalities shift as eager smiles and overt friendliness evolve into awkward suspicion. Half the locals don't speak Thai, and those who do use a jagged dialect that even people from Bangkok don't understand. My roadside-restaurant attempts at making contact are met with wary nods and silent stares. A wanderer's policy of not leaving until we shake hands stretches the day, but after a lengthy period of broken dialogue, my persistence pays off. Eventually, chunky-cheeked southerners crowd around for photos and insist on buying my meals — a gesture unheard of further north but typical of Islamic hospitality. Values and sincerity are more important than who owns what.

My last four days on an expired one-month visa evaporate on the travel-poster-paradise island of Phuket, complete with a moonlight romance that has boiled into breathless tropical lust. Bumming around in the city bars, I've met Loong, the girl of my most recent dreams. Motorcycle rides along clear blue waters lined with sugary sands have stirred up an intoxicating brew of instant attraction and mutual affection. Women of 30 without children are rare in Thailand, yet to ask questions would only encourage lies. Sticking to small talk, the bumbling humor of a stuttering foreigner cuts directly to the chase, and, before long, Loong's naked body is next to mine. Sexual adventures for travelers often start with an unrealistic idea that somehow fate will intervene and inevitable goodbyes can be postponed. Yet wishing and hoping is a mirage for a pragmatic wanderer, no matter how lonely. And as the softness of her smile belies the hardship of Loong's life, I never want to let her go.

Tall and thin with long black hair dangling to the top of her well-fit jeans, Loong's looks caught my eye, but not as much as seeing her give coins to street beggars. An Asian ranch girl in a cultural menagerie of desires and taboos capture a Viking heart. Cautiously aware of how foreigners can be taken in by the childlike playfulness of Thai women, for the last three months I've avoided what could take me down. Yet such cautions are hard to remember lost in a woman's innocent laughter. In a soft, lingering embrace for what seems like forever, her long silky legs hold me inside as she coos for me stay. When pearly toothed natives flick on the charm, we're as defenseless as they are the moment we saddle up and leave. The economic might of a single Western workingman could easily sweep aside the tragedies of an entire Thai village — and realizing this makes riding off into the sunset that much harder.

But destiny rules in Asia. Whether human or natural disasters, the fate of those we learn to care about is always beyond their control. The commercial impact of the recent tsunami is mending far faster than the spirits of its human survivors, while faith and hope wobble as reliably as the region's tectonic plates next shift. Thais celebrate water, but their lifelong friend, the sea, has betrayed them, and now worship has turned to terror. Will giant waves of death come for them again?

A moonlit stroll on an empty paradisiacal beach turns to shivering paranoia as Loong trembles at the waters edge. Her warm melodic laughter silenced, her body freezes with blank-stare chants to Buddha. Clumsy attempts to console her about what I don't understand only add to the frustration of ineptitude. I might as well be watching this on TV. Whispering waves to Loong have become the low hisses of lurking spirits sucked out to sea. *"Grua bpee Gaan."* (I fear the ghosts Glen.)

Later, while I pack my gear, she watches me count the last of my Thai currency while calculating my hotel bill and immigration fines for an expired visa. Not realizing it's only an attempt to avoid another ATM withdrawal, she worries I don't have enough money and holds out a handful of wrinkled bills. After cooking my meals and washing my clothes, she's fired both barrels at once. But another night in the seductive embrace of Loong would surely turn into another year, and once again, I'm facing a now or never moment.

Life is especially unfair for women in developing nations, and it's likely been a while since Loong was treated like a lady — but an armful of purple orchids from the traveling foreigner gave her "big face" in the minds of a watching village. And as I stood there grappling with my emotions, her almond eyes shimmering like coffee beans clouded my reasons to move on. Struggling for composure, she reads from a scribbled note the only English she's yet spoken, *"Plees no foget me Gaan."* And this time, no matter how hard I twist the throttle, it will be a while before I can leave the past behind.

BORNEO

Borneo
July 7, 2005
Serawak, East Malaysia
● ● ● ● ● ● ● ● ● ● ● ● ● ●

Slicing through Malaysian jungle terrain, a seamless asphalt corridor connecting the Thai border with Kuala Lumpur unravels for a straight 300 miles south. With First World infrastructure, toll stations and chain restaurants replace noodle stands and traffic-clogged small towns. Car drivers pay fees, but motorcyclists ride free in special lanes to the sides of toll booths. At my first gas stop, passive Malays welcome me with thumbs-up gestures and the usual question, "Where are you coming from?" Docile women in long dresses and pastel-shaded headscarves are reminders of a return to Islam.

A suggestion from Robert Heikel has caused a spur-of-the-moment decision to deviate from my route toward Indonesia for a detour to Borneo. Rumors of an upcoming exotic Rainforest World Music Festival and an unusual bargain became reality. Faster than sea-freighting and half the price, Malaysian Airlines offered a deal at 500 bucks round-trip for man and machine. International transport is normally at least five times that, but a federally subsidized program to boost internal trade serves travelers as well.

Still, this week, the U.S. government has echoed Australia's warning of a verified, significant risk of terrorist attack along the eastern Borneo coast by Islamic militants from the Philippines. My choice was returning to the civil unrest in Southern Thailand or heading for the separatist insurrection in Aceh province, Sumatra. Since I had already bought a nonrefundable ticket online, fate demanded that I continue on to Kuching, capital of Serawak, in the mythical land of Borneo.

This oil-rich island shared by Indonesia, Brunei and two semi-autonomous states of Malaysia, Borneo is also home to 200 tribes of protected indigenous people. It's an interesting establishment of turf — anywhere in Malaysia, Chinese merchants control commerce, while Muslim Malays run the government. Indians handle textiles and electronics as local natives entertain the tourists. After two hours of importation and customs declarations, the Blue Beast is loaded onto an aluminum pallet and shoved into the gaping hold of an idling MAS cargo plane. There is always a risk of damage from clumsy handlers while freighting a bike, but the promise of adventure outweighed the risk of broken turn signals or bent handlebars.

With its distinctive blend of clashing cultures, Malaysia is as diverse as India, only far better organized. Well-pronounced English is spoken even in the smallest towns, but on Borneo, each tribe has its own tongue differing completely from what is spoken a few villages away. One of only a few Westerners at the Rainforest World Music Festival, I shared three starry nights with throngs of passionate locals eager to hear traditional folk songs from around the world. Algerians, Africans, Iranians, Mongolians, Poles, Australians, Thais, Colombians, Italians, Pakistanis and even a bluegrass band from the

U.S. kept fans energetically swaying and clapping past midnight.

After a red-headed Mongolian girl belted out hair-raising ballads of Genghis Khan, a bagpipe band from Poland moved a captivated crowd with their versions of Celtic melodies. The pulse-grabbing beat of the West African drum ensemble dominated with throbbing harmonies and somersaulting dancers. But when a singer from the Foghorn String Band of Portland, Oregon, stepped on stage bellowing, "Greetings from the USA," the audience went wild with cheers and roared with applause. While the band plucked at twanging banjos and whining fiddles, 10,000 Malaysians jumped to their feet and into dance moves straight out of Texas. Watching a hillside covered with profusely perspiring people party with music from the heartland infected me with an overdue case of homesickness. As normally subdued Chinese girls leaped into country-and-western square dancing, it was with a mixture of relief and pride that I realized that although the world may be furious with my government, they still loved what's truly American.

In the Hands of the Chinese
July 13, 2005
East Malaysia
● ● ● ● ● ● ● ●

Although life is richer in Asia, it's also far more of a struggle. From its early dynasties to a modern republic, China has often been the birthplace of people who eventually migrate elsewhere. From fleeing homeland hardships to providing the slave labor that built America's railroads to escaping famine by drifting into Southeast Asia, the Chinese have always been on the move. Humming with energy, they never stand idle. The wisest of immigrants, they perpetuate ancient superstitions as well as a basic creed: perseverance creates prosperity.

Accustomed to toil, the Chinese are natural born businesspeople who understand human necessities and satisfy them wherever they ultimately settle. Throughout Southeast Asia, they comprise

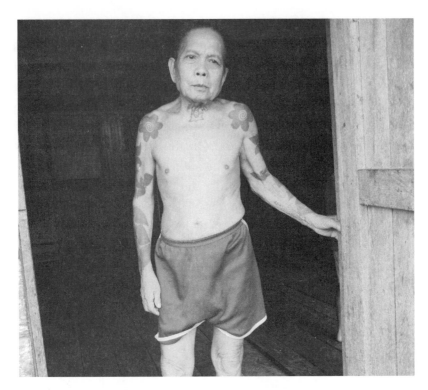

Borneo Iban tribesman in the upriver town of Sibu, Sarawak, East Malaysia

15 percent of populations yet control most of the commerce. Travelers in the region soon learn it's the Chinese who offer the best values in hotels, restaurants and money- changing. In Bangkok, Thai-Chinese government officials own chains of multistory brothels.

First welcomed as cheap labor then resented for their success, the Chinese are the first to be blamed when economies stumble. The Malay-sian riots of 1969 led to the open slaughter of 2,000 Chinese in the streets of Kuala Lumpur. Indonesia demanded that the Chinese abandon their cultural identity by taking Muslim names and stripping their businesses of anything written in Chinese. Even Chinese medicine was forbidden by law. When hard times hit Jakarta, it's still Chinese shops and restaurants that go up in flames. But the determined rise again.

Westerners measure success in quarterly reports and stock market updates. Chinese measure their progress over centuries. Communist control in mainland China represents only a passing moment in the longest lasting civilization on earth. After civil war, feeding, housing and restoring peace for a billion peasants required brutal control at enormous human cost. Yet now, the world can only marvel at the Chinese and wonder how their growing prosperity will affect the future.

Far more pragmatic than the West understands, we now stand gaping while a giant awakens — flexing its muscles. Immigrants ridiculed for their ways and made wary of those who've turned on them, the Chinese have learned to keep to themselves. But revisiting the same restaurants and businesses ultimately yields peeks into their lives they are normally unwilling to share with strangers. It takes a week of fried-duck lunches with a reluctant Mr. Woo to convince him of my sincerity. *"For what you want to know about Chinese?"*

"I have ridden that motorcycle around the world to hear your stories."

Shaking a wrinkled index finger, he explains: *"The natives here, they come from Indonesia 500 years ago — the Chinese only 200. My father born in China, I born here. My family work many shops."*

The Chinese never flaunt their wealth. This scrawny old man with four long hairs sprouting from a chin mole is as likely to own this part of town as he is to be a pensioner. Every day when greeting me, this frail, stooping merchant with a three-day stubble squeezes my hand with an iron claw. Aware this hurts, he still comments, *"Ah you wery strong man."* But the barriers come down with an invitation to his *"Special place for Chinese man only."* Next to his faded checkered shirt with buttoned-up collar, I don't feel out of place in my worn riding clothes, wherever we're headed.

From a darkened back-alley doorway, we follow plumes of incense up a grimy old staircase to a flimsy wooden door. Two rings on the bell make a smudgy window slide open and after a muttered exchange we're hustled inside. *Mamasan* is hesitant, but Mr. Woo insists, *"Ying Ying for my fren."*

For an hour and a half, a solid nine in any culture kneads and pummels back muscles knotted from the last thousand miles. But she doesn't stop there. Oriental massage is synonymous with sexual relief. What the sleek vanilla-skinned beauty does next with her oiled hands exceeds what other women have attempted by conventional means. Dazed and amazed, it takes a few minutes to stand on wobbly legs while Ying Ying waves off my stammered marriage proposals. Slipping back into a high-necked golden gown, she kisses my cheek and glides down the hall to send the next customer to his dream of a heaven. Before disappearing behind a red velvet curtain, the sensuous porcelain doll with soft black eyelashes turns to bow, *"You like Ying Ying, you come again."*

Upriver into Borneo
July 15, 2005
Kapit, Serawak
● ● ● ● ● ● ● ● ●

Rain or shine, I've never been any place where I didn't wish I was on a motorcycle. Today, this includes the wilds of Borneo. Although a tamer version of the indigenous people can be found just outside any city perimeter, to experience them on their home turf, travelers must venture into the island's interior. But the only routes to the remote tribal villages are via a vast series of rivers and tributaries. Local maps show only the main east-to-west road, along with an intricate network of transport waterways. The biggest of six major rivers, the Rejang is Borneo's equivalent to the Amazon and the gateway to the island's unpredictable rain forest. Where the asphalt continues past the river sits the quiet frontier town of Sibu and primary transportation hub of the region.

Although this is Muslim Malaysia, on Borneo, Christians arrived first, and even the Chinese were ultimately converted. One at a time, they introduce themselves in roadside restaurants, "Hello my name is George Wilson." The sixth biggest island on earth, Borneo's cultures are as diverse as its animal life. What travelers can see from a two-lane roadway skirting the edges of a jungle too dense to see into is enough to satisfy most. But for more curious travelers, with threats of anything from witch doctors to headhunters, depending on your imagination, there is much beyond here to feed the soul or chill the spine. Unfortunately, the only way further inland is by boat or small airplane. Yet since this is a motorcycle journey, the Blue Beast will travel on water.

So far, scattered small towns along the roadway have been Asian versions of Mayberry. Tranquil and friendly with an immaculate orderliness separating the old wooden buildings,they make me want to return one day to explore them. City versions of Iban tribesmen greet the few Westerners who venture this far afield with world-famous hospitality. Twice now, when attempting to settle a restaurant tab, the waiter only points to a departing car or a family walking away and said, "They already pay." Last night, a Chinese shop owner I had just met took me out for one of my best meals yet. Over spicy soft-shell crab and pungent steamed vegetables, Kenny Smith mapped out a route upriver to a remote village with rumors of an old deserted logging road connecting back to asphalt. "If it's not raining, you may be able to ride it back to Bintalu and continue north to Brunei."

The next morning, I spent a few hours interviewing reluctant riverboat captains before finding one willing to load a motorcycle for the hundred-mile upstream sail to Kapit, the last main trading post for whatever lies deeper inland. Yet this is still only a transfer point to catch another boat to a questionable riverside town with which no one in Sibu is familiar.

For travel beyond Kapit, the Malaysian government requires special permits and explanations of how travelers intend to get in as well as out. The questions they ask are unnerving. "Do you realize that there are no roads leading to any villages along the way?" I steady my growing uneasiness by mumbling something about crossing those bridges later — but what about the bridges today? Loading 600 pounds of awkward motorcycle onto the cramped rear deck of a 60-foot cargo vessel is tricky without a crane. You can't just pick it up and carry it on unstable surfaces, and there are no convenient steel ramps, like on a ferry. Because of the severe rains, river levels can change 10 feet overnight, so timing is essential if you want to be level with the concrete wharf. Loading the bike this morning, it was. Arriving in Kapit at the end of the day, it wasn't. Combine that with a need to dock on the outside of five similar vessels already tied side by side to the pier and the problem intensifies. For 50 U.S. dollars, a half-dozen beefy young Iban dockworkers offer to carry it over the rocking, narrow decks to the wharf.

They were certainly strong enough, but if one of the flip-flop-wearing youngsters slipped on the wet surface, the Beast would drop straight to the river bottom. Besides, the price was a hustle. After consulting all the captains regarding the next morning's departures, I manage to convince them that when the boat closest to the dock left we could back ours into position for a simple roll-off. They agree but warn that if it rains, the water level will rise another five feet overnight.

Staring out my hotel window past midnight must have helped, or maybe Jesus, Allah, Buddha or Thor took pity on me — but, by morning, the water level had descended to a perfect height, and after some well-coordinated maneuvering, the Blue Beast popped over the rail for a steep ride upriver to Kapit.

In retrospect, none of this had been necessary — in fact, it would have made more sense to leave the bike in Sibu and travel upriver without the burden. And today was the easy part — tomorrow, I'd repeat the process with even more difficulty 150 miles upriver. If I have to backtrack, it's long way out — and even more unpredictable is the trail to a passable road. But then again, if passion didn't override common sense, I never would have decided to ride a motorcycle around the earth.

Stranded (Only Temporarily)
July 21, 2005
Kapit, Serawak
· · · · · · · · · ·

Kapit has defied its reputation as a backwater, rough-and-tumble frontier town. Actually, it's a mini-city complete with paved roads, a small strip mall and modern housing centers. Not only are the spotless, crime-free streets coordinated into precise traffic patterns, there are no police necessary to enforce regulations. When leaving my helmet off to ride half a block, shopkeepers and patrons frantically wave, warning me that I'm violating the helmet law. Tranquility here requires an obedience found in few places outside Germany, and here I don't worry about leaving belongings unattended.

Ten thousand tribal Iban, Orangs and ethnic Chinese live side by side with no tolerance for conflict. To spur trade and development, during the 18th-century days of the White Raja, British authorities urged Chinese nationals to immigrate. They and their descendants have done their jobs well. Iban natives handle agriculture and labor, while a few still live communally in traditional elevated wooden longhouses. Anywhere else in Asia, such a harmonious coexistence would be unusual, but considering that Kapit is also entirely landlocked by a hundred miles of incredibly dense forest, it's a miracle. Perfected Stepford lives in the wilds of Borneo.

It's as though a complete community was simultaneously picked up and transplanted. Government offices, hospitals and a power station promote self-sufficiency, while manufactured goods are imported. Two roads a mile beyond the city limits end at the jungle edge like in a scene from *The Twilight Zone*. The only way to import fuel and supplies is via river barges hauling in construction equipment and building materials. But since there is also nowhere to go, three days has been sufficient to wonder and marvel. Now I must find new transportation.

This morning, after all the captains on the wharf had turned me away, my options dwindled. A tugboat dragging empty timber barges left Sibu this morning and is scheduled for docking tonight. Kapit's only shipping agent has promised a meeting and a desperate plea with the owner on my behalf. One of the reasons ship captains have rejected my passage is that there is no pier upriver to offload the Beast. A 60-foot vessel is too large to beach, and there is only a ladder for people to disembark. There must be alternatives.

Plan C is an unthinkable tail-between-the-legs retreat to Sibu —

but plan B is to locate that long-abandoned logging road to see where it leads. If able to find the entrance, I can haul enough food and water for two days. If it dead-ends on the first day, that leaves another day to return. The problem is, the rumored trail begins a quarter-mile across a swift-moving river with no means to cross.

Borneo Shakedown Ride
July 22, 2005
Sarawak, East Malaysia
● ● ● ● ● ● ● ● ● ● ● ● ● ●

Two hours of haggling in Mandarin, Malay and back into broken English netted no favorable result — no riverboat captains will haul a crazy American anywhere. At this point, even a return to the high-way in Sibu is questionable. Requesting directions to the abandoned logging road further confused my anxious Chinese helpers. *"You cannot go Missur Gren, there no pavement or hotel."* Adventure travel is illogical to business-minded merchants, but after several conversations, they draw me a map and unenthusiastically wave goodbye.

Without crossing any rivers, the trail appeared exactly where indicated, complete with a sign in three languages — "Road Closed." After verifying I had four gallons of fuel remaining, I reset the trip meter and switched on the GPS Breadcrumbs function to show a dotted line indicating the exact route I had just traveled. It's easy to get lost on the hundreds of forks and overrun trails throughout Borneo, but harnessing the technology of a half-dozen orbiting satellites evens the playing field. Yet this GPS is well-worn, and sometimes vibration shuts down the power connection, erasing recent tracks. This could cause a problem on the way out.

The first three hours' ride is over a mixture of wheel-wiggling, rocky adobe and sandy gravel — a persistent reminder of departing off the beaten path. At the 20-mile mark, a bulldozed raised barricade blocks the road. The emptiness beyond is marked by multi-shaded green mountains cursed by trackless miles of mud trails and

Negotiating recent landslides in Borneo

landslides. As advised, the road has been abandoned, but has the jungle? Why has the logging company sealed the forest? Indigenous people around the world resent international corporations raping their natural resources. Would the natives accept or reject a wandering Westerner violating their isolated wilderness on a shiny blue riding machine? Were tribal troubles ahead?

Through an early morning mist, the deteriorating trail grows thick with creeping vines and storm-eroded gullies. It was a pleasant ride dry, but after a solid rain, the return trip would be a miserable, perilous slide. How big a fool rides solo into an unforgiving rain forest hoping it will not rain? Yesterday, the decision came down to whether I would keep spinning my wheels in Kapit or spin them in the forest.

The objective was to ride in as deep as possible the first day and take two more getting out. There was no way to judge how far the road would hold — 10 miles or 100? Just before sunset, after getting buried to my axles in sucking mud one last time, I mark a GPS waypoint and record odometer readings — 55 miles of delightful, challenging jungle track in eight exhausting hours. After setting up camp in the sweltering tropical heat, eating imported apples and canned sardines by the iridescent glow of a silvery rising moon served as the grand finale of an adventurous day.

Once zipped into my two-man tent, like an orchestra warming-up, one by one, sections of awakening insects announce their presence. The first round of beetles shriek like thousands of activated smoke alarms, followed by volleys of deafening, singing crickets. Overhead, giant circling nocturnal birds ride a slow, methodical whoosh-whoosh-whoosh of enormous flapping wings. The symphony of life overwhelms me: "Welcome to the jungle." Masters of the planet we are not — within a square mile, the population of bugs likely exceeds the number of humans on the planet. Suddenly, I feel insignificant.

To Borneo tribesmen, trees, animals and insects have individual spirits, though evil ones are warded off with body tattoos. My recently ink-stained arms provide some small comfort. Still, the sounds in the dark become louder as my mind races to identify and classify which are harmless and which might be otherwise. Speculating about how lurking ghosts might welcome jungle intruders is enough to disrupt my needed night's rest. Backlit against a full moon, silhouettes of fist-size roaches creep across the paper-thin dome of my nylon tent. Somehow, even when sealed inside, tiny ants manage entry in sufficient numbers to march across my bare torso, leaving trails of annoying welts. Lying naked on a cushy Thermarest, the inescapable evening heat and humidity leave me soaked in sweat as I ponder tomorrow's plan. The night turns long and eerie.

Enveloped in predawn fog, my riding clothes, still soggy from yesterday's drizzle, are wetter than when they were hung to dry last night. But there has been a changing of the insect guard. Bees. With undulating little rumps, dozens of pink-and-yellow flyers buzz across the glistening, dew-covered rain flap, probing for something or someone to sting. But I am still hungry.

Crystal Lite and fermented duck eggs made for a decent breakfast, while later, I chase shafts of sunlight cutting through the overhead tree canopy to dry my dampened camping gear. This year's pig-hunting season had opened with a phenomenally large migration from the Indonesian side of Borneo. Tracks running through my camp indicated a family of nighttime visitors. Just after packing the last of my gear, a sharp crashing in the underbrush produces a 200-pound sow followed by a herd of snorting piglets. Slow on the draw, I miss photographing them as they trample up the hillside meadow.

On the second night out, I receive a midnight visit from three well-equipped Iban hunters, curious about the alien invader. The Malaysian government restricts the ownership of firearms, but game-hunting indigenous peoples are allowed single-barrel 12-gauge shotguns. Armed with solid slug projectiles, they can shoot down a wild boar at a hundred feet but not much further. After sharing the last of their strange purple fruit with me and using a sign language to warn of snakes, they switch on their headband spotlights and quietly fade into the woods.

Often, the quality of an adventure can be measured by what went wrong. But this week's deviation into the rain forest's mystical gardens ends as smoothly as it began. No flat tires, engine failures or tumbles off precarious rocky ledges. Poisonous spiders and snakes kept to themselves, while evil spirits attacked only those who believed in them.

Back in Kapit, local wharf workers lent a hand loading the motorcycle on the first boat heading downriver. A pipe-smoking skipper, shirtless and sporting tattered, baggy shorts, was pleased to aid a man with wild dreams. As a penetrating tropical sun caked layers of red clay on my boots, dreams of expanding horizons glowed like red-hot embers. After this test run for the harsher conditions which reportedly existed on the other side of the island, I'm confident Kalimantan is passable. My new challenge is laid out — to be the first person to circle the entire island of Borneo on two wheels.

Wounded Beast
July 30, 2005
Kota Kinabalu, Borneo
● ● ● ● ● ● ● ● ● ● ● ● ●

Maintaining a hard pace through the icy fall rains of Eastern Europe is paying off now. Not only did it get me to the hospital in Germany in time to save my ailing kidneys, sticking to schedule has also launched me ahead of planetary foul weather for the rest of the trip. The last 10 months have been mostly warm days under sunny skies, with only short bursts of monsoon storms. Even when I'm caught in tropical squalls impossible to see through, they end within an hour, and after a bit of stand-up riding, I am dry again.

Cruising East Malaysia is a glide through peaceful jungle parklands. Timid and respectful, local drivers are appalled by this aggressive motorcyclist riding the only Beemer in Borneo. From traditional roadside Iban longhouses, natives wave and beckon me to stop and talk — I resist the temptation as it only turns into a contest over who can ask the most questions. They always win.

From Sarawak, to reach Malaysia's eastern autonomous state of Sabah it's necessary to cross the Sultanate of Brunei Darussalam. One of the smallest countries in the world and once ruler of all Borneo, the government of Brunei basks in waves of cascading oil dollars. For the citizens that means free education, free health care and subsidized housing. But even when they're offered free government-built apartments, villagers often refuse, preferring to live in their stilted riverbank huts — now equipped with plumbing and satellite TV. In the mornings, water taxis deliver citizens to government-subsidized cars parked on the opposite bank for short drives to work.

It was a stroke of luck arriving in the capital of Bandar Seri Begawan in time for the sultan's annual birthday festival. A strict Islamic country, alcohol is forbidden and Western-style nightlife does not exist. Still, the city center is alive with outdoor venues and traditional Muslim food stalls. Colorful banners with images of a grinning sultan drape the tallest buildings. But besides meeting people in the streets and photographing their mosque, there is nothing left to do except continue rolling east.

Irregular international boundaries mean that reaching Sabah requires four separate border crossings back and forth through Malaysia. Limping into Kota Kinabalu with screeching wheel bearings and a leaky water-pump seal was made worse when a brake pedal bolt vibrated out 500 miles back. It's possible to get by using only the front brake, but without both, an emergency stop could be an issue. Three problems at once are difficult, but if you tackle them one at a time, the severity diminishes.

Annoyed this time by the typically inquisitive audience that forms whenever I'm fiddling with roadside repairs, I am short with a group of friendly Chinese and answer anticipated questions before they can ask. "Yes, it has 650 CCs and holds ten gallons of fuel and can go 600 miles without stopping and costs blah blah blah." Middle-aged Mr. Gkwa is not deterred by an impatient foreigner and follows me into a restaurant. *"I can companion with you?"*

Ashamed at my attitude, I offer a hand, "Hello, my name is Glen and I come from America." He likes to repeat the last few words of my answers while stroking his chin — *"Ah, come from America."*

"I have been traveling for more than one year."

"Ah, more than one year."

Over fried noodles and boiled eggs, Mr. Gkwa says he knows of a special machine shop that can make a new bushing and bolt for my crippled brake pedal. As one Chinese to another, a wave of his hand signals to the restaurant owner that breakfast is paid for, and we are off to solve my problems.

The industrial zone winds through a 10-mile maze beyond Kota Kinabulu and into even rows of modern cement-block shops run by older men speaking only Chinese. The creative genius of any machinist is amazing, especially when working from enormous piles of rusting salvaged steel. Instead of using his lathe to make a separate new bushing and bolt, this confident artist insists that carving a complex one-piece part is best. Considering the odds of calculating such precise measurements correctly and certain that German engineers had done it right the first time, I reiterate, "No, please just make a separate bushing and bolt."

He laughs, *"I make. You no like, you no pay."*

Nothing goes to waste in developing countries, especially scrapped metal. Verifying his eyeball calculations with micrometer checks, Mr. Wong carefully trims a rusted old hexagon-shaped crowbar on a spinning lathe, creating a part that, in the West, would take a team to design. The equivalent of five bucks solves problem one.

As a maintenance step, I should have replaced the rear-wheel carrier bearings 10,000 miles ago, but procrastination prevailed. Mr. Gkwa also knows of a bearing shop that might supply cross-referenced BMW parts. An afternoon passes puttering across town in his rattling old pickup truck being entertained by haggling Chinese merchants hunting down fresh wheel bearings. Mr. Gkwa is the ultimate fix-it man, and we proceed to the next step. With critical parts now in hand, an aging mechanic stares through coke-bottle glasses muttering, *"Can do, can do."* From riding through storms and river crossings, hardened steel balls have rusted into shattered fragments that dribble out when the wheel is removed. A debate rages in Mandarin as expert fingers scrape away debris and tap in new bearings.

Yet my final problem is too difficult to resolve here, even for Mr. Gkwa. Worn water-pump seals at this stage of use are normal, but there's no telling how much longer my slow-leaking set will last. When it's cold, the coolant pump shaft leaks a drop a minute, but as the engine warms, it subsides. Barring total seal failure, it's possible to top off the radiator twice a day and continue. It was time to weigh the odds and evaluate the risk of a total rupture, which would yank my journey to an immediate halt somewhere in primitive Kalimantan, the mostly untamed Indonesian side of Borneo. The BMW motorcycle representative in Kuala Lumpur has emailed a message that parts are available in Singapore, but that's 3,000 miles ahead on mud logging roads if I continue in a forward direction.

Looping Borneo
August 4, 2005
Tawau, East Malaysia
• • • • • • • • • • • • •

An endangered species, orangutans that have managed to elude poachers in the wild are difficult to find. The Sipilok Rehabilitation Center on the far eastern tip of Borneo is the largest of four sanctuaries in the world where orangutan orphans are cared for and taught to survive on their own. Just outside the busy seaport of Sandakan, a small, dedicated staff of mostly volunteers studies and rehabilitates former captive adults and babies missed by hunters. Monkeys are common everywhere in Asia, but the human-like features of orangutans puts them in a class of their own, and they are among the most impressive animals in east Malaysia.

Once past the visitor center, a quarter-kilometer wooden catwalk elevated above the rain forest floor guides adventurers on travel packages to a double-tiered platform for the silent morning show. Here, vacationers perspiring in spiffy new safari clothes can wait for feeding time and distant glimpses of orangutans in training. In thick, humid air, almost to the designated minute, a fat nylon cable stretching a thousand yards back into the jungle begins to jump and sway. One by one, rusty-haired young and old orangutans reach hand over hand, gripping their way forward in a coordinated rhythm to receive morning treats of bananas and sugarcane. Fascinating but touristy, this is still the only way to see orangutans in their natural environment.

Later that night, smiling to sleep in a polished hardwood lodge, visions of exploring the upcoming wilderness haunt my dreams. Kalimantan, the Indonesian side of Borneo, is reported to be similar to the interior of Sabah yet lacks a consistent coastal route. There are no paved roads to link remote towns and villages, only sloppy tracks and watery paths of shallow jungle rivers. Just exiting East Malaysia requires island-hopping by ferryboat to reach the shores of Kalimantan. That's been the task here at the last stop in Tawau, locating a sea-going captain willing to haul me to Nunukan Island, where I might find another to take me to Tarakan Island. Because information about the landscape from there is scarce, the path becomes uncertain unless the government has something to offer.

Officials in the Indonesian consulate are cooperative but skeptical, as not even the government liaison officer understands my mission. Explaining my desire to traverse Kalimantan to end up back at my initial starting point in Kuching, he politely advises that it was more practical to ride the asphalt road back from where I just came. Circling the island by land made no sense to him, especially alone. Upon further consideration, he added that he was uncertain if Indonesian customs in Nunukan had ever processed a motor vehicle. Anyway, the only means he was sure of to reach there was by passenger ferries that had no accommodations for motorcycles.

In the past, when I needed the approval of government officials, I always found it helped to first shake a man's hand and look him in the eye — that made it harder to turn me down, and today was no different. By the end of my two-hour plea, a hesitant Mr. Ali was finally convinced to help, offering encouragement by scribbling a note of introduction on the back of his business card. This might come in handy if I got far enough to use it with reluctant customs officials in Kalimantan. And there were still peculiar hurdles lurking ahead.

It's wise to be careful where you camp, and not just because of poisonous snakes or wild animals. Even though Borneo is a giant rain forest, it's nearing the driest time of year, and scientists warn of a danger greater than disease or snake bites: deadfall. Thousands of decaying hardwood tree branches, waterlogged and weighted down by moisture from squalls, silently plummeting to the earth are the most common killers in the jungle. But unless I'm completely stuck, I have no plans to drift from the trail.

With loggers busy stripping the forest, there should be dirt roads leading to asphalt and cities. There was no established primary route or maps showing the individual connections, but truckers must move pillaged timber somehow. To alleviate self-doubt I mumble, "There is always a first time for everything." An Internet search yielded only rumors that two bikers had looped the island years ago, but they'd started halfway into Kalimantan — not from the actual border.

Regardless, my journey proceeds one step at a time, beginning at the wharf, finding a sympathetic ferryboat captain. Evaluating the tides indicates that at 12:30 p.m. the ship's main deck will be at dock level for easier cargo transfer.

When slinging 600 pounds of awkward motorcycle over the raised transoms of passenger ferries, weight is a significant factor. But because of critical gas shortages throughout Indonesia, it's necessary to fill my 10-gallon tank before loading. There are likely additional obstacles no one has imagined. After studying maps showing dozens of small rivers interrupting established mud roads, I'm certain more boating is ahead. If the jungle does prove to be impassable, failure means a thousand-mile retreat back to Malaysia. Once I start, there'll be no turning back.

Nunukan Island
August 4, 2005
Kalimantan, Indonesia
● ● ● ● ● ● ● ● ● ● ● ● ●

As my Russian experience began aboard a ferry in Japan, so did my journey into Indonesia from Malaysia. Packed nearly on top of each other in the sticky heat of an overcrowded ship's hold, curious crewmen and inquisitive passengers edged closer to share handfuls of dried squid and initiate a sign-language conversation. No one spoke English, yet after drawing a map, they understood where I was headed, though they remained unsure why.

Loading the motorcycle onto the rusted decks of the passenger ferry had been an over-the-plank roll-on under power, yet, in shaking their heads and repeating "*Nunukan*," dubious shipmen hinted that off-loading would be another matter. It was, but nothing a dozen anxious helpers couldn't handle with a cooperative captain running the hundred-foot-long ship bow first directly against the wharf for a team-effort manhandle onto solid ground.

Once on the island, a stop to investigate a roadside gathering of costumed natives results in a joyous invitation to join an Islamic wedding procession. Muslims can be as liberal as they please in Indonesia — women wear garments from white-laced headscarves to see-through blouses with black brassieres. It's far too crowded for up-close photos of the ceremony, but tittering bridesmaids and decked-out relatives are anxious to pose for the foreigner while eating and drinking. Although there was little to offer, the men insisted I sample a small table buffet of smoking hot chili dishes — as always, it's those with the least who share the most.

Last week, when I traveled further east through Sabah, the economic situation had deteriorated as evenly as the infrastructure, until it became a pitiful crumple in Kalimantan. But Indonesians shouting greetings today seem content and friendly enough, and it took an hour threading my way through throngs of beckoning islanders to reach the town's lone hotel. Two bucks buys a tidy cubicle with a drooping mattress and a coldwater-bucket bathroom. But the manager lets me use his office's electrical outlet to charge my laptop, and the café next door sells bargain seafood dinners.

Although their answers varied, when I asked locals in East Malaysia, they were confident a bigger boat sailed from Nunukan to Tarakan Island. From there, it would be land-based travel until completing the loop back to Kuching. That is, except for passing over a variety of unfamiliar rivers and swamps.

It turns out there were only two small passenger ferries, both lacking deck space for motorcycles. Anxious to help a wandering foreigner, my new-found friend, Abdul Kahar, explains that there is a 10-foot wooden fishing boat sailing at dawn to arrive west on the mainland — even better for setting my record because it's right on the border instead of further away, where the previous team began.

To my dismay, local Kalimantan maps still don't show roads connecting villages in remote Dayak tribal regions. Although I still believe it's possible to complete my loop around Borneo, on further examination, the estimated distance has stretched to a zigzagging 3,000 miles from here. Barring typhoons and other mishaps, I could reach the other border of East Malaysia in three weeks.

Loggers
August 6, 2005
Simanggaris, Kalimantan, Borneo
● ● ● ● ● ● ● ● ● ● ● ● ● ● ● ● ● ● ● ●

Staring down onto the deck of a freshly painted open-deck fishing boat, I was beginning to believe what people had been repeating the last week. Riding a motorcycle around the island of Borneo was impossible. From the edge of the splintered plank pier, 10 sturdy young wharf workers proposed lowering a 500-pound motorcycle five feet down by hand onto the bow of an awkward, rocking 25-foot water vessel.

But since every other ship's captain had refused the job, this was the last chance to escape Nunukan Island and reach the mainland. After setting up my camera and taking 10 deep breaths, within a few nervous moments, a shiny Blue Beast sat resting on its kickstand while it was securely roped-down for a morning sail across the channel. The upriver logging outpost at Simanggaris is known only to boatmen and can't be identified on a local map. I was almost out of the frying pan.

Because yesterday only the immigration office was open and not customs, when arriving, I just offered my passport for stamping without discussing the bike. Indonesian customs officials did not hear about a motorcycle until this morning, as we were preparing to sail. Since no one was sure how to proceed, friendly-but-firm uniformed men with carbine rifles refused to allow us to proceed. But after several calls to superiors in Jakarta and six cups of tea, they determined all we needed was to stamp my carnet de passage and I could be on my way.

Soon, cool ocean breezes countered a slow-chugging diesel engine pushing us forward among hundreds of tiny islands covered with wild banana trees and thick, tangled undergrowth. Wild boar snorted on empty beaches as huge flapping birds with purple beaks crooned and cackled in the shallows. Eventually, the bay began to channel backwards into a narrow brown river restricted by tides.

At the Simanggaris mud landing a lone, nonuniformed cop was

waiting with radio in hand and permit forms to fill out. Since there was no wharf, we waited for the sundown high tide to roll the bike directly onto the steep, slippery bank. After explaining my mission by drawing a map, the police captain invites me to sleep at his outpost and offers to sketch a route over hundreds of unmarked trails. "You are sure to get lost — there are many turns without signs." But intersections without markings were still better than no roads at all.

But the reason for roads is troubling. Except for the remote, untamed interior of Borneo, logging roads have been cut to facilitate what's recently been outlawed — pillaging of the jungle's valuable timber and replacing the giant hardwood trees with palm groves. After the destruction of the rain forest, a better cash crop for multinational corporations are palm tree seedlings from which they can harvest cooking oil. Not a bad idea if you leave out the fact that the process is destroying one of the most spectacular rain forests on earth.

Riding over the first rise from the river, I see a view of the appalling devastation. The forest has been leveled in all directions to the horizon, leaving a barren landscape devoid of life. With nothing there to hold the topsoil in storms, what remains are thousands of rounded red clay knolls littered with tree stumps — tombstones marking the end of life in the forest. This is how I'd imagine the earth would look after nuclear war — an ecological disaster of unfathomable magnitude.

As a result of pressure from ecologists, logging in the rain forest is now restricted. The four policemen offering me shelter had been appointed by the Indonesian government to monitor the logging. They are also sons of the corporate manager who owns the palm groves, and, as they revealed with their comments about earning big money, they cooperate with the logging companies.

Simanggaris is a conglomeration of 50 logging camps connected by a maze of mangled dirt roads. Scattered rows of barrack-style shacks are home to a thousand workers laboring 10 hours a day in the harsh tropical heat. Through the course of the night, half the population passed through the police compound to verify the rumors of a blue-eyed foreigner on two wheels. The boss was the only one who spoke English. From the cool air-conditioned cab of his company pickup, the Malaysian project manager explained his program.

"First we cut down those useless old trees and then replace them with palm groves. In 13 months we begin taking the oil."

"But what about the rain forest?"

Pointing to the policemen lounging on the station veranda, he laughs "Oh we don't worry, no one cares about that."

"What about your workers? How much do you pay them?"

"Our employees are very fortunate and their future depends on them. If they work hard, they can earn 30 to 40 dollars per month."

When traveling, it's often difficult to resist the urge to criticize. It can be a mistake to judge those living in less fortunate circumstances. How Indonesia balances its economic growth by exploiting its natural resources should be its own business, but the world science community universally believes the destruction of the rain forest is a crime-for-profit against the planet we all expect to sustain us.

My stomach was already turning. As the evening progressed with flitting bugs bouncing off humming tubular fluorescent lights, the stench of these men's complicity overtook the smell of their cheap whiskey and stale cigarettes. The bed they had laid out for me under the office fan would surely have been more comfortable than the smothering humidity outside, but I found a cleansing relief in declining the hospitality and pitching my tent in the sand.

The Reality of Borneo
August 9, 2005
Kalimantan
● ● ● ● ● ● ●

The warnings I'd had about the dozens of unmarked junctions were justified. A flip-of-the-coin choice ended at a murky brown river too deep to ride, prompting a frustrating 40-mile backtrack and half a day lost.

Logging company workers fiddling with the bike last night had broken one of the metal contact prongs supplying power to the GPS. A scrap piece of folded tinfoil from a chewing gum wrapper is almost a substitute until engine vibration causes an intermittent connection failure, so those vital Breadcrumbs tracks frequently disappear. If I can save the sporadically displayed lines and dots on the screen, data stored on my flash disk would be the first satellite record of this area. Even the two logging company engineers I met, working with modern laser survey equipment, lacked enough information to create a map. Their laptop computer stored details of the immediate region but showed only towns of 10,000 people or more — and there are few of those in Kalimantan. While we swapped notes over lukewarm soft drinks and stale potato chips, they assured me that by tomorrow night, I would reach an aggregate road southwest to coastal Samarinda.

Aware indigenous people in Indonesian Borneo are less tame than their tourist-tainted counterparts in Malaysia, I ask the engineers, "What about the Dayak tribes? Can I stop to visit?"

"You'd better find a soldier to go with you. Those people are uncivilized and resent foreigners. You can tell by their tattoos that they are primitive and should not be approached without invitation."

As the rutted track finally turned to graded gravel, I realized that those warnings of an "impossible" ride would have been correct had it rained. After moderate storms, yesterday's steep, eroded gullies of slick clay would have been impassible, with four-wheel drive. This is now the second day without rain that, even in this dry season, should fall nightly. If the weather returned to normal, this could become rough country to be stranded in.

Unless you're in constant forward motion on a motorcycle, the heat and humidity here can be unbearable. Soaked in sweat at midnight, when sleep finally comes, it lasts only a few hours. Two restless nights in a tent and one in a bare-bones logger's camp without electricity has drained my mental energy. Lurking mosquitoes don't bother me anymore; ultimately they'll drink their fill. But the lack of sleep causes errors in judgment, and while navigating without reference, the forest begins to look the same. Villages appear more often now, but just getting the names right from the natives to record in the GPS is difficult as their accents vary greatly every 20 miles.

My spiced tapioca rice bars kept fresh in damp banana leaves ran out yesterday, but a brown-shelled honey-tasting fruit curbs my hunger enough to keep riding. Already too heavy for the unstable riding conditions, my water-hauling capacity has been limited to four two-liter plastic bottles. But with all this sweating, even after consuming two a day, I produce almost no urine.

This afternoon, like a promised reward, a regional map tacked on the wall of a military outpost shows a thousand-mile stretch of paved road with a city large enough for an airport just 200 miles ahead — Samarinda. That means air-conditioned hotels and Internet terminals with nearby seafood restaurants are only two days away. Considering the potential for mishaps, though, I realize anything can happen along the way — with so many variables to plan for, my dreams of returning to Kuching are more remote than ever.

Grappling and the Art of Motorcycle Travel
August 10, 2005
Tengan Selor, Kalimantan, Indonesian Borneo
● ●

Black belt competition judo matches last for an unbelievably exhausting, seemingly endless five minutes. During that time, combatants try to position themselves under or around their opponent in order to gain sufficient leverage to slam each other onto their backs, force an elbow joint backwards or strangle the weaker man into unconsciousness by restricting blood flow to the brain. The loser can stop the fight at any time to prevent permanent injury by slapping the mat — submission. The same applies for jujitsu, but because most of the battle is waged on the ground, rounds extend to 10 minutes. Western wrestling is a series of fast-paced, incredibly intense two-minute rounds where contestants seek to pin another highly trained fighter's shoulders to the mat. Because of the simultaneous use of hands, arms and legs, grappling is the most demanding and requires the most refined technique of all the contact fighting arts.

At Tenri Judo Dojo in East Los Angeles, California, during evening practice sessions, when training for the national team, our warm-up was to throw 50 men in a row then fight every fresh black belt on the mat for two minutes each until collapsing. The following morning workout included wind sprints around a football field followed by an hour of weight lifting. Between that and the injuries, this was the toughest conditioning imaginable, and the reason I retired. The human body eventually reaches its limits.

But that training is what got me through the harder times to come — five weeks of starvation and torment at the hands of a rebel army. Later, shell-shocked by the experience, discipline developed through martial arts gave me the necessary strength of spirit to climb back on a motorcycle and continue to my round-trip to Argentina. During those difficult days, I recalled my earlier training mantras, "If I can do judo, I can do anything."

So that was then and this is now, and what the hell am I doing back in the ring gagging for air in some tropical jungle? The word *impossible* has always been a challenge to me, even if there wasn't much to gain beyond bragging rights. If so many people hadn't claimed looping Borneo was impossible, I probably would be relaxing right now in a comfortable Kuching hotel. But as I am discovering, there are good reasons why no one else has done this. It has taken me five 12-hour days merely to cover the first thoroughly fatiguing 300 wheel-spinning miles. A Trans-Siberian crossing is a cakewalk compared to this.

Muscling 600 pounds of motorcycle on a hard surface is tiring enough. In slick mud, sitting on the seat paddling with burning legs while pushing on the handlebars is exhausting. But to be honest, I would not have felt so alive without those familiar lung-burning gasps for air. If I can ride Borneo, I can ride anything.

After all, what was motorcycling through Kalimantan without being buried in muck at least once? But mile after mile? Toward the end of the day, I ran into four-wheelers attempting a short hop to the next town who'd been stuck in the mud since yesterday — and seemed to accept their situation as normal.

Knowing the road conditions ahead would help. But few natives here have ever traveled 20 miles beyond their homes, so the best information is rumor. No one knows if the distance to Samarinda is 200 or 300 miles, only that it takes three long days if it doesn't rain. In South America, it rained every day and I was wet for seven months. On Borneo, Jesus, Thor and Allah have been merciful. But what if the road ends again at the river? The last stretch had been called "a good road," which makes me wonder what the next 3,000 miles to Kuching will be like. Not counting the tame sections of Borneo: Sarawak, Brunei and Sabah, riding Kalimantan alone is similar to riding from San Francisco to New York half off-road in mud.

When clearing the last bog and asking a woodsman in sign language how much further this misery goes on, I am uncertain if he answered 10 miles or 10 minutes. On the edge of the equator, a relentless tropical sun boils a gallon of moisture from my flesh every eight hours. The fatigue is so intense I lack the strength to sit upright, let alone continue paddling with my legs and feet. But gazing ahead into the vibrant, forbidding jungle exhausted, stinking and hungry, I cannot recollect when I've felt more content.

And thank god for those youngsters who twice lifted the bike off my leg while I was laying sideways. They seemed to enjoy following me, as they could walk faster than I could ride through the slop. At the point of total exhaustion, thinking it impossible to push through the mud any further, they suddenly rushed to my aid, shoving from behind. While I stand red-faced and gasping for air, the inspiring Dayak girl holding my helmet shocks me when urging in decent English, "Come on mister, you've got to try harder. I know you can do it." Today, she was my judo coach.

Hanging with the Locals
August 12, 2005
Kalimantan, Borneo
● ● ● ● ● ● ● ● ● ● ● ●

Males of all ages in Borneo are heavily tattooed with each pattern signifying a particular accomplishment or spiritual meaning. Flowers inked on fronts of deltoid muscles ward off specific evil forest ghosts, but a skull on the back of a hand proves that the bearer has taken a human head — and likely also consumed a few of his victim's internal organs. As a matter of practice with natives anywhere, when entering a village, I remove my jacket to reveal my own collage of Western tribal art and let them speculate what the skulls etched on my forearms could mean.

Skirting the hinterlands, the natives are friendly. When I stop outside thatched-roof villages, it's a slow process to get invited in. Digital camera games lure giggling children, which eventually lead to introductions to the chief. Tonight, following the tribal etiquette of standing quietly for examination, the potbellied old leader with jagged teeth motions with a raised hand-signal permission to sleep in the adjoining quarters of his communal longhouse. With no common words between us, communicating with natives is difficult but also one of the best experiences in Borneo.

The chief was boss, but he still did housework. After sweeping his own floor, he presented me with a specially stamped friendship letter written in local language. This important document will be stored next to my heart along with the hand-painted spoon given to me by the Russian Buryats who housed and fed me during a Siberian tornado. In developing nations, gift-giving is far more important that tips of currency and so is feeding a stranger.

Finding solid food in Kalimantan has been difficult, yet whenever stopping for directions, without asking, natives fill my saddlebags with dwarf bananas and wild berries. Although protein is unavailable, jungle banana trees provide sufficient carbohydrates for energy and to slow any obvious weight loss. I'd assumed at the start that living off the land was possible, but clean water has been hard to find. I'm forced now to ration, as my last half-liter of stored water must be saved to replenish my slow-leaking cooling system. I can function without water, but the motorcycle's engine cannot.

To stay ahead of overdue storms, I must keep moving. A freak dry spell is still the only reason I've made it this far. The reality is a solid rain will stop me cold. Gathering to watch me prepare to ride, grinning villagers step forward, offering handfuls of peeled fruit. Upon this early morning departure, those who fled at my approach now jump with thumbs-up gestures, shouting goodbyes. That's the awkward emotional issue of adventure travel — bidding farewell to people that in a very short time I have grown to like and will surely never see again.

The Price for Adventure
August 13, 2005
Balikpapan, Borneo
• • • • • • • • • • • •

The most adventurous times on a motorcycle are when you're riding off-road. That means straying from the beaten path to see and experience what few tourists can — the extremes of both good and evil. Straight-shooting across the Syrian Desert, wandering the Sinai and sleeping with the Bedouin in Jordan linger in my head like the scents of exotic flavors. In retrospect, even getting lost in the Gobi is now a pleasant recollection. But adventure has a price.

The Gobi alone claimed broken sub-frame bolts, a bent pannier frame and, because of my kidney complications, peeing lots of blood. Abrasive dust and clinging mud prematurely wears motorcycle drive lines, while overworked suspensions eat piston seals causing fluids to leak. The jolts from riding over sinkholes and sharp stones in Borneo require constant stops to check for a busted frame. This has been the most punishing test of the journey, and I still have no clear sense of how far it is back to Kuching.

Off the beaten path in the wilds of Borneo, riding is a relentless struggle, and what's behind shouldn't count. But sometimes it does. The last hundred miles into Balikpapan turned into twisting mountain tarmac so smooth and sweet I drifted into road-racing local boys on souped-up little Hondas. The shock of the day came at the end while unsnapping my aluminum panniers in the hotel parking lot. Noticing an unusual gap between the fender and frame, I discovered that the false exhaust pipe containing 15 pounds of hard- to-replace vital spare parts had vanished. My ratchet tools, tire irons, patch kit and spare brake pads lay somewhere in the last hundred miles. Twelve hours a day of jackhammering had taken its toll.

Double-nutted bolts supporting the stainless-steel tube had sheared in half. Because my last set of brake pads had cost me 180 bucks in Israel, I'd been waiting until they were completely shot to change them — now, front and rear were nearly worn down to bare metal. Because of their superior stopping power, I use sintered pads likely unavailable in Asia. Even in a major city, the typical customs-clearing delays to get express-mailed spares could take weeks, if they made it at all. And how long could I expect to have clear skies?

But if I'd skipped this loop of Borneo, I surely wouldn't have laughed with mischievous monkeys dropping twigs on my head and never had the pants scared off me by a 10-foot cobra in the road. I was satisfied just having witnessed a 400-pound boar reverse his course and charge back into the jungle, more afraid of my motorcycle than I was of him. And I would certainly have never met the Dayak or the coal-mining couple from Sanata who took me home for the night. The rain forest was the same here as Malaysia, but Kalimantan is more primitive and far less filled with people who had seen my kind before.

It's too early to know if the worst is over or just beginning, but I have come to accept that real adventure starts when things stop going as planned.

Friends
August 14, 2005
Banjarmassin, Borneo
• • • • • • • • • • • • •

Two heavenly nights in Balikpapan in a hotel with air-conditioning, fattening up on bargain-priced giant river prawns was a sufficient recharge for the remaining unknown stretch back to Kuching. Although it is cooler here on the coast, I dialed the room thermostat down to blizzard mode — what a relief to wake with a sore throat from cold, dry air instead of soaked in sweat and peppered with mosquito bites.

After a two-hour ferryboat river-crossing, the 300-mile road to Banjarmassin improved to the level of deteriorated asphalt, some of it wide enough for two cars and a dividing line. This is coal-mining country, with a million migrant workers from throughout the islands of Indonesia steadily bussing to and from underground mines or hauling truckloads of jet-black coal. After a week of seeing only a few vehicles a day, being trapped in long black clouds of diesel exhaust is a sullen reminder of the price of progress. Here, dedicated miners toiling six days a week on 12-hour shifts earn $300 a month — a fortune compared to most other jobs in Indonesia. Under threat from pollution caused by plundering its riches of gold, oil, coal and even diamonds, pristine Borneo is to Indonesia what Alaska is to the U.S. — an endangered national treasure.

Coal miner Mohammad Siah explained that with a Korean corporation covering his room and board, at the end of five years, even while supporting his parents, he could retire rich enough to buy a house and motorcycle — raising his status to most-desirable in the eyes of Indonesian girls looking for husbands. This afternoon, he is anxious to teach me his language. Written and pronounced the same as English only without tenses, Bassha Indonesian is easy to learn if you practice with the natives. Restaurant stops become impromptu classes as my scribbled dictionary notebook is filled by new tutors wanting to teach common phrases over some of the tastiest beef satay in Asia. Once you decide what to eat, like anywhere in developing

The bridges of Borneo

nations, meals are cooked to order. No one here has heard of frozen food. Market fruits and vegetables were picked the day before, while the chicken in the fiery tomato noodles was likely clucking a few hours ago. But there are still motorcycle issues to handle.

I am still unsure how far I have to go, but matching GPS tracks against a trucker's regional map indicates another 1,500 miles back to Kuching, at least half of which will be off-road. Up until now, Avon Gripster tires have delivered 10,000 miles per set, even when grinding through Siberia. From spinning over abrasive gravel and rock-face in Borneo, at 5,000, this current pair is almost worn smooth.

If you search hard enough, you can always find what you need. In Banjarmassin, there are motor-scooter shops across the city center, but none have reason to carry tires or brake pads for bigger bikes. Seventeen-inch tires are common in Europe but not in Indonesia — except when used on a particular model of police bike, and there just happens to be one in Banjarmassin. An eager-to-assist Suzuki motorcycle shop owner appoints his English-speaking bookkeeper to spend the morning interpreting, while others work the phones tracking down tires and providing directions.

My new Kalimantan map shows a few major cities linked by waterways with still no indication of rural land routes. Men familiar with the region are busy drawing on my map, connecting the dots with ink lines where the smaller roads should be. They are positive that some of them extend at least another 200 miles to Sampit, but after that, no one is sure. That's good enough; other volunteers will fill in more blanks when I get there.

To assist the crazy foreigner, work at the scooter shop has shut down until my new tire is mounted and road tested. Mechanics and salesmen circled around the laptop for a slideshow of alien cultures and animals. How do you explain snow to those who've only lived in the tropics? They wanted to know what camels smelled like, and when they see the erotic sculptures of Indian temples, the young Muslim men could only gasp and point. At last my bike had a fresh rear tire and a set of used brake pads that should last until I reached Singapore.

If he'd only charged for labor and a half-day's legwork, the bill would have been 10 bucks, yet the owner adamantly refuses my offers of payment — his only request was to take a photo of us all together so I would always remember my friends in Banjarmissan. Topped off with dollar-a-gallon low-octane fuel, I am ready to ride. Late evening light rains cleanse the countryside, while the skies remain cloudy enough to shield me from the frying rays of the equatorial sun. With luck, I'll return to Kuala Lumpur on the mainland in two weeks en route for the next Indonesian island, Sumatra.

Caneeeeebols
August 17, 2005
Sampit, Kalimantan, Borneo
● ● ● ● ● ● ● ● ● ● ● ● ● ● ● ● ●

Indonesia, the largest Muslim nation in the world and fourth most populous, is actually a group of island countries with separate cultures and religions united under one government. Bali is Hindu, Java is Muslim, Kalimantan (Borneo) is predominantly Christian and so on. So different are the various values and beliefs, that for 60 years there has been a constant struggle, in one region or another, to secede. The most recent concerns are the separatist movements of East Timor and the tsunami-ravaged province of Aceh in Sumatra.

There are literally thousands of tiny islands in the archipelago, some inhabited, many deserted. With the Indonesian side of Borneo overflowing with natural resources and vastly underpopulated, in 1973, to properly exploit its riches, the government instituted a national program of transmigration. Because of a critical labor shortage, inhabitants from other islands were offered economic incentives to settle in Kalimantan to begin new careers. Known for their courtesy and hospitality, local Dayak tribesmen greeted the newcomers with tolerance and friendship.

But the more industrious recent immigrants soon passed their welcoming hosts in terms of prosperity and opportunity. The natives were left behind. During the '90s, tensions simmered with sporadic violence and killings. Eventually, an all-out violent conflict exploded between pioneering Mudarese and indigenous Dayaks. The rage peaked in 2001 during a five-day homicidal rampage in which authorities claim 500 Mudarese were stabbed to death. The orgy of violence was so intense regional police fled in terror.

Early European missionaries converted the Dayaks long ago but although they're now dressed in Western clothes and baptized as Christians, a few early animistic beliefs linger. Some Dayak sects believe that when conflicts turn to war, to properly kill an enemy you must also cut off his head to capture his spirit. Then to control that spirit, it is necessary to eat certain body parts. Following ancient practice, during the last violent confrontation, not only did Dayaks sever the heads of their Mudarese enemies, they used their hearts for satay while adding brain matter to their morning coffee. A local man laughed while explaining it to me: *"After they cut off heads, the men was like frog, they keep wiggling for 10 or 15 seconds."*

Sampit had been the flashpoint of the carnage and now, four years later, a designated overnight on my way back to Kuching. When I mentioned Sampit on stops in outer villages to ask directions, frowns replaced pearly smiles as the locals uttered warnings. They wagged little brown index fingers then drew them across their throats, following up with cries of *"Caneeeeebols."*

Sampit wasn't my first choice for a stopover, but there was nothing else beyond my last stop in Banjarmassin. Still, the rumors had me nervous.

Although most of it was paved, covering those 300 miles of steady dipping road was like riding a pogo stick on wheels. There wasn't much to see on long straightaways across dried-out flat jungle terrain, except a few dilapidated villages with old men in baggy cotton shirts lounging in the shade. Not knowing the local languages, travelers miss a lot of what goes on around them — like today being Independence Day for Indonesians, commemorating ridding themselves of Dutch rule. This was a time for them to celebrate overcoming colonialism and to rant about foreigners. I rode into Sampit around 10 at night, just after the parade and festivities ended with an electrical blackout.

Yet, the Dayak were friendly, shouting greetings from streets lined with step-through motor-scooters and partying teenagers. They dressed like natives anywhere else on Borneo, in Levis and T-shirts labeled with names of American football teams. This scene was like Bike Week in Borneo. In the wood-planked lobby of a musty, old two-story hotel, the young desk clerk wearing wire-frame glasses spoke perfect English. And during the usual questions and answers, a bond of trust was established. After helping haul my equipment upstairs, as though sharing the secret of life and death, he pulled on my arm, whispering, *"Mistah, you want to get very hot tonight?"*

Optimistic about what he might mean, I reply, "Are you talking about women?"

"No, no, we have drinks!"

"Drinks?"

"Yes, yes, here in Sahmpeet, we are not Moooslim, we are Christen and make our own drinks."

Indonesia may be liberal in some ways, but it is still an Islamic country that draws the line on certain moral issues. Whatever your religion, alcohol is still illegal, and getting arrested along with a tribal bootlegging ring was pushing adventure a step too far. Indonesian law is strictly enforced — right up to death penalties for selling marketable quantities of marijuana. There is no such thing as probation or halfway houses for substance abuse, only prison. Recalling recent headlines of a 20-year sentence imposed on an Australian woman who wasn't conclusively proven to have possessed pot, slurping Borneo moonshine didn't seem worth the risk for a man who only occasionally drinks beer.

"Thanks for the offer, but I prefer a walk downtown to meet the people."

"No, you can only go out in the daytime, never at night."

"Why, is it dangerous?"

"Yes," he says, drawing his finger across his throat, "Dayaks."

"But you are Dayak."

"My mother is Dayak but my father is from Java, so I am only half-dangerous."

"Okay, can you tell me about the road to Sukamara?"

Waving his hand up and down through the air, he replies, "That is 500 kilometers from here and the road is like this. Traveling there by motorbike will take three days."

Pointing outside, at the pavement, I ask, "Is the road like that," then, indicating the dirt, "or like that?"

Walking outside he selects a baseball-size rock and says, "No, it is mostly these."

Tense Moments
August 20, 2005
Bulik, Central Kalimantan, Borneo
• • • • • • • • • • • • • • • • • • •

Since leaving California over a year ago, other than the encounter with aggressive tribal guards at the Afghan border, I've had few tense moments. The maddening traffic of India and daredevil drivers of Russia kept me on edge, but I was never afraid. Even though the authorities I'd met throughout the world have been mostly friendly, it is common knowledge that policemen and soldiers have a darker side. Tales of corruption and exploitation are too numerous to ignore. Just because I had yet to run into a shakedown didn't mean they didn't exist.

Bulik is a medium-sized multicultural township administered by officials from Java, one of the few villages large enough to have food sold in markets and my first chance in a while to buy a meal. Over greasy fried eggs in an open-air roadside noodle-stand, a well-dressed middle-aged man initiates what has become standard conversation, *"From where do you come mistah?"* Dialogue from there is predictable. Naming the countries, the price of the bike and telling him yes, I am traveling alone. But this inquisitive stranger persists.

"I think maybe you are from Greenpeace?"

Not knowing where he is leading, I laugh, "No I'm just wandering the planet writing about people."

His tone intensifies, *"I know you are journalist from Greenpeace."*

Changing the subject, I ask, "Is there a place here to buy a map? I lost mine yesterday."

"What are you writing about Kalimantan?"

"Just how nice and friendly the people are. Is there a store near here?"

"Are you sure you are not Greenpeace?"

"No. I am just a wandering motorcyclist, and I must go now to find a map."

Nodding to two other men dressed in similar shirts standing

behind me, he says, *"Better you follow them first to go and talk with police."*

A stern-faced commander is waiting outside at the cement-block government station with cell phone in hand, and I can't help noticing that he is dressed well for such a low-paid government worker. After curt introductions, he guides me to his office for questioning. From behind a desk stacked high with documents, he forces a smile: "May I have your documents please?"

Knowing it will only lead to more questions, I never offer more information than requested and return a forced smile. "Yes, you mean my passport?"

"And the papers for your motorbike."

"The carnet de passage?"

"Yes, that and your letter to be here."

I have heard about this routine and suspect what comes next. "You don't have a letter? Oh that's a shame, but to keep you out of jail, we can write one for you for a fee." Trying to conceal a hard swallow, I decide to play this out. "A letter isn't necessary, just a visa for me and a carnet de passage for my bike."

"But you are working for Greenpeace?"

Pointing outside the window, I state, "No, I am only riding that motorcycle around the world."

Suddenly, remembering the business card with a scribbled introduction from the Indonesian consulate liaison officer, I hand over the dog-eared scrap of paper sealed with a government stamp. "My friend Mr. Ali said a letter was not necessary with this card."

"Ah, very good. What do you carry in those boxes?"

My medical kit packed with prescription drugs long pounded into powder would at least arouse suspicion — maybe arrest. Because a relapse of my migrating kidney stones was likely, doctors in Munich had given me supplies of powerful pain pills and anti-spasm medications. Labels describing the contents with my name had rubbed off months ago. If this situation was not resolved quickly, five plastic bottles packed with now ground-up opiate-based white powder could mean I'd be explaining myself from an Indonesian prison.

This situation needed a happy resolution quickly. Was it better to keep smiling and slip him a handful of local currency? Would 20 or 30 bucks guarantee a ride out of town? If they believed an environmentalist has infiltrated their midst, would he be let free at any price — or maybe even disappear? But as he scans my documents, it is clear that this country cop has never seen a U.S. passport and does not know what to do. As he continues to flip through pages with colored visa stickers — Afghanistan, Pakistan, Egypt and Syria — his interest grows. Indonesia is busy dealing with a rising militant Islamic movement. Recent bombings in Bali had been orchestrated from within by underground al-Qaeda cells. Terrorism was on everyone's mind.

Finally, after enough grunting and throat-clearing, the commander telephones to superiors for directions on how to proceed. Should he detain the foreigner for further interrogation or ignore the coincidences? After I sat staring at a slow-moving wall clock resisting the urge to perspire, the brief reply comes an hour later — "Photocopy the suspect's documents and set him free."

Got My Ass Kicked Today
August 21, 2005
Western Kalimantan, Borneo
• • • • • • • • • • • • • • • • •

Experienced motorcyclists know better than to ride exhausted from lack of sleep, especially at night, when distance vision is reduced by two-thirds. But long, taxing days strung together trying to outrace overdue rain while covering so little distance has been discouraging. Checking my odometer was useless; after 12 hours bouncing over irregular Borneo terrain, the in line digital numbers did not change much.

There is little to see in the wilds of western Borneo. Villages are 10 miles apart so only a few appear during the course of a dawn-to-dusk ride. No one speaks English, and sometimes the Dayak do not speak Indonesian either. There are no stores to buy food, so I rely on village hospitality to eat. But you can't just roll into town, pass out cigarettes or shiny trinkets and expect a meal. I must first park my bike, stand near the first hut and smile while the boldest of the curious sniff me out. Sudden moves or reaching into my saddlebags can send them retreating until they're calmed again by more standing and smiling.

The whole procedure, from start to a late evening meal of pasted roots and boiled vegetables, can take several hours. At breakfast and lunch that's too much time. This means one meal at the end of an exhausting day, with a woven grass mat to sleep on under a thatched roof. But gaining acceptance in a village teaches patience and makes a guest feel more connected to his experience. There is something very alluring about primitive simplicity unspoiled by Western influence. As civilization moves closer to their dwindling tribal paradise, vulnerable Dayak are still fortunate to be without the complications and gadgets that become necessities when connected to the electrical grid. Without artificial light, they sleep when the earth sleeps and live harmoniously within the natural cycles and rhythms of the human body.

Shy and simple, Dayak are one with their environment and respect the individual spirits they believe dwell inside all plants, rocks and animals. When questioned about their beliefs, tribal elders explain their religion is based on common sense and that the people conduct themselves as though surrounded by ghosts who can affect their lives. Tattooed body art is their method of communicating gracious recognition or respectful fear. Under the spell of this mystical rain forest, during memorable evenings of understanding and sharing, it's easy to fall in love with a people so soft and free.

With no established timetable for riding Borneo, looping the island seemed like a worthwhile challenge with nothing certain except that there would be no turning back, even if unable to proceed further by land. Plan B is simple. I rely on the idea that if reaching a point where radical terrain prohibits moving forward, I could at least find a river and wait for a fishing canoe in order to hitch a ride to the coast. From there, I could wait for a larger vessel to hail for a sail to the next major port. After all, by now I am already experienced in negotiating with boat captains.

But it's been five weeks since I left Kuching, and with unknown mileage to cover until the finish line, my growing frustration makes me ride faster than conditions allow and makes me continue when it is time to rest. We follow our own rules in life because experience teaches the consequences of breaking them. Sometimes lessons need to be repeated.

Going down on dirt is generally less damaging than colliding with asphalt, still the bike and body always suffer some harm. When I'm off the beaten path, more than mechanical failures, I fear a broken limb from a crash. Even minor tears in the flesh offer convenient pathways for toxic microbes and tropical diseases. In the event of serious injury, there is no way out of here. If I was found overturned in some bottomless ravine or shivering with fever, who would know what to do?

Even on a lighter bike with knobby tires, motorcyclists are never in complete control riding in mud. Mud is the great equalizer. Using dual-purpose street tires while slinging 600 pounds of motorcycle adds negative factors to the equation. The numbers are simple, after 2,000 miles of mostly rugged dirt track complicated by mud, it is not a matter of if but when and how many times a rider does an over-the-handlebars face-plant. Until today, I had been lucky with only a few slow-moving spills where the main problem was developing enough traction for my boots while I tried to get the bike upright.

But today was payday for breaking the rules. Headlight filaments expire quicker under vibration and heat, but seldom do both go at once. My high beam had burned out last week, the low beam yesterday. Just before sunset, the best I could determine from quizzing a team of boar hunters, the next village was three hours away via the feeble glow of my remaining front-end parking lamp. Do I stop and camp or roll the dice?

If evening storm clouds release their water it will mean an instant halt to further progress — the clay is too slick to ride and would require a day to dry. And how many days could be spent sitting in a tent waiting for sunshine in a rain forest? What if monsoon season starts early? The recent lack of rain has caused havoc for firefighters battling forest fires in neighboring Sumatra but have been a miracle of good fortune for a man trying to stay ahead of the mud on Borneo. It is best to keep moving.

After the sun dropped below treeline, seeing where damp clay turned slick was difficult, but my front wheel washing out sideways delivered the news. Over the handlebars and somehow landing on my knees, I ended up lying in the road assessing the damage. My chest had taken out the windshield and mirrors, while ramming into solid earth had torn loose the left side aluminum pannier. The impact snapped stainless-steel fasteners while bending the support frames — again. Except for a swelling left knee, my padded riding clothes absorbed enough of the impact to minimize the damage to me.

But help is never far away. While I use a hardwood tree branch to straighten the frame, a lone Dayak teenager on a motor-scooter putters over the hill, stopping to aid the alien. His surging headlight illuminated the scene enough for me to strap luggage pieces together to get moving again. Rami tells me it is another 25 miles to his village, but he will ride slowly to guide me. Attempting this journey in darkness stretches a three-hour ride into six. Peeking from behind silky veils of fluorescent clouds, a silvery full moon brightens the road barely enough to see shadows. Soon, I trail Rami into the night, trying to avoid dangers stuck in my mind but impossible to see.

Storms have eroded this road for years, resulting in long stretches of ruts and crevices ending in pools of stagnant water. Dodging what I can only imagine is a situation requiring total focus and breathing through teeth. The long, zigzagging gouges are only a foot or two deep, but lodging motorcycle tires between them means being locked into wherever they lead — deeper mud or maybe a tree. Balancing on the ridges means if starting to tip, there is nowhere to plant a foot to stabilize.

In daylight, this would be difficult, without lights at night, it's a panicky plunge into the unknown. All I can do is follow the weaving silhouette ahead and not look down. The darkness plays tricks. Did Rami swerve to avoid a mud puddle or finally disappear? I wasn't sure until I'm abruptly buried to the bike's axles, two feet underwater, sinking and spinning my tires while the engine furiously pumps gas bubbles from a submerged exhaust.

How could only two men free 600 pounds of rubber and steel from oozing mud? Wading to our hips in muck, Rami pushes from behind as I pull from the side, delicately feathering the clutch against the desperate gurgle of the laboring motor. Forty-five minutes of inching free of the bog underlined the grim realization that there would be five more hours of creeping through twilight shadows until we'd find shelter and sleep.

The Home Stretch
August 22, 2005
Kuching, East Malaysia
● ● ● ● ● ● ● ● ● ● ● ● ● ●

After Dayak teenagers used buckets of river water to rinse away two and a half weeks of clay and slime, it was time to assess the damage. Broken mirror stems with the glass intact could be rethreaded and bolted back, but the windshield, duct-taped together since Mongolia, was finally finished. Bent frames and panniers are easy enough to restore if worked carefully in a Chinese body shop. My replacement for a new 30-dollar street tire, spun bald, is on the way. Steering-head bearings are beaten square by the constant pounding from muscling the front end through turns, but they are a simple fix. My crunched left knee still functions, yet, when I'm back in California, it will likely finance another orthopedic surgeon's ski vacation.

Because detailed maps did not exist, after interviewing locals, I wrote down the names of villages further ahead in sequence. Later, at forks in the road when I'm unsure which way to choose, I would point to the next village in the sequence and turn my palms upward. Asking how to reach major cities a hundred miles away was like asking a teenager in Los Angeles how to get to Brooklyn. They merely shrugged their shoulders about places they have only heard about.

This morning, the decimated dirt track abruptly turned into creamy black tarmac beneath the cooling canopy of jungle foliage. But that type of brief relief had happened before. Elsewhere in Kalimantan, unexplained short stretches of new asphalt had miraculously appeared only to evaporate into mud a few miles later. While I refused to raise my hopes, a last hundred miles of welcome asphalt continued until quietly ending without warning at a sleepy Malaysian border post. Even though fresh seafood meals and solid rest was only a few hours away in Kuching, I felt a familiar melancholy recalling the faces of new friends left behind. With an emotional last glance back, the laughing villagers who'd befriended a stranger suddenly outweighed the taxing brutality of Kalimantan's terrain. Once again, the journey moves too fast to digest the lessons.

Rolling up wobbly wooden planks onto rocking riverboats and across shallow streams has taught me much about circus riding. Considering the excessive wear on a motorcycle I expect to perform over another 20,000 miles through Indonesia and Africa, I have to wonder, was it worth it? Which overly fatigued metal parts would snap without warning while traversing the Serengeti Plain? After my Trans-Siberian crossing and wandering the Gobi, an overtaxed suspension had already been rebuilt after 17,000 miles, and that was 20,000 miles ago.

Months of wiped away road dust and sand have left the GPS screen too scratched to read. But by cupping hands in the shade of an overhead mahogany tree, I am able to distinguish a tiny black triangle pointing toward a faded blue background, indicating water, reconfirming my direct course toward the South China Sea. Still, the most valuable data is coded within the GPS memory chip — the first recorded logging-road route circling the island of Borneo; a challenging path I would surely never attempt again. Continuing further from flickering memories of Kalimantan, I begin to focus on what lies ahead. Without immigration problems, if riding hard, I could reach the streets of Kuching before sunset — another foreign town to temporarily call home.

On the first mile into Malaysia, the strong summer squalls that had held off when they would have done the most harm instantly crack down, rinsing off my mud-caked boots and riding suit. Flipping open my helmet visor invites sweet tastes of stinging raindrops in to flush away stale body oils and crusted sweat. A full gas tank was too heavy for wrangling through the mud of Kalimantan, so to keep the weight down, it had never been more than half full. But with the gas gauge malfunctioning again, I could only guess how much remained. In the end, my triumphant return to Malaysia was undone by a single broken wire, as my anticlimactic last hour limping back to Kuching alone ended when I sputtered out of fuel short of the city limits. No matter, I'd had a lot of good fortune.

Was it simply due to luck that I had had extraordinarily good weather while overwhelmed in the forest? How had I determined the correct paths at a hundred unmarked forks? Was it Allah, Shiva or Jesus? Or was it Buddha and Thor conspiring with the Travel Gods that kept me safe? Without divine intervention, would this pathetic solo wanderer have been destined to fatal disaster? Standing roadside in the pouring rain, staring at my resting Blue Beast empty of fuel, I wondered, "For all this complicated effort, what have I gained?

Borneo is still Borneo, although the natives have been affected by an inquisitive foreigner appreciative of the lessons they taught and the kindness they showed. And what are their memories of this peculiar vagabond alien and his farewell promises to never forget them? Much to my chagrin, I soon discover that even with temporary way stations, there still is no going home. In the past five weeks, most of the hotel staff who had sent me off with parting smiles had found other work. There are no parades or friendly faces to shout, "Welcome back!" But when I log on to the Internet, there is a flood of emails streaming in from curious readers eager for an account of my tumultuous adventure. And although I'm slightly worse for the wear, my war chest is packed with wealth beyond that of silver or gold. Even in the jungle, at the end of each day, like a marauding pirate returning with riches, I set up my equipment to transfer digital treasures from camera to laptop — cherished mementos of a journey within a journey I hope will never end.

Sarawak
August 29, 2005
Kuching, East Malaysia
● ● ● ● ● ● ● ● ● ● ● ● ●

Was it a longing for the concept of a home that has ceased to exist or was it just the primal charm of Borneo beckoning to linger? Since I'd left California, Sarawak province has been the closest place yet to paradise and somewhere I'd return. A warm, soothing climate with a manageable helping of equatorial storms to nourish a vibrant landscape, this passive land of East Malaysia is the perfect balance between what the earth has to offer and a satisfying spectrum of humankind flourishing in the heart of a rain forest. A few hours beyond glitzy Western-style shopping arcades and five-star resorts, primitive jungle life still exists to awe the most experienced adventurers. You can even drink the tap water in any of the cities.

Unlike other developing-world tropical playgrounds mired in poverty, the modern infrastructure and an educated populace puts Malaysia directly in the 21st century, even when its orderly one-way streets end at the jungle's edge. How does such a diverse sample of humans manage this perfect order without police on street corners? Unless you are breaking one of their laws, you can travel all day without seeing a cop. A typical Muslim country, Malaysia functions by using an unforgiving legal system. Drug peddlers granted probation in the West are hanged here, while small-time offenders can look forward to public canings. True censorship laws silence government critics, but even the most liberal democracies have ways of muzzling dissidents. Though the stakes are frightfully high, there is no denying the relative safety of an Islamic nation. If you mind your own business, the zero tolerance for violent crime becomes a relief when you're concerned about where to park a valuable motorcycle or stow your expensive camera equipment.

Yet, since leaving California, I have never been alone. As Kuching bike club members coordinated the delicate reshaping of angled aluminum panniers, a brother karate sensei takes me out to the best seafood restaurant in town. They wanted to know motorcycle specs and the numbers behind my world touring, while I was curious about social issues in Borneo. Over fried prawns and Tiger Beer we conversed about every subject except politics and religion.

When you ask Malaysians what makes them the most proud, they invariably say: "Our desire to live in harmony. In Sarawak, Chinese, Malay and Dayak sit at the same table sharing food with tolerance for all religions." Yet it's hard to fathom how they juggle this bouquet of conflicting cultures given the potential for disaster. Scanning cable TV stations, one channel has women in headscarves preaching the Koran, while on another, shapely Chinese girls dance in bikinis. Consuming pork is a major offense in a predominantly Muslim country yet local Dayak are allowed to promote wild boar barbecues at roadside noodle stands. All religions are accepted, but national law prevents Muslims from converting and forbids intermarriage.

But as education spreads, youngsters long for fuller lives, migrating from longhouses to cities, where they usually end up doing menial jobs. Except in tribal regions, most inhabitants are bilingual, and of the three major languages, English has become the medium for communication and commerce. Everyone loves Malaysia, but T-shirts with slogans in English outsell traditional dress. As young students marvel at American opportunities, I remind them that wealth won't cure all and that nothing outshines daily life in Sarawak.

Politics and Terrorism
August 30, 2005
Bummed in Malaysia
● ● ● ● ● ● ● ● ● ● ● ● ●

In two decades of sporadically wandering the world, I have never met an Australian I didn't like. A jovial "G'day mate" has always been accompanied by a hearty handshake and the knowledge that I had just met a friend. Whatever their political stripe, they are among the few traveling Westerners who didn't harbor bitterness toward the U.S. government. Maybe it's their kindly ruggedness and similar frontier past, blending into a familiar multicultural society, that makes me identify with their national character. When I think of a visit to Australia, seeing kangaroos and koala bears is less important than meeting kindred spirits who speak the same language. Whatever the reason, bonding with Australians has always been easy, and I was looking forward to making new friends.

After island-hopping over lower Indonesia next month, the plan was to take a ferryboat from the bottom of the elongated archipelago at East Timor into Darwin, Australia. From there, reaching the southern coastal cities would require a week of riding several thousand miles of empty outback desert in the middle of summer heat. That and a visa.

For Westerners, acquiring Australian visas is quick and convenient. Electronic Travel Authorities (ETAS) can be approved on the government's Internet website by simply supplying personal information, including nationality, passport number, and birth and travel dates. Add credit card information, press Enter and a number-code should pop up to write on your immigration forms at your first port of entry. Occasionally, certain applicants receive a message stating that they are among the random few who require embassy "personal interviews." Such was the case when I'd applied online a few months ago, last June in Thailand. The text stated that as matter of routine, my online visa application had been selected for face-to-face interview at the nearest Australian embassy.

A trip to the Australian embassy was not a major hassle, but it was still a day's ride up and back through heavy traffic from pleasant seaside Pattaya to smoggy, stinky Bangkok. After considering the reasons my application might be subject to further review, I decided that just submitting a request from Thailand instead of the U.S. might have been enough to trigger additional scrutiny.

In the Bangkok office of the Australian visa department, after waiting in line for an hour, local staff are polite when they tell me I needed to go to the main headquarters a few miles away. No problem, it was on the way out of town. But once there, I was directed to "window two." And hanging from the wall at window two was a pink paper bulletin stating citizens of Iraq, Iran, Sudan, Algeria, Syria, Libya and Pakistan must fill out the form they had just handed me, a first for this American.

For embassy personnel to make a decision on whether to grant my visa, they requested five pages of detailed information regarding previous jobs and residences for the last 30 years, for me and for members of my immediate family. Filling out the form took two hours, but, finally, a nervous middle-aged Australian woman accepted my rough recollection of family history along with 2,100 Thai baht (50 U.S. dollars) and a promise to follow up by email or cell phone within 10 days. That was two months ago.

In case the matter just disappeared in their system, I'd also requested her business card with email address to keep in contact. After waiting a month, I began sending her polite inquiries about the status of my application. As of today, I'd received no reply.

In these days of worldwide terrorism, it's understood when nations have tightened security. In the aftermath of recent bombings in Western cities, news reports linking suspects to Middle Eastern countries and recent visits to Syria, Pakistan and Afghanistan were obvious red flags for wary intelligence agencies in any country. What was surprising was how they knew of my visits to those countries the second I hit the laptop's Enter key. Was there a multinational computerized watch list? As high-tech espionage grows, undercover spotters cannot only spy on adversary's embassies but also look into their personal lives. What books do we read, what is our religion? Was this all about some of the countries that I had visited or the fact I had reported online that Arabs and Muslims had treated me well? How far had this "public security" gone?

Tell a friend you want to ride a motorcycle through El Salvador, Nicaragua and Honduras on your way to South America, and you'll see them gasp and fear for your safety. Mention crossing the Andes and they'll collapse. So far, nearly every country on my itinerary has carried a dire U.S. State Department travel warning. Had the one for Colombia been any different? And should I have been more concerned about the political ramifications of visiting the Middle East?

Maybe I should have stayed home and allowed the media to provide their version of the truth? Osama bin Laden would love that.

Given the circumstances, there were understandable reasons for further evaluation, and the Aussies might yet grant my visa. But most disturbing was thinking about what Muslims must experience when trying to travel anywhere. As I'd discovered today, it's an ugly feeling to be suspected, singled out and mistrusted by those around us.

Utopian Police State
September 1, 2005
Singapore
● ● ● ● ● ●

When I'm on the road, I gather information differently than I would at home. In foreign countries, I depend on local information on current road conditions and where to eat and sleep but, most importantly, to locate supplies and equipment repairs. Telephone calls are useless for communicating what I need to buy or repair. A personal appearance to draw diagrams and point to a problem on the bike is the only sure way to track down whatever item is needed. But even with an appropriate map, finding the appropriate place of business can take all day — providing I don't get lost.

Because the GPS displays only major cities and primary roads, it's minimal help in smaller cities. But once I do find a specific location, pressing a waypoint button will mark that precise position with a symbol, making it easier to return later. An internal memory also automatically records the last a hundred miles traveled as a line of tiny dots called Breadcrumbs. If I forget to pocket a hotel business card before I leave to run errands, it can be difficult finding the way back. But with the GPS Breadcrumbs trail and labeled waypoints, returning after picking up laundry, visas or supplies is much easier.

No matter the country in Asia, when I need special services, I've learned to find the Chinese. Time and again, a volunteer from a crowd of curious Chinese examining my bike has led to introductions to private networks of mechanics, supply houses, even restaurants that forgo the tradition of double-pricing for foreigners. In the Chinese language, negatives don't seem to exist as we understand them in the West. Whenever describing exactly what I have needed to the Chinese, their invariable one-word response is, "Can." Today was typical:

"Mr. Hoi, are you able to install these bearings?"

"Can."

"Are you sure Mr. Hoi, it requires careful removal of —"

Without bothering to look he interrupts, "Can."

"But what about the —"

"Can."

"And are you able to rebuild the —"

"Can."

Since the first major motorcycle center in Malaysia had just opened, its inexperienced shop manager in Kuala Lumpur could only order steering-head bearings exclusively from Germany. But Mr. Hoi, a few miles away, had those same hard-to-find bearings upstairs in his race-bike shop, and after soldering a few broken wires, he installed them for 20 dollars. From there, his assistant led me through the backstreets across Kuala Lumpur to have his cousin replace the foam cushion in my now hard-as-a-rock motorcycle seat. But searching for water-pump seals had been a dead end until this morning, when an unexpected email message arrived.

I didn't know exactly how many readers from around the world were following my journey via my Internet website, but after evaluating hit-counters and page-view reports, the number had to exceed 10,000. And that's how I met two Chinese motorcyclists, Eris and Murphy, serving as sailors in the Singapore navy. They had been reading my online journals, and when they saw that I needed a mechanic, they sent an email offering help. Eris could provide labor to remove the mono-shock for rebuilding, and the owner of the shop where he works offered an old stock windshield to replace the one I shattered in Borneo. After confirming warranty parts were available at the local BMW shop, Eris and Murphy directed me 200 miles south from Kuala Lumpur toward the tip of the Malaysian peninsula and the city state of Singapore. By the time I arrived at the causeway connecting the city to the mainland, Murphy was waiting.

A super-organized, high-tech city state famous for laws so strict they prohibited chewing gum, the red tape required for entering with a motorcycle had made Singapore not worth the trouble of visiting. Even with a carnet de passage, the Federal Transportation Department still requires an endorsement by their Auto Club plus 36 dollars a day for insurance along with prepayment of expensive road tolls. But once we reached the official entry point, a quick passport stamping at immigration ended in two lines for customs inspection. Counting on being able to play Stupid Foreigner if caught, after acknowledging a nod from Murphy, I took a chance and followed the lane with a sign reading "Nothing to Declare." When I finished quickly flipping the lids on my panniers, a serious teenaged machine gun–wielding soldier waved us both through without asking for further paperwork. In bypassing the mandatory carnet de passage inspection, I became an illegal alien in a utopian police state where electronic surveillance of its citizens is standard procedure. From remote-controlled traffic signals managed by distant observers to restricting certain vehicles from driving downtown, even the hallways of my budget hotel are monitored by closed-circuit TV. If border inspectors later asked for vehicle documents at the same checkpoint, getting out of Singapore was going to be interesting.

An island country connected by concrete bridges to the tip of Malaysia, Singapore's international boundaries are the city limits. As they have run out of solid real estate to expand their nation, builders now reclaim land from the sea. Other than that, there is nowhere to go but up, in multi-storied ultramodern structures with geometric rooflines high enough to vanish in the monsoon clouds. Against an Indian Ocean sunset, Singapore's skyline of contemporary architecture resembles a futuristic silhouette of Saturn. Because I relish jungle terrain and small-town friendliness, cities have been places I tend to avoid. Yet, with English as the national language and the quiet frankness of its residents, Singapore is a fascinating multicultural blend of Chinese, Indian and Malay, who have joined efforts to pass laws controlling every aspect of social behavior.

An orderly metropolis similar to Tokyo, good manners practiced by tradition in Japan are mandated by strict regulation in Singapore, with severe penalties for even minor infractions. Singapore is the safest city in the world as long as long as you obey the rules. Depending on the cop, even bumbling tourists jaywalking in traffic can be ticketed or jailed. Foreign drivers photographed by hidden cameras breaking traffic laws are not exempt. To make sure no one escapes without paying fines, license plate numbers are instantly computer-checked at the border, where violators must fork over the appropriate amount of Singapore dollars to cover their crimes before exiting back to Malaysia.

Exploring Singapore proved better by night, as downtown restaurants and evening markets ignite with a vibrancy as intense as the blowtorches blasting beneath the giant woks in back-alley kitchens. To reduce city-center gridlock, the government has initiated expensive tolls to discourage traffic during peak hours. But a midnight cruise down the deserted, echoing boulevards of the towering financial district makes for an artificial alternative to the rocky canyons of the Egyptian Sinai. Among imposing granite-coated skyscrapers, polished walls reverberated the throaty rumblings of motorcycle exhausts and shouting bikers. But besides shopping in the swanky 20-story commercial plazas and staying at out-of-reach exclusive hotels, there is little else to do in Singapore except dine at the dozens of ethnic food courts.

In the morning, I will ride 300 miles north, back the length of Malaysia, along the Straights of Malacca to the island of Penang for sea passage to Sumatra. But even that is becoming complicated. There is a rumor spreading among travelers that Indonesia had recently reduced its tourist visas from 60 to 30 days. Considering it took me five weeks just to loop Borneo, covering the next five islands before my new visa expires will be a challenge.

Thumb Twiddling
September 15, 2005
Penang, Malaysia
• • • • • • • • • • •

Since Glen Eagles Medical Centers are the most advanced hospitals in the region, the Penang, Malaysia, branch was the best and last place to investigate my misbehaving left kidney before continuing on to Sumatra. The 10 millimeter aggressive stone doctors in Munich couldn't pulverize electronically but had said was too big to migrate did, and it now floats free, acting as a ball-check valve where it shouldn't. To complicate matters, since departing Germany last October, another eight-millimeter stone had formed on my right side. Yet, an optimistic Chinese urologist claims that by taking pH-altering pills and drinking lots of water, the stones could dissolve in a few weeks. The painful distress of kidney stones on the move has been known to ruin vacations. After discarding the powerful meds doctors had issued to me in Munich, the urologist has upgraded my emergency-only supplies by prescribing two glass ampoules of heavy-duty injectable painkillers for that special moment I hope does not arrive somewhere in Africa.

The good news is local riders have provided me valuable information about a new roll-on/roll-off vehicle ferry operating from Malaysia to Sumatra. No more slinging bikes over the decks of onion boats. The ship sails across the Strait of Malacca at 8:00 p.m. Tuesday and puts into port 12 hours later. Meanwhile, using sporadic Internet connections, I answer email and update my journals.

There is little else to do these last two weeks except wait for new tires to be express-mailed and organize supplies for Sumatra. While still digesting Borneo, images of mud roads and Dayak villages fade in the shadows of impersonal skyscrapers and forward gazes toward the rest of Indonesia. Without tribal villages to pass, it's boring riding the smooth modern freeways of Malaysia on long, empty stretches between anonymous cities that all look the same. But bikers rule the roads in Malaysia — there are separate high-speed lanes and underpasses exclusively for motorcycles. While cars are packed tight in smoggy gridlock, bikers zoom by like competitors on private Disneyland racetracks.

In response to a growing militant threat, security tightens in Indonesia. The rumors I've heard about visas have been confirmed. According to new Indonesian immigration regulations, 60-day visas have been restricted to 30. Once again, it was time to plead my "special case." After an embassy meeting, yet another consul general is happy to bend the new rules and issue an on-the-spot 60-day visa. My laptop slideshows over afternoon tea have become the ultimate dog and pony show to woo everyone from jungle natives to apprehensive government officials. Now, there is enough time to consider including a tour of the tsunami-stricken rebel-held territories of Banda Aceh. In the past week, there have been televised news reports that militant Islamic separatists have finally signed a peace agreement with Jakarta, and this week, have begun surrendering weapons in exchange for troop withdrawals.

Crowded with aggressive merchants and pungent spice markets, Penang Island connects to mainland beaches by bridges and ferries from various cultural districts. Rows of Indian restaurants pump varying beats of tabla drums with familiar piercing scents of fiery curries. Dark-skinned Hindu men in long, baggy shirts call out wanting to know *"From where is the place to which you have been traveling."* As a 5:00 a.m. loudspeaker Muslim call-to-prayer nudges the faithful from sleep, smoky trails of smoldering incense drift from colorful Chinese Buddhist temples with clinking cymbals and banging gongs. Afternoon strolls require alternating ethnic greetings — *Nee hou* to Chinese, *Namaste* to Indians and *Salamat siang* to Malay. And like clockwork, at sundown, thick-mustached Georgetown rickshaw riders lurking outside tourist hotels make their pitch: *"Pssst, Mistah, you looky for massage?"*

SUMATRA

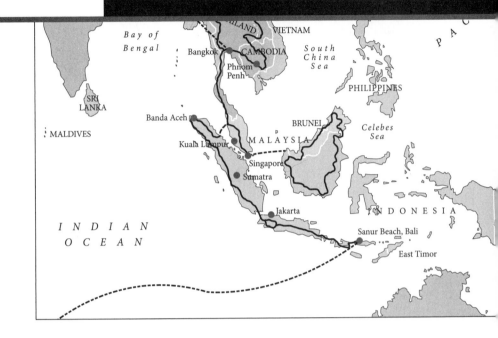

Across the Strait of Malacca
September 21, 2005
Belawan, Sumatra, Indonesia

●●●●●●●●●●●●●●●●●

After an Internet introduction from Eris and Murphy in Singapore, Chinese riders B.K. and Francis were waiting for me in Penang. In keeping with the two-nights-max rule, I divided time between staying at their houses and downtown hotels. Fluent in English and three dialects of Mandarin, B.K. is happy to field questions about his views. The issues are the same everywhere: racial, religious and cultural identities in conflict.

Indigenous Malays receive preferential treatment for government jobs and official licensing for businesses and industry. Non-Muslims are out of the loop and find it difficult to get ahead. When they do, the government steps in to appropriate a corporate share to give to someone more deserving — one of their own.

According to Malays, racial quotas exist to protect their culture from more aggressive, business-minded Chinese. If they didn't, the Chinese would soon dominate. At the very bottom, highly educated Indians grab whatever is left. Unless they are members of a circle of well-connected merchants, young Indian men with master's degrees are left to accept menial jobs. Yet with all the grumbling, there are still no tanks in the streets or armed gangs of rebels as in other developing countries.

B.K.'s neighbor is engaged to be married, and together we have been invited to a Chinese wedding bachelor party. Far different from a Western stag with its strippers and bad behavior, this family affair is attended by future in-laws who lecture on morality and ancient ways. Dressed in pattern-printed red silk pajamas, during the ritual combing-of-hair, the groom is admonished by both sets of parents on issues of fidelity and duty. A costumed priestess waves smoldering joss sticks while reciting instructions to respect ancestors and live according to ancient customs.

The Chinese have no rules governing alcohol, and after the ceremony, wine, whiskey and beer flow freely next to fried noodle dishes and flaming seafood delights. No one knows much about the motorcycling American, but because I'm the guest of a man held in high esteem, they honor me as a family member.

Spending days with 50-year-old motocross champion B.K. has allowed me to witness an impromptu mediation he is conducting between an older traditional businessman and a young, hot-tempered construction boss. Their animated conversation is conducted in a little-used dialect of Mandarin, but the irate 72-year-old milky-eyed senior pounding his fists on the desk leaves little doubt what's going on. Ignoring the presence of a surprised yellowed-haired stranger as he shuffles toward the door, the old man's last warning is "I have my temper too, if he takes my face, I will kill him."

After a week of waiting for the ship to Sumatra, I can almost count final days to California. I'm getting homesick for a home, any home, period. And relaxing on the ferry is a chance to reflect about the future as well as the past.

To spur tourism for the whole region, Thailand, Indonesia and Malaysia have combined resources to create a vehicle ferry service between Penang and Sumatra. No one is certain if it's fear of terrorism or the tsunami disaster that has been keeping travelers away, but there's only a motorcycle, one car and four passengers onboard a ship designed to carry a hundred times that.

Among empty rows of sticky vinyl cabin seats, a full crew of 40 stands waiting to serve airline-style dinners comprised of a spicy chicken wing and stale rice. A dozen video screens simultaneously display images of Muslim girls in head scarves singing and dancing to traditional music — picture a Lawrence Welk version of MTV with young women dressed as nuns.

Overpowering currents from the Indian Ocean surging through the Strait of Malacca forced the frustrated captain to wait two hours before docking the ferry for offloading. Twelve hours later, when we arrive in Port Belewan, we wasted another half day waiting for rising tides to align for the roll-off ramp. Moving a motorcycle by means other than on its own two wheels is a sorry process, but at least there was no crating procedure or teams of sloppy port workers picking it up by the turn signals.

Indonesia is to Malaysia what Mexico is to the U.S., a less fortunate neighbor with too many people and not enough money. From the clear skies of Malaysia, the change is dramatic. In the oppressive heat and throat-burning smog, a hodgepodge of dilapidated vehicles converges in single lanes. Jockeying for road space is a nerve-frazzling science that requires delicate refining. Still relaxed from Malaysian highways easier to ride than California, Sumatran traffic is an ice-water-in-the-face shock to the system.

North from Medan
September 26, 2005
Sumatra, Indonesia
● ● ● ● ● ● ● ● ● ● ● ●

When I first enter a major city, I immediately long for the fresh scented countryside and its slower pace. But after a few days of nutritious meals, fast Internet connections and motorcycle servicing, I've made enough new friends at bike shops and restaurants to get lazy and uncomfortable. But all I need to do to be reinvigorated is to load my gear and roll past the city limits with a new direction that invariably leads to somewhere interesting. Once back in the wind, shifting into high gear, the situation reverses when discarding that temporary security for the open road, with unfamiliar food, unpredictable weather and questionable routes. Still, it's not always important to seek a particular destination; often, a mere compass heading is sufficient inspiration to appease cravings to move on.

Maps are useful for general directions and timing seasons, but tomorrow's destination can easily be subject to change depending on your mood at sundown or sunrise. Maps aside, gossip about villages in neighboring countries is rarely reliable. Claims of "danger ahead" and "promiscuous women abound" are generally overstated, while other road information seldom applies to bikers. "It takes 10 hours to get there by car" can mean a longer or shorter ride by motorcycle, depending on traffic or insanity levels of bus drivers. With the growing realization that this journey must end sooner rather than later to deal with my kidneys, I have set a deadline to return to California by late winter of 2006.

As time becomes a glaring factor, it's important to make every day count, but lingering in the countryside to smell blossoming orchids may soon be reduced to deep inhales while downshifting around jungle curves. I originally allocated four months for Africa, but additional time spent exploring Indonesia meant less for Kenya and Tanzania. Even if I eliminate Australia and reduce my days here, I will only have two months for the entire African continent.

So why another deviation? Weaving through convoys of commercial vehicles fouling muggy morning air, this long, grueling detour in the opposite direction north from Medan made little sense. I had planned for a safe ride through the mountains and a visit to a famous lake before heading south to catch the ferry to Java. This morning that plan changed. I stopped on the highway shoulder, pondering the wisdom of riding north into the troubled Aceh province. Questioning my own better judgment, I even considered retreating. Looping the entire island of Sumatra seemed less possible every hour. Warnings of "No Return Road" on the opposite side of the island constantly raised the question of whether it was worthwhile to ride 400 miles in miserably thick traffic just to turn around and commit the traveler's mortal sin of backtracking? How important is Banda Aceh anyway? I've already seen the pictures of a leveled city on TV.

But at every meal stop, welcoming natives with encouraging toothy smiles restated the case, convincing me to proceed to meet more Sumatrans. *"Hallo mistah, wahr you come from?"* preempted animated language lessons and hilarious photo sessions. Further from the city, puffy black trails of diesel fumes evaporated into vibrant green rice fields speckled with meandering broad-horned water buffalo. Within hours, the boredom of Malaysia's modern cities, and the apprehension of Indonesia's congested roadways, dissolved into the optimistic spirits of people returning from the brink. You'd never guess Sumatrans were suffering from horrific disasters — a maliciously deadly civil conflict and the whimpering aftermath of a devastating tsunami.

The Indonesian military had sealed off Aceh province from the rest of the island. Under a negotiated agreement, the Islamic secessionist movement is currently scheduled to surrender its weapons as the army withdraws. Skirting police checkpoints required riding through the forest, but once I was past the provincial border there were no more patrols or armed convoys — just a few hundred thousand dazed survivors trying to assess the damage.

Yet, through it all, disoriented villagers worry as much for others as themselves. When I answer questions in other countries with, "I come from California," locals everywhere shout, "Arnold!" Here, when I say "America," their tones turn sympathetic and they utter, *"Katrina, Katrina, we are so sorry for you."*

Just as residents of Sumatra's Aceh province were wondering what could be worse than 15,000 dead in 30 years of a bloody secessionist movement, they were struck by a series of earthquake-induced tidal waves. The first was a humdred feet tall, crushing everything in its punishing path. As the earth trembled and buckled beneath the ocean, survivors could only scramble in panic to higher ground. In one gargantuan, unforgiving surge of the sea, five-story buildings collapsed into instant tombs for those inside. Yet, before assisting, organizing world bodies demanded warring factions recognize that they needed each other to rebuild, leading to the current settlement brought about by Finland's most determined negotiators.

Spending the last 15 months off the beaten track, most of my time has been spent with people of color. At first, it was uncomfortable seeing groups of other white Westerners, but they have arrived as dedicated relief workers and international observers on missions of peace.

Unarmed multinational groups have invaded the countryside, monitoring the fragile new ceasefire treaty that requires rebels to surrender machine guns, hand grenades and small arms as government troops slowly retreat to the southern provincial border. So far, the exchange is ahead of schedule. Yet, in the midst of this precarious stand-down, United Nations personnel are just as surprised to see a wandering American biker. "How did you get past the military?" they ask. "You must be careful. If they find out you are here, you'll be immediately escorted to the airport."

UN peacekeeping forces classify security risks. Afghanistan is a level three. Because of heavy rebel fighting in the surrounding mountains and local assassinations of political leaders, Aceh province is considered a level four. Last week, two foreigners were shot outside the city for violating the 6:00 p.m. curfew. My rear tire blew out around 5:00 p.m. today, and it was a long taxi ride back to town to search for a 17-inch tube that I soon discovered does not exist on Sumatra. We over inflated a smaller version to fit, muttered

"In shallah" and continue to hope for the best.

In their negotiated settlement with the government, separatists of the Free Aceh Movement (BAM) won a bid for autonomy and a return to Islamic Law — Sharia. The people have chosen to be governed by the religious rules of the Koran. Comparable to the Christian Amish and Quakers, these are peaceful people wishing to live according to the strictest interpretations of their respective sacred teachings.

In the Christian-dominated American Midwest, there are still dry regions where the sale of alcohol is forbidden and district attorneys will criminally prosecute store owners for selling magazines featuring bare-breasted women. Under Islamic Sharia, women are required to cover their hair and male to female contact outside of marriage is forbidden. It's scary to consider life in the USA if radical religious leaders were allowed to declare and enforce laws — and fundamentalist states provide worthy reminders of the value of separating church and state.

Tsunamis
September 27, 2005
Banda Aceh, Sumatra
• • • • • • • • • • • •

Shortly after he turned 63, my father died of a long-anticipated second heart attack. Though I had left home as a teenager and we weren't close, the aftermath of disbelief and denial lasted years. But learning to fend for myself from the age of 16 had given me an independent spirit. While devastated at his funeral, I recall wondering what the death of a loved one was like for those with deeper roots? How painful is the passing of a child or spouse?

In developing nations, extended families are so tightly knit they often live together in one house. Elders are respected and depend on those they raised to care for them in their twilight years — one reason they have so many children in countries without social safety

A horrific tsunami swept 200,000 out to sea and left another 200,000 homeless in Banda Aceh, Sumatra, Indonesia

nets. Children are social security; the ones who live long enough to work will feed you when you're no longer able to look after yourself. Maybe that's why the people here smile and laugh and complain less than their Western counterparts — they might like a new color TV but know they can survive without one as long as they have each other. There is also far more demonstrative love and warmth expressed between family members, and with that open love comes a positive attitude towards the world.

Throughout Asia, it's unusual to find villagers not smiling. Is it the simple life minus anxiety over stock market prices or which conniving politician has stirred more animosity toward the other? There are no worries about evaluating portfolios and counting money — there isn't any. As long as the basics of human survival exist, natives enjoy each other. Yes, they would prefer accessible health care — everyone wants to live better and longer — but the hand they've been dealt doesn't include the privileges available in the West.

But how did people so poor cope with one of the worst natural disasters in human history? In a ruthless rush of nature's fury, one sunny December afternoon in 2004, enormous ocean waves of unprecedented size penetrated as much as three miles inland to pummel and destroy all in the unsuspecting path. In a single wicked hydraulic pulse, 200,000 innocent mothers and fathers, brothers and sisters, were crushed instantly or swept out to sea.

Riding over rutted trails among the remaining concrete foundations of a city that used to exist is an eerie drift among forsaken tombstones. Twisted steel rebar poking from jagged brick ruins reach out like skeletal fingers toward the sky, beckoning for remembrance. A gasping scene of heartbreak watching ragged young orphan boys with filthy faces sniffing bags of glue brings the despair into focus. Gazing at this lingering disaster is a similar experience to visiting the S-21 Torture Museum in Cambodia. It causes the same sense of breathless horror.

Yet, again, the human spirit prevails. Among sun-bleached, frayed canvas tents flapping in the salty tropical breeze, splintering plywood shelters and makeshift noodle stands are being hammered into shape. Survivors too busy for pity are hauling wood, digging trenches or loading trucks with sacks of cement and homemade tools. And still workers laboring in the sticky heat stop to smile and wave, pitching familiar questions: *"Mistah wahs you name?"* What does one say to a humble people who've just lost what little they had and nearly everyone they loved? *"Salamat siang, apa kabar?"* (Good afternoon, how are you?) To relieve my discomfort, an elderly, crooked-tooth rickshaw driver pauses roadside and asks, *"You have come to see tsunami?"*

Knowing much can be spoken with just the eyes, I touch mine, then his. "No, I have come to see you." In a moment's locked gaze, I try to tell him that the world has not forgotten the tragedy he recalls every second. I can't help but wonder what these tormented people dream of at night. Happy faces and steady smiles can't change what they must relive when clenching their eyes. But with 200,000 still homeless and hungry, a world preoccupied with newer disasters may already be starting to forget.

Entire bridges and coastal roads disappeared in Northwest Sumatra, Indonesia

On to the West Coast Wasteland
September 28, 2005
Lamno, Aceh Province, Sumatra
● ● ● ● ● ● ● ● ● ● ● ● ● ● ● ● ● ● ● ●

Finding roads in places that no longer exist is difficult in Banda Aceh. The world as the natives knew it had ended, so the survivors were unsure of what was left even down the next stretch of beach, and most didn't want to know. Trying to tell them how I needed to ride back along the devastated west coast of Aceh province was as difficult as explaining why. Their answer to everything was *"Soo naam mee,"* so I decided that it was best to proceed and check in with other survivors along the way. By all accounts, the single-lane highway on Sumatra's northwest coast had been consumed by the tsunami, and the few remaining isolated villages were being supplied by airdrop. But learning the road to Lamno had been cleared was encouraging. Lamno, the site of the first major bridge collapse, is the last stop with relatively fresh food and supplies heading due south along the Indian Ocean. When I arrive and see how few buildings remain, a beat-down flophouse hostel seems like a welcome refuge at the end of the day. An optimistic native's suggestion that if I rode the waterline at low tide I could connect to more intact roads on higher ground further down the coast provided the spark I needed.

There wasn't much that could go wrong if I ran into solid jungle or an impassable sea, except that it would mean a time-consuming retreat to Banda Aceh. A UN relief worker had told me: "It takes five hours on the good road just to reach Lamno. That's only the first 60 miles. Then comes the hard part, finding a way around washed-out bridges to reach the next organized city 150 miles south in Meulaboh." But their five-hour ride had been in a convoy under military escort. Mine, including photo stops, took only about three, and most of this was on sporadically solid asphalt that ran from the mangled seaside and twisted back through delicious isolated coastal mountains in rebel territory. Without using his weapon, a BAM fighter along the way waved me aside, offering tea and rice cakes. So much for the rumors of Muslim guerrillas murdering civilians.

Investigating a variety of exaggerated tales with the locals eases my worries. Two German backpackers allegedly killed for violating curfew were actually accidentally shot by the military much further south. Tourism has been nonexistent since the fighting began, and the hikers had been camping in a combat zone when a jungle army patrol stumbled upon them sleeping in their tent. Failing to obey commands to exit with their hands up, they were presumed rebels and tense government soldiers promptly opened fire. The wounded woman survived but her husband did not. Still, hearsay panics the listeners.

There is plenty of fuel in Sumatra, but unfounded rumors of diminishing supplies cause city-block-long lines at gas stations. Yet as I'm a Westerner, attendants assume I'm an NGO worker and wave me to the front.

Wild tales of two unchaperoned young couples being whipped and caned by religious authorities also proved to be unfounded. The couples in question had actually been caught near a mosque illegally drinking beer, and as a lesson to others who would disregard Islamic law, they were unceremoniously paraded around the town square in the back of a pickup truck. Even though the rules governing male-female contact are strict, Muslim women in groups are always anxious to talk to me, displaying sweet, open personalities that defy their conservative dress.

While I'm on an after-dinner ride on the outskirts of Lamno, four young native women wearing traditional headscarves wave me over to warn of the 6:00 p.m. curfew outside of villages. After wordless gestures of firing invisible pistols and rifles, they were convincing enough that staying to chat with them seemed like a better idea. As our conversation progressed to the point where they agreed to be photographed, one woman in particular displayed a noticeable fondness for foreigners by standing closer than normal, wearing a longing smile. In a surprising violation of local custom, in front of the others she invited me to sleep at her house. For wandering motorcyclists, come-ons from local girls are common, but in the past, they'd always turned up in private, away from the prying eyes of gossiping towns-folk. Yet most of those flirtations had turned to sullen faces when they learned I would be back on the road at dawn. I'd learned to avoid them.

Still, this bright-eyed olive-skinned beauty skipping and laughing in the silvery moonlight was persistent. Placing clasped palms together next to her tilting head then touching two index fingers together while pointing to herself and then to me was a gesture too obvious to ignore.

There may have been another meaning, but earlier in the evening, when we'd looked at her digital images on the camera playback screen, she had pressed her very firm breasts against my arm — and as she'd been the only girl not wearing a headscarf, her gestures sure looked like a green light from here. But what may have been okay with her was likely to be reported by nosy neighbors and might earn her a public caning or worse. Yet, I knew that I'd replay this moment in my head for weeks to come.

Back in the mosquito-infested hotel room under the monotonous hum of the lopsided rotating ceiling fan, the bulk of the night was consumed pondering undergarment colors and the garden scent of a young woman's hair. In the morning, I resisted a hormone-influenced urge to return — but I knew from experience that if you turn down a woman once, you will rarely be given a second chance (no matter how hard you beg).

After a cool water-bucket shower and four greasy fried eggs, I repacked my gear and proceeded to the knoll where the first major bridge had been yanked out to sea. Proving once again its mastery over man, aqua-tinted ocean waves continued to brush against remaining fragmented pillars. Standing there alone on the brim of a forbidding wasteland extending to the horizon, gazing across the gaping expanse was a sobering warning of what lay ahead.

Coastal Drift
September 30, 2005
Meulaboh, Aceh Province, Sumatra
● ● ● ● ● ● ● ● ● ● ● ● ● ● ● ● ● ● ● ●

In the summer of 1978, I was curious about sensational media reports of feuding Protestants and Catholics blowing each other up in Belfast and boarded a flight to Dublin to see for myself. Was the whole country at war and were Christians, and the Irish in particular, somehow more violent and dangerous than the rest of us? Backpacking through rich green farmlands and contemporary cities seemed like a good way to investigate.

Spending a month hitchhiking cross-country doesn't qualify anyone as an expert, but questioning the Irish who were kind enough to offer me a lift and sleeping with families in bed and break-fasts was a decent way to catch a glimpse into the minds and souls of the people. Despite sensationalist U.S. media reports, outside of certain sections of Belfast, I could only find working men and women quietly sharing their lives in white plaster cottages nestled in between sections of neat stone fences dividing emerald green pastures. Where was the alcoholism and the proverbial Irish temper?

It's true the Irish love their Guinness and are better-than-average boxers, but while recording impromptu private interviews I could not find anyone who condoned sectarian violence. Instead, like a chorus of typical country folk, they all repeated a slogan hard to forget: "Aye, it 'tis, it 'tis that we are all God's creatures." Although the Northerner's disagreements, and sometimes violent confrontations, involved more politics than church, the rest of the otherwise law-abiding Catholics and Protestants were being instigated by extremists. With an occupying British government stuck in the middle, violence was begetting violence.

Religious zealots killing each other is nothing new, but recently, the art of mass murder in the Islamic world has been refined with car and suicide bombings. Now, instead of bloodthirsty Christians, images of fanatical terrorist Muslims dominate the media. The struggle in Islam between Sunni and Shiite factions raging in Iraq exists on a much milder scale between moderates and fundamentalists here in Indonesia. It's not a matter of the crazies being Christian or Muslim; it's about ignorant people using religious doctrine out of context to justify extremism.

But if nine of the finest legal scholars in America cannot interpret the carefully worded U.S. Constitution unanimously, how could simple villagers understand difficult-to-read religious texts thousands of years old? No matter how clearly ideas are written, a clever person can manipulate them to rationalize their position. In the Bill of Rights, U.S. gun laws underscore this point.

Despite the stirred-up resentments, settlements of regional conflicts brokered by disinterested parties can succeed. Just this month, in Indonesia's Aceh province, optimistic Finns negotiated hard with intransigent political leaders to soften government and rebel positions. Finally, thanks to the persistence of interested foreigners and an urgent need to recover from an enormous disaster, there is a chance for peace and a return to an Islamic law acceptable to all. With most of the international aid workers stationed in Sumatran cities, I've only seen dedicated foreign AMM members out spinning their tires in the mud. An aggressive Aceh Monitoring Mission has sent out a fleet of late-model four-wheel drives equipped with satellite communications and window stickers showing circled machine guns with lines drawn across them.

Their mission is to scour rural strongholds collecting weapons surrendered by rebels then trade them to military officials in exchange for reduced troop positions. The results have been astounding, as everyone I've encountered insists the program is way ahead of schedule. If there is a silver lining to the tsunami disaster, it is that it has brought sworn enemies together for the good of all citizens.

Today is a new day, and even the cobalt sky is clear as a radiating mid-latitude sun holds monsoon rains at bay and soggy trails firm up enough to ride. Except for AMM personnel, I have not seen any other Westerners. Foreign relief workers in larger cities coordinate from a distance, but it's the silent surviving mothers, fathers and children that provide the grinding labor necessary to reconstruct their lives. Scattered down the coast, surviving villagers stoop in the heat replanting flooded rice paddies while others hand-cut timber to build new fishing boats. None are idle or complaining — crisis has brought peace to Indonesia, though they have a long road back.

Bottled water is everywhere, but my stash of bananas and canned fish paste ran out yesterday. At a thatched-roof noodle stand, an old woman, flustered by having a customer, smiles while clearing a place to sit on sawed-off tree-stump chairs. Five dollars buys a scoop of cold rice and three shriveled chicken necks refried every day because there has been no one with enough money to buy them. If chewed long enough, fishy-smelling flesh cooked hard as plastic becomes stringy bits soft enough to swallow. I can only imagine what mealtimes are like for the locals.

Roads along fluffy, pale beaches were swept away, but as suggested by villagers, at low tide they connected to solid tarmac on higher ground. A Richter-scale nine-point-zero earthquake originally triggered the main tsunami, but sporadic aftershocks of fives and sixes have continued ever since. Reports of yesterday's aftershocks are unnerving. With one eye on the water's edge, I nervously scan the terrain for potential escape routes through shady palm tree groves to higher ground.

Once above sea level, the controlled slides over mud and sand give way to a euphoric glide through a pulsating jungle on multi-mile strips of asphalt rarely used anymore. But soaring beneath refreshing canopies of towering hardwoods also provokes sobering reflections. Each time I reach another fallen bridge which once connected villages across deltas, a ghastly reality strikes hard when I realize the reason for this blissful isolation is that those who once lived here have all perished. I shudder at the irony that it requires dreadful catastrophe to bring such peace.

Time
October 5, 2005
West Sumatra, Indonesia
● ● ● ● ● ● ● ● ● ● ● ● ● ● ●

Like sands running through an hourglass, my final days on a two-month Indonesian visa dissolve into final glances back. Just zigzagging the northern quarter of Sumatra has taken two weeks, with the islands of Java and Bali still left to ride. As time passes, it's difficult to avoid resorting to schedules that take health issues into account. Joyful daytime jostles over uneven terrain can later lead to uncomfortable nights repositioning to relieve my ailing left kidney. Before I tackle the rest of the continent, South Africa represents the last Western country with reliable medical facilities for ultrasound treatment. The stones have got to go. Targeting a midwinter crossing of Sudan means I need to be in Cape Town by early November to bite the bullet and get treated.

Thus far, living in the moment, minus the anxiety of rushing, lets me avoid a strict itinerary — the plan-of-no-plan. Staring at a map too long leads down the slippery slope of scheduling fuel stops and overnights that deny exploring situations that might otherwise have turned into spontaneous adventures. If I'd paused first to consider the enormity of Borneo and Sumatra, I would never have appropriated the time. Yet, those experiences proved to be among the most unique in this journey, and who knew what lay ahead in Ethiopia.

Dodging the worst of monsoon season by traveling below the equator during early October, I am still on my follow-the-sun route around the earth. Because seasons reverse in the southern hemisphere, December becomes the beginning of summer and a continuing dry ride back to California. With any luck, the weather patterns will turn in my favor on my way through Africa.

Yet, no matter the season, at altitude everywhere in the tropics\ the world is always wet. Apart from scattered mountain villages, the bulk of Sumatra's small population lives along the outer island perimeter. Two days crossing mist-cloaked mountains back to Medan was time well spent. Between traffic congested coastal routes and the empty central highlands, steady precipitation turn from a drizzle to a mild downpour. But clinging moisture also settle the dust as I passed through darkened caverns of giant fanning ferns. Overhead, like furry, delicate lace, long, fluffy strands of mustard-colored moss dangled from massive tree limbs in chilly canyon breezes. These seldom traveled gravel tracks winding through green, scented forests didn't register on the GPS, but the trails leading up and down through the fog kept me circling fresh-mowed hillsides in sweet isolation.

Pee stops were excuses to linger, savoring rhythmic winds stirring a labyrinth of creaking mahogany trees amidst the perfume of bright orange and purple flowers. Faint crashes on crackling leaves in the underbrush stirred my imagination — curious monkeys or preliminaries for the charge of a wild boar?

Returning to Medan late meant departing for Dano Toba late. Under the glow of an emerging half moon, I missed the drama of steep hairpin photo-ops but reached the crater's edge in time for a last ferry out to the mighty lake's only island. At 50 miles long and 16 across, Dano Toba is the largest freshwater lake in Southeast Asia and Sumatra's primary tourist attraction. Rising from the center, Samosir Island is the size of Singapore and dominates the landscape with storybook waterfalls and jagged peaks set against gray-clouded skies. A million years of geologic evolution has turned this collapsed volcano into a home for indigenous Christian Batak tribes and their ancient arts of fabric weaving and music. An easygoing people famous for love songs, they convey a mild nature with their look-you-in-the-eye greetings and lingering handshakes. Yet, among rows of charming waterfront hostels, I found only one other Western couple and no local travelers. There were reasons for others to stay off the road.

Strategically waiting for October's eve of Ramadan, to prevent the economy from experiencing further decline, overnight Indonesian government officials cancelled fuel subsidies for its impoverished people. Islam's holy month of prayers and fasting started at midnight with doubled gas prices. Traffic in the crowded seaside towns immediately dropped, with most Muslims wanting to remain home anyway.

During Ramadan, earthly pleasures like food and sex are restricted to evening hours, so restaurants remain closed until sunset, when families gather for prayer and feasts. Riding through quiet country neighborhoods provides a chance to peek into windows of slat wooden houses. Tables heaped with fried meats and steaming vegetables make me long for Ramadan to end. For now, bags of salty cashews and pints of chocolate milk will have to suffice until the cafés are back in business. Striking a bargain the previous night when no one was looking, a sympathetic cook had slipped me four fried eggs wrapped in newspaper. But a whole month of this?

Where it once seemed pleasantly eerie, the 5:00 a.m. Muslim call to prayer has become an annoying disturbance. There is no escaping it. Whether sleeping in mountain villages or big city hotels, piercing predawn blasts from metal bullhorn speakers shake all within range from fitful slumber. The earsplitting off-key verses shouted by energetic imams last just long enough to ensure that those they have awakened remain so.

As with America's Bible Belt, Third World life centers on God and family, with strong convictions concerning morality. Although no one ever mentions my religion, during typical roadside café chats, natives in every country constantly ask, "Where is your wife?"

With eyes half-closed while waving my hands in holy gestures, solemnly I declare, "As a high priest in the Sacred Order of Confirmed Bachelors, I am forbidden to marry." Those listening nod with a knowing respect as I continue, patting the shiny blue tank of my faithful machine, and pronounce with utmost sincerity, "This is the only wife I am ever allowed to take."

Gasping as though a spiritual revelation has just occurred, the surrounding barefoot crowd dressed in shorts and T-shirts murmur among themselves, "Ah, the only wife to take, the only wife to take . . ."

Java
October 8, 2005
Jakarta, Indonesia
● ● ● ● ● ● ● ● ● ●

Next to slapped-together palm leaf–covered noodle stands, the most common roadside business in Asia is tire repair. Highway shoulders used for dodging oncoming vehicles are minefields of debris dropped off lumbering trucks and fragments of past collisions. Although bikers know to be vigilant inspecting their tires, we seldom find rusted steel shards until a faint hissing sound stops us to pry them out from between wounded treads. India and Indonesia have been the worst for punctures.

If not stopping to inspect an unmistakable rear-end wobble, I wouldn't have noticed sprays of engine oil dripping across the tank. Sidetracked by natives during a morning fluid check, I'd forgotten to secure the oil cap. For the previous hour, darkened oil splattering in the wind had also been coating the front of my jacket and pants. Stuck sweating and cursing under shady banana trees on a stretch of road between towns, I did not have to wait long for assistance.

At times, the locals can be annoying, firing the same questions I'd fielded from the last group only an hour before, but they also appear when most needed. Flat tires are always a hassle, but being stranded miles from a town compounds the problem. Temporary glue-on sticky rubber squares are unreliable patches and usually leak after tires warm up. A new tube is cheap enough, but if they're unavailable, the heat-vulcanizing patches are best. And how to find a tire shop in unfamiliar territory?

Within minutes after parking and removing the rear wheel, two-man teams of eager volunteers on little flashy scooters surround the disabled alien. Passing motorists notice the swelling crowd competing to assist me and stop to investigate. They all volunteer to take my punctured tube to the nearest repair stand. For the job of courier, I chose the one man wearing a watch, and an hour later, he returns in triumph with a 10-bike escort. After charging just one dollar for the patching, my angels of motorcycle mercy refuse to take tips for their efforts. Now if only there were decent restaurants.

Sumatran village food was getting old — literally. Before they're offered to customers, the severely overcooked deep-fried chicken and smoked fish heads displayed on restaurant shelves sit long hours without refrigeration. Once you're seated, a buffet of a dozen flaming vegetable dishes and chilied meats are set before you. After the meal, you pay for whatever you choke down — and because of Ramadan, the hungry must wait until sundown. But the Indonesian capital is more forgiving.

Eleven months out of the year, religious fundamentalists tolerate the open sinning of Jakarta's infamous red-light district and blazing discos, but during Ramadan, doors leading to sinful paradise remain chained. But, flagrantly serving food in daylight hours, the provocative decadence of Western fast-food restaurants beckons to the famished. At the risk of burning in hell, women in headscarves sneak out of downtown McDonald's with Big Macs stuffed into bulging purses.

Seventy percent of 235 million Indonesians crowd the single island of Java, while Jakarta's teeming streets overflow with forlorn migrants who've abandoned a hopeless countryside for the despair of an overpopulated city. Yet, they still smile and wave, asking if there is anything they can do to help a disorientated stranger.

When I'd rolled off the ferry from Sumatra into a series of tangled intersections, a fellow rider immediately came to my rescue, offering guidance through the 60 miles of tricky boulevard mazes leading to Jakarta. Motorcycles are prohibited on the much faster toll road, and what should have taken an hour turned into four. At the halfway mark, in choking gridlock, we stopped to eat. My new friend, Wayan, with the expensive motorcycle carried three cell phones, and while tossing wads of rupiah to the waitress, explained that he works as a bouncer in a tourist nightclub. Wayan flashed too much cash for a teenager working a job that pays a dollar a day. Pantomiming popping pills, with a boyish nonchalance he twirled an index finger next to his ear, and then leaning slightly forward whispered, *"Mistuh, you want some Axtasee?"*

It's not right to judge another man without first walking in his shoes, and how Wayan answers the challenge of survival in the developing world is up to him. But it was disheartening to realize that under Indonesia's brutal drug laws, this kind young stranger demanding to pay for my food might someday swing from the gallows. As we dined on sizzling chicken satay sticks and my first taste of Diet Coke in a while, maddening racket from outside the café drowned out a conversation I didn't want to hear.

Thick blue smoke from two-cycle motorcycles blended with trails of black burned diesel fuel swirling together with brownish road dust kicked up from dueling buses and three-wheeled taxis. Although clouds of filth invaded the canvas flaps of our roadside barbecue stand, Wayan still sucked down one cigarette after another. To relieve my inflamed sinuses, I sipped shallow gulps of this airborne sludge, but from stinging eyes to burning skin, the assault was endless. Ever since Turkey, I have inhaled enough carcinogens on this journey to guarantee one day waking up with potatoes growing in my lungs.

Once on the two-lane boulevard leading to Jakarta, the road-space battle escalated as traffic backed up for miles. Some of the common evasive maneuvers here would have aggressive Southern California drivers drawing sidearms. After 10 minutes of high-risk weaving to the front, we discover two truck drivers stopped in the middle of the road, talking to each other through open windows.

Reluctant to unmask as the Ugly American yet still anxious to vent, I flipped open my face shield and shouted, "Hey asshole, that's not the way we do things in Montreal!"

Mountain Tops
October 18, 2005
Mount Bromo, Java, Indonesia
● ● ● ● ● ● ● ● ● ● ● ● ● ● ● ● ● ● ●

Indonesia has not always been Muslim. From European mixes of green-eyed Taoist Chinese in Banda Aceh to the Christian church steeples of Dana Toba, for 2,000 years conquerors and occupiers have stamped their presence and beliefs upon this South Asian archipelago. In the early ninth century, when Java was Buddhist, worshippers constructed the massive stone temple of Borobudur on the outskirts of Yogyakarta. A decaying stone behemoth rising a hundred feet above the forest floor, its chiseled granite walls tell the story of Buddha. Hand-carved scenes of interacting humans describe the life and teachings of a young Indian prince reaching nirvana through meditation. Later abandoned and reclaimed by the jungle, Borobudur remained buried in encroaching foliage until 1814, when it was rediscovered by English explorers. Recognized as the greatest of all Buddhist monuments and a significant tourist draw, now, once again, it is deserted.

With the recent doubling of fuel prices, family gatherings for Ramadan and unwarranted fears of terrorism, Indonesia's famous attractions remain empty. Except for a wandering unemployed tour guide, I'm the only one scrambling up the ancient temple steps. Resting on the upper decks, bell-shaped stone stupas house smaller Buddha statues floating in serenity against a backdrop of stunning palm-covered countryside. A lazy afternoon spent absorbing local history passes into night, but with only three weeks left on my visa and another island yet to explore, it was time to visit Indonesia's mountains.

It had been so long since I'd been cold, I'd forgotten what it was like or even to keep handy a sweater and insulated gloves. Riding west across Java, cloudy skies shielded the earth from baking rays of a tropical sun, but that was in the sweltering lowlands. Once beyond the smog-choked asphalt fingers of Jakarta, traffic thinned from the chaotic pace of first-gear sprints and fast hard-braking to long empty stretches of green agriculture fields between small rural towns. At sea level, the air was sweet and warm, but spiraling up the sides of dormant volcanoes, the temperatures plummeted in relation to ascent. An abrupt rise of 8,000 feet into monsoon clouds turned the air see-your-breath cold. Mount Bromo is actually one of three volcanoes within a much larger crater and still belches steamy vapors through cracks in the mountain.

The last outpost at Cemoro Lawang was a ghost town of idle villagers waiting for tourists who would not arrive. Employees of the only open café provided me with directions for investigating Bromo-Tengger-Semeru National Park without a guide. Pasted on lobby walls, faded flyers touting excursions by rented jeep and tired old ponies promised to replace hours of trekking for views over the rim of a puffing volcano. But those options were for people without motorcycles. An overnight drizzle had packed soft ground lava fields solid enough to ride straight across as long as the surface was flat. Determined to avoid walking, I rode halfway up the radical incline of the first smoldering cone until buried to the engine skid plate by a spinning rear tire losing traction. A second attempt with more running speed might have yielded better results, but it was now only a 10-minute hike to the base of the famous 254 cement steps to the crater's edge. Peering over the rim provided eerie glimpses of boiling sulfur fumes that encrusted the crevice walls a powdery yellow. Yet, if the weather cleared, panoramic postcard shots from five miles across the crater up on Penanjakan Peak were a photographer's ultimate prize.

What guidebooks warned was a serious four-hour hike up to the summit became 20 minutes by motorcycle, twisting up jungle hairpins to 9,100 feet. But by late afternoon, mild drizzle turning into a full-force storm meant becoming stranded at the top. The highest point in the region, Penanjakan Peak is also a base for remote radio towers and relay stations. While I stood drenched and staring though graying walls of falling water, the final light of day faded into a solid fog. In better times, the half-dozen boarded-up shacks near the lookout patio served as souvenir stands for winded trekkers, but after prying apart broken wooden slats, a hollow musty shell became this shivering solo traveler's twilight refuge. While waiting for rains to ease enough to retrieve camping gear from my bike, a middle-aged bearded man appeared from the darkening shadows. Draped in dripping green plastic trash bags and without speaking, he motioned with his hands to follow.

Unsure if I'd been busted for burglary or rescued from the elements, Agil Kurniawan's cramped five-by-eight-foot brick cubicle provided instant relief from biting winds. As exterior temperatures nose-dived, the orange glow of his electric cooking plate was warming enough to begin to dry my waterlogged riding clothes. Cluttered with a nine-inch flickering TV, a few handheld transmitters and a rack of eating utensils on top of boxed clothing, there was barely room in here for one. Folding away his makeshift rain suit, Agil repeated familiar greetings, *"Dari manna mistuh?"* (You come from where sir?)

"Nama saya Glen. Saya orang Amereeka." (My name is Glen and I am original of America.)

Using a dented metal cup to scoop a bowl of rice from his cooker, he asked *"Apa kabar? Mau makan?"* (How are you? Do you want to eat?)

I nodded, and he sprinkled a plate with steaming white grains and chunks of smoked fish heads that were spicy enough to melt plastic. Sitting cross-legged, eating in silence, it was obvious this wandering alien was now trapped by the intensifying evening storm. Pointing to the raised plywood platform filling half the tiny room, Agil said *"Tidur desanah."* (You sleep.) Waving away my objections, he rolled out a greasy horse blanket onto the cold concrete floor and insisted that I use his bed. Debate was useless, so we spent the next two hours studying my computer images of faces and scenes from distant cultures. While tracing my route around the globe, Agil smiled and stared as if he was hearing about life on Mars. Even explaining the other islands of Indonesia was difficult — he understood only Java.

Agil's wife had died years ago, so he'd accepted work as station caretaker to live alone on this chilly mountaintop. To combat his eerie solitude, he conversed with others like himself, broadcasting bizarre messages over the radio. Throughout the night, switching between three handheld transmitters, he communicated with similar workers on other faraway peaks. In bursts of alternating short verses and chanted Islamic prayers, the men entertained and consoled each other through the night. With the endless crackling chatter beneath a bright fluorescent light, my chain-smoking new friend made sleep difficult.

In the morning, crisp dawn air was locked in thick fog while I manhandled the Beast up the final steps to what should have been a perfect volcano photo shoot. Bromo's illusive panorama was still obscured, but after coming this far I waited, hoping the sky would clear by noon. It did not, and I realized that if not leaving soon, another storm would surely cause me further delay. I was worried about complications airfreighting out of Bali next week as the regulations were rumored to have changed. A quick island hop south was imperative.

After a long farewell handshake, I held forth a few rupiah, but like those befriending me before, he shook his head in annoyance, indicating by pointing that hospitality comes from the heart. Hooking leathered brown fingers together, he stumbled through what he had written down using my dictionary, *"Mistuh Glan, we brother forever."*

Murphy's Law 101 (Refresher Course)
October 29, 2005
Ubud, Bali
● ● ● ● ● ● ●

Airfreight rates vary according to cargo. The highest are for hazardous goods — chemicals, combustibles and nuclear or infectious materials. Since they run on combustible fuel, motorcycles are considered hazardous goods, billable at quadrupled prices. In other countries, to declassify them as normal goods for standard rates, motorcyclists only have to drain fuel tanks and disconnect batteries. Today in Indonesia, that's not allowed, and instead of per-kilo costs of three to five dollars, they have jumped to 17. Shippers also use tricky methods of calculating fees based on volume as opposed to actual weight, using whatever numbers are higher. While the total weight of the bike, including crate, is 320 kilos, the volume formula translates into a billable 450.

To further the headache, within hours of discovering this rate hike, a half-dozen follow-up emails arrive announcing that there is now an embargo on airfreighting motorcycles from Indonesia, period. Singapore doesn't even allow their airport to be used for transit. Qantas in Australia, however, is holding steady at 17 bucks a kilo with no space available for three weeks. Sea freighting is worse, as it can take an unreliable four to six weeks and adds a series of additional complications, namely changing cargo ships in hub cities. Potential for wildcat strikes, deliveries to the wrong continent, port charges and Murphy's Law make that a poor choice.

But surrender is not an option when there is nowhere to go except backtracking 3,000 tedious miles to Malaysia for possibly a similar outcome. For eight eyeball-burning hours a day, I have spent the last week staring at fuzzy computer screens emailing and awaiting answers from freight-forwarders around the world. So far, there is only bad news to add to my reminders of an expiring Indonesian visa. As this journey unwinds, every hour is important and nonproductive days dallying in Indonesia will eat into quality time in Africa. While still mumbling "damn a schedule," at some point soon I'll also need to deal with my cursed kidney stones.

Airfreighting from Australia would be far simpler, but that requires a visa and two more weeks of riding the remaining islands of Indonesia just to reach East Timor for a ferry to Darwin. From there, it's another two weeks across the deserts to Sydney for transport to South Africa. Australian officials in Bangkok still refuse to acknowledge my emails.

But just as I've learned that after a series of misfortunes in life better days soon follow, somehow, this situation seems certain to lead to deeper experiences. And so, after firing a Friday afternoon final salvo of enquiries, a windy road through jungle mountains called out to me — to meet and enjoy the enchanting natives of Bali.

Sweet Bali
November 3, 2005
Ubud, Indonesia
● ● ● ● ● ● ● ● ● ●

Since I last trekked through Bali in 1982, much of the Hindu island has changed. Then, the entire southeastern beach had only one major hotel; now, there are hundreds connected by traffic-clogged roadways smothered in gagging exhaust fumes. A wobbling tourist industry was just beginning to recover from the 2002 terrorist bombings when another wave of violence struck last month. With threats from extremists of more attacks to follow, few tourists visit the main vacationing towns of Sanur, Kuta and Nusa Dua. Rows of downtown bars and fancy restaurants are manned by forlorn waiters staring at empty tables while pondering their future. Between fuel prices doubling and worry about the next terrorist bomb, there is much to be concerned about.

Renowned as a cheap holiday with world-class surfing, Bali resort areas have also grown famous for dope and partying. Paradisiacal beaches draw reveling hordes of young backpackers whose nighttime thrills can have dire consequences. Despite Indonesia's merciless drug laws, foreigners are still arrested weekly for selling or possessing marijuana and cocaine. The price for a short-lived good time can be 10 years in prison. But weary motorcycle riders aren't here for such distractions and instead appreciate the Western food, discounted lodging and perfect weather to offset months of gulping greasy noodles and bumpy rural roads. Still, rest and relaxation gets boring after a week, and life is always more interesting in the countryside. Beaches and nightclubs are great for vacationers, but a world tour should be about experiencing people and seeing society on other levels.

If Hindu Bali is the cultural capital of Indonesia, then the mountain enclave of trendy Ubud is the epicenter. A once sleepy artist colony now battles to preserve its indigenous charm by fending off promoters of fast-food chains and throbbing discos. As passive locals grew fat on tourist dollars, they also became seduced by Western values. Today, Balinese merchants struggle to keep up with the Jones's by buying cars, motorcycles and material goods on credit. Formerly an economical destination by international standards, the invasion of bargain-hunting tourists and migrating expatriates has caused painful inflation and annoying overpopulation.

Today, Ubuds's meandering streets are barely wide enough for streams of motor-scooter riders weaving through stagnant lines of idling minibuses and taxis waiting hours for a customer. Yet every evening in dozens of incense-clouded temples, clanging gongs and wooden xylophones coax glittering costumed dancers through flowing movements with contorted postures and focused wide eyes. Religion, with its deep beliefs in karma and Hindu Gods, has survived the commercial assault. Any excuse to celebrate is welcomed with elaborate festivals for births, deaths and cursing or cajoling otherworld spirits. But unless there is a ceremony in progress, the traditional Balinese sarongs and headbands have been abandoned for T-shirts and Levis, while the more ambitious learn English to peddle trinkets or work as guides.

Packed between street-corner brick temples and shrines draped in garlands, scattered tourist shoppers pick through hundreds of thousands of hand-carved woven handicrafts of batik and bamboo.

Owned by expats but staffed by locals, expensive health spas advertising coconut-oil massages and mango-cucumber facials are stacked between European-style art galleries and foreign-owned hotels. Yet, with so much to sell and no one to buy, the economy flounders.

From the city center out, in all directions, miles of overstocked furniture factories and souvenir stalls block views of the rich jungle terrain and the incredible rice terraces of Bali. But Indonesia still lures foreigners in search of easy living on fixed incomes, and more of those arrive daily, complicating the carefree island lifestyle. At first infatuated with local ways, newcomers soon busy themselves with familiar enterprises that cater to their kind. Polluting village life to accommodate the fanciful whims of those who can afford them, gleaming all-night supermarkets supply costly American wines and aromatic French cheeses. The closest relief is Pondok Saraswatsi, a traditional retreat three miles beyond the city limits and a universe away.

Although most foreigners establish businesses to support themselves, Pondok Saraswatsi is run by a native family aided by a few Australian men more interested in giving than taking. Careful to describe their nonprofit project a retreat not a hotel, serenity and appreciation of traditional Balinese life is the rule. Set in manicured gardens of statues and shrines, each of five stilted bungalows is hidden behind giant rubber trees and enormous blooming wildflowers. Beneath upstairs sleeping quarters, a stone-tiled shower and open-air bathroom blend with natural surroundings and scents of exotic plants and vines. Without television or Internet, this is the ultimate environment to tune out problems of airfreighting motorcycles and savor quiet evenings.

In the stillness of midnight, a glowing silver moon reflects from the surface of flooded rice paddies, and you can smell the sprouting first blades of grass. Cool forest breezes whisper through bamboo windows across polished teak floors and walls of woven reed. I drift into slumber under billowing chiffon mosquito nets serenaded by groaning bullfrogs and buzzing cicadas. Morning is announced by toiling field workers nudging water buffalo to plow the earth for next season's harvest.

Invisible hands deliver breakfast quietly so as to avoid disturbing my early morning meditation. Moments later, I surface from the void to Chinese tea with four fried eggs on a plate hand-painted with fresh purple orchids. Three days evaporate in silent hours of doing nothing but reminiscing. Proceeding according to the plan-of-no-plan means living in each individual moment. But the enormity of Africa lurks in the distance. It will be another week of waiting or a mind-numbing backtrack to Malaysia. Either way, the perils and pleasures of an enticing Dark Continent dance just beyond my imagination.

Working It Out in the Developing World
November 9, 2005
Sanur Beach, Bali
• • • • • • • • • • •

A guaranteed way to spoil a good time in the developing world is to get caught in a hurry. Suddenly, the easygoing ways of passive natives turn into irritating nonsense as Western expectations for efficiency end in shocking disbelief. It takes a while to remember that this confused young man seeking information by tapping keys on a computer terminal was likely born in a village without plumbing or electricity. He grew up focused on evening temple prayer chants and dances. His is a spirit world where the future is about preparing for the next event in a series of Hindu celebrations and music festivals, not an eight-to-five job he is expected to appear at on time every day.

For Balinese, training as office workers or skilled laborers involves memorizing basic procedures and reading and adhering to short, oversimplified rule books with no allowance for what impatient Westerners consider common sense. As in Russia, more than death, natives fear making decisions. They'd rather risk losing customers than make a mistake. If the request is not simple and easy, any solution is too complicated. And airfreighting a motorcycle to Africa is as confusing as it comes. Conferring with front counter personnel is fruitless, but business is more organized at the top — if you can get there.

Cargo departments of airlines don't deal directly with the public; a middleman is required for document filing and customs clearances. After the company that gave me a reasonable quote two months ago withdrew their offer, my first 10 days in Bali have been wasted in endless Internet enquiries to other freight forwarders throughout Indonesia and elsewhere. Of the half that responded, half of those declared the task impossible, while those who agreed sent follow-up emails asking for ridiculous shipping fees. And no one understands why this is so unreasonable. Don't Westerners all possess magic plastic cards that make strange machines spit out multicolored bills of Indonesian currency? What's the problem?

No matter the time spent showing maps, photographs or diagrams, riding a motorcycle around the world makes no sense to the puzzled natives. Airfreighting from one continent to another seems even more bizarre. In Bali, no matter the size of the stone in the road, any complication leads to a brick wall. Putting in a personal appearance has not helped either.

More than in other developing countries, this lack of initiative is more pronounced in Bali. I'm trapped in the Twilight Zone. Even those who speak English offer only blank stares and empty smiles.

"Hello, I need to airfreight my motorcycle from Bali to South Africa. Can your company do this?"

Ten seconds of blank stare ends with a robotic smile followed by slowly repeating, "Motorcycle . . . Bali . . . Africa." After another 30 seconds without even tilting his head — "I am sorry that is impossible."

Knowing that the Harley-Davidson dealer in Jakarta receives his motorcycles by air, I ask how he accomplishes this.

"Those are new motorcycles without fuel and disconnected batteries."

"Okay, I'll disconnect my battery, drain the fuel and flush the tank."

"Yes, but there are still dangerous magnets in your motorcycle."

"There are magnets in the Harley-Davidsons also."

"Yes, but those are different magnets."

It is obvious we have too far to go, and I venture across town seeking the next freight-forwarder on a lengthy address list. The alternative is unthinkable — a 3,000-mile destruction-derby retreat to Malaysia at a time when Muslims return home en masse for the final week of Ramadan.

But after another three hectic days, the Travel Gods take pity and the owner of Ritra Shipping agrees to call MAS Cargo and actually allow me to ask the question directly. Felicia, a Chinese freight manager with perfect English, interrupts a carefully worded request with, "If you fax over a statement that you disconnected the battery and drained the fuel, we can ship at regular rates. When would you like to go?"

Dumbfounded and stammering, "Uh, ah, oh, right away. Uh, ah, oh, is tomorrow okay?"

"I'm sorry, this is the end of Ramadan and all offices are closed until Monday, but I have in friend in Kuala Lumpur who may get you confirmed. The problem is that receiving an answer will take a few days. In the event you can't reach me, here is the telephone number of the man I will assign to follow up." Where was this saint 10 days ago?

Although buried in shipping business meant missing an anticipated ride around Bali, coordinating my departure has turned out fine in the end. If nothing else, an adventure in frustration has become a lesson in patience. But the news improves when I discover flights to Johannesburg actually continue much further south to where I'd initially wanted to begin riding the Africa leg. Flying direct to Cape Town saves me two days on a boring road that would have required backtracking. Meanwhile, removing bulky weights on the handlebar tips allowed trimming the motorcycle crate, further reducing shipping costs. But the hassle is far from over.

Exiting Indonesia is only the second major hurdle. After telling shippers that I wouldn't leave Bali until the bike left first, they promised to call the moment the plane was airborne. That message finally arrived tonight, stating that the crate was too big for the afternoon plane, but the Blue Beast was now finally bound for Malaysia in the hold of a 747. Still, this required a transfer to another aircraft in Kuala Lumpur for a flight to Cape Town tomorrow. Experience had taught me to beware of the mischievous hands of fate, so I won't be resting easy until my motorcycle rumbles to life on African soil.

AFRICA

Stumbling Through the Clouds
November 11, 2005
Airborne over Madagascar
● ● ● ● ● ● ● ● ● ● ● ● ● ● ●

From five miles up, I drift into a sensation of whirling displacement staring out the dual-Plexiglas window of a roaring jet missile. While I'm suspended among idle puffy clouds, a muted fiery sun rises against the curve of the earth. Trapped in the disorienting daze of the continental hop on a precarious slide into the role of uneasy alien, I wrestle to contain mental images of primal cultures I'll soon encounter.

In 1988, when first returning to California from living in Asia, culture shock did not strike me until I was among familiar surroundings. Even promptly falling back into old routines with lifelong

343

friends, the social adjustment took a year. No one but other long-term travelers can understand the disorientation that comes with returning home. Those feelings intensified in 2002, after completing my South American ride, resulting in an about-face from Palm Springs for a four-month retreat to Central America. Still restless, I embarked on yet another extended visit to Mexico, only to return to California long enough to organize my present journey. So where does all this wandering lead?

There is a psychological line long-term international travelers cross that marks a point of no return — when we surrender to the lure and take the expatriate plunge by deciding to live in a foreign country. I grapple with these quandaries daily, often hourly — what do I do once back in the U.S.? And where should I finally settle and grow old? This morning, when boarding a plane crowded with package-tour Europeans leaving Bali, culture shock exploded like a series of glaring lightbulbs. One would assume that with time spent in sociable Indonesia, these tired tourists would have learned something and at least lost the unpleasant frowns.

Since most hotels in Bali were empty, it was annoying to encounter partitioned rows of emotionless Caucasians with sunburned faces and worn expressions. How is it I can be so uncomfortable with my own kind? Have I become the dog who has played with the ducks so long he thinks he is a duck? In 30 years of wandering 70 countries, from Mongolian nomads to Amazon Indians, I have interacted with almost every major race and culture except black African. And now, to the dismay of those at home, that exploration awaits when this 747 lands in Cape Town.

My first attempt to explain to friends and relatives my wild idea of continuing my global ride after the unfortunate events in Colombia were met with long faces and forced smiles. They may share the splendor of this adventure reading my journals, but they also suffer unfairly worrying about what might happen to me. Even though my South American adventure turned out for the best, the hell my loved ones endured for five weeks, not knowing if I was dead or alive, took its toll, perhaps more on them than on me. Announcing I was subjecting them to a second round of grating anxiety had a price.

Although everyone feigned excitement, no one but my closest brothers really understood. Cracks in rock-solid relationships widened in the deepening gloom of an approaching departure date. None of us could stand the strain of another emotional train wreck. India, first of the two biggest risks on this route, has passed with only a stomach-ache and frazzled nerves. Now, a glowing African sky pulsates with forbidding images of genocide, famine and disease. But somehow, I know it is going to be different, and the Dark Continent will welcome this curious gringo.

When first committing to embark on this odyssey, I told Brad that I would only be gone a year and had no intention of leaving the pavement. I aimed to confine the ride to developing nations but also to sidestep even the mildest hazards. And today, with recent pledges to be home by January, my course has veered again. So far, I've been a traveler without an established itinerary, just a general direction around the earth subject to change by political concerns or weather patterns. Originally, Africa was not an option, but a lengthy conversation with a fellow traveler stimulated further consideration. "Glen, you have to do Africa, life won't be complete without visiting the Masai of Kenya."

That very same afternoon an experience I'd had while talking to a cashier in a Seattle convenience store cemented my decision. While paying for a tank of gasoline, the shiny black-skinned girl's unfamiliar accent sparked my curiosity. "Okay, you're not British or Jamaican, where are you from?"

In a laughing voice behind sincere brown eyes, she answered in a series of soft jingling tones, *"I an fron Eet tee oh pee ah."* A homely girl with a happy face, she flowed lithe as a hand-carved ebony figurine, and during 20 minutes of conversation, between attending to customers and answering her cell phone, she spoke to me of a distant homeland. *"I con to Ahmeerica to be weet my famalee but I mees my contree so much. I an goin back to there soon."* Her comments caught me off guard. Living in the security and affluence of America, how could anyone miss the suffering of Ethiopia?

As of that moment, my answer was simple: I had to go and find out for myself. Now when meeting Africans traveling, I startle them by boldly announcing "I'll be in your country next year." But I am not proceeding blind — this time I am protected by omens.

While I was standing in line transferring planes in Malaysia, an Indian Sikh sitting in cross-legged meditation suddenly opened his eyes to wave me closer. With his bulging head layered in a white linen turban, he radiated a sage's wisdom. From behind a scraggly beard framing a tan, wrinkled face, he stared direct into my eyes, uttering these simple words: "Many great things lie ahead for you." As abruptly as he surfaced, he cast down his gaze and retreated to where he had been journeying, and I, with no further apprehension, took a confident step toward the immensity of Africa.

Pacing for the Main Event
November 20, 2005
Cape Town, South Africa
● ● ● ● ● ● ● ● ● ● ● ● ● ● ●

Cape Town fulfilled its promise as the planet's most charming destination. From the heart of a prosperous downtown business district to the fabled backpackers' enclave of colonial Long Street, the evenly sectioned city is surrounded on three sides by glistening blue oceans, where the icy waters of the Atlantic meet the warm currents of the Indian Ocean. At the urban edge, like a towering plateau plucked from the American Southwest, the sheer granite walls of Table Mountain jut 3,500 feet straight up into a turbulent sky. Eavesdropping in fashionable boulevard cafés, it's amusing to hear locals complain of their version of traffic issues — after the wilds of New Delhi, the worst afternoon gridlock here is like a cruise in the country.

Arcing concrete slopes of elevated overpasses guide whizzing automobiles outwards into upscale suburbs of fenced-in security. If people were not driving on the opposite side of the road, this could be a European-tinted California churning with Southern hospitality.

In restaurants or gas stations, everyone wants to chat with musical accents from 11 distinct languages blossoming into English. And even the roaming squads of beat cops seem reasonable.

The aggressive maneuvers I'd learned navigating Asia prompted the traffic police to stop me a dozen times. Cowboy road tactics acceptable on chaotic Java are serious offenses in the orderly West. Wrong direction rides on one-way streets or in between pillars on sidewalks are as shocking as parking in hotel lobbies — a common practice in developing countries.

Cyber-linked readers still follow my movements vicariously from computers around the world. Because of my online journal, Cape Town motorcyclists have emailed invitations to stay in their homes. South African generosity is overwhelming. But abiding by the traveler's three-nights-only rule, I swap Steve and Sharon's home-cooked meals and satellite TV for a return to the seclusion of a run-down backstreet hostel. Abandoning the ruggedness of the open road has made returning to civilization awkward, and there are blunt realities ahead to prepare for.

Idling in the comfort of Western countries, seasoned travelers lose their edge. A sterile environment of relative safety dulls senses vital for a quick reaction. Survival reflexes and the smell of danger become clouded back in the cushy West, where little can go wrong.

In rush-hour traffic, with belligerent commuters competing to get ahead, I should have been on high alert. Halfway into a multi-lane intersection, a speeding woman lost in her cell phone ignored the red light. A car-length ahead, the driver on her left snagged her front bumper with his, sending them both spinning sideways. But the sturdy hands of Thor slowed his rotation enough to abruptly come to a rest with the tip of his fog light tapping my front wheel. Another few feet and I would be dictating this from a body cast.

But this is high season in the southern hemisphere, and, without the threat of terrorism, throngs of European tourists invade and drive up prices. Anticipating bargain rates for provisions, I delayed purchases I could have made in Malaysia. Already-expensive anti-malaria pills were double what they cost in California. Accustomed to being the only guest in empty hotels, the tables have turned. A budget single room took a full day to find, while the owner advised me rates were subject to weekend hikes. But it's wise to enjoy abundance while possible; there will be few comforts if later crossing war-scorched Central Africa. With lean times ahead, I have been fattening up on pizzas and cheeseburgers interspersed with the best fish & chips in the world. Yet, all is not well in paradise.

Only a few generations from lives as bushmen herding cattle, awakening black South Africans peer out from cardboard shacks at streams of gleaming wealth. Beneath the pale yellow glow of highway streetlamps, expanding shantytowns and rural ghettos seethe under staggering poverty and pathetic despair. Inner-city misery exists in every country, but the sprawling futility of South Africa's infamous townships would move even the most callous.

With growing apprehension, wary whites cling to a prosperity generated under the intimidating impact of exceptionally violent crime. Forbidding invisible boundaries are established out of well-earned fear — security is tightly managed. Suburban housing developments appear as armed camps behind concertina wire and barred windows. Those desperate for a share of the wealth are tired of waiting and grab what they can with startling ferocity. Even the most liberal have personal stories. Simple thievery has turned into savage attacks, with thefts of cell phones and pocket change escalating into rape and murder. Numerous times a day, I hear gasping warnings, by every color, to be on guard and not get caught alone.

After the fall of apartheid, outnumbered eight to one, a new generation of whites is paying for the sins of their fathers. Under the covetous eyes of an all-black government, landowners and businessmen are wary about plans to balance the scales. Already, land disputes centuries old are being resolved with official offers they can't refuse — sell your farm at this price, or we will seize it.

National news is dominated by horrifying reports, yet no one has done anything outrageous to me except smile and wave. Meanwhile, deep, foaming seas are always an awesome way to change the pace. Day rides over twisting ribbons of coastal highway led to encounters with roving baboons guarding the Cape of Good Hope. South African cliff-side glides next to exploding breakers are the most spectacular on earth. Along strands of vanilla beaches, suntanned blonde bunnies with crystal blue eyes are as friendly as the local boys, asking the same questions as Indonesians. Without my quest to traverse this continent, this wayward spirit could easily be convinced to pause and linger.

Into Africa
November 26, 2005
Fish River Canyon, Namibia
● ● ● ● ● ● ● ● ● ● ● ● ● ● ● ●

Since camping was far too risky from endemic robbery, the next best answer to South Africa's budget-busting comfort were bunk beds in crowded backpacker dormitories — complete with throbbing American rap music played so loud you needed to shout to be heard. If you're interested in late-night beach parties and beer-drinking contests, refuges like the Wildside Backpackers Hostel are the ultimate tourist thrill. And for three nights while riding the seaside past Cape Town, they were.

Bundled in foul-weather gear to dull the chilly coastal drizzle, my run to the border was a typically melancholy look back at newfound friends. A half-dozen fellow motorcyclists and their families had guided me on rides and shared their lives, but Steve and Sharon's home-cooked meals were hard to beat. When you know you will never again see people you have grown to like, a simple goodbye is never enough.

Once on the outskirts of Cape Town, the straight, empty lanes of Highway N-7 cut across rich agricultural plains of combed wheat fields carpeting rolling low-lying golden hills. Almost without notice, the far fringes of the Kalahari Desert turned soaring rocky cliffs into jagged pink mesas of blazing crumbling shale. Within minutes, temperatures jumped from high 60s to 110 degrees.

South African customs and immigration procedures were so fast that, before I knew it, a sign appeared: "Welcome to Namibia." Twenty-two miles later, a hard left turn onto the graded gravel dirt track led to Fish River Canyon, a mini-version of Arizona's finest landmark. The least populated country in Africa, most of Namibia is uninhabited desert, with 50-mile stretches between fuel stops and campsites on the asphalt road running clear to Zambia. But a better route is this scenic parallel side road zigzagging the length of Namibia from the hot, arid inlands to the foggy breezes of the Atlantic Ocean.

Preparing for the next thousand miles of dusty dirt track meant loading up with 10 gallons of fuel and two of water, plus a three-day supply of canned goods. Vienna sausages, sardines and baked beans would substitute for Cape Town's fresh-cooked pizzas and barbecued chicken. Signs forbidding camping outside, just two official sites in Fish River Preserve assured a rule-bending motorcyclist would enjoy the bliss of the Namib Desert alone.

Proceeding undetected, I spent a half-hour spinning straight across soft shifting sand to the tallest rock formation on the horizon. Providing a heat block three stories high, the western side was the coolest spot to sleep. Setting up camp directly in late afternoon sun meant I'd have morning shade from an anticipated fiery dawn. Unruly desert winds eventually calmed into delightful silent stillness interrupted only by trumpeting caws and clicks from unseen animals. Signs of life were everywhere. Dark crevices between massive orange boulders lead to darkened burrows of unknown desert dwellers. Fresh tracks and still-damp animal dung confirmed this as home to unknown species, hopefully friendly to two-legged versions. In a region roamed by jackals, hyenas and leopards, would there be midnight visits from hungry beasts? Guidebooks insist there is nothing here big enough to eat men — or so they say.

Reeling in the seclusion of a nylon domain creates a feel of familiar security. Alert to my communion with nature, I awoke with a full dose of the powerful midnight sky. With no trace of pollution, a brilliant galaxy of stars shone bright enough to throw shadows as the lowering overhead dome seemed close enough to reach up and touch. Faint scents of acacia bushes and camel thorn trees became a soothing tranquilizer to doze back to sleep.

Canned peaches and stewed beans made for a delicious sunrise breakfast as the cold evening air lingers long enough to don a sweater. But as the heat of the day boiled into the hundreds, the trail toward Fish River Lookout became alive with game. First appearing like odd-shaped bushy cactus, tall, stilted ostriches stood frozen in their mindless gawking. Cousins to the antelope, fleeing springbok leapt across the road in vertical pogo-stick bounds higher than my helmet. The only sign of their passing were evenly spaced puffs of dust disappearing into a pencil-line horizon. Having drunk their morning fill from the edges of muddy watering holes, small families of short-legged, stocky zebra strolled by, observing the two-wheeled invader from a distance.

Late November is the beginning of a scorching southern hemisphere summer, so the long, dusty ribbon of decomposed granite was as vacant as the clear indigo sky. The Namib Desert is an environment cruel to the living, yet it's also an enticing return to the kingdom of solitude. Except for sagging cable strands connecting distant tilting telephone poles, there is little evidence of man. After 24 enchanting hours without seeing another human and at last intoxicated by the euphoric aromas of desolation, inhaling a full dose of Namibia feels like I have finally arrived in Africa.

The Piss of Solitude
November 29, 2005
Namib-Rand Nature Reserve, Namibia
• •

The power of positive thinking has remarkable effects. Believing that the cup is always half full does not guarantee everything goes right, but when it's combined with perseverance, it increases the ability to cope with whatever difficulties arise. Hand wringing serves little purpose, but in the back of a long-rider's mind lurk worries about breakdowns or mishaps in isolated locations. We are all aware of the consequences of electrical failures in snowstorms, broken bones in distant jungles or breakdowns in remote deserts.

Although inconvenient, small punctures in tires are easily repaired in an hour by patching the tube and reinstalling the wheel. Not so with total blowouts, where radically ruptured casings instantly deplete tires of the vital air that keeps them round and bouncy. And since blowouts seldom occur, the loud snap followed by a wobbling rear tire was a mystery. Staring down at a six-inch gash, I could see that yesterday's off-road shortcut over knife-edge shale had had its price.

Had I not recently been smirking about the fact I'd seen no other cars or humans for the last 24 hours, a ruptured tire in the desert would have been more tolerable. Yet, if that pattern continued, my trash sack containing drained water bottles and empty cans of food would become unwelcome reminders of the folly of traveling alone. What was a retired judo instructor doing in Africa anyway? Suddenly, California never looked so good.

Four hours flipping through mental files of dead-end solutions produced nothing. My carefully stored aluminum tire irons had been claimed by the mud holes of Borneo, yet two screwdrivers worked carefully with long-handled wrenches could substitute. Still, inserting the backup tube into a tire ripped this bad would be futile. Once reinflated, the soft rubber would immediately bulge through the slit and burst. Anywhere else in the world, a rusted old pickup truck filled with locals would surely ramble along to the rescue. Here, in this isolated section of the Namib Desert, there weren't even birds or telephone poles. Yet, sooner or later, a cavalry arrives.

Remembering their names would be more polite, but at least I took their photo. A handsome young Italian couple out sightseeing in a rented four-by-four rolled up just before sunset — the most welcome sight all day. Discovering their tool kit contained a long-handle tire iron was the inspiration I needed to contend with the approaching dusk.

There had been no traffic in the daylight, and there would certainly be none at night. Since abandoning the bike is never an option — the possibility of sitting roadside for days had been my most recent fear.

The Italian couple's car tire iron worked well easing the casing off, and packing in a new tube was like any other repair. But how would I pinch and hold a gaping gash together enough to cover the 40 miles to the next campground and telephone? Nylon straps used when cinching down the bike for air transport would serve a second purpose. Trimmed to fit the circumference of the tire, I could tighten three of them enough to close the gap and keep the tube from popping out. A 10-inch strip cut from the old tube with the ends folded over and under the nylon straps should keep them from fraying on jagged gravel stones.

After adding air from a 12-volt pump, followed by grateful hugs farewell, I was off into the uncertainty of a blackening desert night. Ten miles further, rows of lights on a barren rocky hillside led me to Sossusvlei Mountain Resort. This was the first and possibly last opportunity to stop and evaluate my repair. The improvised patch was holding, but the tire needed more air and I needed sleep. Camping in the posh eco-reserve was an option until Bob, the resident astronomer, quoted resort hotel rates at $1,000 a night. Abruptly, the potential pitfalls of a midnight ride dodging wild animals seemed more attractive.

On a road without a severe washboard, the makeshift patch would have survived for more than a few miles, maybe even all the way to a phone at Sesriem campground. But bouncing and spinning over roughened stone ridges soon shifted the straps, allowing the gash to open and, for the second time, blow out a tube.

Tenting between the bike and the shoulder of a long, broad straightaway made certain no vehicles passed unnoticed while I was sleeping. With laptop and LED light batteries expired, the dim glow from a useless cell phone screen became my flashlight as I rolled out a sleeping bag next to empty water bottles.

Awakening to the buzz of aggressive horseflies in the inferno of a fierce morning sun was a nasty reminder of yesterday's events. Yet, just as a menacing midday heat was sucking away my remaining body moisture, that rusted old pickup rambled up and out jumped astronomer Bob with a crew of African workmen. Even better, the generous management of Sossusvlei Mountain Resort insisted I stay as a guest in their pilot's quarters while sorting out my tire issues. Sooner or later, the cavalry always arrives.

Posting online journals has also helped again. Recalling an email from a reader offering assistance if I was ever in his area, we were soon connected through a hotel satellite phone and arranged a replacement tire. Another stroke of luck was that Antonie van der Smit happened to live in the capital city of Namibia, home of the last BMW dealer on the African continent. Within minutes, he assured me that a nearly-impossible-to-find 17-incher would be on tomorrow afternoon's chartered flight delivering the next group of ecotourists to the luxury resort.

So while relaxing in the cool, air-conditioned staff quarters of Sossusvlei Mountain Resort, appreciating the difference between fortune and plight, I offer another humble thumbs-up to the Travel Gods. What could possibly beat munching on imported kiwi fruit and fresh grilled salmon steaks as I wait for the delivery of a new tire?

Eastbound on the Kalahari Highway
December 3, 2005
Kavango, Namibia
● ● ● ● ● ● ● ● ● ● ●

After the near-extermination of the indigenous tribes, southern Africa developed from European stock in a similar timeframe, though on a smaller scale, than the U.S. Roads, terrain and architecture here even look much the same, except the cities are further apart and there's less development in between. In Namibia, when I am not camping in the desert, scattered remote farmhouses established by 18th-century German immigrants provide soft, spongy beds in hundred-year-old but polished-clean wooden bunkhouses. Overnights with old-time homesteaders are refreshing upgrades, with outdoor stone bathrooms and communal kitchens in which to cook freshly butchered lamb chops the farmers sell. But the repeating scenery grew old as roads toward the coast remained washboard gravel with endless miles of beige-colored sand.

Approaching the celebrated Red Dunes of Sossusvlei, diesel truckloads of young European overland voyagers rumbled in for their dose of tourist-gouging. Prices are shockingly high. With southern Africa lacking a competitive industrial base, most goods are imported and heavily taxed, but the greedy merchants take extra advantage by exploiting budgeting travelers who have no choice where to shop. Compared to Asia, this region is unreasonably expensive, so trucking overlanders spend most of their trips camping with occasional evenings in backpacker hostels for hot showers and Internet connections. Before the rampage of civil war in Sudan made it too risky to traverse, the common route for these hearty adventurers was through eastern Africa, beginning from Cairo and ending in Cape Town. But recently, combined with the open banditry of northern Kenya, the new route has become Nairobi to Cape Town. (Now the genocide in Darfur can continue with fewer witnesses.)

Interviewing truck drivers is still depressing. As civil wars flicker and flare in central Africa, there still is no way to cross the mud roads west beyond Kenya or Uganda. Whatever the direction, once out of southern Africa, there is a 5,000-mile stretch to the Mediterranean Sea in which spare parts do not exist for larger motorcycles. Since tires are double the price of anywhere else, to stay on budget, Antonie sent me a 50-dollar used one with a quarter of the tread life remaining. On my plan-of-no-plan, predicting wear patterns and estimating arrival dates makes coordinating international supply shipments a logistical challenge. With 2,000-miles left to Livingstone, Zambia, where fresh tires are scheduled for delivery, timing is going to be tight. Anyway, the newly paved double-lane Trans-Kalahari Highway beginning from the coast is easier on rubber than the previous long stretches of sharp gravel road. Riding east out of the hot desert sands leads to a cool, pleasant plunge through a heavily wooded landscape.

White African cities were interesting, but this was a welcome change as the last one, Swopkupmund, disappeared behind me into foggy ocean breezes. Back in the countryside, among the occasional leaping gazelle and black-masked oryx, herds of 300-pound demonic-faced warthogs stood their ground staring while grazing roadside. Rippling with thick shoulder muscles and coarse-haired swaybacks, double rows of upturned tusks make them the ugliest beasts of the jungle. With every mile, Africa shows me more of its wilder side.

As concerns about robbery and murder in the cities faded, it was time to see how simple jungle villagers live. Swirling orange-purple flares during a primal Namibian sunset signaled that the moment had arrived to seek black Africans in their tribal environment. Riding the first suitable footpath through a tree-studded thicket led to a sprawling enclave of random mud huts reinforced with wooden poles. With a worn-out sign painted in English, one building stood out from the rest: Mbeyo Baptist Church.

At the sight of the invading alien, 20 of 40 lounging natives fled as the others watched warily from a campfire. Eventually, a hesitant-yet-curious tall, scraggly elder approached to investigate. Holding forth my hand with a mighty Viking smile eased his worries.

"Greetings from America. Is it okay if I camp with you tonight?"

Answering in a British accent, he sounded so proper, "Yes, of course you may sleep wherever you please. All visitors are welcome in Mbeyo."

"So, why then have those people run away?"

"When some of us see white men, we are afraid that you have come here to kill us."

"No, I am only a friend who has traveled across the world for one-and-a-half years to learn from your village."

"But you are from a great country, what can we teach you?"

"We are both from great countries and can learn from each other. Maybe you can remind me of what's been forgotten."

"We are the Kavango and this is our church. We are Baptists but others here are Catholic and Evangelicals. Can you help us contact American Baptist missionaries?"

"Well, I don't know any, but if you write a letter, I'll photograph the page and post it on the Internet. Why do you want to contact them?"

"Because the missionaries will come and make electricity for us."

"Why do you want electricity?"

"So we can have computers and Internet."

"And televisions and stereos too?"

"Yes, yes, of course. We want everything just like American people."

Pointing to a single-room mud hut, I ask, "But if you acquire those things, you'll need a bigger house and an extra job to pay for it all."

This confuses him. "But if the missionaries come, unemployment will end, and everyone will have lots of money."

Pointing to groups of idle men standing next to women busy tending fires and stacking wood, I ask, "What do you do all day now?"

"There is nothing to do for many months while we wait for the rains. Then we will plant seed. Anyway, you are in time to hear our choir practice."

The Mbeyo Baptist Church was built with the same mud-and-pole materials as the rounded huts, only bigger and square with a hard-packed dirt floor and rows of uneven sawed wooden benches. Inside, as two young boys warmed up on goatskin drums, the low humming choir began to shuffle with gyrating hips, matching the rhythm of a hollow barrel beat.

Between powerful harmonizing vibrations and subtly stamping bare feet, a fine dust filled the air, almost obscuring the undulating slow-motion dance. Clear, alternating octaves from converging voices gave me tingling goose bumps and shivers with hairs on end. Although swirling airborne particles made breathing difficult, it was impossible to rise or resist the hypnotic lure of entrancing upbeat hymns. As the Mbeyo Baptist Choir erupted into a spellbinding synchronization of explosive melody, I found myself sucked into the layered extremes of primordial life emerging in the eternal African song.

Khara
December 8, 2005
Livingstone, Zambia
● ● ● ● ● ● ● ● ● ● ● ●

One of Africa's poorest countries, Zambia still holds its head high. Lacking the fanatical friendliness of Asia, acceptance here requires explaining my journey with photographs through fire-lit evenings winning over the hearts and hesitant smiles of wary natives. Slave-trading and genocide may be old stories to Westerners but not to Africans. Over the centuries, when they weren't exterminating or enslaving each other, European colonialists arrived to take up the slack. Today, if they're not soldiers, foreigners in Africa are aid workers living here who tie their assistance to converting the people to new religions.

Africans should be grateful that 37 separate Christian and Muslim sects landed in time to explain to them that for the last 10,000 years, they'd been worshipping the wrong gods. Yet, less populated and poorer than other African countries, Zambia's future is promising.

Benefiting from Mugabe's chaos in neighboring Zimbabwe, tourists exploring Livingstone have stumbled onto superior views of Victoria Falls and less commercial game parks much richer in animal life. Still underdeveloped in terms of hotels and lodges, two main asphalt roads connecting national borders east to west make it possible to cross the country in any weather. Run by European expatriates, backpacker hostels continue as the slums of adventure travel, with greedy owners exploiting the unsuspecting.

Cramming tiny rooms with rows of narrow bunk beds and with one broken-down hallway bathroom for 20 or more guests, these pitiful cons appear at first as bargain accommodations for 10 bucks a night. Without private transportation, a captive audience of trucking overlanders is hoodwinked into paying inflated prices for food, Internet and laundry. But vagabond motorcyclists dodge the gouging by venturing into town to determine where locals eat and shop.

Yet for singles, backpacker hostels provide welcome opportunities to meet other travelers, specifically those of the opposite sex, also weary of being alone. Of all the exotic women I have met thus far, single female backpackers are by far the most impressive. Educated by experience and boldly spirited, they are inspiring to engage in deep conversation, swapping tales of adventure from different perspectives. So dazzling are these daughters of the road, if ever to marry again, I would surely choose a woman who has had the courage to travel developing nations alone. As African nights of introspection in a shrinking nylon tent closed in, my anticipation grew for what hopefully lay ahead in backpacker hostels.

It had been over a year since I'd encountered another long-rider, so I was surprised to meet a trio of bikers touring southern Africa. No matter the nationality, motorcyclists share a common bond. While three German riders were assisting in my parking lot tire mounting, out from an idling minibus stepped a young English backpacker hauling a daypack. Women this stunning are difficult to find, and she was definitely worth approaching. "What happened? Weren't you heading to Victoria Falls?"

Annoyed but not flustered, the clear-eyed beauty with strawberry lips brushed back her sweat-dampened hair and stopped to talk, "Yes, but I forgot my money so I'll have to return later."

Concealing a set of sprouting horns, I tell her, "When I finish mounting these tires, I'll be riding over around two o'clock. You're welcome to jump on the back and come along."

"That's great, I'll wait by the lobby."

When men and women first meet, it's common, though not always possible, for them to disguise their underlying intentions. Women are better at this than men. Although standards vary, men have body parts they inspect while trying to conceal staring, but women eventually catch us studying their breasts, the shape of their legs or the roundness of their butts. Although men aren't sure about the specifics, women have criteria of their own. With all this in mind, everything about Khara radiated uniqueness. Sometimes women just glow, and taking my eyes off her was nearly impossible. Ferociously independent with an unpretentious beauty, a centerfold figure and a country-girl smile, Khara had it all. An aspiring archeologist who'd traveled South America solo, she managed to learn four other languages while teaching English around the world.

Backpacker women may be more accomplished and sincere than city girls, but they still maintain a special persona reserved for men. Private discussions with my female friends confirmed my suspicions years ago — no matter how innocent the smile, there are few women who don't understand exactly what is on a man's mind. And no matter our efforts, women ultimately choose their men.

Still, backpacking women are a breed of their own, unimpressed by what car a man drives or how many digits appear on his bank balance sheet. More intrigued by what is different and put off by arrogance, being so particular also reduces their dating pool options. Fast-talkers need not apply, and a man better have achieved the extraordinary if he wanted to be a candidate for a roll in the hay. A potential suitor who has climbed Everest has a better shot than a rock star. But everyone's knees wobble a little in solitude.

Loneliness on the road is a constant, subsiding during the moments we meet new friends and peaking when experiencing the glory of a fascinating planet with no one to share it with. While lovers can be a burden, without the fulfillment of turning to say, "Hey baby, check out the sunset," somehow the thrill is diminished.

An afternoon spent ogling Khara as much as the booming waters of Victoria Falls led to pizzas and beer at midnight under a starry African sky. A lot can happen in a day, and connections on a spiritual level are powerful. "Khara, you should forget your plans and travel with me for a while. We'll find a helmet tomorrow, stash your extra gear and head for Tanzania in the morning."

"Yeah, I was thinking about that too, and it sounds good. I just need to be in Lusaka with friends for Christmas."

From using her lap as a pillow, I leaned up to kiss her a second time — followed by her admonishing wagging finger. "But when we travel together, there'll be none of that."

Having heard and made such statements before, everyone knows that an agreement restricting sex is a fragile arrangement subject to change. No matter your efforts, keeping a relationship platonic is rare, especially when sleeping next to someone who's spent the day riding with her arms and legs wrapped around your torso. One person or the other eventually gets ideas, and the dynamics can change with a strategic brush of the hand over bristling forearm hairs — and not always for the best.

Single Female Backpackers Part Two
December 12, 2005
Chipati, Zambia
• • • • • • • • • •

A wise man knows he is in trouble when he meets a female version of himself — in this case, a matching spirit meant she was driven by a similar yearning to get off the beaten path. A woman as qualified as Khara could be replaced but never be duplicated, and worse yet, she knew it. I knew if I traveled with her for any length of time, the best and the worst lay ahead, with an inevitable, uncomfortable fork in the road. Assessing emotional risk with Khara would be difficult, surely leading to a kind of aggravation that can empty a man's soul. Before squirming into sleep lost in drifting erotic images, I knew that a certain train wreck was approaching.

Midnight scents of her warmth were already taking my breath away, and we had only known each other a day. We would travel for a few weeks, and with me at the end of a journey and she at the beginning of hers, just as I was returning to California, she'd be hungry to continue. As a dedicated wanderer, faced with a choice, she was certain to follow the open road. Now, how to diplomatically withdraw an offer.

She was even more beautiful in the morning, clean and fresh with shining eyes more intense than I recalled. As she stood with her bags in hand, eager to ride, I waited until after breakfast to be a jerk. As if in a pathetic scene from a familiar movie, I stammered out my feeble explanations without her even flinching. She understood. "Yes, it would have been difficult, sleeping together every night . . ."

With an awkward hug and quick kiss goodbye, I felt a rush not soon to be forgotten and half-wished she had ruined the moment with something revolting like lighting a cigarette. But instead, her soft olive skin and deep, dark eyes shone brighter than ever, outmaneuvered only by a low-cut blouse revealing what I was now sure to miss. As a single male most of my life, I can read a woman better than most, and when I feel the slightest manipulation, I have developed an ability to tune them out. Even though we would never meet again, Khara made certain her image would haunt me forever.

For fear that I would write, I skipped the ceremony of swapping addresses, instead handing her a business card with website information, "In case you wake up one evening and discover that you can't live without me . . ."

As a single woman traveling alone, she had heard this all before and interrupts, "I'll know where to find you."

There wasn't much left to say as she stood without emotion, feeding slender arms through the worn straps of a bulky canvas backpack and then strode down the rutted dirt road to find a taxi. The farther away I got from Khara, the more I wished she'd turned around.

Back beneath a frayed mosquito net, an otherwise cheery early morning dragged into dull afternoon with an aching for the night to come and go. Tomorrow was another grind deeper into Africa with unknown mind-twisting events ahead. Finally resting in the shadows of graying twilight, wrestling with the curse of solitude, I tossed into slumber aware I'd always wonder if I had done the right thing.

Sweet, Gentle Malawi
December 15, 2005
Nkhata Bay, Malawi
● ● ● ● ● ● ● ● ● ● ● ●

Though I'm still on target for following the sun, southern hemisphere rains have begun, with ferocious evening thunderstorms lasting until mid-morning. Crossing the equator again next month in Kenya marks the beginning of dry season and a clear though long journey north. Even if occasionally drenched, the ride across Zambia is pleasant with sporadic stops to chat at dilapidated roadside produce markets. After quizzing loitering truckers about their homes and families, I ask for a picture and get an unexpected reply. "How much are you going to give me?"

Surprised because it's usually the natives who are first to ask for photos, I countered, "How much is it worth for a memory of meeting a friend?"

Embarrassed, with head hung low the barefoot young man clad in ragged brown shorts shuffled away only to return moments later with handfuls of soft yellow fruit. "I am sorry, please take these mangos and always remember the people of Zambia." In the heat of an afternoon tropical sun, we joked about life on the road and shared the sticky, succulent pulp. Across the road, licorice-skinned women in colorful long dresses balanced woven reed baskets high on their heads while they chattered and bargained for shriveled vegetables. Vivid patterns of blues and reds contrasted with their shiny black skin. But another squall was approaching, and after posing with the truckers it was time to ride.

Unlike Asia, camping in Africa has been convenient and economical, but threatening wildlife on the banks of the Zambezi River in Zambia now made that questionable. At night, the jungle is an aggressive world of predators battling their way up the food chain. Survival of the fittest is the only given. Although they're strict herbivores, in Africa, hippopotamuses kill more unsuspecting people than scorpions, snakes and lions combined. Getting between a hippo and its water refuge usually results in a stomping, crushing or tossing into the air. With that in mind, it was better for me to sleep in a farmhouse campground while deciding where next to go.

Of the two routes to choose for reaching Malawi, the road southeast passed Luanga National Game Park, the newest and reputedly best in Africa. But a 90-mile connecting seasonal side road had incurred serious storm damage, and rumors were that the last 30 miles were washed away. This meant a four-hour spin through mud to find out, and with worn sprockets and a fully stretched drive chain, it was a chance not worth taking. With sufficient time left to reach Nairobi by January, an untargeted detour into Malawi became the latest deviation on the plan-of-no-plan, still leaving enough time to refresh in the capital. In an intriguing blend of East and West, descendants of Arab traders strolled the modern concrete boulevards of Lelongwe in traditional Islamic gowns crowned with crocheted white skullcaps. Controlling major commerce for 200 years, tan-skin Muslim Indians and Arabs consider themselves true Africans as much as the indigenous black natives. But the convenience of a city was only an afternoon rest stop to stock up on fuel and food sufficient to last while riding the irregular lake shoreline leading north to Tanzania.

Namibia, Zambia and Malawi have been more comfortable to navigate than rumored. Tales of corrupt guards at African border crossings also prove to be unfounded stories. So far, there have been no pistol-waving demands for bribes or paperwork complications. In run-down wooden immigration stations, polite uniformed men stamp me in and out in minutes, with the only hassle being having to wade through throngs of babbling money changers with hand-held calculators competing to cheat confused travelers converting horrendously inflated currencies. But this is Africa, and even they are part of the show, as much as the incredible landscape that frames the gasping poverty of Malawi.

An elongated body of water covering half of the country, life centers on gigantic Lake Malawi, for its fishing and the water it supplies to maintain surrounding rubber tree plantations. A long, tiring day ended at the edge of darkening lake waters lapping at pebbled beach coves. Ringed by mud huts hidden in shaded forests, this scene had likely not changed for a thousand years. Camping in native villages evolves into a deeper experience as the lives of the locals unfold. Crowded and lively, after sundown, every hundred yards another group of laughing youngsters kick up dust as they practice singing and dancing for upcoming tribal festivals. When lacking a drum, they clap in encouraging beats as performers in the middle shimmy and prance to chanting rhythms. Wandering through the smoke-clouded village, firelight and a full moon reflect off shiny black faces flashing dazzling white teeth. As I pass between huts made of sticks and mud, teenaged natives grab my arms, guiding me into their circles to watch the clumsy white man flail.

Dressed in disheveled rags, old fat women with enormous butts stooped, cooking porridge in overflowing iron pots while men staggered about drunk on powerful local brew — African White Lightning. Wherever I visited through the night, there was always someone offering drinks, dances or questions about why I had come.

Native life is good, but staying clean is a challenge requiring occasional overnights in farmhouse lodges for showers and homegrown food. Poorer but even friendlier than Zambia, Malawi is a well-kept travel secret which supplied the strongest lure yet to linger. Even the cops who impounded my motorcycle were amiable while soliciting a bribe for "One of the most serious crimes in Malawi." Riding without a helmet is a finable offense around the world, but for payment of their fine, I insist that they provide a receipt. Wearing tattered street clothes, the Malawi police refuse and threaten to impound my bike if I decline to pay. How was I to know if these unarmed barefoot boys were even real cops? Sensing a bluff, I respectfully held my ground — but they were serious, and they chained up the Beast right next to the jail for the night. Typical of Malawi friendliness though, they walked me back to the lodge to view a nighttime laptop slide show of this journey so far. In the morning, we shook hands as I paid their seven-dollar fine and headed north to Tanzania.

From rocky ridgetops to forested valleys, I wove up and down among chilly mountain shadows until camping at sunset in a gargantuan crack in the earth. Created by colliding tectonic plates, the Great Rift Valley stretches from the Middle East to lower eastern Africa. Straddling the outer edges while gliding through fresh-paved curves provided incredible sunrise views of docile fishing villages and dug-out canoes loaded with flopping catches. But challenging decisions lay ahead.

Prospects for crossing Central Africa grow worse daily as violence erupts across the Congo and panicked refugees flee to safety. But there is none as militias march in to rape and murder whoever can't run. Bring your own machete and hope for the best. As options dwindle, my final alternative is to sprint past the bandits of northern Kenya into Ethiopia and plea for a Sudanese visa. Crossing the Sahara Desert into Egypt is more difficult than the Moroccan route, but there is no other viable way to reach the Mediterranean by land. Supplies are scarce and hauling sufficient food and water will only make maneuvering the bike more difficult. Even though my journey is winding down to the last 5,000 miles, it appears that the final stretch home will be a significant gamble, with politics as the wild card.

Holidays on the Road
December 23, 2005
Dar es Salaam, Tanzania
● ● ● ● ● ● ● ● ● ● ● ● ● ● ●

In off-road conditions, a set of sprockets and chains has been lasting 10,000 miles, but somehow my current ones made it to 15,000. Now, after crossing into Tanzania, worn to the limits, even riding slow the chain is failing so quickly I had to stop every 100 miles to tighten the slack as overstretched sections slapped and cut into the metal frame. Short tugs under acceleration followed by increasing clacking suggested that some time during the next 500 miles to Dar es Salaam, lopping steel links could jump track, jamming into the engine cases. But, rolling across arid southern highlands, there was much more to think about.

With its sharp rise in socioeconomic status from Malawi, the eastern Tanzanian countryside became a worthy distraction, bursting alive in vivid natural colors and wild animal life. From a half-mile away, women were easily visible, reflecting sunlight off soft cotton fabrics of brilliant ruby reds and dandelion yellows coming into focus from distant blurs across the canvas of African savanna earth tones. Nearing the eastern coast, traditional Islamic garb replaced Western pants and button-down shirts for all but Africa's most noble tribesmen. Evidence of past invading cultures contrasts with traditional Masai erect in royal postures, clutching trademark long-handled herding sticks. Tall and thin with beanpole legs sprouting from baggy Roman-style tunics, these princely jungle warriors now contend with tourism and 21st century technology while battling to survive government relocation plans. Between pressing cellular telephones against gaping pierced earlobes and controlling vast herds of cattle, they keep an eye open to exploit any circumstance.

Parking roadside to witness an open-field butchering of a hapless African buffalo turns into a sorry scene of opportunistic frenzy. Abandoning their fabled composure, 10 Masai tribesmen leap at me at once, rushing forward, shouting while rubbing thumbs and index fingers together, "Money, money, money!"

Disappointed, I stuffed my camera back inside my jacket and moved on in search of indigenous animals unique to the continent. With dozens of major game parks throughout Africa, all prohibit motorcycles except Mikumi, the only one with a highway passing through. But animals accustomed to the rolling thunder of speeding diesel rigs panic at the sight of any slowing vehicle. Even when cutting the engine to coast in silence, herds of grazing gazelles with swept-back corkscrew horns immediately bolted in methodic sprints for the security of faraway treelines.

Yet, enormous jungle birds were bolder. As I approached, waiting until the final moment, lounging flocks covering the roadway suddenly took flight, engulfing me in upward swirling clouds of snow-white flapping wings. Surrounded from all directions, through cawing and yakking, ascending yellow-brown beaks and dangling feet missed my helmet and windshield by inches.

In a scene out of *Star Wars*, silhouetted against the soft blue glow of an early sunrise sky, towering long-necked giraffes paused to consider the intruder. Once violating their safety zone, a half-dozen magnificent spotted beasts casually stepped across the meadow in graceful slow-motion strides, vanishing into forests of camel thorn trees.

With hairless pink butts thrust high in the air, roving families of arrogant baboons sauntered fearlessly back and forth across the road. Roguish creatures known for their unpredictable behavior, they are a force to be reckoned with. Sinister dog-like faces bearing sharp, curved fangs confirmed the warnings that close encounters could go either way.

Curious, black-and-white striped zebras grazed in nearby fields but always at safe distances, warily eyeing the two-legged trespasser on a shiny rumbling machine. After being spooked into short dusty gallops, they stopped to return my gawking amazement. All my suspicions are confirmed — Africa, rather than just another continent, is a separate universe. Every hundred yards, more wildlife scenes commanded a halt, yielding either to trumpeting bull elephants trampling highway shoulder grasslands or wondering about the groan and growling from within quivering underbrush. With a day left before Christmas, my mesmerizing plunge into Africa continues in an evolving saga a million years old.

Ali Hussein
December 24, 2005
Dar es Salaam, Tanzania
● ● ● ● ● ● ● ● ● ● ● ● ● ● ●

After visiting a few mostly white enclaves and small African towns, Dar es Salaam was my first predominantly black major city heading north. Aside from decaying, old European-era buildings, because there is not much to see, the drab capital of Tanzania serves mainly as a commercial center and transit point for tourists visiting the offshore island of Zanzibar. A small contingent of foreign aid workers and businessmen are hardly noticed alongside African-born Indians busy managing hotels and stores. From dusty, congested street markets to grimy corner cafés, Dar es Salaam has become purely African, with little Western influence and no Western franchises. In matters of race, it's a reversal of roles now, being a minority judged by a suspicious majority.

But passive Tanzanians lead simple lives and don't require over-bearing authority to keep order. Except for scattered unarmed men in worn-out blue polyester uniforms directing traffic, it's hard to find a cop. With rougher edges than villagers, city folk are always harder to approach, but even when idle young men stand staring from street corners, most are happy to talk if approached properly. Swahili was easier to learn than I first thought, and like everywhere, greeting people in the native language buys instant acceptance and conversation. *"Jambo! Haguri gani? Jina langu ni Glen. Nimekuja kutoka amerce kuku tembelea."* (Hello, how are you? My name is Glen and I've come from America to visit you.)

By five o'clock I had made my first Tanzanian friend, a tall, heavy-set motorcyclist who, though a third-generation Indian, considers himself African. Preparing to meet his family for dinner, the unshaven Ali Hussein was closing his motorcycle workshop when hit with an unexpected vagabond's wish-list for repairs. Shiite Muslims are strict family men, and staying late to work on some distressed foreigner's faltering bike was the last thing on his mind. But once he'd heard my plea, he offered, "Since you are traveling such a long way, me and my men will work tonight." But wrenching in the dark leads to errors and lost parts, so we agreed to wait until sunrise.

In the morning, uncomfortable with his non-English-speaking crew, when an overly concerned Ali Hussein suggested disassembling the entire drive section for inspection and cleaning, I argued that the rest of the motorcycle is fine and all that was necessary was to unbolt the rear swing arm to replace a worn chain and sprockets — a one-hour job with the correct tools. Fluent in Swahili, Hussein turned, yelling words to his men that made them laugh aloud.

Curious as to the joke, I asked, "What's so funny?"

"I told them you are afraid of their skin."

Embarrassed because he was right, I tried to deny it, "No that's not it, I just prefer not to take things apart unless absolutely necessary. You never know what can break or get misplaced in the process." Still, the truth was, I foolishly questioned their competency because they weren't Germans in white smocks.

"You worry that they won't remember how to put it all back together?" More comments and more laughter.

But Hussein is forceful, and, to my dismay, wins our debate, directing two shoeless young black men with severely callused feet to disassemble the suspension mechanical arms for further inspection. An hour later they hand me two sets of rusted bearings — the same ones we had just replaced in Borneo. After riding the washed-away coast near Banda Aceh, saltwater from low-tide beach runs had leaked past protective rubber seals, corroding hardened steel balls and needles designed to spin free. Had this damage gone unnoticed, they would have disintegrated and left me stranded on the most rugged section ahead in Africa.

Hussein said, "See, you don't have to worry about my workers, they know their job." Thirty minutes later, a winded errand boy returned with new bearings and fresh oil, while another prepared a homemade arc welder to remove a stripped-out drain plug. Annoyed at my constantly questioning each maneuver, Hussein took me by the arm, "Come, let's get out of their way so they can make everything new for our traveling brother. You need to see my empire."

Importing a dozen shipping containers a month, outside of South Africa, Ali is the largest motorcycle parts distributor on the continent. This will be good news for Internet-linked international riders who, until now, have been unaware of his presence. In a developing country with limited industrial base, I am amazed to see a warehouse stocked with hundreds of tires and engine rebuild kits. Yet skilled labor remained a question.

A one-hour chain-and-sprocket swap had turned into eight with a lengthy list of replaced parts, but by the end of the day, a minor job turned major repair was complete. Preparing for the worst, my meek request for the bill was met by Hussein's stern gaze. "There is no bill for you. My shop is absorbing the entire cost for our traveling brother."

And he wasn't listening to my objections — even when insisting that I at least pay for parts only made him angry. "I have made up my mind, this is between Allah and me."

Convinced of his determination, I made one final demand. "Okay, but I'm taking you to dinner."

Every big city has good restaurants, but for travelers to find them unassisted requires extensive exploring with more misses than hits. Hussein knows of the best, where only black Africans go to eat. In north Dar es Salaam, an empty block normally jammed with daytime traffic becomes a nighttime bazaar of street-barbecue kitchens and temporary dining rooms of uneven wooden tables and flimsy plastic chairs. Hussein is well-known among crowds of jabbering patrons — even cooks and waiters shouted back and forth as we approached.

At first, ordering food was awkward, as Ali issued commands to the cook without asking me what I wanted. With fierce expressions and aggressive verbal exchanges, both men dickered as though in serious confrontation about to turn violent. Suddenly, each was laughing and clasping hands while shirtless waiters in baggy shorts set down huge platters of sizzling lamb and chicken. Hussein translated: "I told them that this is my motorcycling brother who knows judo, and if the food is not good, he will kick your ass." When the bill arrived for far more than two men could eat and drink, the scribbled numbers on a piece of torn paper only amounted to a fraction of a tourist-area price.

Two days accompanying Hussein on his daily rounds of slapping countertops while shouting negotiations ending in laughter was a fascinating side-journey into the business culture of Dar es Salaam. Even the briefest glimpses into the lives of those in distant lands are the ultimate prize of adventure travel.

But the sourest moment of this unforeseen detour neared, and after reminding Hussein of the sacred coin he promised, the time had come to say goodbye. As he closed his eyes reciting an ancient Shiite prayer, a hundred-shilling Tanzanian coin carefully folded in a printed handkerchief became a prayer from the both of us that continued safety lay ahead.

"When you reach Ethiopia, you must stop and give this coin to a poor man and Allah will guide you the rest of the way."

As he shuffled his feet while looking down, I noted that Hussein also disliked goodbyes. With two sets of watery eyes, we touched cheeks Muslim-style with an enormous American bear hug. Tomorrow is Christmas and a long ride toward the northern plains of Serengeti.

Serengeti (Genuine African Adventure)
December 29, 2005
Arusha, Tanzania
● ● ● ● ● ● ● ● ● ●

Once Africans discovered that shooting their exotic animals with cameras is far more lucrative than with high-powered rifles, a proliferation of national game parks sprouted across the continent. Because environmental restoration is connected to economic success, for the last three decades, under the guidance of international preservation groups, governments have been appropriating vast savanna tracks and untamed jungles for national parks. Now, black rhinos, bull elephants, elusive cheetahs and other endangered animals can proliferate without interference from poachers and big, brave game hunters. But how to feed them becomes the sour note of Africa's symphony of survival. Ironically, today, once-threatened wild herbivores are nearing overpopulation and compete with domestic cattle for limited rangeland.

Under government relocation programs, the Masai tribes are being forced off traditional lands once taken for granted. After believing for 500 years that they were the sole owners of the earth and all its cattle, they are in dispute with well-meaning preservationists as well as park administrators. Over the centuries, grazing land was so plentiful that ecological practices like those of the Mongolian nomads were never developed, and lately, stubborn Masai are required to learn pasture rotation. But as game reserves were established to protect million-strong herds of migrating wildebeest and Thompson gazelles, Masai herders are being nudged further from their homes.

And planeloads of foreigners arrive daily to witness the spectacle. In starched beige shirts and creased khaki pants, they are armed with telescopic lenses while cruising in four-wheel drive safari vehicles for up-close glimpses at water hole predatory dining. Scenes of lurking crocodiles eyeing baby zebras and lions disemboweling gazelles send anxious shutterbugs into camera feeding-frenzies, with the latest high-tech recording devices thrust out simultaneously from half-rolled-down windows. In Tanzania, long caravans of dull-colored Land Rovers rumble across the barren Serengeti Plain kicking up billowing clouds of suffocating orange dust as conditioned warthogs and roaming giraffes stare back with equal interest.

African safaris have evolved in the last 30 years. Nowadays, tourists are snatched from airports in air-conditioned buses and whisked to fancy city hotels for transfer to luxury accommodations in commercialized bush-camps. Genuine African ultra-expensive adventure — complete with all the amenities of hot showers and gourmet meals served while bored natives perform evening tribal dances. Morning visits to slightly staged African villages with convenient souvenir stands are sucker stops for the unsuspecting.

In a bartering society where livestock are symbols of wealth, by African standards, Masai lead comfortable lives. Drinking mixtures of cow's milk and blood provides nutrition to keep them healthy and able to walk long distances from villages to grazing lands. As well as resisting Islam and Christianity, they still have no need for material goods or Western clothes. Many can afford conventional houses but prefer familiar mud huts close to the pastures, where they can watch over their prized cattle. Yet recognizing the opportunity to earn a buck, once-dignified warrior herdsmen now pose for dazzled foreign tourists, demanding cash payments for "capturing their souls." Mindful of enormous profits generated by ridiculously overpriced tour companies, costumed Masai now loiter roadside ready to sprint to safari wagons, demanding money from anyone holding a camera.

Since this journey is more about people and cultures than sightseeing, I struck a reluctant balance, deciding to visit at least one game park. But between the staggering, touristy safari prices and parks prohibiting motorcycles, a venture into Serengeti seemed more distant every day. Or was it?

Another stroke of luck was Ali Hussein introducing me to a group of foreign bikers who all work in Tanzania. Billy Hollington, the project manager for a cellular tower company, just happened to be departing the next day to conduct transmission-repeater station inspections across the Serengeti Plain — would I like to ride along? Even better, his route was over a remote section unused by tour companies, and the passenger seat was empty in his four-wheeler pickup. Bouncing across unmaintained roads, we would at least avoid scenes of 50 other vehicles circling to photograph a lion gorging on giraffe organs.

Billy sees the Serengeti often, and as he yawned at thundering elephants trampling acacia trees, I shouted with excitement to halt for photos. Although a gross violation of park regulations, I yielded to the temptation of exiting a vehicle for up-close photographs of bull elephants and dozing crocodiles. And even though we traveled on company expense, on day three, after eating lunch in a tourist company safari lodge, I asked to pay the bill. Often numbers get misquoted by confused locals uncertain of currency equivalents, so when the waiter requested $106 I was sure he meant 16.

But this is another giant money hole of Africa, and the manager confirmed without flinching that this was the price for his dried-up barbecued chicken. Billy was furious, and the bill was so outrageous I had to laugh, knowing it would make for an interesting commentary on the page of genuine modern-day African adventure. Tomorrow is another chapter on the road to Kenya.

The Plot Thickens
January 4, 2006
Nairobi, Kenya
● ● ● ● ● ● ● ● ●

Crime statistics reveal that one in three Nairobi residents was violently mugged last year, and that news was sufficient warning to spend evenings inside the barbed-wire capped cement-block walls of a suburban campground. After sundown, the sinister sideshows begin, as menacing street predators and persistent prostitutes emerge from the cracks and sewers of a desperate city. As darkness settles in, foot-police regroup at outer city inspection stations, with roaming predators left to be stared-down by nervous private security guards fingering the triggers of antiquated assault rifles. And that was the protected tourist side of town. Nicknamed "Nai-robbery," police checkpoints sealed off metropolitan exits so anyone entering or leaving had to show identification and open their car trunks. Authorities were searching for stolen property, smuggled goods or bodies.

But at 6,000 feet high and near the equator, sunny days turn into balmy evenings, and once away from the gridlock, the air becomes cool and fresh. Three nights in Nairobi is also the last chance for northbound travelers to stock up on supplies and spare parts before entering northern Kenya's lawless and remote Chalbi Desert. Yet, other than for sluggish Internet connections and grocery shopping, there was no reason to sleep or linger downtown.

Run by an immigrant German biker, Jungle Junction was, so far, the first camping lodge with functioning electrical outlets, intact door hinges and glass in the guest-quarter's windows. This walled-in park is an overlander's dream, with garage shop walls lined with polished mechanics tools and acres of mowed green grass perfect for pitching tents and parking big, square Range Rovers with rooftop sleepers. For several weeks, African highways have been sprinkled with adventurous European families on year-long sabbaticals venturing south on the opposite route as mine. During late-night campfire chats, they provided valuable information on conditions ahead.

An asphalt road 200 miles beyond Nairobi eventually dissolves into a no-man's-land of decimated dirt tracks home to smugglers and Somali bandits. Foreigners are prohibited to pass except under armed military escort in long, dust-clouded caravans of four-wheel drive diesel trucks tediously bouncing side to side over the eroded terrain. From the last outpost where the pavement ends at Isiolo, overlanders report it's only a three-day run to the border across the Chalbi Desert. But traveling by motorcycle means it's also best to haul a four-day supply of food, water and fuel. Although north Kenya is in a second year of drought, if seasonal rains appear early, no one wins in the sucking mud. Buried-to-the-axles vehicles are often abandoned during storms only to be retrieved months later in the dry season by jackhammering them free. When asked to summarize the experience of crossing the Chalbi in well-equipped trucks, the overlanders' responses are the same, "We would never do that again."

And that's just to reach Ethiopia in order to enter Sudan for an endurance traverse of the Sahara Desert. From there, the road turns eyeball-jiggling washboard and soft sand all the way back to Egypt to continue on last year's route to the Mediterranean Sea. Rumor is that that particular land border is also closed, but a once-a-week ferry floats down the Nile from Sudan to Aswan for a familiar day-long immigration procedure and another military escort to Cairo. From now on, the journey mantra again becomes *In shallah.*

Even with proper documents, processing a Sudanese visa can require months — that is why I applied before Christmas in Dar es Salaam. Visa approval is hit or miss for Americans and a definite no with an Israeli stamp on a passport page. While still in Tanzania, believing a face-to-face explanation of my mission would convince officials, I request an audience with the consul general. Detailing one man's journey around the earth to personally meet the inhabitants irrespective of culture or politics had a promising effect on him. After an abbreviated slideshow and a tiptoeing discussion of Middle East politics, the cautious official seemed convinced and scribbled a two-page letter of recommendation, but he also advised me against admitting involvement with anything related to writing books.

As for Iranian visas, applications must be faxed to national headquarters and scrutinized by suspicious bureaucrats weighing political issues, so I still may not have an answer until after exiting Kenya next week. As a backup plan if I'm denied, I can reapply with a fresh passport issued from the U.S. embassy in the Ethiopian capital, Addis Ababa. In a surprising gesture of support, Uncle Sam granted rare special permission to carry a second passport with blank pages to disguise my questionable past global path. With luck, that arrives tomorrow. If denied again, with borders to Chad and Eritrea closed due to fighting, Ethiopia will be the end of the African trail and a reluctant airfreight to somewhere in Latin America. From Addis Ababa there is a limited choice, and I will be forced to settle for any destination out.

When It Rains, It Pours
January 5, 2006
Northern Kenya
● ● ● ● ● ● ● ● ●

Guidebooks are correct when they claim the beaten path terminates in northern Kenya. Since first entering South Africa, except for riding smooth graded tracks the length of Namibia and a few subsequent intentional dirt detours, all roads have been lightly used smooth-flowing asphalt, whether they wound through lush tropical jungles or spectacular desolate plains. As all good things come to an end, this wanderer's pleasing dream has just concluded at the equator.

In Africa, the crummy food doesn't matter. Vagabonds don't eat for pleasure or even health, only to minimize hunger. Up until now, meals and accommodation had been understandable, though unsuccessful, attempts at Western standards — yet, at the frontier town of Isiolo, Africa abruptly turned barebones-basic, reverting to a sandy meshing of old and ancient.

In the animated jabber of a garbage-strewn market, arriving in Isiolo was a return to Islam, with colorful veil-shrouded women bartering with Masai tribespeople for withered fruits and vegetables. A sundown visit to the town center mosque yielded questioning from worshippers after prayers. "You don't worry when traveling so far alone?"

"Why should I? Allah protects me."

"Ah, so you are Muslim?"

"No, but Allah still blesses my journey and keeps me safe."

"So if you believe in Allah, you must become Muslim."

"Maybe, but I'll hold off making decisions until returning to my home."

"All right, but in the meantime remember that Allah protects us all."

With a hard day ahead, just before dawn, imagining the misery of riding in a dust storm of commercial trucks in convoy, I skirted the final military checkpoint requiring foreigners to travel under guard. As the last chance for supplies and fuel drifted by in a reluctant haze, a starker image of Africa emerged. Fashion statements became blade-scarred faces above elaborately beaded neck disks and pierced bodies against midnight skin so black it was almost blue.

Walking sticks morphed into bows and arrows as wary herdsman stopped to eye a trespasser traversing a parched and drought-stricken land. If you disregarded a long, pale strip of mangled dirt track, this was an evolutionary step back into primordial survival, with nature prevailing. Everyone is thirsty. A single river contained enough shallow pools of trickling water to supply scattered villages for 20 miles. The rest were dried sandy creek beds with stooping women digging barehanded in fruitless searches for traces of underground streams — and as the two-year drought continues, there were none.

During unpredictable bursts of desert struggles, there is no backup plan, just faltering hope that when masses begin to die, a world community will again send more aid. Africa is a cruel and unrepentant provider that challenges humanity to contend with its whims. But as the newest species on the planet, only man considers himself a higher form more deserving to live.

Other than the indigenous natives, the empty, rocky desert is traveled only by occasional caravans of aid workers and the odd determined adventurer traveling from Cairo to Cape Town. There is no other reason to pass through an environment so hostile to life. Armed soldiers may fend off roving bandits and murderous warlords, but there is nothing to protect even the hardest tires from slices and punctures punched by razor-edged volcanic rock. Directly after resecuring a gushing high-pressure fuel line, a dreaded rear-end sway signaled the first flat tire of the day. There may be only 400 miles to the southern border of Ethiopia, where a paved road leads direct, to Addis Ababa, but wretched conditions stretch that into a miserable three-day event. Severe washboard turning unexpectedly to soft sand and back and deep gullies of fist-sized stones test even the best of suspensions — but since mine was rebuilt 10,000 miles ago, the hard rubber seals should have weathered the strain. They did not.

Mind-numbing jarring and bucking was so intense that more gas spilled through the tank breather-vents than was burned by the engine. Even sloshing battery water slapped high enough to drip from an overflow tube. And that was the good news. Normally, when shock-absorber fluid begins seeping past worn seals, lack of oil shouldn't cause a compression lockdown. Treated liquids and pressurized gases regulate rebound action, and without them, handling deteriorates into a tolerable, bouncing pogo-stick ride. Although a blown shock should not remain compressed, mine did, resulting in zero vertical travel to relieve explosive jolting from a jagged road. And that guarded convoy so carefully avoided was several hours ahead.

Even at 10 miles per hour, the vertical forces generated were difficult to endure with the rear section kicking up and slamming back down. Ridges on a deep-cut washboard surface turned into spine-snapping slaps equally destructive to metal frame-welds. With nothing but thorn tree desert ahead, the only solution was a 10-mile retreat to the relieving shade of the last tribal outpost, with a hope that the natives were friendly.

Competing for resources in the midst of a drought, water is too scarce for washing. Barefoot in filthy, ragged Western clothes, Muslim Kenyans coexist in a détente with spear-toting Masai tribesmen festooned in sparkling metal trinkets. Only a few offered greetings. Language barriers kept most from understanding each other, but the message resonated: one angry woman did not want a foreigner to linger. Her reasoning was valid. In a robbery-plagued region, I could draw unwanted attention, and they had no protection against marauders with guns. Without governing authority or troops to keep order, violence and murder is the law of the land. Cattle rustling and cross-border reprisal raids have resulted in retaliatory slaughters of entire villages.

And a traveler in their midst was a legitimate concern considering news of a treasure-laden American could draw roving cutthroat Somali bandits eager to pillage his precious cargo. In a heated exchange of English and Swahili, the verdict was returned that the alien be sent on his way. And who could blame them? Why should they fret for the plight of a white man with more riches in his wallet than they earn in a year? Still, it was early evening, and after a long, hard negotiation, my desperate plea for sleep was considered. A simple bribe of 400 shillings was sufficient incentive to conceal my bike in a straw hut and allow a four-hour rest if I promised to be gone by midnight.

Off the Beaten Path
January 7, 2006
Chalbi Desert, Kenya
● ● ● ● ● ● ● ● ● ● ●

Since the whole village was asleep, I probably could have dozed until sunrise without anyone noticing, but once awake it was best to avoid potential hassles and roll for Marsabit, the last small Kenyan town with electricity. Yet even if I reached there, the next long stretch to Moyale at the Ethiopian border is the fiercest section. The only light at the end of this tunnel was knowing that eventually an asphalt road at the frontier would lead to Addis Ababa and hopefully to a set of mechanic's tools to repair a broken suspension.

Out of fear and common sense, no one drives after dark in Kenya, but I hoped that also meant any bad guys were likely fast asleep dreaming of daytime plundering. Attempts to convince myself that a night ride under the stars would ease the misery were quickly squashed when I recalled, the previous day's events. A few optimistic test bounces in the saddle confirmed that no divine healing had occurred during the last four hours, and there was no telling if the shock absorber would last another day or another mile. I was beyond the point of no return in every direction.

Unlike blazing desert days, midnight air was crisp and clean. The push of a button made the motorcycle grumble to life. But my confidence faded as yesterday's brutal jarring resumed even worse than I remembered. There would be no escape in a first-gear crawl, easing over every ridge and rock. With zero travel in a frozen shock, violent kicking and bucking made simply hanging on to the handlebars a challenge. At 10 miles per hour without rear suspension, I tried to calculate how many hours it would take to ride 300 miles. Maybe throttling up to 15 miles per hour would shave an hour or two. Either way, between robbers and vicious terrain, one of Africa's worst roads was ready to bang and test the limits of both my internal organs and a thoroughly abused motorcycle frame.

At least riding slow allowed me a chance to evaluate which bumps and gullies to dodge to minimize impacts. Standing on the foot pegs with bent knees was temporary relief but became too tiring, requiring rest stops every 30 minutes. With fatigued arms and legs, a creeping desert dawn glowed into a bursting orange sunrise. Soon, wandering Masai camel herders emerged from the thicket with familiar demands. "Pay money! You give me money!" No matter what they were doing, young and old, the moment any tribesmen spotted a wandering foreigner they turned and sprinted forward waving and shouting "Money, money, money!"

By noon, the last carefully packed apples had shaken into mush and the fragmented shells of hardboiled eggs had ground together with the yolks into gooey paste. Combining the concoction together to swallow in lumps was still better than the foul-tasting local fare. But the smelly combined proteins were nutritious, and there was still a gallon of water left to last the day. My need for intense focus on the road meant that stunning savanna scenery passed by in a jiggling peripheral blur. By noon, there were still no other vehicles in sight. Once, when I stopped to rest, a young Masai woman with bared sagging breasts came running from a hut for no apparent reason, yelling and waving a machete. Baffled but still wanting to record the scene, I paused long enough to snap a decent photograph, then I quickly slipped the clutch and rode away before she came too close.

Finally, just after the 20th straight hour of rolling misery, a two-room dilapidated structure appeared with barely legible, grime-covered words above the tilting doorway — Marsabit Medical Center. Even though I knew more of the same still lay ahead, arriving on the town's outskirts felt like reaching the finish line at an Olympic event.

Marsabit town is a scene out of America's Wild West — scrawny cattle being driven past windowless ramshackle wooden cabins and clouds of red grit swirling down stony clay avenues. Nothing has been maintained or repaired since it was built decades before. Few buildings had electric power, and none had running water. Hand-painted weathered letters on broken signs described what was offered inside. In Magic Marcie's Fashion Design, piles of musty used clothing donated by international charities were ready to be illegally resold. Marsabit General Supermarket was a doorless shack selling milk in cartons and canned meats with labels reading "A Gift from the People of New Zealand." What wasn't crumbling was rusting or sat gathering dust while no one seemed to care.

As in many developing countries, men stood drinking afternoon tea and cheap beer by night. From disordered, debris-strewn markets, subservient women in lace headscarves trudged under heavy loads of vegetable baskets and bundled firewood. Engaged in their share of the labor, caped young boys in worn sandals tugged on ropes, leading bleating goats to pasture. What little water there is must be hand carried or lugged in lopsided wooden wheelbarrows wherever needed or to those who can afford it. Jey-Jey Center is the only hotel secured by barbed wire and with a deteriorating underground cistern servicing a filthy squat toilet — at five bucks a night, the single cement cubicles were a bargain. Cleans sheets stopped mattering to me months ago, as long they don't stink and are not overrun with fleas. At least the two-year drought had eliminated mosquitoes and the threat of malaria.

For boring evenings, a beat-down honky-tonk built of splintered planks provided economical entertainment as one strolled past broken saloon doors hanging off rusted hinges. With African rap music blaring through crackling metal speakers, the ear-splitting throbs were a deafening assault as I wandered. Safe within steel-barred cages, middle-aged Indian men peddled rotgut whiskey and warm local beer while drunks slobbered on themselves in darkened corners. The scene was made complete as potbellied hookers with long, drooping breasts flashed nauseating smiles through decayed teeth and puffy maroon lips. But late nights in Marsabit are for partiers with more determination than me, and other than this exclusive freak show, there was nothing else enticing enough to keep me awake.

In the afternoon, the moment I ventured outside Jey-Jey's, throngs of unkempt children crowded around me, yelling "Sweets, sweets, give me money, give me pens!" Although it's clear that the foreigner's role in Africa is strictly for giving, all that I offer is bumpy rides on a limping motorcycle.

Having trained their children to beg, scowling parents glared as giggling youngsters abandoned rehearsed scam-lines and jumped with delight, lining up to be next for a spin through town. Sometimes you just have to let kids be kids. With one eager child on the front and two on the back, it still took a whole afternoon to appease them all. Following the Pied Piper back to Jey-Jey's, the trailing troops assured me they would stand guard as I swatted away the last of persistent horseflies and tried to forget the situation while spiraling into sleep.

No matter how good it feels, ignoring problems will not make them disappear, but leaving the bike parked for three peaceful days allowed me enough time to quit peeing burgundy and relieve an aching back. Still, the question of reaching the border returns with a confirmation by locals that bandits are active again. "They don't tell you to stop, they shoot the driver and then attack passengers." Pulling off his shirt, one truck driver says, "Here, look at my body. I've already been shot five times." On that thought, it's likely the road ahead is to become more interesting still.

And the Road Smoothes
January 10, 2006
Delia, Ethiopia
● ● ● ● ● ● ● ● ●

Early mornings in Marsabit were a wicked tease. A cold, gray fog enshrouded decrepit buildings and browning eucalyptus treetops, offering just enough momentary light mist to tingle faces. But in the arid Chalbi Desert air, rain was a frivolous notion as faint whiffs of moisture were sucked into clouds of swirling red dust before ever hitting the ground. Inhabitants weren't encouraged; only optimistic foreign visitors were foolish enough to think the drought was ending and a storm approaching. But it was the same result by noon, an empty powder-blue sky breathing steady desert gusts to deposit grit into squinting eyes.

Riding toward the border, there was little to see beyond a deep-cut corrugated road evaporating into the horizon. Endless ruts and jagged stones threatened to slice vulnerable rubber tires over thousands of flat square-miles across evenly spread baseball-sized volcanic rocks. The scene ahead looked like photos broadcast from robot cameras on Mars.

Despite the government's attempts to search for water, their inadequate gesture is a year too late. As massive brand-new yellow road-graders rusted in Marsabit equipment yards, there was no one to man them or the scattered, abandoned roadside drilling rigs. Foreign aid sent to finance relief was likely lining the Swiss bank accounts of various government officials appointed to oversee these projects — and no one here works without pay. They will die first — sooner rather than later, if the delay continues.

Established watering holes have vanished into pathetic pits of caked earth — there is nowhere left to drive cattle for drinking, and there is no plant life left to graze on. Useless to continue herding, cows have been freed to die in the open. Every other mile, scrawny strays lie sideways, intermittently flailing their legs in futile attempts to rise — and in between, the piercing stench of death announces another less fortunate. Skinned for their hides, the decaying meat was poison to humans, and there weren't even any vultures to pick the bones.

Despondent villagers with downcast eyes waited next to stacks of empty plastic jugs. African pleas were no longer hustles for money — only parents and children on their knees with clasping hands shouting "Water, water, water." I still hear them when trying to sleep.

Continuing past dusk into late evening's transparent black velvet, teams of miniature antelope the size of jackrabbits leaped aimlessly across the road. Sets of shining pink eyes either froze in my path or charged for the light. A faster-moving vehicle would have creamed these only companions of the night. Able to march vast distances without water, long camel caravans weaving through thorn bushes stood the best chance. These tall, lanky animals could be smelled before they were seen in the headlight, as nomadic tribesmen in high-piled turbans swatted their rumps with irritable commands to keep moving forward. As the only beasts able to survive, even their final hopes were to find the edge of the desert. Yet the only hope for an alien on a limping motorcycle was the Ethiopian frontier, where promised tarmac would lead to Addis Ababa and an opportunity at repairs which will be necessary if I am to finish a journey that I am no longer sure of.

And just before dawn, rooftop shadows of the dilapidated outpost at Moyale rose into view like welcoming tombstones. More rundown than a typical soulless border town, this forlorn graveyard of decaying structures made Marsabit look modern. Though it was too early for me to enter customs and immigration procedures from the Kenyan side, I could see relief ahead — a dark asphalt strip wrapping low-lying hilltops, vanishing into the Ethiopian skyline.

Finally, groggy, old black men in soiled gray uniforms shuffled to their posts in time to first fire kettles of tea for the upcoming day. As the only person transiting either direction, my *carnet de passage* and passport were stamped and registered almost faster than I wanted. With no other suckers out this early, black-market moneychangers argued over who could scalp me the quickest. But using the leverage of supply and demand, I bargained them down to exchanging the last of my Kenyan shillings at better-than-bank rates and felt lucky until discovering that there are no ATMs in Ethiopia. Riding to the capital was a 12-hour sprint to cash my emergency traveler's checks, which until then, would leave barely enough money for fuel.

Still, the casual countryfolk were pleasant, and at every stop I was met with outstretched hands and urgings to take their photo. Ordering food was a challenge. As no one spoke English, in order to eat without fried onions, there is now a complicated new language to learn, quickly. Derived from Arabic with no familiar letters, consonant sounds are configured in peculiar order and pronounced with hisses. Greetings come first in developing countries. "*Salaam endemana?*" (Hello, how are you?)

But this works fine while waiting for food in side-street restaurants, as I engage locals while pantomiming questions for recording definitions in my improvised Amharic dictionary. Experimenting in crude cafés is still the best way to meet people, and soon I've bumbled through an hour-long simple dialogue in an unknown language. Between easygoing natives and flavorful, spicy curries, southern Ethiopia was much too pleasant to rush, and for the first time in a while, it was a refreshing change not to hurry.

Shadows of the Firelight
January 14, 2006
Lake Langano, Ethiopia
● ● ● ● ● ● ● ● ● ● ● ● ● ●

Even though fuel is cheaper in Ethiopia than in other African countries, there are few private cars. Back from the brink of famine, the country's national resources have been allocated to survival rather than conveniences. So, despite foreign governments constructing an extensive highway system, everyone walks in Ethiopia. Other than an occasional overloaded truck or swaying old bus, the road is occupied only by lines of herded cows and goats trailing donkey carts piled high with hay.

Enterprising fruit peddlers boldly stand on the highway centerline, forcing drivers to dodge them or stop and buy fresh-cut spears of papaya and pineapple. In the bigger towns, other than beat-up taxis and sardine-can minibuses, a common site is big white four-by-four Toyota Land Cruisers marked "UN." Even with scandals of mismanagement, it's still relieving to see foreign countries contributing useful vehicles to the World Food Program instead of tanks.

There were only 500 miles left from the border to the capital, but with nothing to do except wait for a new shock absorber to arrive, I decided to extend the ride into five days of loafing through temperate jungle highlands. Without a map or guidebook, my faltering GPS became the only source of information for what lay ahead. The two-by-two-inch color screen showed a dozen bodies of water as potential sites to overnight with a new asphalt highway snaking between. Because Lake Langano was the only one rumored to not be infested with microscopic parasites or crocodiles, the forested beach was a favorite campground for vacationing Ethiopians and fellow overlanders.

Two touring European couples made me jealous. The first were mid-20s newlyweds bicycling from Paris to Cape Town, sleeping in tents along the way. Their purpose was to raise awareness at home via the Internet with stories of what they encountered. *"We yust wahnt zee worlt to know zat Frahnz ees reech because Arfreeca ees poor."* Hearing their reasoning was a way to convince myself that maybe world motorcycle rides are, after all, not so crazy.

And the other two travelers also lived on the fringe, each riding 30-year-old 50cc East German motor-scooters round-trip from Germany to Ethiopia. Packed under bulky loads, they somehow managed hauling a laptop, three big cameras and full camping gear, including cooking utensils. But at 20 miles per hour, it took them a while to reach destinations plotted from Munich. While eating dinner alone, my hearing moans from inside their tent stirred sentiments in me that the only thing missing on this journey has been a woman to share the lunacy.

In the morning, we swapped addresses, and they rode south in time to avoid an invasion of rambunctious Ethiopian students on weekend holiday. Because of public uprising over alleged recent election fraud, opposition leaders have been jailed and the capital placed under martial law. First-year university classes were postponed indefinitely, leaving nervous undergraduates little to do but wait and wonder. By late afternoon, busloads arrived to set up camp and share their music via high-tech stereos powered by antique, sputtering portable generators.

As the sun went down, all-night partying began in the grip of whining Middle Eastern strings regulated by African drums. Luscious young mocha-skinned women with eyes half-closed circled towering campfires, dancing seductively just beyond the fingers of crackling flames that matched the motions of their graceful, slender arms. Elegant swept-back foreheads and pointed noses made their fine-featured faces appear more Egyptian than African. Flashing smiles reflecting a rising full moon complemented bodies wiggling in suggestive postures. Black silky braids dangling above gyrating, sinewy torsos made thin hip-hugger jeans hardly visible. In a primal writhing of erotic Cleopatras, sensuous silhouettes set my imagination afire in a perspiring, hypnotic twirl.

Through clouds of sweet marijuana smoke, strolling dreadlocked Rastafarians dressed in Bob Marley T-shirts discreetly kept revelers supplied. Deep into midnight, the music grew louder and movements bolder until it was time to breathe or succumb to the spell. For an outside, viewing alien, a cold beer was necessary to calm a throbbing pulse.

In the restaurant, Harvard-educated intellectuals sat sipping tea while murmuring about local politics. Caution was the word of whispers; anyone caught openly disagreeing with the government was swept to a prison cell. Conspirators warn that journalists too are suspect and subject to a similar fate if they ask improper questions. Combined with soldiers in the streets, this is another good reason to quickly repair my suspension and move on. Friday, a decision should be final for my Sudanese visa, so by first thing next week, the trail continues to Khartoum or diverts with a flight to Mexico. Either way, this adventure into humanity is sure to take another twist.

Who Are We?
January 22, 2006
Addis Ababa, Ethiopia
● ● ● ● ● ● ● ● ● ● ● ● ●

Dark-skinned Americans' declarations of unique African heritage are a mystery. Who on this planet is not African? There may be dispute over whether man first walked upright in Ethiopia or South Africa, but paleontologists concur that all humans evolved from somewhere on this continent. Doesn't that make any two-legged earth-dwelling creature with opposing digits a hyphenated African of some sort? Today comes the realization, that I, too, am African-American.

Months of sleeping and eating with both city folk and primitive tribesmen only enhances my new claim — especially after viewing the 1974 discovery of my three-million-year-old cousin Lucy from northeast Ethiopia. So what about all these differences? When straying from home for extended periods, wanderers often reevaluate their roots — the longer we travel, the further we drift. For unexplained reasons, the more difficult a country is to explore, the deeper

Greeted on the road entering Omo Valley, Ethiopia

the experience and the closer travelers grow to the people. While I breathed a sigh of relief departing Russia in 2004, at the same moment, because I'd spent so much time with them, I felt Russian. For overlanders, it's hard to avoid living and breathing the hardships natives endure, and whether trapped in long, miserable lines at government offices or trapped in Siberian inclement weather, everyone was subject to the same circumstance. Today, when encountering Russians in other lands, after first bellowing out *"Pree vee et!"* I announce that I, too, am Russian. And now, African.

In the last four and a half years, I've only spent 11 months in the U.S. Born in California from a family that is still in Norway, and now discovering ancestry in Africa, perhaps the title "world citizen" fits better. Lately, I have experienced a moment's hesitation when curious locals ask, "So, where are you from?" And what causes such bonding with former enemies or those depicted negatively on television? Although separated by economics and geographic boundaries, inside, we are all the same, except some folks are just nicer. When recently asked what was the biggest surprise in Africa, my answer repeated what I had said about Muslims, "How kind and docile the people are." Like everywhere in developing nations, natives are meek, and whether they live in cities or jungles, they always make time to stop and talk with a stranger. And why do they share so much? When trying to make sense of it all, the same philosophical question arises. Are nice people poor because they are nice or nice because they are poor?

Since Ethiopians lack enough money to buy cars, the streets of Addis Ababa are much less congested than those of other major cities, and with media-inspired fears, there is little tourism. Except for exploring a few ancient churches up north near Sudan, there is not much left to do except visit tribal lands connected by seasonal roads. Yet, who wants to spend a vacation witnessing drought and famine and perhaps intertribal war?

Foreigners are either white UN troops recently expelled from Eritrea or aid workers trying to alleviate the harsh realities of nature. I spent a week just locating one of the only two long-riders in Ethiopia. With light-brown skin and bulging blue eyes, Mauro introduced himself after recognizing the logo on my gas tank. "Hey Striking Viking, I have seen your stories on the Internet. It feels like I know you." With an Italian grandfather and Ethiopian grandmother, he referred to himself as a half-caste but still claimed dual citizenship. Like always when meeting bikers on the road, I felt as though I knew him too.

Tracking down and clearing three of four incoming supply packages through customs was like working a second job. There is still one to go, but that should be easy after spending three days convincing department heads that I don't live here and the new Ohlins shock absorber and Avon tires are not for resale.

There is a constant stream of complications when riding the world, yet the overall experience is so rewarding that after mild grumbling, travelers only remember the good times. Still, while winding down this journey, a smoother landing would've been welcome. With 5,000 miles to go, it's hard not to dream about California, and the more I ponder returning, the bigger common hassles here seem to grow. I've been homeless with limited possessions for the last two years, so considerations of what to do first when returning to Palm Springs pile on top of my already considerable frustrations connected with developing-nation bureaucracies. And in the middle of Africa, for the first time in a while, concerns about the future override living in the moment — a sure signal that it's time to return to a village.

Dorze Village
January 26, 2006
Omo Valley, Ethiopia
● ● ● ● ● ● ● ● ● ● ● ●

For most travelers, backtracking is a bitter pill, but since crossing into Ethiopia from Kenya with a broken suspension, I postponed exploring the border regions of a very remote Omo Valley off-road until the bike was fully functional. With curt Sudanese embassy staff still replying, "Come back tomorrow," the timing was perfect for a side journey back south into the richest remaining tribal societies of Africa.

When wandering developing nations, sharing and gift-giving are cultural fundamentals that Westerners learn quickly, so half my food stock was small bags of sugar-coated peanuts and key-tag LED flashlights — presents for ranking village elders. To accommodate a week's supply of canned fish and water, I stored nonessential gear at the last hotel along with emergency forwarding instructions. Although inter-tribal warfare over cattle rustling and grazing had flared again, violence is generally contained amongst native warriors.

I checked once more with the Sudanese embassy, which meant a late start and overnighting only three hours further down the road in Shasheme, a trucking-route crossroads town composed of dimly lit one-room brothels and stinky dormitory flophouses crammed with snoring drunks. But it's also home to the world's most famous pot-smokers. When instituting his 1930s Back-to-Africa movement, Jamaican Marcus Garvey convinced his followers that the biblical prophecy of a king emerging from Ethiopia had been fulfilled when Ras Tafari Makonnen was crowned emperor, whereupon he changed his name to Haile Selassie. Their new lifestyle was rigid, yet it allowed one peculiar spiritual recreation. Pork, milk, and coffee may have been forbidden, but smoking marijuana was deemed a sacrament for devoted masses later recognized by their trademark long, tangled dreadlocks. And the rest is history.

As the final potholed asphalt again deteriorated into a rocky dirt track, Africa also faded from the fringes of ragged civilization into the basics of a primitive world. To adventurers searching for the ends of the earth, the deeper we stray into south Omo Valley, the closer that world becomes. Each mile, creeping over uneven terrain carved away another century in time, as barefoot livestock herders and villagers were escorted by lean, young warriors armed with spears and rifles. Middle-aged mothers marched for miles in smothering heat stooped under 70-pound bundles of firewood while less fit teenaged daughters backpacked five-gallon clay jugs of water.

On the pine tree ridge of a 9,000-foot mountain summit overlooking the brackish waters of Lake Chamo, the curious inhabitants of Dorze village rushed forward to greet this invading alien. At the end of a weekly market day, merchants and traders were busy with last-minute bargaining over tobacco cakes, spices and piles of crystallized rock salt. At sunset, according to tradition, women shared dried pumpkin gourds of homemade beer as men stayed home guzzling bottles of local whiskey. But shy village children reacted the same as those in Kenya after the first was coaxed aboard my motorcycle for a ride among bulging banana-leafed huts. Giggling pandemonium erupted as they scrambled atop my flexing aluminum saddlebags and even stood on a buckling front fender. But the show was not to be stolen.

Brutally African, self-appointed adult bodyguards clubbed them with long bamboo poles until I shouted in anger to leave them alone. But the shocking cruelty continued as fistfights and attacks against those smaller broke out over who was to ride next. To quell the calamity, I promised them a laptop slideshow after sundown.

But that was only a temporary reprieve as the random swatting continued until children countered with rock throwing and fleeing into the brush. Startled by the spontaneous and unnecessary violence, I still questioned the propriety of me, an outsider, judging jungle methods of maintaining order — especially when I come from a society that continues to legally execute other humans and develop nuclear weapons.

Yet, the smaller the society, the stricter the codes of behavior, and no one likes a thief. Even in Nairobi, if captured by fed-up crowds, a street-criminal is sure to be beaten without mercy. Assault here appears common among them, but they do not attack visitors, and theft of any kind is rare. To show trust when visiting villages, without worry, I intentionally leave (but monitor) my camera and GPS left lying on the motorcycle seat. That's why the surprise this morning when I noticed, while repacking my laptop, a set of dangling ignition keys had disappeared. Like news of a death, waves of shame spread through the crowd in breathless murmuring as young and old approached with heads hung low, offering tearful apologies. A teenaged translator explained, "This is not our way and we are so sorry."

Although there were spare keys stashed under the motorcycle seat, the missing ones had no value and if an opportunity arose, were certain to be returned. After announcing that I must have dropped them earlier, villagers immediately appeared with candles and torches, combing surrounding grasses on hands and knees. But as the search turned fruitless, suspicion fell on the young translator who had earlier pleaded to work as my guide — if only I would stay. For all to save face, I needed an alternate explanation so that they might resurface. "After I dropped the keys, the children must have found them to play with. Please announce that I will give five dollars to whoever finds the keys."

At sunrise, I awoke to dozens of chattering villagers taking turns peering in through my tent's skylight screen. It was an African zoo in reverse. Unzipping my nylon flaps, I discovered a bag of bananas next to a scribbled apology note. Amidst worried frowns and hand-wringing, the morning mood of somber concern was soon interrupted by a parting crowd and shouts of delight. Four-year-old Jakono Makurmno rushed forward waving a set of familiar shiny keys. Celebratory cheers led to shaking hands with hundreds of villagers and a triumphant one-motorcycle-parade for the newfound tiny hero. But it was still time to move on, and, as always, in the wake of a reluctant departure, another family of waving friends vanished into memory through the smudged glass of a vibrating rearview mirror.

The Road to Jinka
January 28, 2006
South Omo Valley, Ethiopia
• • • • • • • • • • • • • • • • •

Since first reaching Central Africa, sometimes in cities and always in the country, every child and nearly every adult I have encountered has asked for money. When first spotting my freckled white skin, whether walking roadside or working in fields, as a conditioned response, natives instantly abandon their current tasks to charge forward with right palms outstretched. "You pay money!" "Shillings, shillings!" and in Ethiopia, it's "You give me one Birr!" They are seldom persistent, and after a while the practice seems normal, but still, what is the effect on dignity? It's hard not to notice that this never happened anywhere else on this journey, even in tsunami-ravaged Banda Aceh.

Seldom far from famine and always in conflict, many Africans have grown accustomed to foreigners causing or relieving their plight. In Kenya, conversations with men dressed better than me invariably ended with, "Can you give me a few dollars?" But the reaction is different when a traveler's in need, and that's when the true nature of Africans shines.

Long, thick thorns embedded in motorcycle tires and sharp volcanic rocks eventually took their toll, and yesterday I lost count after

Mursi tribal beauty queen who took a liking to motorcycles in Omo Valley, Ethiopia

a dozen flats since dawn. Even in the countryside, whenever I stopped, crowds materialized from nowhere to assist. A stranger unpacking tools to remove a rear wheel ignites more interest than a lunar landing. Beginning at a polite distance but edging closer for better views, there was often a volunteer in Western clothes who spoke some English. *"Father, may we be of assistance to you?"* *"Father where is the place of your country?"*

"I come from California."

Nearly as geographically challenged as U.S. college graduates, they reply, *"Oh Father, you are English?"*

And finally, as they crowd close enough to block the sun, I rise, impatiently demanding that they all move back. But within minutes, kicked-up clouds of fine dust indicate they again feel the need to inspect up close the progress of patching a tube. No one wants to miss anything, and soon my wrenches and screwdrivers are buried beneath leathered feet and dirt rearranged by those pushing and shoving. Most just wanted to help but were killing me with kindness, and I considered hiring the biggest man to drive them away.

Like overzealous surgical nurses passing instruments, my anxious assistants tried to guess which tools I needed next — but before they're passed to me, they have to be circulated among the audience for inspection. I can now remove tires with two screwdrivers and patch ruptured tubes in 30 minutes — or an hour if I have help. But afterwards we have fun describing the problems with motorcycles, and it's a pleasure to offer money when it is not expected.

Small bills of local currency stretch a long way in Africa, and gesture is as important as amount. After tightening axle bolts, the most determined assistants glowed with delight when receiving wrinkled bills of four Birr — 50 cents in U.S. currency — but enough for a tasty café meal in Ethiopia.

People are always asking for something in Africa, and without knowing the common words, it's hard to be certain what those I meet roadside actually need. While I rested in the shade of scraggly acacia trees, spear-toting natives regularly approached, pointing to water bottles strapped to my gas tanks. Since they carried their own supply in dried pumpkin gourds, why they wanted mine was a mystery. When offering drinks, they only stared. It took some grunting in sign language to understand that they didn't want the water, they wanted the plastic containers.

The last hundred miles to Jinka turned prehistoric and should have taken only four hours, but, with stops to interact with natives, it expanded into eight. Accustomed to supply trucks and four-by-four minibuses, a roaring blue spaceship with a yellow-helmeted pilot sent primitive tribesmen fleeing for the safety of the thick wooded savanna. Like chumming timid animals, I set out bags of peanuts and water bottles a few feet away while kneeling on the ground with outstretched palms. Sometimes it took half an hour of peering from behind pine trees, but eventually curiosity prevailed, and, one at a time, the men approached first. Fast movements or standing too quickly started the process all over again as none were certain of my intent.

Accustomed to simple diets of fried meat and ground barley,

reaction to my sweetened peanuts varied from nibbling to spitting them out. But weapons interest everyone, and soon young warriors allowed me to inspect their crude blades and spears if I first handed them my multipurpose knife. Teenage boys took turns aboard the Beast and burned with enthusiasm when I showed them how to press the starter button and horn.

Sneaking photographs by tilting my viewfinder allowed for more candid shots capturing natural poses, yet the women appreciated the camera-screen playbacks most. Shoeless and naked from the waist up, young native girls decorated in blue beaded neck bands strutted in circles while examining the bike. When offered a ride, they shook their heads with folded arms while still primping and twirling their hair. But eye-games speak volumes, and universal signals meant the situation might have changed if no one was around to tell.

Turmi Market
January 29, 2006
South Omo Valley, Ethiopia
● ● ● ● ● ● ● ● ● ● ● ● ● ● ●

Sometimes I wonder, "What is it about nature that attracts us?" Even when I lived in Southern California backcountry, every morning, when spotting the same trio of white-tailed deer, I stopped to gape until they disappeared, bounding like four-legged pogo sticks through the trees. It's the same for humans and exotic cultures; we're fascinated by ancient civilizations or museums lined with antiques and statues — the simpler, the better. We may be trapped on dollar-chasing treadmills, but returning to basics subtly entices us with a subliminal lure. Often on this journey, as I drifted from beaten paths without seeing others of my kind, there was little indication in what century I lived. Yet, when mixing with primordial tribesmen of the remote Omo Valley, there was a distinctive marker — this is prehistoric time. As though in a scene from *Jurassic Park*, any minute, I expected the sharp, booming roar of a tyrannosaurus rex.

Attired in loincloths of untreated furry hides, the tribesmen's musky scent announced their presence before they arrived. As beige-soled calloused feet plopped against compacted dirt floors of thatched, roof huts, silent black natives entered single file. It was Monday, market-day in Turmi village, and the Hamer people had lugged heavy loads of tobacco and millet to trade for rock salt and metal tips used in crude wooden tools. Beginning before dawn, their work schedule was a six-hour trek bent under heavy goatskin rucksacks — but their day wouldn't end until returning home laden under treasure.

With trimmed ringlets, the women's hair was stained orange from the natural resins they used to hold it in place, while the men, if they recently prevailed in battle, wore short woven ponytails hard-ened in clay. Copper tubing arm rings and intricate beaded bands all held meaning, from the number of wives a man possessed to a wearer's wealth. Pierced body decorations and patterned scars told stories of powerful spirits or of combat with ferocious animals or other humans. Once removing my jacket, as in previous tribal encounters, the dark blue India inks long ago etched into my arms were the subject of curious attention.

Twenty years back, tattoos were brands of drunken soldiers or outlaw bikers, but today such permanent markings are fashionable Western adornments, as likely to appear on movie stars as ex-cons. Unsure of the significance of these marks on the wandering alien, natives have so far regarded them as emblems of a fellow warrior, and they have treated me with wary respect. As always, people crowded around me to pull up my sleeves, touching and scratching at the uni-versal patterns depicting my rebellious past. Satisfied that these fading but permanent images wouldn't rub off, they murmured amongst themselves with nods of approval for a member of another tribe.

Yet it was their women who fascinated me most. From creamy licorice skin to deep brown shades of bittersweet chocolate, they moved in deliberate steps on muscled legs. Even through thick layers of waist-covering animal skins, the outlines of bulbous rear ends fol-lowed the curves of rock-hard cheeks. With pronounced lower back arches and upturned buttocks, their accentuated postures stirred primal urges to mount from the rear.

While resting on a makeshift wooden bench, a mid-20s female with long protruding breasts pointed for a place to sit. To see what she'd do, I patted my knee. Laughing out loud with her friends, she lowered her rucksack and stooped to sit on my lap. Before discovering what came next, a loud crack from a man snapping a whip instructed her to find another seat. Beatings can underscore masochistic desire in their culture — to Hamer women, enduring skin-ripping lashings is proof of unwavering love for a prospective husband. During festival matchmaking ceremonies, they smile while accepting bloody floggings by men they are anxious to marry. Along with broad metal necklaces, crisscrossing scars across their backs are the grisly romantic symbols of taken women.

And the world never gives up trying to subdue simple folk. Rejecting ruthless domination by colonial masters, diminishing numbers of the remaining Hamer tribesmen cling to their customs. Though determined to maintain traditional values a thousand years old, few clans have managed to resist missionaries shaming them into covering their breasts and the intimidations of invading Muslims that they must veil their hair. However, animistic in their beliefs and proud of their ancestral ways, Hamer lifestyle has changed very little.

Whether besieged in jungles or on the open savanna, it's their refusal to submit that maintains their solid spiritual connections to nature. In the same breath that Western technology destroys our environment, science produces cures for devastating disease while seeking more efficient ways to annihilate humankind. As I wandered amongst such basic creatures, burdened myself with the latest electronic gadgets, the question kept arising: who is really ahead? And by the end of the stay, I was uncertain who were the heathens.

Having acquired few souvenirs since starting this journey, mementos from Omo Valley would be the most meaningful to me. But what is a worthy enough souvenir to remember a connection with the core of humanity? Bartering the last of the LED key tags and felt-tip pens yielded an armload of foul-smelling beaded goatskin loin cloths embroidered with seashells — tribal sexy-underwear for a few lucky folks back home.

Finally, at the day's end, a weathered old man approached offering drinks from a gourd they all shared — a favorite source of protein among herders of Africa — honey and milk mixed with raw cow's blood. The taste wasn't bad, and if I had been unaware of the ingredients I would likely have asked for more. For a more customary meal, instructing native girls to fry eggs in animal fat was easy, but that and a sack of bananas had to last the rest of my trip. A week camping without bathing was enough, but if there had been an adequate supply of water and familiar food I might have stayed.

The Red-eye out of Africa
February 19, 2006
Amsterdam, Holland
● ● ● ● ● ● ● ● ● ● ● ●

In the midst of the last three weeks of double-talk and aggravation, forgetting the adage that kept this journey alive was too easy — the adventure begins when things stop going as planned. Escaping Africa with a motorcycle was proving to be far more difficult than arriving was. I spent jaw-clenching days uncovering lies from shippers, which ended in sleepless nights, but I almost overlooked the friendship forged with an Ethiopian man who rose to my aid.

After a slideshow presentation to a few of his friends, Hailu, the King's Hotel's manager, took interest in my complicated airfreight quagmire and soon spent half of his days working for solutions. Phone calls to freight-forwarders were never returned, and each enquiry required that we make a personal appearance for the follow-up; we'd wait long hours just to hear negative results. To Hailu, sorting out the mess was another challenge and an opportunity to do what is so common in poorer countries — help a stranger. And this hospitality is what diluted my growing bitterness over having dealt with a few dishonest businessmen who were trying to dig into the shallow pockets of a frustrated traveler.

But with Hailu's aggressive persistence, we were finally able to fire the correct sequence of volleys necessary to forward my bike from Ethiopia to Frankfurt, with hopes that the Germans would figure out how to reroute to Mexico City. Having booked the last passenger seat out for a week, there was nothing left to do but wander Addis Ababa's neighborhoods for a final taste of the enduring pace of a continent adrift with so much potential.

With my bike crated at the airport, I was back on foot again. After packing and repacking my remaining gear, I joined the marching masses threading through town among black-soot-belching buses and livestock herders grazing their animals on grassy roadway medians. There is no need for city landscape maintenance as long as hungry cows and goats handle the trimming, with enough space left for pedestrians. Ethiopians are still confused by the beeping horns of trucks and cars urging them to move aside on what they consider to be a giant asphalt sidewalk. As with everywhere in developing nations, a general tolerance and understanding of life overcomes people's impatience over traffic jams, some of which are caused by 30 longhorn steer strolling through intersections. Yet, no matter how absurd the chaos, Western-style road rage is unknown in a land with little concept of space or time.

From Cape Town to Omo Valley, Africa has been a roller-coaster ride of gut-wrenching intrigue through every extreme of life. Beyond even India, Africa defines suffering and hopelessness as much as it inspires the human race to examine itself. As it is certain for romantics to reel in the ecstasy of love and to suffer its piercing pains, travelers are sure to learn the rapture of Africa as well as its pitiful agony. And nowhere is this more pronounced than in the passive enchantment of Ethiopia.

While Europeans vacationing in South Africa dodge violent crime, the bolder tourists venture to Kenya's game parks. But even there, extraordinary thrills wear thin. Observing roaming giraffes and lions leaves a lasting impression, but after a while, travelers grow accustomed to horizons of zebras and wildebeest thundering up clouds of dust while hippos and crocodiles bask in murky swamps.

Masai tribesmen were worthy encounters, but they were so astute at hustling tourists that they left those seeking deeper experiences disappointed. Until reaching Omo Valley, an empty feeling had lingered inside me, as though the best was yet to come. Everywhere I have traveled, pine trees are pine trees just as sand is sand. But startling cultural differences exposing humanity's similarities is what has made me feel alive. World journeys are really about the people, about a chance to merge with the landscape of humanity.

As I crossed from Kenya into Ethiopia, the face of Africa evolved into another captivating collage of racial blends — not just with the soft Arabic eyes of the beige-skinned city dwellers, but in the spirit of country folk so ebony black they swallowed my camera flashes, even when set on high. There was no limit to the cultural extremes during a plunge through this astonishing variety of human species. But an echoing theme remained constant: the most impoverished took care of their own. With disaster as a steadfast companion, Africans have learned to suffer in harmony with humble smiles, teetering on the verge of the next catastrophe aided or hindered by outside influence.

Since biblical times, taking into account the whole region, present-day Ethiopia was the first to receive Christianity and only later the stricter teachings of Mohammad. Two-thousand-year-old churches carved from solid rock are famous attractions in the north, while the ancient cities of the east mark the flow of Islam from conquering Arabs. Docile Africans were never left alone. For the last millennium, Africans have also oppressed, exterminated or carted each other off as slaves. But no one has been as efficient and well armed as the early European invaders or the plundering Arabs. Even now, freed from the crippling yoke of its particular colonial masters, each African nation retains its paternal roots in the form of crumbling infrastructure and intermarriage. With Addis Ababa's pleasant blend of Italian cuisine and Mediterranean architecture, visitors can almost forget Mussolini's carnage, exploitation and genocide. Yet even after a hard-fought independence, the assault on Ethiopia continues.

Rich in natural resources yet plagued by starvation and disease,

Africa is still ravaged by a treacherous, familiar monster: corruption. Finally ruling themselves, fragile nations with boundaries carved by foreigners buckle once again under the brutal suppression of ruthless dictators propped up by external forces. From 18th-century European power grabs to Cold War pawns, today, in Africa, it's the War on Terror. Whoever aligns on the right side receives weapons and aid, with a blind eye turned when governments attack their own. And the West still winks at tyrants who do their bidding. But a land of plenty and good fortune awaits this privileged vagabond born within specified geographic borders that are blessed by the world's strongest economy and its mightiest weapons. Few Americans will ever realize what the world is really like. Instead they prefer to accept media interpretations that unseen TV producers have decided are the images we need to see. Peering into my own immediate future, I shudder at the prospect of an approaching reality — the now alien opulence of California.

In 11 hours, a sterile aircraft will deliver this hesitant wanderer into Mexico City for a month-long attempt to reconcile the painfully enlightening events of the last 55,000 miles. My heart races and aches at the notion that I will never see Africa again. And what will become of the kindest of strangers who have befriended me? Crossing the land border by motorcycle at Tijuana will mean resurfacing from an awkward introspection that is likely to last for a while.

Incarcerated for Transit
February 22, 2006
Mexico City, Mexico
● ● ● ● ● ● ● ● ● ● ● ●

If you want to punish a free-spirited biker, take away his motorcycle; if you really want to antagonize him, stuff him in an aircraft designed to accommodate human bodies half his size. Crammed in between two men even bigger than me, the 30 monotonous hours of transit from Ethiopia, via Holland to Mexico, was a fate worse than prison.

Once shackled to my seat, there was no escape from a confining aluminum cylinder restricting freedom and separating me from an adopted world I had now left behind. There weren't any bars on the windows. No need — they were made too small to crawl through.

It seemed as though the pilots had conspired with control tower sentries to escalate my depression with a two-hour takeoff delay at the end of the airport runway. To alleviate the torturous thumb-twiddling moments, I convinced myself that this was unbalanced karma furthering justice. Even the guards were scary. Young, pretty stewardesses have gone the way of full meals on aircraft. Broad-torsoed middle-aged European women with shriveled frowns have taken the place of smiling female college graduates who used to fluff up pillows and make passengers comfortable. Patrolling these narrow aisles for renegades using laptops, a team of manly matrons hovered, hissing commands to shut down or else.

Once airborne, grim news for the starving was announced with sadistic nonchalance — since it's a midnight flight, there is no need for food. For the next nine hours, exasperated passengers were expected to pinch their elbows together and sleep while ignoring growling pangs reminding of a need for nutrition. But after a few hours, numbing fatigue subsided into a shallow doze just in time to be awakened by barking loudspeaker orders to open tray tables for mid-flight snacks. My request for a second cup of water to wash down the contents of a plastic packet containing exactly 12 honey-coated peanuts was met with fierce glares and stern admonishments — "Okay, but don't ask again."

Arriving in Amsterdam before daybreak with an eight-hour lay-over was an opportunity to see the city at its best — when it's asleep. After curt but polite immigration officials glanced at my U.S. passport, they waved me through without scanning or stamping — and suddenly the gentle familiarity of Africa was light-years away. Where were my tribal friends?

With stunning medieval architecture divided by silent stone-lined canals, storybook Amsterdam was as majestic as I remembered from 30 years ago while still evoking sensations of a Disney movie set. By nine o'clock on a frozen February Sunday morning, the cobblestone streets were still empty, with the only signs of inhabitants being 100,000 bicycles chained outside cookie-cutter brown brick apartment houses and the rows of neon-lit deserted shopping arcades.

Still dressed light for temperate Ethiopia, my brisk walk at a jogger's pace was enough to keep me from freezing but little else. It was damn cold, and the demeanor of early-rising citizens echoed the harsh weather conditions. As cathedral bells gonged neighborhoods from slumber, the mid-morning icy air slowly filled with the scattered white puffs of deep-breathing humans in wool overcoats emerging from wrought-iron staircases. Responses to my requests for directions back to the train station were in shocking contrast to those in developing nations where, to guide someone, locals eagerly take strangers by the hand. Slamming doors and turned backs without comment were not how I remembered the cosmopolitan Dutch, and after a dozen failed attempts, I walked off on my own. Welcome back to the West.

But at last, after my layover and flight, the flying prison bus touched down in the Mexican central highlands, depositing exhausted globe-trotters into an overcrowded, polluted capital linked by a modern transportation system of subways and crisscrossing freeways. Ringed by choking smog, the faceless avenues speckled with yellow streetlights flowed nonetheless with Latin hospitality in a nation known for its warmth. Tucked in between locked-down storefronts, a few scattered side-street restaurants remained open — but with families staying home, there was no better time to land in Mexico City than Sunday night. A 30-minute taxi ride was all that separated me, the famished traveler, from plates of steaming enchiladas in red sauce and tacos laced with fiery salsas. Spiced by the jukebox backdrop of a crooning Marco Antonio, life never tasted so good.

But my internal clock kept insisting it was still morning in Africa, which meant settling in at midnight and staring at the 20-foot ceiling of my room in a converted colonial mansion until sunrise. Moping in jet lag is the purgatory of world travel. Soon, the roll-up metal doors of high-speed Internet cafés were hoisted, and it was time to search for a lost motorcycle. By now, news of airfreight delays are common, and it was no shock learning that German dangerous goods inspectors were demanding additional payment before they would release my cargo. Yet, this environment was so relieving and pleasant, negatives didn't register. With no one to contact by phone or email, all that remained was for me to wait for instructions from bike-knappers on where to deliver the ransom.

On the Road in Mexico
February 28, 2006
Tepic, Mexico
● ● ● ● ● ● ● ●

Since motorcycles arriving by air in Mexico City are unusual, airport officials didn't know how to process my cargo. After four hours of phone calls and serious interoffice debate, solutions varied from a 600-dollar pay-off to customs brokers to forwarding the unopened crate on to California. One persistent Lufthansa employee finally had an answer — travel back across city lunch-hour traffic to army headquarters and request the same document issued at land border crossings. Worried that we were running out of time, airline employees insisted on the company prepaying the exorbitant taxi fare. To be sure there were no further delays, the station manager escorted me back through the airport security maze to personally instruct the driver, "You must get our friend there and back before end of business." Eventually, after a series of wind-sprints up staircases to all the wrong offices, a combination of German efficiency and Mexican hospitality freed the bike five minutes before closing on a Friday night. A month-long battle of continent hopping was finally over, but this was also a case of hurry up in order to slow down. Now, onto the West Coast.

But with Mardi Gras celebrations sweeping my targeted city of Mazatlán, it was best to stall a few days in Mexico City and avoid legions of drunken gringos embarrassing themselves. Besides, departing after the weekend allowed time to witness a fascinating concentration of Mexican life in the nation's capital. Sundays in any Mexican city are opportunities to people-watch as families gather on *las Plazas* for whatever stirs their passion. As 50,000 political marchers demanding a new president blocked surrounding streets of El Zocalo, hundreds of motorcyclists converged on Iglesia de Guadelupe for an event of their own. Avenues teemed with a vibrancy found nowhere else on the planet as, every few blocks, weekly food festivals blossomed in countless variations of regional dishes. While wading through throngs of eager hand-holding children, waiters demanded the Americano stop and sample platters of simmering seafood quesadillas set ablaze with lip-burning salsas. Machete-wielding servers stood ready to dice colorful fresh fruits and crispy vegetables while bands of roaming musicians kept everyone moving. Twelve-string guitars backed by chords from puffing accordions and bellowing tubas blended into old German rhythms now unique to Mexico.

Puzzled glances at my helmet led to shouts of *"De donde viene?"* (From where are you coming?) and they were met with my reply that also astounded me, *"Soy de California pero estoy regresando de Africa."* (I am of California but returning from Africa.) Interrogation began while delighted cooks handed over dripping tacos of chilied goat meat and bubbling cheeses on chewy tortillas hot off the grill. "No" was unacceptable, and after an hour I had to leave because it was impossible to eat anymore. At the end of an exciting day, there was just enough time to organize my scattered gear and wait for Monday's ride.

Dodging infamous Mexico City traffic required that I get rolling before dawn. And in Centro Historico, just as the first rays of sunlight bounced off the commanding granite bell towers of a Spanish cathedral, I was riding past fast-walking office workers bundled in overcoats with upturned collars. Accustomed to the mild temperatures of Africa, it took me a moment to realize that riding into biting mountain air required foul-weather clothes and heavy gloves. Passive old men on early morning strolls responded to my requests for directions with pats on my back accompanied by animations that rivaled Shakespearean players. Unable to merely indicate the next corner where to turn, with waving arms they felt compelled to describe the building and its historical significance. Together we formulated an escape route from an awakening megatropolis whose commuters were soon to choke the boulevards leading to the open road. Against a background of dilapidated shantytowns and honking taxi horns, the exclusive skyscrapers of the glimmering commercial district were the final farewell as I headed northwest toward the Pacific Ocean.

From an altitude of 6,000 feet, it was a rapid descent on the most expensive toll road on earth. Coughing up eight U.S. dollars guaranteed me a 10-mile bypass of a continuously gridlocked maze at any hour. Soon, a cement-slab spiraling superhighway unraveled through thick forests of poisoned pine trees coated in varying grays of brake dust and settled engine carbons. Since my last bike servicing was back in Tanzania, the Beast was in desperate need of filters and fresh fluids — yet locating any of three local shops was a navigational feat requiring more time than was available. But like an unexpected mirage, while descending at a pace too fast, from the corner of my eye appeared an elongated showroom of familiar motorcycles. Reflecting off the morning sun, a giant sign spelling "Lerma BMW" didn't register until a half-mile later — but this is Mexico, and abrupt freeway U-turns against traffic are acceptable maneuvers.

As in other motorcycle shops, whenever long-riders appear, red-carpet treatment is followed by a slideshow of cultures and people from faraway lands that fuel the typical biker's dreams. Servicing racks were cleared, and storeowner Ulrich Gut assigned two mechanics to disassemble and clean the Beast while replacing broken fittings and parts that had vibrated loose. Before I was able to stop them, the final remnants of Ethiopia flowed down a stainless-steel drain while I stared paralyzed in disbelief. "What have you done with my African dirt?"

CALIFORNIA DREAMING

Sixty fellow motorcycle riders led by Dennis Hof, arrived at the U.S. border in Tijuana, Mexico, to escort me back to California

As Much as Things Change . . .
May 26, 2006
Palm Desert, California
● ● ● ● ● ● ● ● ● ● ● ● ●

As traveling the world according to my plan-of-no-plan had been a success, so was the idea of returning to Mexico first in order to ease into the anticipated gasping jolt of the U.S. After a month renting an apartment in sunny seaside Mazatlán, a gradual deceleration toward home up the Mexican coast has proven to me that California is after all just that, home. Recalling previous failed attempts at readjusting after a tumultuous journey through South America, I feared being

411

forever lost, trapped in a disoriented drifter's limbo, never comfortable with hollow sensations of the present and plagued by the curse of discovering too much. Touring developing nations was as fascinating as it was morbidly enlightening. The monumental suffering of the human race is beyond description — just witnessing a fraction of the misery can make you throw up your arms in despair while smothering your soul in pitiful involuntary midnight recollections.

Other earth wanderers, once returning home, have written bitter essays on rejecting their own previous values while balancing difficulties reconciling the tragedies and injustices of a troubled planet against the abundance and relative peace of industrialized nations. We all return to recognize the same hideous ironies — as one half of the world endures malnutrition on two dollars a day, the other suffers obesity-related illnesses while spending billions on weight reduction gimmicks. What's wrong with this picture?

Will the personal torment ever end as we examine why the West has so much while the developing word languishes in poverty and starvation, crippled by exploitation? And still, imprisoned within a capitalistic accumulation mode, most Westerners have trouble defining happiness. And simple questions reverberate. Why do those with the least share the most? Or even smile the most? No matter how many plasma TVs or image-enhancing vehicles we own, we still chase our tails in glittering shopping malls, lost in the feverish desire to own one more piece of junk to add to a collection of artifacts defining status. Via an unscrupulous media, consumerism strangles the unwary with debt while our collective heads slide further up our rectal canals.

But a search for utopia will always be fruitless — though varying in form, familiar nonsense echoes everywhere. Even the most primitive tribesmen have developed hierarchical societies with crude metal jewelry to announce their wealth or their number of wives. And to impress their men, women eagerly stuff clay plates in their lips or silicone bags in their breasts while painting their faces with unnatural colors. Returning home, I realize that, as much as everything has changed, life still remains the same, and it's apparent that paradise exists within our own heads.

While I'm a little bit more aware of the world, once I reached California, its famous weather and blue skies have never glowed so sweet and clear. Although current U.S. foreign policies taint America's image abroad, even its staunchest critics agree with our foundations of democracy. After seeing my country from the outside in, I now understand why angry foreign crowds can burn American flags while wearing T-shirts printed in American slogans. American concepts of liberty and justice are still the shining light representing a glimmering hope for a developing world desperate for change. Once I crossed the border from Tijuana to San Diego, even in all its capitalistic folly, with California's sprawling metropolises lapping at the foothills of her majestic Sierra Mountains, my homeland has never felt so good. In an effort to resolve troubling personal issues, I went searching the earth and discovered how people are connected.

The solution of peddling those earthly possessions in order to have nothing to look back at or worry over was also successful, except that no matter what we attempt to discard, we will always keep something, even if it's just our clothes. Prior to departing on this incredible odyssey, to wean myself from materialistic grief, I disposed of almost everything, except for a few cardboard boxes containing symbols of memories I deemed essential to review in decades to come. In case I died while traveling, martial arts memorabilia, along with pictures and letters reflecting the intimacies of 30 years and countless heartbreaks, were tucked inside four brown cartons with the names of who gets which scribbled on the outside.

But, careful storage in a farming community warehouse was not secure enough to fend off desperate drug addicts ransacking valuables to barter for one more night of babbling paranoia. Frustrated that lengthy attempts to hot-wire the ignition of my old pickup truck failed, local speed-freaks frantically scooped up whatever could be hawked for another buzz. A few bags of methamphetamine were swapped for a set of ancient Samurai swords and a very special leather jacket embroidered with words only meaningful to me: "South American Motorcycle Adventure 2001." In a disappointed fury, they had maliciously ripped apart the remaining treasure of 70 martial arts trophies. Yes, but so what?

In our darkest moments, we often fixate on benign objects as a means to keep from sliding over the edge. While chained to a tree as a prisoner in the mountains of Colombia, the now ridiculous notion that kept me struggling to stay alive was that I had to survive in order to someday wear that jacket. In retrospect, at least half of our actions in life later seem silly, but, still, that simple leather coat represented a one-time dangling connection to sanity. Even though the battle is over and though I seldom wore it, being able to reflect on a meaningful symbol would have helped settle those sad events.

Fearful of ruining my otherwise fascinating journey through Africa, when this burglary occurred last Christmas, my friends had the presence of mind to keep secret what had happened. Although I would not have returned early to deal with a theft, brooding over the matter surely would have tainted remaining travel days that required living in the moment. The good news is that I never got mad. Those watching and nervously waiting for an unpredictable reaction were relieved when I merely mumbled that all that stuff was just that — stuff. A lesson I learned while evaluating my losses was that although material things are wonderful to have and enjoy, it's the value we place on them that weighs us down. Can it be true that less is more?

Even more valuable yet less tangible, I still have memories of those encountered while rambling around the planet. Images of my Siberian, Asian and South African brothers blend in a tingling collage, flashing among recollections of Mongolian nomads, Dayaks of Borneo and Hamer tribes of Ethiopia. No one can take them from me, nor can they erase the lessons of kindness and friendship they taught. They are now part of my soul, and to forget them is to betray them. How can I fail to remember the least of the least who shared the most with a wandering stranger they would never see again? When asked what I learned most from this journey, the reply is easy — to share.

So why is it that when humans meet face to face we do the right thing, yet from a distance we hate and suspect each other? And ultimately plan and organize our resources to destroy entire societies? It seems all cultures recognize a supreme God or otherworld deities who affect our fate and who may someday hold us in judgment. If religion is supposed to explain the unknown and temper aggressive spirits, have the teachings failed? As it stands today, in Christianity, Judaism and Islam, radicals wield disproportionate punishing power, bullying faith into fanaticism, which could lead to a showdown between the West and the followers of Mohammad.

But no matter the culture or period in history, it's the same all over: humans coerced into battle over another person's God and money. Whether it's corporate greed, thieving dictators or authorities demanding bribes, when riches are at stake, there is forever a temptation to take more than one's share with no regard for who suffers or dies. Wherever we venture, we will discover similar frightening patterns of senseless mayhem, with only the numbers differing. Is it the nature of men to kill each other? We don't have to look back far to identify homicidal frenzies. Nazis, Khmer Rouge or Rwandans on the rampage proved that when properly inspired, we will slaughter as many people as technology allows. But it doesn't take long before local news of celebrity gossip buries such tragedies in the public's consciousness, reducing them to more palatable, simple statistics with perhaps a movie or a few books — if there is profit involved. And at this very moment in Sudan, anyone with a mild education is aware of a continuing genocide, but there is little concern. Maybe when word spreads that it's Muslims killing Christians, Westerners will take a side. In the meantime, Arabs are relieved at the silence.

As televised images of war and horror bombard us in our homes, a shameful callousness insulates our hearts as we only grimace when hearing about our own dead countrymen. Are the victims more deserving or not as significant if predominantly of another race or religion? As suggested during the murderous breakup of Yugoslavia, were Americans and Europeans quicker to act when the victims had the same facial features or were of similar heritage? Or is it acceptable if particular groups are exterminated because they have been branded "those people who want to destroy our way of life?" Even with the current ebb and flow of Middle East butchering, we still only wince and privately complain, with merely a relative few showing enough courage to question the morality of military aggression. And where are our courageous leaders? They stand ready to act according polls. Who wants to come down on the wrong side of war?

At the end of the day, is it that we care only about what occurs directly in front of us? Seeing an old man slip and crack his head on a sidewalk, who would not stop to render assistance? From tsunamis to earthquakes or civil wars, the less-fortunate are slipping and cracking their heads by the millions every day, but because their blood doesn't splatter directly on our clothes, somehow we don't feel the agony of their tragedy.

And exactly how much aid do we owe each other anyway? Is it our responsibility to raise the level of entire societies to what Westerners consider civilized or just restore them if suffering untimely disasters? Or is it best to share our knowledge so others can decide how much technology and democracy is right for them? Does the world need a more equitable distribution of wealth or a more equitable distribution of knowledge and opportunity? If events were reversed, would those of the developing world assist us? Actually, they did, every day, as I drifted among their lives most often lonesome, tired and hungry. So what's the price of organized civilizations?

As universal is a mother's love of her child, so is the need for humans to form tribes, which, for one reason or another, ultimately attack each other. And the less we know about others, the easier it is to kill them. Yet, those who look the same as us or speak the same language are harder to slay. Could Americans easily war with Canadians? Wherever I traveled, once I practiced a few simple phrases in local languages, barriers dissolved. Although the stumbling communication was basic at best, it was the gesture of attempting to understand that built friendships. Without the ability to exchange ideas, and a growing eagerness to use high-tech weaponry, are humans destined to eventually exterminate themselves?

Yet, in the interests of prosperity, when war is temporarily unfeasible, humans always resort to the irrevocable laws of mathematics, communicating with the most common symbols in history. Even committed enemy nations, no matter the race, religion or culture, use simple-to-understand codes of measure. In every country on earth that prints currency, on the upper corners of paper bills, they indicate values with universal Arabic numerals. And what's to gain from realizing these basic notions?

With nearly two years on the road minus the comforts of home and family, a sought-after metamorphosis must have taken place; yet, my only epiphany is common sense, that and the desire to reiterate the obvious. As a species cut from identical genetic cloth, we all want the same things — so if individuals can get along, why can't governments? But stepping outside the comfort zone to investigate has had its price. It takes years to digest and recover from a journey like this, maybe a remaining lifetime. Day-to-day existence was so intense, a thousand experiences have to settle, but also, to stay on track, every day since returning, I stare at the photos of my friends from the road and still gaze into their eyes. Tormenting emotional extremes return as I recall pledges to speak for the suffering from alien cultures who, in spite of their plight, found reason to hold forth a hand. It's true that the world is a mess. So what do we do? Throw up our arms and turn our backs. Or do we roll up our sleeves and get to work? Doesn't everyone who is able have a responsibility to hold out a helping hand?

Imagine how our world would appear to visiting spacemen. From the cushy seats of gas-guzzling suvs we rant about oil prices as Kenyans in the Chalbi Desert dig into parched clay riverbeds while dying of thirst. As delirious people flounder in grief sorting out the devastation of tsunami-ravaged Banda Aceh, meek little Cambodians pray that someday those who planted land mines in their country will return to retrieve them. And that's only a fraction of the insanity. What's wrong with this picture? In terms of geological time, we have only been around the blink of an eye; so how significant is humankind anyway? Would the universe be better off without us? Dr. Jonas Salk said, "Take away the insects of the world and life will perish, but remove humans and life flourishes." Is it time to prove our worthiness?

As world citizens with such abundant resources, should we shut off our televisions and get out more to see how the other half lives? Views from the trenches differ from media portrayals that distort for the sake of ratings, and after opening our eyes, we just may become motivated enough to act. We can never solve world problems unless we understand what they are, and we will not uncover the truth by relying only on interpretations of the monetarily motivated. To know for ourselves we must go there — anywhere, just go.

It's almost a cliché to state that we need to travel in order to appreciate home, and while that is true, so is the concept that learning about other cultures and languages through first-hand experience stimulates our interests and ultimately revives a wobbling faith in humanity. My temporary detour into a kaleidoscope of alternate civilizations eventually evolved into an experience of marveling at our similarities and celebrating our differences. Will life ever be the same? When asked by those at home if I have any regrets, my invariable reply is, "Yes, I wish I could have stayed one more day, everywhere."

Acknowledgments

I would like to thank the following supporters who in one way or another helped make this project possible:

Frank Weimann

Jack David

Gary Farinacci

James Gairdner

John Cockrell

Brad Neste

Dennis Hof

Jimmy Weems

Paul Boughey

Donal Rodarte

Shirin Bassirian

Dan McCown

Anthony Montanona

Hushang Shahidi

Troy Freet

Cliff and Dale Fisher

Tex and Pam Earnhardt

Doug and Stephanie Hackney

Loren Gallagher

Al and Julie Jesse

Andy Goldfine

Peter Doyle

Jimmy and Heather Lewis

Kjell Heggstad

Big Don Hinshaw

Brian and Skye Coddington

Laird Durnham
Suzette Gwin
Mike and Sue Brown
Chuck Zito
Ricardo Rocco
Michael Kneebone
Antonie van der Smit
Graham Matcham
Sukoshi Fahey
Chris Macaskill
Göran Hedin
William Mayer
James Renazco
John Pierce
Hugh Blair
Robert Heikel
Danny Hurowitz
Sharon Hurowitz
Scott Weingold and family
Grant and Susan Johnson
Ian Smith
Steve and Sharon Fields
Murphy Sims
Teo Seng Boon
Lee Woon Sin
BK
Sean and Laurene Franklin
Ken Grunksi
Joe Gallagher
Bonnie Kramer
Laurence Kuykendall
Dan Rather
Greg McLaughlin
Larry King
Montel Williams

Bill Willis
Pete Corboy
Ricardo Lemus
Nate Katz
Tucker Carlson
Dara Klatts
National Geographic Channel
Tom Meyers
Brad Vardy
Russian Motorcycle Federation
Mike Harashou
Nick Rosser
Dr. Christian Chaussy
Dr. Flosner
Anita Trost
Maureen Ross
Louis Gonzales
Dr. Page
Renee Leman
Roger Pioszak
Steve Peyton
David Peterson
Dean Garner
FFs from Advrider
Southern California BMW

Links:
www.guilty.com
www.rideabmw.com
www.aerostich.com
www.telestial.com
www.ohlins.com
www.avon-tyres.co.uk
www.touratech.com
www.F650.com

www.renazco.com
www.billmayersaddles.com
www.jimmylewisoffroad.com
www.smugmug.com
www.cariboucases.com
www.shapefitting.com
www.bestrestproducts.com

All royalties from Glen Heggstad's projects are donated to international aid organizations.

For more photos and information, please visit
www.strikingviking.net
Photo gallery images are available in high-resolution
eight–mega pixel format.

Contact Glen:
USA (760) 275-9375
Mexico 011 52 1669 158 7195
locovikingman@yahoo.com